# The Other Prussia

Royal Prussia, Poland and Liberty, 1569–1772

This book considers the phenomenon of nation-building before the age of modern nationalism. It focuses on Royal (Polish) Prussia – the 'other' Prussia – a province of the Polish-Lithuanian Commonwealth from 1466 to 1772/93, and its major cities Danzig, Thorn and Elbing.

As an integral part of the Polish state (a constitutional and elective monarchy) the Prussian estates took pride in their separate institutions and extensive legal and economic privileges. Although its urban elites, after the Reformation, were predominantly Protestant and German-speaking, far from identifying with Germany they used history to formulate a republican identity which was deliberately hostile to the competing monarchical-dynastic myth in neighbouring Ducal Prussia, ruled by the Brandenburg-Hohenzollerns from 1618. After 1700, the Polish crown increasingly antagonised the Prussian burghers by its centralising policies and failure to protect the integrity of the Commonwealth's borders. The decline of Poland and the partitions of 1772–93 guaranteed that it was not the tradition of liberty but the Hohenzollern version of Prussian identity that survived into the modern era.

KARIN FRIEDRICH is Lecturer in History, School of Slavonic and East European Studies, University of London.

CAMBRIDGE STUDIES IN EARLY MODERN HISTORY

*Edited by Professor Sir John Elliott, University of Oxford*
*Professor Olwen Hufton, University of Oxford*
*Professor H. G. Koenigsberger, University of London*
*Dr. H. M. Scott, University of St. Andrews*

The idea of an 'early modern' period of European history from the fifteenth to the late eighteenth century is now widely accepted among historians. The purpose of Cambridge Studies in Early Modern History is to publish monographs and studies which illuminate the character of the period as a whole, and in particular focus attention on a dominant theme within it, the interplay of continuity and change as they are presented by the continuity of medieval ideas, political and social organization, and by the impact of new ideas, new methods, and new demands on the traditional structure.

*For a list of titles published in the series, please see end of the book*

# The Other Prussia

Royal Prussia, Poland and Liberty, 1569–1772

KARIN FRIEDRICH

CAMBRIDGE
UNIVERSITY PRESS

CAMBRIDGE UNIVERSITY PRESS
Cambridge, New York, Melbourne, Madrid, Cape Town, Singapore, São Paulo

Cambridge University Press
The Edinburgh Building, Cambridge CB2 2RU, UK

Published in the United States of America by Cambridge University Press, New York

www.cambridge.org
Information on this title: www.cambridge.org/9780521583350

First published 2000
This digitally printed first paperback version 2006

*A catalogue record for this publication is available from the British Library*

*Library of Congress Cataloguing in Publication data*
Friedrich, Karin.
The other Prussia: Royal Prussia, Poland and liberty, 1569–1772 / Karin Friedrich.
p.  cm. – (Cambridge studies in early modern history)
Includes bibliographical references and index.
ISBN 0 521 58335 7 (hardback)
1. Poland – History – Elective monarchy, 1572–1763.
2. Poland – History – Partition period, 1763–1796.
I. Title. II. Series.
DK4290.F75  1999
943.8′02 – dc21
99–21652 CIP

ISBN-13  978-0-521-58335-0 hardback
ISBN-10  0-521-58335-7 hardback

ISBN-13  978-0-521-02775-5 paperback
ISBN-10  0-521-02775-6 paperback

Für meine Eltern

# Contents

# Preface

This book is a study of the construction of early modern identities in one historically and politically distinct province in the Germanic-Slavonic borderlands: Royal or Polish Prussia, which from the fifteenth to the eighteenth century was part of the Polish-Lithuanian Commonwealth and possessed great strategic and economic importance due to its location on the Baltic Sea. Recent local initiatives in today's Poland to revive a specifically 'Prussian' patriotism in this region, including the voievodships of Pomerania, the region around the Mazurian lakes, and the old Hanseatic cities of Gdańsk, Toruń and Elbląg, have not only attracted tourism, particularly from Germany. They have also thrown down the gauntlet to almost fifty years of denial by communist governments of the fact that Poland's historical borders included a large number of non-Polish inhabitants whose composition bore no resemblance to the country's present, artificially created national, linguistic and religious homogeneity.

The loss of this diversity of cultures, languages and nations in the nineteenth and twentieth centuries creates problems for the historian with regard to the recording of place and personal names. In the contemporary sources, within one and the same document, or even on the same page, German, Polish and Latin versions for the same town, territory, country, office or person appear without rules or regularity. Despite the best intentions of creating clarity for the present-day reader, compromises have to be made. To avoid blatant anachronisms, I have rejected the solution of using the present form of place names, which would turn Königsberg, for example, into Kaliningrad. I have decided, therefore, to use the names which were used in the early modern period by the majority of the inhabitants of a given community. Large cities, such as Danzig, Thorn and Elbing, or towns such as Marienburg, Kulm or Graudenz, will keep their German names (although the district of Chełmno (Kulm) will keep the Polish name, as explained below). Their Polish names will be indicated in brackets the first time the city is mentioned in the text. For cities with a majority of Polish-speaking inhabitants, such as the Lithuanian capital Wilno, the cities of Lwów, Bydgoszcz or Poznań, I have used the Polish name, whereas I have Anglicised the capital cities of Cracow and Warsaw. I have also Anglicised and Latinised important provinces and territories such as Mazovia (Mazowsze), Great Poland (Wielkopolska), Small Poland (Małopolska) and Ruthenia (Ruś), whereas 'Ukraine' usually refers only to the palatinates of

## Preface

Kiev, Bracław and the territories lost to the Muscovites in 1667. The names of the territories and districts in the province of Royal Prussia which were administered by office-holders appointed by the crown, such as palatine (*wojewoda*), castellan (*kasztelan*) and starosta, are given in the original Polish form: e.g. the palatinate of Malbork (Marienburg), the starosta of Świecie (Schwetz) or of Puck (Putzig), and the bishoprics of Chełmno (Kulm) and Warmia (Ermland), since the majority of the population in these districts spoke Polish, and most royal officials were exclusively Polonophone, conducting their business in either Polish or Latin. An additional reason is political: I did not want to perpetuate the practice of some historians of Polish Prussia, who do not read or work with Polish sources and impose on the history of Royal Prussia a symbolic Germanisation. In the early modern era, even the Germanophone urban elites of smaller Royal Prussian towns knew and applied Polish, Latin and German versions interchangeably. I shall make an exception for the castellans of Danzig, Thorn and Elbing (not Gdańsk, Toruń and Elbląg), the starostwo of Samogitia (Żmudź), and the palatinate of Pomerania (Pomorze), which even in English usage have acquired Latinised names. To avoid confusion, a multi-lingual gazetteer has been included.

Personal names are usually given in the Polish or German version, except for ruling princes, where names can easily be Anglicised. Most institutions have been Anglicised, with the exception of the central Sejm (Diet), the szlachta (nobility) and the izba poselska (chamber of envoys), as well as Rzeczpospolita (Republic), the Polish name of the Polish-Lithuanian Commonwealth. Latin and German expressions, such as *pacta conventa*, *forma mixta*, *Ständestaat*, etc., are explained in the glossary. All translations from Latin, Polish, German and French are my own.

My deepest academic debt is to Professor Andrzej Sulima Kamiński of Georgetown University, Washington DC, who as my supervisor inspired me to pursue this topic in 1989, at a time when great changes started to transform the country whose past so stirred my curiosity. I would like to thank him for his provocative questions and perceptive criticism, his patience, kindness and encouragement when I needed it most. Professor Janusz Małłek in Toruń supervised my progress during my archival research in Poland and not only offered me his knowledge, but also his and his family's hospitality. I learned much from the expertise of Professor Jacek Staszewski and the members of his seminar on early modern Polish history at Nicholas Copernicus University in Toruń, where I also benefited from the deep and detailed knowledge of Professor Stanisław Salmonowicz. Many conversations over dinner with two special friends, Dr. Teresa Borawska and Dr. Henryk Rietz, not only helped me to feel at home in Toruń, but taught me much about the culture and religious history of Polish Prussia. I am also grateful to Dr. Jerzy Dygdała, Dr. Krzysztof Mikulski and Dr. Jarosław Poraziński, director of the Toruń archive, whose staff were more than helpful in providing source material quickly and unbureaucratically. I also want to express my thanks for the support I received from the scholars and staff of the libraries and archives I visited during my research,

*Preface*

particularly the director of the University Library in Toruń, Stefan Czaja, and Małgorzata Kapelińska of the Special Collections Department at the Książnica Miejska, as well as the archive and the library staff of the Polish Academy of Sciences in Gdańsk, Cracow, and Kórnik, the Czartoryski Library in Cracow, the collection of special prints of the National Library in Warsaw, and the Ossolineum archives in Wrocław.

I thank Professor Edmund Cieślak for providing accommodation in the Historical Institute of the Polish Academy of Sciences in Gdańsk, and for sharing his great knowledge on Danzig burghers. I am grateful for the perceptive comments made by Professor James Collins and Professor Marc Raeff, who read and examined my doctoral thesis, and to Professor Helli Koenigsberger and Dr Hamish Scott whose valuable criticism and advice helped me to transform the thesis into a book. The German Academic Exchange Council (DAAD) and the Polish Academy of Sciences (PAN) generously granted me a research fellowship which enabled me to spend ten months in Poland. I owe much to the Günther-Findel Foundation at the Herzog-August Bibliothek in Wolfenbüttel, which made it possible for me to spend three months in the splendid scholarly environment of this library and its treasures. My personal thanks go to Dr Sabine Solf and Dr Gillian Bepler. In 1996, the International Society for Enlightenment Studies allowed me to participate in their greatly valued annual 'East-West seminar', held in Paris-Sèvres that year. I want to thank Professor Jochen Schlobach for the opportunity to present my research. I am also grateful to the British Academy which gave me a grant enabling me to take part in the annual conference of the American Association for the Advancement of Slavic Studies, where I presented a paper and benefited from new contacts and discussions about my work.

Throughout several years, Georgetown University supported me with fellowships and, in 1991, with a special grant to improve my Polish language abilities, for which I shall always be grateful. For the last four years, the School of Slavonic and East European Studies at the University of London provided a work environment which gave me support and encouragement. Without the patience and understanding of my colleagues and students, I would not have been able to finish this project. I am particularly grateful to Professor Lindsey Hughes, and to Dr Roger Bartlett for enriching conversations on the Baltic region.

Special thanks go to Professor Michael G. Müller, who sent me the typescript of his book on the second Reformation in Danzig, Thorn and Elbing before it was published. I am also grateful to Professor Robert J. W. Evans, Professor Jörg Hoensch, Professor Udo Arnold, Dr Hans-Jürgen Bömelburg, Dr Almut Bues, Dr Richard Butterwick, Dr Jolanta Choińska-Mika, Dr Jörg Hackmann, Paul Heineman, Professor Pentti Laasonen, Dr Jerzy Łukowski, Dr Roger Mettam, Dr Andrzej Nieuważny, Dr Barbara Pendzich, Professor Jan Piskorski, Professor Gerald Strauss, Janusz Zathey and Janina Zatheyowa, and the members of the seminar on early modern Europe at the Institute of Historical Research in London.

*Preface*

My thanks also go to Dr Lyndal Roper and Dr Michael Hunter who gave me the opportunity to present my research on Danzig to their seminar at the Institute. I am grateful to Cambridge University Press for accepting this book in their series on early modern European history, and to William Davies and Jocelyn Pye for their understanding and help in preparing the manuscript for publication.

I wish to thank my family for all the support they have given me during many years of study and research, in particular my parents to whom this book is dedicated. Had it not been for my research in Toruń, I would not have met my husband, Robert, whose knowledgeable comments and help, but above all, whose love and encouragement as well as our shared fascination with Polish-Lithuanian history have never failed to inspire me and keep me going.

# Gazetteer

| German | Polish | English, Latin (or other) |
|---|---|---|
| Allenstein | Olsztyn | |
| | Bracław | Bratslav (Ukr.) |
| Braunsberg | Braniewo | |
| Breslau | Wrocław | |
| Brest | Brześć-Litewski | Brest-Litovsk (Russian) |
| Bromberg | Bydgoszcz | |
| Bütow | Bytów | |
| Christburg | Dzierzgoń, Kiszpork | |
| Danzig | Gdańsk | |
| Deutsch-Eylau | Iława | |
| Dirschau | Tczew | |
| Elbing | Elbląg | |
| Ermland, Warmia | Warmia | |
| Frauenburg | Frombork | |
| Glogau | Głogów | |
| Graudenz | Grudziądz | |
| | Hadziacz | Hadiach (Ukr.) |
| Heilsberg | Lidzbark | |
| Karthaus | Kartuzy | |
| Käsemark | Kezmark | |
| Königsberg | Królewiec | |
| Konitz, Conitz | Chojnice | |
| Kulm, Culm | Chełmno | Culm |
| Kurland | Kurlandia | Curonia, Courland |
| Labiau | Lubawa | |
| Lauenburg | Lębork | |
| Lissa | Leszno | |
| Livland | Inflanty | Livonia |
| | Małopolska | Little Poland |
| Marienburg | Malbork | |

| | | |
|---|---|---|
| Marienwerder | Kwidzyń | |
| | Mazowsze | Mazovia |
| Mewe | Gniew | |
| Michelau | Michałowo | |
| Mirchau | Mirachowo | |
| Mitau | Mitawa | |
| Neuenburg | Nowe | |
| Neustadt | Wejherowo | |
| Oder | Odra | Oder River |
| Pillau | Piława | |
| Pommern | Pomorze | Pomerania |
| Posen | Poznań | |
| Putzig | Puck | |
| Schlochau | Człuchów | |
| Schöneck | Skarszewy | |
| Schönsee | Kowalewo | |
| Schwetz | Świecie | |
| Stargard | Starogard | |
| Stettin | Szczecin | |
| Stolp | Słupsk | |
| Stuhm | Sztum | |
| Strasburg | Brodnica | |
| Thorn | Toruń | |
| Tolkemit | Tolmicko | |
| Tuchel | Tuchola | |
| Wehlau | Welawa | |
| Weichselmünde | Wisłoujście | |
| Werder | Żuławy | |
| | Wielkopolska | Great Poland |
| Wilna | Wilno | Vilnius (Lith.) |
| | Żmudź | Samogitia |

# Glossary

| | |
|---|---|
| castellan (*kasztelan*) | In origin the commander of a royal castle. In the Polish–Lithuanian Commonwealth, castellans sat in the senate. Royal Prussian castellans sat in the *Landesrat*, or senate of the Prussian Diet, and, from 1569, also in the senate of the Sejm. |
| chamber of envoys (izba poselska) | The lower house of the Sejm, composed of envoys from local dietines (*sejmiki*). |
| Commonwealth (Rzeczpospolita) | The Polish–Lithuanian state (*res publica*), composed of the kingdom of Poland and the grand duchy of Lithuania, the vassal duchies of Courland, Prussia and the condominium of Livonia, ruled jointly by Poland and Lithuania. |
| confederation (*konfederacja*) | A league of nobles formed to achieve a specific political goal, such as opposition to royal policy; confederations used majority voting. |
| crown (*korona*) | The kingdom of Poland, as opposed to the grand duchy of Lithuania. |
| *ekonomia* | A royal domain whose proceeds went to the upkeep of the royal household. The rich *ekonomia* of Malbork, for example, was situated in Royal Prussia. |
| *forma mixta* | Mixed form of government, composed of the three Aristotelian elements: monarchy, aristocracy and *politeia*. |
| hetman | Commander of the armed forces. Poland and Lithuania each had a grand hetman and a field hetman. |
| *ius indigenatus* | Rights and immunities connected with citizenship, bestowed by birth. Members of the noble or burgher estate, usually (and controversially) those who owned land. |
| *liberum veto* | The right of individual envoys to refuse consent to legislation of the Sejm or *sejmiki*, invoking the principle of unanimity. |
| *pacta conventa* | Conditions which a newly elected king had to promise |

xvii

to honour. If the king broke his oath, his citizens could refuse obedience.

palatinate (*województwo*)  An adimistrative unit headed by the palatine (*wojewoda*), who ranked above the castellan in the senate, but below the bishops, and responsible for the defence of his province. A palatinate was usually subdivided into districts (*powiaty*) and lands (*ziemie*).

*rokosz*  The right claimed by the szlachta to rebel in defence of the constitution.

Sarmatism  The myth that the nobility of Poland-Lithuania were descended from the ancient warrior tribe of the Sarmatians.

Sejm  Parliament or Diet (from 1569 including senators and envoys from Lithuania and Royal Prussia), comprising the king, the senate and the chamber of envoys.

*sejmik*  Provincial diet or dietine of the local szlachta in the palatinates and districts. After 1569, Poles called the Royal Prussian diet (*Landesrat*) the 'Prussian *sejmik*', or '*sejmik generalny*' (general dietine).

senate  The upper chamber of the Sejm and the royal council, composed of bishops, palatines, castellans and government ministers.

*Ständestaat*  A state with representative parliamentary bodies and political estates with a participatory political culture and constitutional government.

starosta  An official appointed by the king, with wide judicial and administrative powers, who presided over the local *gród* court (court of the first instance). There were also non-judicial starostas, who held a lifelong lease on a royal landed estate (starostwo).

szlachta  The nobility. Its privileges were legally defined and guaranteed in the *pacta conventa* and other constitutions. Despite the doctrine of legal equality and the right of all nobles to elect their king, there were enormous differences in wealth and political power within the noble estate.

tribunals  The supreme courts of the szlachta of the Polish-Lithuanian Commonwealth.

# Abbreviations

| | |
|---|---|
| *ADB* | *Allgemeine Deutsche Biographie* |
| ADWO | Archiwum Diocezji Warmińskiej w Olsztynie |
| APGd | Archiwum Państwowe w Gdańsku |
| *APH* | *Acta Poloniae Historica* |
| APO | Archiwum Państwowe w Olsztynie |
| APT | Archiwum Państwowe w Toruniu |
| *AUNC* | *Acta Universitatis Nicolai Copernici* |
| Bibl. Czart. | Biblioteka im. ks. Czartoryskich |
| Bibl. PAN Gd. | Bibioteka Polskiej Akademii Nauk w Gdańsku |
| Bibl. PAN Kór. | Biblioteka Polskiej Akademii Nauk w Kórniku |
| *BGW* | *Beiträge zur Geschichte Westpreußens* |
| BUWr | Biblioteka Uniwersytetu Wrocławskiego |
| EM | Etatsministerium |
| FUB | Freie Universität Berlin |
| GSta | Geheimes Staatsarchiv Preußischer Kulturbesitz, Berlin Dahlem |
| GTN | Gdańskie Towarzystwo Naukowe |
| HA | Hauptabteilung [Main Section] (GSta) |
| KM | Książnica Miejska w Toruniu |
| MS | manuscript |
| OBN | Ośrodek Badań Naukowych (imienia Wojciecha Kętrzyńskiego w Olsztynie) |
| PAN | Polska Akademia Nauk |
| PAU | Polska Akademia Umjejętności |
| PIW | Państwowy Instytut Widawniczy |
| *PSB* | *Polski Słownik Biograficzny* |
| PTPN | Poznańskie Towarzystwo Przyjaciół Nauk |
| PWN | Polskie Wydawnictwo Naukowe |
| Rkps | Rękopis (manuscript) |
| *RTNT* | *Roczniki Towarzystwa Nauk w Toruniu* |
| TNT | Towarzystwo Nauk w Toruniu |
| TPNL | Towarzystwo Przyjaciół Nauk w Lublinie |
| UMK | Uniwersystet Mikołaja Kopernika |
| UTB | Universitäts-Taschenbuch (Verlag) |

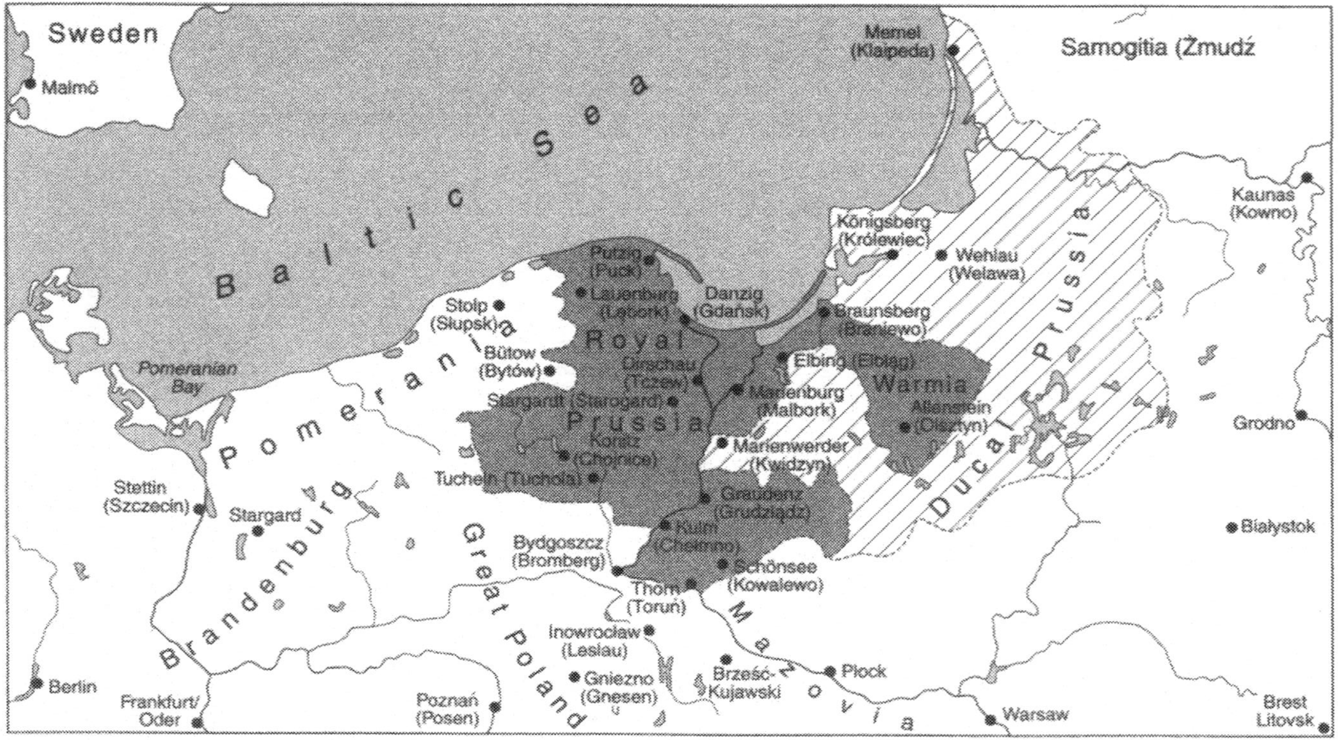
Sweden
Malmö
Baltic Sea
Memel (Klaipeda)
Samogitia (Żmudź
Kaunas (Kowno)
Königsberg (Królewiec)
Wehlau (Welawa)
Pomeranian Bay
Putzig (Puck)
Lauenburg (Lębork)
Danzig (Gdańsk)
Stolp (Słupsk)
Bütow (Bytów)
Pomerania
Royal Prussia
Braunsberg (Braniewo)
Elbing (Elbląg)
Warmia
Dirschau (Tczew)
Marienburg (Malbork)
Allenstein (Olsztyn)
Stargardt (Starogard)
Konitz (Chojnice)
Marienwerder (Kwidzyn)
Ducal Prussia
Grodno
Tuchein (Tuchola)
Stettin (Szczecin)
Stargard
Graudenz (Grudziądz)
Kulm (Chełmno)
Białystok
Bydgoszcz (Bromberg)
Schönsee (Kowalewo)
Thorn (Toruń)
Brandenburg
Great Poland
Inowrocław (Leslau)
Mazovia
Berlin
Frankfurt/ Oder
Poznań (Posen)
Gniezno (Gnesen)
Brześć-Kujawski
Plock
Warsaw
Brest Litovsk

Map 1

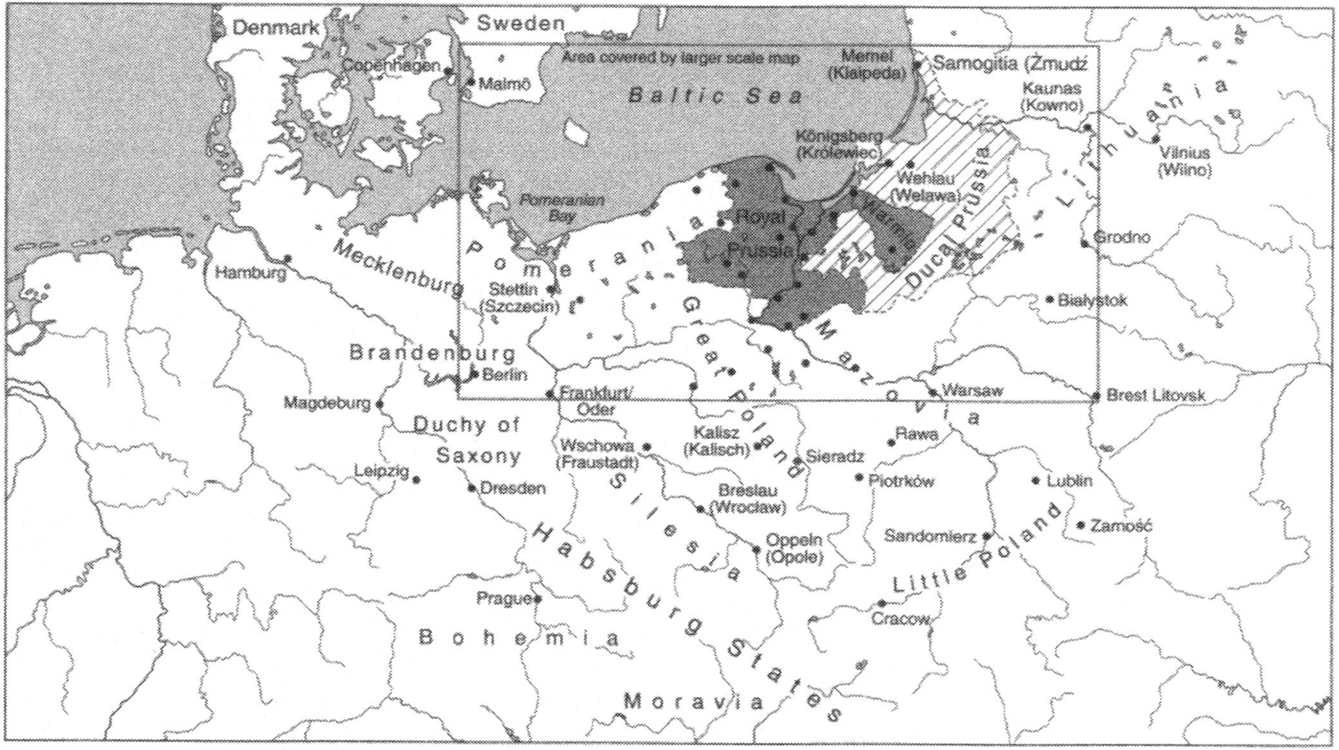
Denmark
Sweden
Copenhagen
Malmö
Area covered by larger scale map
Baltic Sea
Memel
(Klaipeda)
Samogitia (Żmudź
Kaunas
(Kowno)
Vilnius
(Wilno)
Lithuania
Königsberg
(Królewiec)
Wehlau
(Welawa)
Pomeranian
Bay
Royal
Prussia
Ducal Prussia
Grodno
Hamburg
Mecklenburg
Pomerania
Stettin
(Szczecin)
Great Poland
Mazovia
Białystok
Brandenburg
Berlin
Frankfurt/
Oder
Warsaw
Brest Litovsk
Magdeburg
Duchy of
Saxony
Wschowa
(Fraustadt)
Kalisz
(Kalisch)
Rawa
Sieradz
Leipzig
Dresden
Piotrków
Lublin
Breslau
(Wrocław)
Silesia
Habsburg States
Oppeln
(Opole)
Sandomierz
Zamość
Little Poland
Prague
Cracow
Bohemia
Moravia

Map 2

# Introduction

The essence of a nation is that all individuals have a lot of things in common, but also that they have eliminated many things from their collective memory. Forgetting, and, I would say, historical error are an essential factor in the creation of a nation, and thus the advances of historical study are often threatening to a nationality.[1]

I

In 1902, a curious masquerade took place at Marienburg Castle in West Prussia. Emperor William II, flanked by knights in medieval armour, entered this formidable fortress overlooking the plain of the Nogat and Vistula Delta. Among them were several members of the Order of the Hospital of St Mary of Jerusalem; others were ordinary Prussian soldiers dressed up as knights of the Teutonic Order, as this organisation was commonly called. It was a memorable moment: for over 450 years, no Teutonic Knight had set foot in the castle. Marienburg had been the seat of the grand masters of the Order from 1309 until 1457, when the Knights surrendered it to a Polish-Lithuanian army. In 1454 the noble and urban estates of Prussia rebelled against their Teutonic masters and accepted the king of Poland, Casimir Jagiellończyk, as their new overlord. The resultant war lasted thirteen years, ending in 1466, with the Second Peace of Thorn.

From 1455 there were two countries known by the name of Prussia. The eastern territories, stretching from the lower Vistula near Marienwerder (Kwidzyn) in the South-West to the Niemen river and Memel in the North-East, with the capital in Königsberg, remained under the administration of the Teutonic Order, whose Grand Masters now owed an oath of allegiance to the Polish crown. The end of Teutonic rule came in 1525, when the last Grand Master, Albrecht of Hohenzollern, converted to Lutheranism, secularised the country and, with Polish support, declared himself Duke of Prussia as a vassal of the Polish crown. In 1657, Frederick William, the Elector of Brandenburg, negotiated full sovereignty over the duchy. The more urbanised and commercially more successful western territories of Prussia, however, were incorporated into the Polish crown on the basis of the act of

[1] Ernest Renan, 'Qu'est-ce qu'une nation?' in Stuart Woolf (ed.), *Nationalism in Europe, 1815 to the Present: A Reader* (London and New York: Routledge, 1996), p. 50.

union of 1454, which confirmed all privileges and rights the Prussian estates had previously enjoyed.[2]

In 1902, however, these events were hardly on people's minds during the ceremonies celebrating the completion of the castle's restoration, partly destroyed under Hohenzollern rule in the last decades of the eighteenth century. William II visited the Marienburg as the ruler of a united Germany that was just thirty years old. The visit was the proud self-assertion of this new state whose mission, as the Emperor defined it in his speech, was to spread superior Prusso-German culture to the 'barbaric' East, to defend German 'national values and treasures against Polish hubris'.[3] Historians loyal to the court in Berlin played a crucial role in popularising this imperial agenda. Heinrich Treitschke, who was greatly admired by William II, made it his personal crusade to emphasise Prussia's central role in the creation of the new Germany:

What thrills us inhabitants of petty German particularist states even more in the history of the *Ordensland* . . . is the profound doctrine of the supreme value of the state and of civic subordination to the purposes of the state, which the Teutonic Knights perhaps proclaimed more clearly than do any other voices speaking to us from the German past . . . The full harshness of the Germans favoured the position of the Order amidst the heedless frivolity of the Slavs. Thus Prussia earns the name of the new Germany.[4]

The depiction of the Teutonic Knights as champions of the 'German cause' in the East, the close identification of everything Prussian with unified Germany, the attempt to blot out the memory of older federal traditions of Germany and the Holy Roman Empire, and the brandishing of anti-Hohenzollern traditions as 'dangerous particularism', lie at the root of the distortions which still dominate popular, and even many scholarly, views of Prussia. This vision of the German past was not only extremely successful in justifying the unification of 1871, the continued partition of Poland, and the primacy of the Prussian state as orchestrator of German politics; but it also legitimised German expansion into territories even further East. According to Bruno Schumacher, whose 1937 *History of East and West Prussia* was until recently the only complete German history of both parts of Prussia from the Middle Ages to the twentieth century: 'We not only rely on the historical right of the Teutonic Order, but also on the persistent right of the German people, who by hard work under the rule of the Teutonic Knights made the country what it became, and what it still is, namely a country of German character.'[5]

Yet the Hohenzollern view of history was not always focused on a united

[2] Marian Biskup, *Wojna Pruska czyli walka Polski z zakonem krzyżackim z lat 1519–1521* (Olsztyn: Wydawnictwo Pojezierze, 1991), p. 23.

[3] Hartmut Boockmann, *Die Marienburg im 19. Jahrhundert* (Frankfurt, Berlin, Vienna: Ullstein Propyläen, 1992), p. 38.

[4] Heinrich von Treitschke, 'Das deutsche Ordensland Preußen', *Preußische Jahrbücher* 10 (1862), 112.

[5] Bruno Schumacher, *Geschichte Ost- und Westpreußens* (1937), repr., ed. Walter Hubatsch (Würzburg: Holzner-Verlag, 1977), p. 216.

Germany, and the supposed continuity between the military success of the medieval knights and the boastful martial culture of Wilhelmine Germany is a false one. It was Hohenzollern rule that had spelt the end of the Teutonic Order's power in Prussia, and it was a Hohenzollern – Frederick III of Brandenburg – who in 1701 claimed the crown of a country to which the Grand Masters of the Teutonic Order never surrendered their title. After the first partition of Poland in 1772, Marienburg Castle was partly destroyed under Frederick the Great and his successors, who used it to store grain and ammunition.[6] In Prussia the negative image of the Teutonic Knights survived well into the nineteenth century, as the Order was protected after 1525 by the Catholic Habsburg Emperor in Vienna, the arch-foe of Prussia's pretensions to leadership in Germany.[7] Thus the Teutonic Knights who flanked William II's entry into Marienburg Castle in 1902 symbolised all too clearly the victory which Hohenzollern Prussia had won over the Habsburg dynasty – not only on the battle-fields, but also in German history-books.

Historical myths do not have to be very old to be effective. We rationalise them, and they sometimes amuse us. In the light of Treitschke's quote, we know why Hitler found the comparison of his Germany with the state of the Teutonic Knights so attractive. But rarely do we take myths seriously enough as a political discourse, linked to a specific historical and cultural context. Myths have an easily underestimated dynamic of their own: the Germanisation of Prussian history is one of the most strikingly successful examples of the survival of a historical myth to the present. Even during the renewed enthusiasm for Prussia that swept West Germany in the early 1980s, on the occasion of a widely publicised exhibition in Berlin, Prussia – officially abolished by allied decree in February 1947 as the 'cause of German militarism and aggression' – was defined as part of an exclusively German past.[8]

Nineteenth-century historians of Prussia constructed a continuity driven by a relentless determinism: they drew a direct line from the Teutonic Knights to the establishment of a strong military and bureaucratic state under Frederick William, the Great Elector in the seventeenth century, to Frederick the Great in the eighteenth century. Thereafter, 'historical necessity' pushed German history towards unification in 1871.[9] In pre-1918 Germany, scholars such as Max Toeppen,

[6] Boockmann, *Die Marienburg*, p. 44.

[7] Wolfgang Wippermann, *Der Ordensstaat als Ideologie. Das Bild des Deutschen Ordens in der deutschen Geschichtsschreibung und Publizistik*, Historische Kommission zu Berlin 24 (Berlin: Colloquium Verlag, 1979), pp. 90–2; Michael Burleigh, 'The Knights, Nationalists and the Historians: Images of Medieval Prussia from the Enlightenment to 1945', *European History Quarterly* 17 (1987), 37.

[8] *Preußen. Politik, Kultur, Gesellschaft*, 2 vols. (Hamburg: Rowohlt, 1986, 2nd edn).

[9] For a good summary of the historiography on Brandenburg-Prussia since 1871, see Jürgen Mirow, *Das alte Preußen im deutschen Geschichtsbild seit der Reichsgründung* (Berlin: Duncker and Humblot, 1981); Jerzy Serczyk and Andrzej Tomczak (eds.), *Dzieje historiografii Prus Wschodnich i Zachodnich do 1920 roku. Kierunki, ośrodki, najwybitniejsi przedstawiciele* (Toruń: TNT, 1989); and Andrzej Tomczak (ed.), *Dzieje historiografii Pomorza Gdańskiego i Prus Wschodnich 1920–1939 (1944). Materiały sesji w Toruniu 15–16 IX 1991 r.* (Toruń: TNT, 1992).

Karl Lohmeyer, Ernst Wichert, Hans Prutz and Max Bär, who had a deep knowledge of the local archives they directed in Danzig, Königsberg and Elbing, and who distanced themselves from the cruder forms of the ideological battle, did not receive the recognition they deserved.[10] From the early 1920s, when a broad German political consensus demanded the revision of the Versailles treaty, historians of Germany's eastern provinces became valuable instruments of political propaganda: Edward Carstenn and Erich Maschke, Theodor Schieder, Hermann Aubin and Kurt Forstreuter all continued their careers during the national-socialist regime. Erich Keyser in Danzig supported the *völkisch* idea of history and considered the 'German people the real (and only) representative of historical life' in Prussia.[11] After the Second World War, Keyser and his colleagues duly resumed their posts and chairs in the new West German state.[12]

Outside Germany, the historiographical focus on Prussia as the state embodying the worst of Germany's national character continued to dominate history books: the violence of the Teutonic conquest, the imposition of serfdom and the decline of the cities, the oppression of the Brandenburg-Prussian estates,[13] absolute monarchy, the militarisation of society and bureaucratic despotism[14] were associated as much with Prussian as with German traditions; the designation of Frederick William I as the 'Potsdam Führer' is but one example of this tendency.[15] The history of Prussia remained the history of a German country and a German dynasty. German historians continued to speak of the territories that gave the state its name – the ancient lands of the Teutonic Order – as 'East and West Prussia', although for over three hundred years they had belonged to two different states and political systems. 'East Prussia', or the duchy of Prussia, was linked with Brandenburg exclusively by a personal union and served the Hohenzollern rulers as a power base outside the Holy Roman Empire. 'West Prussia', only called by that name after the province's conquest and annexation by Frederick II in the wake of the first partition of Poland, was part of the Polish-Lithuanian Commonwealth from 1466 to 1772. Its historically correct name was 'Royal Prussia' until, in the early eighteenth century, its inhabitants started to call it 'Polish Prussia', to distinguish their province from the neighbouring Prussian monarchy.[16] To use the name 'West Prussia', as several

---

[10] Burleigh, 'The Knights', p. 43.

[11] Jörg Hackmann, 'Der Kampf um die Weichsel: Die deutsche Ostforschung in Danzig von 1918–1945', *Zapiski Historyczne* 58 (1993), 49. On Aubin, recently M. Raeff, 'Some observations on the work of Hermann Aubin (1885–1969)', in H. Lehmann and J. van Horn Melton (eds.), *Paths of Continuity. Central European Historiography from the 1930s to the 1950s* (Cambridge University Press, 1994), pp. 239–49.

[12] Hackmann, 'Kampf', p. 57.

[13] F. L. Carsten, *The Origins of Prussia* (Oxford: Clarendon, 1954), pp. 136–64.

[14] Hans Rosenberg, *Bureaucracy, Aristocracy and Autocracy. The Prussian Experience, 1660–1815* (Cambridge: Harvard University Press, 1966).

[15] R. Ergang, *The Potsdam Führer. Frederick William I, Father of Prussian Militarism* (New York: Columbia University Press, 1941).

[16] This book will follow this convention.

recent works have done, is therefore a political statement which implicitly rejects Royal Prussia's status as part of the Polish crown and wrongly suggests a continued political, cultural and national unity of the Prussian lands.[17] The 'Borussian' myth of Prussia as Germany's unifier and saviour effectively suppressed historical reality. Its success depended on silence, forgetfulness and the denigration of the political system of the Holy Roman Empire and the Polish-Lithuanian Commonwealth.

Despite certain difficulties in gaining access to Polish archives before the fall of communism in 1989, it was more due to historians' ideological attitudes and their ignorance of the Polish language that so little research was done on Royal Prussia outside Poland. Above all, in Germany, the longevity of aggressively anti-Polish traditions of historical *Ostforschung*[18] reflected a tradition of conflict and tension in Polish-German relations and produced much deplorable scholarship. After 1945, the history of Royal or Polish Prussia was left to non-scholars, usually members of the *Vertriebenenverbände*: organisations of those expelled from West and East Prussia in 1945, who were more interested in venting political claims and expressing a sentimental attachment to their village or home town than in studying the history of the whole region. Younger historians shunned the topic: until 1993, no attempt was made to produce a modern synthesis of the history of either part of Prussia, or to react to the prolific flowering of Polish historiography on early modern Royal or Ducal Prussia.[19] Even when a new project for a history of the Prussian lands, intent on 'conducting a dialogue between greatly differing Polish and German historiographical traditions', finally saw the light of day, no such dialogue resulted. It is hardly a sign of constructive discussion when one contributor writes that in the Prussian lands 'the only cultural nation were the Germans', and polemicises about seventeenth-century Polish Catholics as 'nationalists and religious fanatics'.[20] As a result, the writing of the history of Royal or Polish Prussia

---

[17] Examples include Wolfgang Neugebauer, *Politischer Wandel im Osten. Ost- und Westpreußen von den alten Ständen zum Konstitutionalismus* (Stuttgart: Franz Steiner Verlag, 1992); Ernst Opgenoorth, (ed.), *Handbuch der Geschichte Ost- und Westpreußens*, 3 vols. (Lüneburg: Verlag Nordostdeutsches Kulturwerk, 1994–7); and Bernhart Jähnig, 'Die landesgeschichtliche Forschung des Preußenlandes (Ost- und Westpreußen) seit 1960 im Überblick', *Jahrbuch für die Geschichte Mittel- und Ostdeutschlands* 38 (1989), 81–141. See the critical remarks on this anachronistic use of 'West Prussia' in Jörg Hackmann, *Ostpreußen und Westpreußen in deutscher und polnischer Sicht. Landeshistorie als beziehungsgeschichtliches Problem* (Wiesbaden: Harrassowitz, 1996), pp. 19–21; Hans-Jürgen Bömelburg, *Zwischen polnischer Ständegesellschaft und preußischem Obrigkeitsstaat. Vom Königlichen Preußen zu Westpreußen, 1756–1806* (Munich: Oldenbourg, 1993), p. 27; and his 'Die königlich preußische bzw. westpreußische Landesgeschichte in der frühen Neuzeit – Probleme und Tendenzen. Eine Streitschrift', *Nordost-Archiv* (1998), forthcoming. I am grateful to the author for allowing me to read this work in typescript.

[18] Michael Burleigh, *Germany Turns Eastward. A Study of Ostforschung in the Third Reich* (Cambridge University Press, 1988); Karen Schönwälder, *Historiker und Politik. Geschichtswissenschaft im Nationalsozialismus*, Historische Studien 9 (Frankfurt and New York: Peter Lang, 1992).

[19] Hackmann, *Ostpreußen und Westpreußen*, pp. 329–32. For a valuable critique of West German historiographical traditions after 1945, see ibid., pp. 305–21.

[20] Heinz Neumeyer, in Opgenoorth (ed.), *Handbuch der Geschichte Ost- und Westpreußens*, vol. II/1, p. 163; for a critique, see Hackmann, *Ostpreußen und Westpreußen*, pp. 319–20.

was left almost entirely in Polish hands after 1945. Klaus Zernack's 1992 prediction that the history of Germans in North-East Central Europe would remain a preoccupation of historians of Poland as long as Germans did not bother to research the close historical links between Germans, Poles, Lithuanians and Russians, except from a Germanocentric perspective, has proved largely accurate; his hope that the opening of the Iron Curtain would lead to the recognition of the place of the Polish population in the history of Prussia has only been fulfilled in few works, all published very recently.[21]

Inevitably, the few works in English on Prussian history in this period reflected the weaknesses of the German approach. None has sought to break the hegemony of the Hohenzollern-centred, 'Borussian' school of Prussian history. The most comprehensive account of Prussian history, by Hans W. Koch, was published in 1978, and denies any need to take account of the Polish and East Central European context of Prussian history: in contrast to the multi-national Habsburg Empire, Koch described Prussia as 'a purely German state, untroubled by the problems of minorities . . . until the final phases of its history'.[22] Other histories of Prussia, such as Giles MacDonogh's *Prussia, the Perversion of an Idea*, aimed at a popular readership, and Margaret Sheehan's *The Rise of Brandenburg-Prussia*, which targets A-level pupils and first-year university students, repeat the exclusive focus on the Hohenzollern success story and Prussia's German roots. With the exception of William Hagen's study on the relationship between Poles, Jews and Germans in the Prussian territories of partitioned Poland, even detailed studies of eighteenth-century Prussian enlightened absolutism, its education system, the emergence of Pietism and the success of cameralist government,[23] pay little or no attention to the Polish population and the historical link of a substantial part of Prussia to the Polish-Lithuanian Commonwealth.

II

The nationalisation of history was, of course, not only a German phenomenon. The invention of modern German nationalism was paralleled elsewhere in Europe, as public opinion, mass literacy and education, newspapers and journals, the militarisation of society and the development of mass political parties served the cause

---

[21] Klaus Zernack, 'Der historische Begriff "Ostdeutschland" und die deutsche Landesgeschichte', *Nordost-Archiv* NS 1, no. 1 (1992), 162. Works by Michael G. Müller, Hans-Jürgen Bömelburg and Jörg Hackmann are well researched and take full account of the sources in Polish archives, as well as Polish historiographical developments; see the bibliography for full titles.

[22] Hans W. Koch, *A History of Prussia* (London: Longman, 1978), p. 284.

[23] For example, C. B. A. Behrens, *Society, Government and the Enlightenment. The Experiences of Eighteenth-Century France and Prussia* (New York: Harper & Row, 1985); James Van Horn Melton, *Absolutism and the Eighteenth-Century Origins of Compulsory Schooling in Prussia and Austria* (Cambridge University Press, 1988); Richard L. Gawthrop, *Pietism and the Making of Eighteenth-Century Prussia* (Cambridge University Press, 1993); William Hagen, *Germans, Poles and Jews. The Nationality Conflict in the Prussian East, 1772–1914* (University of Chicago Press, 1980).

of nationalising the collective memory. In 1771, a year before the first partition of Poland-Lithuania, Jean-Jacques Rousseau proclaimed that the Polish nation, even after its dismemberment, would live on in the 'hearts and minds' of the people, in the memory of national customs, institutions and virtues, which would make the nation immortal – even without the formal context of an independent statehood.[24] At the beginning of the nineteenth century, under the influence of Johann Gottfried Herder, the idea of the modern European nation was based on an imagined community which shared certain traditions, corresponding to the nation's emotional and physical needs. This 'national spirit', or *Volksgeist*, was imagined usually by a small educated elite, who thrived on instrumentalising the nation's past.[25] The result of this intellectual construct was usually the primordial view of an 'eternal' nation, a 'natural' phenomenon, which belonged to people like their language, culture, customs and origins, something that was 'always there'. It was this type of modern nationalism which started to consider German-Polish antagonism a 'fact of nature'. The provinces of Prussia, where Poles and Germans had lived together for centuries, increasingly became a national battleground, in the history books almost more so than in real life.

Hostilities intensified after the foundation of a Polish state in 1918, which, regardless of its large non-Polish populations, projected a narrowly defined Polish national image of the multinational and multicultural Polish-Lithuanian Commonwealth. Polish historians followed politicians in subjecting the historical communities of Lithuanians, Ruthenians and Prussians to the fictitious construct of an eternal Polish and Catholic nation-state. Historians of Royal Prussia, such as Szymon Askenazy and Łukasz Kurdybacha,[26] emphasised the loyalty of the Prussian cities, especially of Danzig, to the Polish-Lithuanian Commonwealth, in order to enforce Polish political and historical claims to the Polish Corridor and Danzig, playing down the German or Baltic origin of Royal Prussia's population. Polish historical research into Royal Prussia as a province in its own right led to many serious, source-based social and economic analyses,[27] but the ideologically most successful approach to Polish Prussian history in interwar Poland, which survived into the post-1945 era, regarded the territories on the Baltic, including Eastern and Western Pomerania, Royal and Ducal Prussia (and the later kingdom of Prussia) as one region, under the name of *Pomorze*. This geographical and political term finds

---

[24] *The Government of Poland*, trans. and with an introduction by W. Kendall (Indianapolis and New York: Bobbs-Merrill, 1972), pp. 11–12.

[25] Dusan Trestik, 'Moderne Nation, hochmittelalterliche politische Nation, frühmittelalterliche Gens und unsere genetische Software. Der Fall Mitteleuropa', in A. Bues and R. Rexheuser (eds.), *Mittelalterliche Nationes – Neuzeitliche Nationen* (Wiesbaden: Harrassowitz, 1995), p. 165; Benedict Anderson, *Imagined Communities. Reflections on the Origin and Spread of Nationalism* (London: Verso, 1983).

[26] Szymon Askenazy, *Gdańsk a Polska* (Warsaw: Gebethner and Wolff, 1918); Łukasz Kurdybacha, *Stosunki kulturalne polsko-gdańskie w XVIII w.* (Danzig: TPN, 1937).

[27] For example by Kazimierz Tymieniecki and Zygmunt Mocarski; see Hackmann, *Ostpreußen und Westpreußen*, pp. 217–21.

no correlation in the German word *Pommern* (Pomerania), which more narrowly focuses on Western Pomerania, between Stralsund and Stolp (Słupsk).

From 1935, the writing of a comprehensive history of *Pomorze* became a political programme under the aegis of the Instytut Bałtycki in Toruń and the Instytut Zachodni in Poznań. The most pressing concern was the gathering of evidence for the continuity of an ethnic Polish population, and of Polish culture and language in Royal Prussia, the bishopric of Warmia and parts of Ducal Prussia. Only since the late 1970s have Polish historians working on the Prussian and Pomeranian territories distanced themselves from an exclusively national perspective and concentrated on the multinational character of the alleged geographical and political unity of *Pomorze*.[28] The influence of historical materialism, however, and the focus on the role of early modern 'feudalism' in the social and economic history of the region, replaced the older, national perspective. The important question of whether Prussia carried any specifically national, political and historical connotations for early modern people who lived in both parts of the ancient Prussian lands remained unaddressed.

III

This book is a case study of nation-building before the French Revolution and the age of modern nationalism. It focuses on the province of Royal or Polish Prussia – the 'other Prussia', which was an integral part of the Polish-Lithuanian Commonwealth from 1466 to 1772/93 – and specifically on the urban elites in the three major urban centres of the province, Danzig, Thorn and Elbing. The local patriciate, the shapers of urban politics, economy and culture,[29] were most active and vociferous in defining the notion of an early modern Prussian nation. Social scientists who have constructed models of modern nation-building usually deny that what they term early modern 'patriots' have any claim to constitute a nation. Hans Kohn, one of the most influential theorists on modern nationalism, saw the nation as a product of the French Revolution and the idea of popular sovereignty, thereby ignoring the deep roots of such ideas reaching back to the conciliarist movement of the late Middle Ages and early modern republicanism and monarchomachism.[30] Anthony Smith's emphasis on a 'Western' concept of nation, which, according to French Enlightenment thinkers, represented a 'community of people obeying the same laws and institutions within a given territory', overlooks the fact that Poland-Lithuania cultivated this principle as the ideological basis of its multi-national political commonwealth two centuries before the Encyclopédie saw

---

[28] Hackmann, *Ostpreußen und Westpreußen*, pp. 290–98.
[29] Mack Walker, *The German Home Towns, 1648–1871* (Ithaca: Cornell University Press, 1972), pp. 61–7; Christopher F. Friedrichs, *The Early Modern City* (London and New York: Longman, 1995), pp. 45–8, 182–213.
[30] Hans Kohn, *The Idea of Nationalism* (New York: Collier, 1967), p. 3.

the light of day.[31] In classical political terms, they were part of their *patria*, the *res publica*, an emotional as well as a rational principle of order, following Cicero's recommendation that a people should be bound together by similar legal, political and historical ties which provide useful social cohesion.[32] Early modern political and historical writing all over Europe applied the concepts of *gens*, *patria* and *natio* interchangeably. As John Elliott has observed with regard to the history of Spain, which possessed a nobility as numerous and self-conscious as Poland-Lithuania, 'the apparent uncertainty of modern historians when faced with the question of nationalism in early modern Europe stands in marked contrast to the increasingly confident use in the sixteenth century of the words *patria* and *patrie*'.[33] The citizens of Royal Prussia formulated a constitutional and political concept of the nation rather than an 'ethnic' one based on blood or genealogy. Thus the distinction between a 'West European political' and an 'East European ethnic' national identity makes little sense. The Prussian burghers imagined a community, albeit small, whose history and sense of origin, constitutions, privileges and parliamentary institutions connected the Prussian province with the Polish-Lithuanian Commonwealth as a harbour for many nations. In contrast to early nineteenth-century definitions of the cultural and ethnic nation, the Prussian nation of the sixteenth, seventeenth and early eighteenth centuries was an intellectual construct based on citizenship and property, and individual and corporate liberty. Its strong sense of an idealised past spent in liberty from oppression was clearly linked to the principle that a ruler must be bound to positive law. Royal Prussia was a typical early modern nation of estates, orders and parliaments, deeply rooted in European constitutionalist traditions. John Elliott's observation that 'national constitutionalism learnt the language of law, of history and antiquity'[34] was as true for Poles, Lithuanians and Prussians, as it was for the Castilians, the Dutch, the English or the Scots.

The most contentious issue between modern theoreticians of nationhood and historians of the early modern nation concerns the mass character of national ideology. Smith insists that 'a common, mass public culture' was a necessary element of national identity.[35] It is undeniable that the early modern nation was more or less the creation of its articulate and political elites, but this is also true for 'modern' nationalism, particularly in the nineteenth century, when small circles of intellectuals dominated the formulation of a national ideology and culture.[36]

---

[31] Anthony Smith, *National Identity* (London and New York: Penguin, 1991), p. 9. See also Jerzy Szacki, *Ojczyzna, Naród, Rewolucja. Problematyka narodowa w polskiej myśli szlacheckorewolucyjnej* (Warsaw: PWN, 1962), p. 38.

[32] Horst Zillessen (ed.), *Volk, Nation und Vaterland. Der deutsche Protestantismus und der Nationalismus*, (Gütersloher Verlagshaus, 1970), p. 23.

[33] John Elliott, 'Revolution and Continuity in Early Modern Europe', in Geoffrey Parker and Lesley M. Smith (eds.), *The General Crisis of the Seventeenth Century* (London, Henley, Boston: Routledge and Kegan Paul, 1978), p. 121.

[34] Ibid., p. 130.

[35] Smith, *National Identity*, p. 14.

[36] Trestik, 'Moderne Nation', p. 164.

Nevertheless, the following analysis of Royal Prussian identity will show that this political nation was not restricted to the nobility, but included burghers, and in a few cases was extended even to the free peasantry. Considering the weak development of democracy in Europe, Royal Prussian national identity before the age of Enlightenment was surprisingly inclusive. In the seventeenth century, Prussian historians explored the historical myths of origin of their nation by collecting popular legends among the peasant population of Warmia and the Vistula delta. National and historical myths were discussed in city council chambers and in local parliamentary sessions. They permeated private letters, diaries, but also printed political treatises and historical accounts of the history of Prussia and Poland-Lithuania. Teachers and pastors, burgomasters, merchants and craftsmen alike became familiar with these myths through school textbooks, at home, during public festivals and ceremonies in their cities and parishes, in news-sheets and by oral tradition. In his comparative study of medieval and modern national identity in Europe, Benedykt Zientara demonstrated that historical mythology was always an integral part of national identity, and that patriotic self-absorption could turn communities into nations at any point in history.[37] Consequently, the historical element of national identity features most prominently in this study. Historical myths are neither rational, nor are they consistent.[38] Changes in emphasis and meaning, and the introduction or elimination of specific historical metaphors are essential barometers of a nation's collective identity. They reflect private and communal interests and political agendas, and adapt to altered circumstances. Erik Ringmar has stressed the necessity of self-definition, particularly during periods of unrest and upheaval which upset traditional patterns of self-consciousness. It is the acquisition, loss or change of an identity which influences people, affecting not only their consciousness but also their actions:

What we take ourselves to be is not a question of what essences constitute us, but instead a question of what metaphors we apply to ourselves and of the stories we tell about what we see . . . A crime against an identity is an act of omission . . . If we want to deny a person recognition, all we have to do is to look the other way – no big gestures are needed . . . Actions undertaken in defence of an identity are of a peculiar kind. The action does not seek to maximise utility or minimise loss, but instead to establish a standard – a self – by which utilities and losses can be measured.[39]

'Formative moments', in which identities are lost, redefined and established, are vital clues for historians, as they provide patterns of explanation for collective

---

[37] B. Zientara, 'Świadomość narodowa w Europie Zachodniej w średniowieczu. Powstanie i mechanizmy zjawiska', in A. Gieysztor and S. Gawlas (eds.), *Państwo, naród, stany w świadomości wieków średnich* (Warsaw: PWN, 1990), pp. 11–26; and Trestik, 'Moderne Nation', p. 168.

[38] Erik Ringmar, *Identity, Interest and Action. A Cultural Explanation of Sweden's Intervention in the Thirty Years War* (Cambridge University Press, 1996), pp. 88–9.

[39] Ibid., pp. 75, 82–3.

action. It is such 'formative moments' which limit the period studied below. In 1569, the constitutional relationship between Royal Prussia and the Polish crown changed fundamentally, when the political elites of the province started to participate as full members in the Polish central parliament, the Sejm. The refusal of the political leadership of the Prussian cities to join their fellow estates in the Sejm, and their insistence on the Royal Prussian diet as the only competent parliamentary forum for the province, split the former political unity of the country and had a lasting impact on Prussian identity. Similarly, in the eighteenth century, the political disintegration of the Polish-Lithuanian Commonwealth, the external threat to its existence, and finally the first partition of Poland-Lithuania in 1772, also brought into question the whole concept of a Polish Prussian nation and its survival, which had been so passionately defended by the urban patriciate of the province.

People who define their identity usually tell a story, often with messages which vary according to the audience they are addressing. The burghers of Danzig, Thorn and Elbing produced many accounts of what they perceived as their origins, their constitutional privileges and their political status within the Commonwealth. Their intended audience included the Polish king, the Sejm, the Polish-Lithuanian nobility, but also their own political nation of nobles and burghers, and outsiders in the Holy Roman Empire and elsewhere, especially in times of crisis. This story of the Royal Prussian cities' struggle for a recognised place within the multinational commonwealth, and of the changing identity of their social and political elites, deliberately focuses on a provincial perspective. Such an approach to the history of one of the largest states of early modern Europe has so far been overshadowed by a more traditional focus on the court and the political centre, the Sejm. Thus the goal of this book is to reinvigorate what German historiography calls *Landesgeschichte* (provincial history) which for the history of other European states, such as France or England, has already proved so fruitful.[40] We will hear voices from a historical laboratory, working hard on the experiment of early modern nation-building. The issues addressed by the citizens of Prussia are still important: how do diverse ethnic and cultural groups with a differing idea of origin and historical identity live together, and how do conflicting social and political concepts find a *modus vivendi* within a confederal structure? The history of Royal Prussia's attempt to carve out its own national and political existence within the Polish-Lithuanian state may also contribute to the vital question all historians of Poland have to face: why did this once powerful commonwealth succumb to its rapacious neighbours, and why did it slowly disintegrate from the mid-seventeenth century, before being partitioned in

---

[40] Bömelburg, *Zwischen polnischer Ständegesellschaft*, pp. 2–4; Luise Schorn-Schütte, 'Territorialgeschichte – Provinzialgeschichte – Landesgeschichte – Regionalgeschichte. Ein Beitrag zur Wissenschaftsgeschichte der Landesgeschichtsschreibung', in Helmut Jäger et al. (eds.), *Civitatum Communitas. Studien zum europäischen Städtewesen. Festschrift für Heinz Stoob* (Köln, Berlin: Böhlau, 1984), pp. 390–416.

the eighteenth century, despite a successful – albeit belated – constitutional reform? Were the Prussian burghers disloyal, undermining the ideal they had once enthusiastically embraced? At the end, were they merely trying to leave the sinking ship? Were they 'separatists', contributing to the general decay of the Commonwealth, as several Polish historians have suggested?[41]

These questions are important, since German historians have traditionally singled out the urban elites of Royal Prussia as defenders of a 'German ethnic identity', German language, culture, and the Lutheran religion, as well as economic and political superiority. Thus Frederick II's propaganda after the annexation of Polish Prussia in 1772 concentrated on the cities. In a 1773 letter to his brother Henry, the Prussian king wrote that during his travels in the annexed Polish territories he saw 'nothing but sand, fir trees, heather and Jews'.[42] In a country which 'has few manufactures, scarcely any commerce . . . the peasants groaning under a yoke of feudal despotism far worse than the tyranny of an absolute monarch', as one of many West European travellers, following well-established clichés about the 'barbarian East',[43] stressed, the three major cities of Polish Prussia have often been regarded as exceptions. German historians continued to apply the stereotype of *polnische Wirtschaft* [Polish economy], connotating Polish anarchy and disorder, contrasting it with German orderliness, industriousness and urban pride in the Prussian cities. In 1897, Paul Simson, a historian from Danzig, wrote in best Treitschkean manner: 'The Germans looked contemptuously at the Poles and their barbarian language, their uncleanliness; the citizens of the Prussian cities in particular looked down on the miserable settlements that were called towns in Poland.'[44] These notions still feature in more recent historical works. Peter Letkemann, for example, wrote in 1976: 'When Frederick the Great took possession of West Prussia in 1772, the cities presented a heart-breaking picture of decay.'[45] The intention of most travellers' reports of the eighteenth century, instrumentalised as 'evidence' by modern nationalists, was to show their own superior level of civilisa-

[41] Władysław Konopczyński, 'Prusy Królewskie w unji z Polską, 1569–1772', *Roczniki Historyczne* 3 (1927), 111–41; Jerzy Dygdała, *Życie polityczne Prus Królewskich u schyłku ich związku z Rzecząpospolitą w XVIII wieku. Tendencje unifikacyjne a partikularyzm*, Roczniki TNT 81, no. 3. (Warsaw, Poznań, Toruń: PWN, 1984), pp. 241–2.

[42] Ernst Pfeiffer, *Die Revuereisen Friedrichs des Grossen besonders die Schlesischen nach 1763* (Berlin: n.pub., 1904, repr. Vaduz: Kraus, 1965), p. 40.

[43] Hans-Jürgen Bömelburg, "Polnische Wirtschaft'. Zur internationalen Genese und zur Realitätshaltigkeit der Stereotypie der Aufklärung', in H.-J. Bömelburg and Beate Eschment (eds.), *'Der Fremde im Dorf'. Überlegungen zum Eigenen und zum Fremden in der Geschichte. Rex Rexheuser zum 65. Geburtstag* (Lüneburg: Institut Nordostdeutsches Kulturwerk, 1998), pp. 235–6. See also Larry Wolff, *Inventing 'Eastern Europe. The Map of Civilization on the Mind of the Enlightenment* (Stanford University Press, 1994), pp. 235–83.

[44] Paul Simson, 'Westpreußen und Danzigs Kampf gegen die polnischen Unionsbestrebungen in den letzten Jahren des Königs Sigismund August, 1568–1572', *Zeitschrift für Westpreußische Geschichte* 37 (1897), 2.

[45] Peter Letkemann, 'Die Geschichte der westpreußischen Staatsarchive', *Beiträge zur Geschichte Westpreußens* 5 (1976), 8.

tion, which was more a proof of the limitations and the ignorance of West Europeans than an accurate picture of Polish or Royal Prussian urban life in the early modern period.[46]

Historians related to the *Ostforschung* tradition adopted Erich Maschke's influential thesis that Prussian local patriotism in the late Middle Ages – mainly in reaction to the oppressive rule by the Teutonic Knights – was the result of the concept of a 'new Prussian tribe' (*preußischer Neustamm*), which cultivated a strong, particularist German identity.[47] A similar approach features in the work of Theodor Schieder, who also emphasised the Prussian burghers' German cultural and political orientation, sharply juxtaposing Polish, Catholic superstition and backwardness with 'bourgeois German rationalism' and open-mindedness.[48] Apart from the fact that not all Prussian burghers and nobles were German in language and culture, and that not all of their ancestors came from the German provinces of the Holy Roman Empire, Maschke's and Schieder's ideological concoctions completely ignore the political content of Prussian identity: not only did they discount Polish-speakers among the Royal Prussian population, but also the political loyalty of the Royal Prussian estates to the Polish crown and the Commonwealth's constitutionalist nature. Although Maschke and Schieder, as well as the whole tradition of *Ostforschung*, have more recently been discredited by German historians, few of these critics have braved the issue of national identity. To escape the problem of defining Prussian national consciousness, Wolfgang Wippermann, for example, spoke of 'a tribal identity' (*Stammesbewußtsein*), an 'East and West Prussian [*sic!*] local patriotism' of the 'German burghers' in the Royal Prussian cities.[49] He fails to identify, however, the elements and meaning of this 'tribal identity'. This obviously embarrassed and cramped relationship to questions of national identity is also typical for Polish historiography of the 1970s and 1980s.

It was in a short and little-noticed article, written in 1937, that the first attempt was made to resolve the riddle of early modern Prussian identity. Reacting against the ideological instrumentalisation of Royal Prussian history in the service of Polish nationalism, Stanisław Herbst introduced the notion of a Prussian self-consciousness which developed in the fifteenth and sixteenth centuries in reaction against Teutonic rule.[50] But even Herbst thought that the acceptance of the Commonwealth's political values by the Prussian nobility of German origin amounted to a process of 'Polonisation'. This concept, frequently used by historians on both sides

---

[46] Bömelburg, ' "Polnische Wirtschaft" '.

[47] Erich Maschke, 'Preußen, das Werden eines deutschen Stammesnamens', in *Domus Hospitalis Theutonicorum*, Quellen und Studien zur Geschichte des Deutschen Ordens, vol. 10 (Bonn-Bad Godesberg: Verlag Wissenschaftliches Archiv, 1970), pp. 158–87.

[48] Theodor Schieder, *Deutscher Geist und ständische Freiheit um Weichsellande. Politische Ideen und politisches Schrifttum in Westpreußen von der Lubliner Union bis zu den polnischen Teilungen, 1569–1772/93* (Königsberg: Gräfe und Unzer, 1940), pp. 94ff.

[49] Wippermann, *Ordensstaat*, p. 84.

[50] Stanisław Herbst, 'Świadomość narodowa na ziemiach Pruskich w XV–XVII wieku', *Komunikaty Mazursko-Warmińskie* 75, no. 1 (1962), 1–10.

of the Polish-German border, is of little help: it tells us nothing of the changing patterns of identity.[51] What in Herbst's opinion prevented the further development of a conscious Prussian nation, was the powerful attraction Polish noble privileges had for the Prussian nobility, which aborted the formation of a united nation of burgher and noble elites modelled on the United Provinces after the Dutch revolt.[52]

The Polish historian most sympathetic to Herbst's thesis is Janusz Małłek, whose work on Royal Prussian identity and the relationship between Ducal and Royal Prussia is remarkably free from political influences, such as the *Pomorze* concept.[53] Małłek observes the sense of unity which bound the nobles and burghers of both parts of Prussia together, mirrored in the chronicles of the Prussians, particularly after their rebellion in 1454, and in common sessions of the diets of Royal and – from 1525 – of Ducal Prussia. He attributes the failure of a united Prussian nation to survive the late sixteenth century not only to the division between the estates of Royal and Ducal Prussia, but also to the pressure exerted on the Royal Prussian szlachta by the Polish Sejm and the king, as well as to the political developments in Ducal Prussia under the German Hohenzollern dynasty. Małłek's approach also challenges Marian Biskup's thesis of the formulation of a 'Polish' and a 'German' version of Prussian identity, the former in Royal Prussia, the latter in Ducal Prussia under Hohenzollern rule.[54] Małłek showed, however, that settlers from the Holy Roman Empire very quickly replaced their German identities – be they Saxon, Silesian or Pomeranian – with loyalty to the new Prussian *patria*.[55]

This observation has recently been confirmed by Michael Müller's work, which provides detailed evidence of the Prussian burghers' conscious attempt to avoid the social, religious and political upheaval resulting from intense conflicts between the Lutheran and Reformed churches in the Holy Roman Empire. In contrast to the aggressive confessional policies of many German territorial princes, the three major cities of Royal Prussia adopted a conciliatory approach, heavily relying on Melanchthon, and closely cooperating with the Reformed nobility of Great Poland and

---

[51] For example, Maria Bogucka and Henryk Samsonowicz, *Dzieje miast i mieszczaństwa w Polsce przedrozbiorowej* (Wrocław, Warsaw, Cracow: Ossolineum, 1986), p. 574; on the German side, see Edward Carstenn, 'Die preußischen Stände und das Königreich Polen 1454–1772', *Mitteilungen des Copernicus-Vereins* 45 (1937), 86.

[52] Herbst, 'Świadomość narodowa', p. 10.

[53] Janusz Małłek, *Dwie części Prus. Studia z dziejów Prus Książęcych i Prus Królewskich w XVI i XVII wieku* (Olsztyn:Wydawnictwo Pojezierze, 1987), pp. 9–17. Also his *Preußen und Polen. Politik, Stände, Kirche und Kultur vom 16. bis zum 18. Jahrhundert* (Stuttgart: Steiner Verlag, 1992).

[54] Janusz Małłek, 'Powstanie poczucia odrębności w Prusach i jej rozwój w XV i XVI wieku', in his *Dwie części Prus*, p. 9; see Marian Biskup, in Gerard Labuda (ed.), *Historia Pomorza*, II/1, (Poznań: Wydawnictwo Poznańskie, 1976), pp. 120–2.

[55] For a summary of Biskup's view on the ethnicity of the inhabitants of Prussia see his 'Etniczno-demograficzne przemiany Prus Krzyżackich w rozwoju osadnictwa w średniowieczu', *Kwartalnik Historyczny* 2 (1991), 45–66, which presents a Polish version of Erich Maschke's thesis on the Prussian *Neustamm*.

Lithuania. The dogma therefore, that the Prussian burghers consistently stuck to a combined Lutheran and German identity from 1525, when the Reformation swept through the province, requires fundamental revision. The so-called 'second Reformation' was a dominant feature of Royal Prussia's political and confessional life in the second half of the sixteenth century: it created Calvinist majorities in the councils of Danzig, Thorn and Elbing, and introduced the strong influence of groups such as the Bohemian and Polish Brethren, particularly in Thorn and Elbing. Müller successfully questions the assumption that Lutheranism was closely connected to separate and (German) particularist aspirations among the Prussian burghers: instead of pressing for an autonomous territorial church organisation after the German model, they accepted the principles of the Consensus of Sandomierz (1570), as well as the Confederation of Warsaw (1573), which introduced a policy of mutual toleration among the noble estates of all religions (except Antitrinitarianism) in the Polish-Lithuanian Commonwealth.[56] The failure of the Reformation in Poland-Lithuania to acquire a strong institutional character meant, however, that true religious diversity was also doomed in Royal Prussia, where the Calvinist-dominated city councils succumbed to pressure from the Lutheran citizenry and suffered from interference by the Polish king, who successfully played off Calvinists against Lutherans. Yet it was only from the mid-seventeenth century that Calvinism lost all influence in the Royal Prussian cities to a Lutheran political and clerical establishment. As the rich and interesting religious life in Royal Prussia during the Reformation and Counter-Reformation, better summarised as the period of confessionalisation,[57] has been comprehensively covered in Müller's work, this book only introduces religious questions when they are of direct relevance to issues of political, historical and national identity in the Royal Prussian province, or to provide a better understanding of the course of events. That religion was central to early modern identities is certainly true for the great majority of the population; nevertheless, the history of confessionalisation should not serve as a means of denying any other approach to the definition of the early modern self, particularly among the educated elites which form the focus for this analysis.

Finally, this study also seeks to contribute to the history of early modern society and its political organisation as a *Ständestaat*, a 'state of estates', from its late medieval roots to its transition to the modern age, when the corporate structures of a society divided into strictly-defined, privileged groups slowly dissolved. Poland-Lithuania was an elective monarchy, *de jure* since the fourteenth century, *de facto* from 1572, when during the interregnum following the death of the last Jagiel-

---

[56] Michael G. Müller, 'Zweite Reformation und städtische Autonomie im Königlichen Preußen. Danzig, Elbing und Thorn in der Epoche der Konfessionalisierung, 1557–1660', doctoral diss., Berlin: Freie Universität, 1993, pp. 60–5. It has meanwhile appeared in print (Berlin: Colloquium, 1998). I am grateful to Professor Müller for having allowed me to read his typescript.

[57] Heinz Schilling, 'Confessionalisation in the Empire: Religious and Societal Change in Germany between 1555 and 1620', in his *Religion, Political Culture and the Emergence of Early Modern Society. Essays in German and Dutch History* (Leiden: Brill, 1992), pp. 205–45.

lonian king, Sigismund August, the diet under the authority of the primate imposed electoral capitulations on the monarch. All previous privileges, such as the security of life and property of all noblemen against arbitrary convictions, or the rule that no new taxation or legislation was to be introduced without parliamentary consent, were confirmed and institutionalised in the Henrician Articles, named after the first elected king of Poland, Henri of Valois. Together with the *pacta conventa*, these regulations set clear limits of the exercise of the royal prerogative and were the condition by which the newly elected king was accepted by his noble estates. The clause of *de non praestanda oboedientia* legalised the right of resistance to illegitimate and unlawful power. Hereditary monarchy was anathema in Poland-Lithuania, and the repeated attempts by Polish kings in the seventeenth and eighteenth centuries to limit the elective nature of the monarchy were regularly met with armed rebellion and political crises.[58] The model of mixed government (*forma mixta*), composed of monarchy, aristocratic and republican elements, embodied in king, senate council and the lower chamber of the parliament, the *izba poselska* (chamber of envoys), also enjoyed unequivocal support in the province of Royal Prussia and its cities. As in similar parliamentary systems in early modern Europe, the legitimacy of power was based on fundamental laws and constitutions: *lex facit regem* (the law makes the king).[59] During the sixteenth and early seventeenth centuries, the Polish-Lithuanian model of constitutional and decentralised rule, institutionalised in the provincial and local diets and dietines, elicited more loyalty and exerted a more direct impact on the political culture of the Royal Prussian cities than other European influences, such as the classical virtues of the Italian city republics, or the republican teaching of the Dutch rebels. The idea of a corporation, a voluntary organisation, which functioned on the principles of election and consent, was familiar to urban citizens. The step towards a group identity which went beyond merely economic and social interests, but fostered a political and national community of fully privileged members, with the right to representation and civic action, was then a small one.[60] This was not an exclusive or linear process: notions of citizenship and patriotism which focused on an urban community within medieval walls could coexist very well with national ideas attached to a wider province, territory or commonwealth.[61]

To avoid any anachronism it is necessary to state that early modern urban political theory was not democratic in a twentieth-century sense, and the transition to modern democratic ideals was not easy to achieve. Even the meaning of

---

[58] As, for example, during the Second Northern War; see Robert I. Frost, *After the Deluge. Poland-Lithuania and the Second Northern War, 1655–1660* (Cambridge University Press, 1993).

[59] Dieter Wyduckel, *Princeps Legibus Solutus. Eine Untersuchung zur frühmodernen Rechts- und Staatslehre* (Berlin: Duncker and Humblot, 1979), p. 163.

[60] Anthony Black, *Guild and Civil Society in European Political Thought from the Twelfth Century to the Present* (Ithaca: Cornell University Press, 1984), p. 149.

[61] Robert J. W. Evans, 'Essay and Reflection: Frontiers and National Identities in Central Europe', *The International History Review* 14, no. 3 (1992), 486.

'republic' was not directed against monarchy – as long as its ruler did not exceed his strictly limited powers. Many political organisations containing elements of republican theory did very well within the framework of monarchy. The Royal Prussian version of the early modern *Ständestaat* defined itself as a political body that thrived on liberty, which was defined as the sum of privileges and constitutions, immunities and rights accumulated over centuries, repeatedly confirmed by a succession of monarchs in cooperation with representative, parliamentary institutions which, in contrast to the rest of the Commonwealth, comprised both nobles and burghers.[62] The great economic and political influence of the urban elites in the Royal Prussian cities was not only exceptional in the Polish-Lithuanian 'noble republic', it also lay at the root of numerous conflicts between the province and the rest of the realm. Urban and noble attitudes towards taxation, property and inheritance laws, trade-related issues, access to the port of Danzig and its profits, division over means of defence, principles of jurisdiction, and many other matters, varied widely. Despite economic, legal and religious frictions, urban and landowning noble citizens considered their own province a more perfect version of the *Ständestaat*, whose traditions enabled them to live in relative harmony. The historical works of the second half of the seventeenth century are invaluable testimonies for these values; in particular, the histories of Prussia and Poland by Christoph Hartknoch and Joachim Pastorius, and Reinhold Curicke's history of Danzig single out Royal Prussia from among the multitude of national groups represented in the Commonwealth, and the authors defend their fatherland against its neighbours abroad, particularly the Holy Roman Empire, and against German claims to the former Teutonic province.

Myths, historical constructs and political ideas were tested for real functionality in the everyday political life of the province. From 1655 to 1660, during the devastating wars against the Cossacks and Muscovites, against Sweden and Brandenburg, Royal Prussian loyalties underwent a severe test. Neither the Lutheran Swedish occupation of the province nor military threats could convince Danzig to break its allegiance to the Polish crown; only the enemy's superior armed forces succeeded in subjecting Thorn and Elbing. Following the achievement of Hohenzollern sovereignty over the duchy of Prussia, negotiated between Warsaw and Berlin to Royal Prussia's dismay in 1657, the alienation between the two provinces of Ducal and Royal Prussia grew. The competition between two hostile political cultures – one based on constitutionalism and an elected throne, the other on a hereditary and increasingly militarist ruler – sharpened the burghers' belief in their historical and political uniqueness. After 1701, when Frederick III of Hohenzollern crowned himself king in Prussia and elevated the duchy to a kingdom, the name of

---

[62] Helmut G. Koenigsberger, 'Republicanism, Monarchism and Liberty', in Robert Oresko, Graham Gibbs, Hamish Scott (eds.), *Royal and Republican Sovereignty in Early Modern Europe. Essays in Memory of Ragnhild Hatton* (Cambridge University Press, 1997), 62–5; and his *Politicians and Virtuosi* (London: Hambledon, 1986), pp. 3–12.

Prussia was gradually and increasingly associated with the image of absolute rule and monarchical myths from the Prussian past totally alien to Polish Prussia's culture and constitutions.

Historians outside Poland have traditionally paid little attention to the need to distinguish between the two Prussias. Apologists of the Hohenzollern state tended to ignore the fact that many members of the urban or noble estates of Ducal Prussia felt nostalgia and envy in view of their Polish Prussian brothers' greater political opportunities and influence on central government policies. As urban self-government was a commonplace to the ruling elites of Danzig, Thorn, Elbing, and so many other, smaller towns in Royal Prussia, it had been taken for granted ever since the rebellion against the Teutonic Order, and successfully defended against all attacks from the Polish king or the nobility for three centuries. Was it therefore not natural that the memory of the common historical origin and shared political traditions would serve as an inspiration for the estates of Hohenzollern Prussia?

The mood in both provinces of Prussia changed considerably during the Great Northern War, the decisive period in the development of the Polish Prussian towns before Poland-Lithuania's demise. A growing sense that the constitutional and political life of the realm needed reform, that the three elements of the mixed government were out of balance, and that abuse, corruption, and political paralysis, partly caused by ambitious monarchs, partly by the lack of unity among the political estates, had weakened and changed the state beyond recognition, was a feature recognised as much by the estates of the Prussian province as in the rest of the Commonwealth. One of Danzig's mottos, inscribed on the gate leading to the city's main street, the Lange Gasse, cautioned against civil war: 'concord makes small republics prosper, while discord is the death of large states' – a prophecy which was taken very seriously by the burghers of Polish Prussia at the end of the eighteenth century.[63] Sharp conflicts over financial and political reform continued to plague the cities' relationship with the Prussian and Polish nobility. The fear that a more centralised monarchy would undermine their ancient immunities intensified their crisis of identity as being caught between a rock and a hard place: between Hohenzollern *absolutum dominium* and the rule of Poland's last king, Stanisław August Poniatowski, who stuck to his refusal to confirm their special laws and constitutions. The burgher elites rallied around their historical myths, their increasingly exclusive urban perspective, and their demand to be recognised as a separate political body and nation within the multi-national state.

Was there a way from the corporate world of privilege to civic society, avoiding the statist, cameralist tutelage of Hohenzollern rule? Was there an escape from the modern, chauvinist nation-state, by maintaining a nation of 'free Prussian citizens', based on a mutual pact between government and governed,[64] and through the

---

[63] Reinhold Curicke, *Der Stadt Dantzig historische Beschreibung* (Amsterdam, 1687), repr. ed. S. Rosenberg (Danziger Verlagsgesellschaft, Hamburg: Paul Rosenberg, 1979), p. 46.

[64] Gerhard Oestreich, 'The Estates of Germany and the Formation of the State', in *Neostoicism and the*

simultaneous realisation of national identity and civil liberty? Neither the estates of Poland-Lithuania, nor the burghers of Polish Prussia were granted the opportunity to find out: the invasion and occupation of Polish Prussia by Hohenzollern troops ended such speculation. As Ernest Lavisse wrote in 1891: 'mother nature made many countries and prepared cradles for new nations. For Prussia she has done nothing. There is no Prussian race, no geographical area called Prussia. Germany is a child of nature, but Prussia was created by men.'[65] Like many historians, Lavisse had no use for the history of a nation which failed to survive annexation by a hostile power. The 'other Prussia' was taken over by men who indeed created a dynastic nation, sworn to loyalty towards the Hohenzollern monarch, not to civil society and the idea of liberty.

*Early Modern State* (Cambridge University Press, 1982), p. 194.

[65] G. Oestreich, *Strukturprobleme der frühen Neuzeit. Ausgewählte Aufsätze* (Berlin: de Gruyter, 1969), p. 281.

# 2

# The origins of Royal Prussia

The identity of the citizens of Royal Prussia was fundamentally formed and influenced by their struggle against their masters for two centuries: the Teutonic Knights. The crusading mission of the Knights increasingly lost its primary purpose when, by the fourteenth century, they had largely completed the subjection, Christianisation and assimilation of the pagan Prussians. The Lithuanians, the next target for conquest by the Order, preemptively adopted Christianity when their grand duke Jagiełło married the successor to the Polish throne, Jadwiga, in 1385. Dissent and internal strife not only spread among the members of the Order but also marred the relationship between the Knights and their subjects, many of whom had followed in the Order's wake as colonists from North-West Germany. These settlers depended on the Order – by far the largest and most powerful landowner in Prussia – for favours and the distribution of lands, but the Knights' increasingly arbitrary style of government triggered a new sense of political, economic and cultural solidarity among the Prussian townsmen and landed freemen.[1]

The first corporate bodies, foreshadowing the future organisation of estates and regular diets, originated in assemblies set up from the mid-fourteenth century by the Hanseatic towns Thorn, Kulm, Danzig, Elbing, Königsberg and Braunsberg, under the watchful eye of the Order.[2] The Lizard League, the first organised body of the provincial nobility, was founded in 1397 and voiced its opposition on matters such as taxation and land administration. The Order, however, did not cede any consultation rights before 1411, when the cities' and nobles' consent was sought for military contribution. The Prussian elites continued to discuss papal taxation and monitored the election of the Grand Master without having any real impact on decision-making. Administrative and legal institutions, such as district or town courts, had existed since the thirteenth century, but no representative estate structures existed which would have given the colonists any influence on the policies of their Teutonic masters.[3] The Order's demand for increased custom

---

[1] Michael Burleigh, *Prussian Society and the German Order. An Aristocratic Corporation in Crisis, c. 1410–1466* (Cambridge University Press, 1984), pp. 138–40.
[2] Burleigh, *Prussian Society*, p. 136; Roman Czaja, 'Udział wielkich miast pruskich w handlu Hanzeatyckim do połowy XV wieku', *Zapiski Historyczne* 60, no. 2–3 (1995), 35–6.
[3] Marian Biskup, 'Rola miast w reprezentacji stanowej Królestwa Polskiego i Prus Krzyżackich w XIV i

duties and taxation, especially after the disastrous battle of Tannenberg (Grunwald) in 1410, when the defeated Knights started to look for new sources of income to pay their growing armies of mercenaries, sharpened the conflicts with the Prussian elites.[4] When after 1411 the Teutonic Order tried again to curb the influence of provincial assemblies, which were appointed and controlled by the Knights, unrest spread among the Prussian subjects. In 1412, nobles and burghers took the initiative and set up their own joint assembly, which marked the first step towards the development of an independent institution of self-government. In 1434, Elbing and Thorn recognised Danzig as the leading city in the Prussian delegation to the Wendish circle of the Hanseatic League: the international trading house of the Fugger family had a base there, and the flourishing trade in grain and other important commodities made it the dominant urban centre in the Southern Baltic.[5] The Order's attempt to tap into the cities' wealth and to exercise control over their resources led to constant friction and hostility between the urban magistracies and the Knights. The Order's competition was particularly unwelcome to Prussian townsmen and merchants at a time when the Hanseatic League was growing weaker.

Resentment was not caused by economic factors alone. The German elite who provided the Order's career pool, and who originated largely in southern and central Germany, had always been a foreign element, isolated from the land and its inhabitants, consisting of immigrants from north-western German provinces, as well as native Prussian, Pomeranian and Polish peasants, freemen, landowners and merchants. The celibate Knights whose ranks were constantly replenished by new waves of outsiders became increasingly alienated from Prussian society, while native Prussians could only climb the lowest steps of the career-ladder of offices.[6] Contemporary accounts show the first signs of the development of a common identity hostile to the Order, which fed on the resistance against the increasingly frequent violations of the law and the corruption within the leadership of the Knights, culminating in the murder of three Danzig delegates in 1411.[7] It was not until 1440, however, that the Prussian estates openly formed a political union against the Teutonic Knights, claiming the right of resistance against injuries to

XV wieku', *Czasopismo Prawno-Historyczne* 30 (1978), 104–7; see also Max Bär, *Die Behördenverfassung in Westpreußen seit der Ordenszeit* (Danzig: A.W. Kafemann, 1912), p. 13.

[4] Josef Leinz, 'Ursachen des Abfalls Danzigs vom Deutschen Orden unter besonderer Berücksichtigung der nationalen Frage', *Westpreußen-Jahrbuch* 13–14 (1963–64), 2–5.

[5] See chapter 3 below, pp. 46–7.

[6] Eric Christiansen, *The Northern Crusades. The Baltic and the Catholic Frontier 1100–1525*, New Studies in Medieval History (London and Basingstoke: Macmillan, 1980), p. 236; and Janusz Małłek, 'Die Entstehung und Entwicklung eines Sonderbewußtseins in Preußen während des 15. und 16. Jahrhunderts', in *Preußen und Polen*, p. 74.

[7] Udo Arnold, 'Geschichtsschreibung im Preußenland bis zum Ausgang des 16. Jahrhunderts', *Jahrbuch für die Geschichte Mittel- und Ostdeutschlands*, 19 (1970), 77–9, 84–5, 92–3; Bernhart Jähnig, 'Bevölkerungsveränderungen und Landesbewußtsein im Preußenland', *Blätter für deutsche Landesgeschichte* 121 (1985), 142.

their liberties.[8] The initiative of the Prussian League against the Order once more came predominantly from the towns: sixty-two of them were represented during the first provincial assemblies (*Tagfahrten*), in the early fifteenth century.[9]

Gradually, the Prussian estates came to regard the Polish king, who had granted them political privileges in exchange for an oath of allegiance after the battle of Tannenberg, as their natural ally. The Prussians had to repeal this oath when the Order recovered some of its strength after the first peace of Thorn in 1411. Henceforth, however, voices pressing for a change of government grew stronger. The Polish view that the Knights had illegally seized not only Eastern Pomerania, but also the Prussian territories, and particularly the Kulm lands, from the Poles in the thirteenth century, found some support in Prussian historiography.[10] The 1440 Prussian League against the Knights envisaged the creation of a bicameral representative institution, the Prussian *Landesrat*, consisting of two separate but equal chambers of the cities and of the nobles, which took decisions with the unanimous consent of all members. In 1449, when the Teutonic Knights sought support from the Emperor and the Council of Basel, this rudimentary Prussian parliament was prohibited by imperial decree; but it immediately reconstituted itself as a secret organisation. In 1454, seeking help from the Polish king and placing themselves under Polish authority, the estates of Prussia directly translated their previous experience with political representation in the *Landesrat* into the new political environment under their new Polish ruler.

### ROYAL PRUSSIA AS A PROVINCE OF THE POLISH CROWN

In the political language of the Polish Renaissance, whose culture had already penetrated Prussian political thinking and writing under Teutonic rule, the Incorporation Act of 6 March 1454, which joined the Prussian territories in union with the crown of Poland, accused the Teutonic Knights of tyranny: their acts of perfidy and violence had nullified all previous treaties and obligations owed by their former subjects. This document was later accorded quasi-religious veneration by the Prussian estates, and particularly the representatives of the three major cities. As a catalogue of gravamina against the German Order, it details the estates' accusations. The Teutonic Knights' evil deeds – murder, conspiracy, exploitation, rape, fraud and tyranny – justified, in the words of the Polish king, the act of resistance against unlawful government. As a 'king who obeys the laws set by God', Casimir Jagiellończyk accepted the Prussian prelates, knights, burghers, nobles, and all inhabitants of the Prussian lands under his rule, to which they 'spontaneously and voluntarily' subjected themselves: 'reintegramus, reunimus, invisceramus et incor-

---

[8] Leinz, 'Ursachen des Abfalls Danzigs', pp. 2–4.
[9] Biskup, 'Rola miast', p. 103.
[10] Janina Dworzaczkowa, 'Kronika Pruska Szymona Grunaua jako źródło historyczne', *Studia Źródłoznawcze* 2 (1952), 119–46; Christiansen, *The Northern Crusades*, pp. 159ff.

poramus et ad usum participacionem omnium bonorum, iurium, libertatum et praerogativum . . . regni Poloniae' (we reintegrate, reunite, reinstate, and incorporate [you], for the participation in all properties, laws, liberties and prerogatives . . . of the Polish kingdom).[11]

Casimir confirmed that the Prussian estates shared all the rights and privileges of citizens of the Polish crown, including the election of the king, and all previous immunities that they had obtained from former rulers. In the future, these privileges were to be reaffirmed, extended and protected by his successors; they included the liberation from the *Pfundzoll* – the hated tariff levelled by the Teutonic Order on all merchandise going through the port of Danzig, the *ius indigenatus*, which secured all royal offices in the Prussian province to natives, and the right to decide all affairs that concerned Prussia alone (*omnes causas notabiles*) in their own estate assemblies. The Prussians were also granted the privilege to mint their own money in the cities of Thorn and Danzig; the validity of Kulm and Magdeburg law in the whole province was recognised, as was freedom of trade. The defection of the Prussian estates was followed by the Thirteen Years War (1454–66) between the Prussian estates, supported by Poland and Lithuania, and the Teutonic Knights, which led to widespread devastation, whose economic and demographic consequences were felt for decades. In 1466 the Second Peace of Thorn divided Prussia into two provinces: the western lands, under the name of Royal Prussia, remained under the Polish crown, while the eastern lands, with the city of Königsberg, continued to be ruled by the Order. The Order's rump state only lasted until 1525, however, when its last Grand Master, Albrecht of Hohenzollern, turned Lutheran, secularised the organisation and created the Duchy of Prussia as a fief of the Polish crown. The 'Prussian homage', first enacted on Cracow market square in 1525 and repeated on the coronation of every Polish king or the succession of every new duke until 1648, was the necessary price paid for ducal autonomy.

Although the legacy of the Teutonic Knights left distinct traces on the political, economic and social development of Royal Prussia, its *Landesrat* accepted the Polish model for the organisation of political offices. In 1454 four palatinates (*województwa*) were founded, the largest being the palatinate of Pomerania, west of the Vistula river, including Danzig. To the South-East, across the Vistula river, was the palatinate of Chełmno (Kulm, Culm). In 1454 the third and fourth palatinates were Elbing and Königsberg, but after the Thirteen Years War, the administrative structure was remodelled. The Polish king transformed the palatinate of Elbing (Elbląg) into a castellanate, while Malbork (Marienburg) became the third Royal Prussian palatinate. After 1510 the rest of this palatinate was declared royal demesne land, what is known as *ekonomia*, under the immediate administration of the king who drew substantial income from

---

[11] 'Incorporatio terrarum Prussiae, 6 March 1454, Cracow', in Karol Górski, *Związek Pruski i poddanie się Prus Polsce. Zbiór tekstów źródłowych* (Poznań: Instytut Zachodni, 1949), p. 177.

it.[12] The territory of Warmia (Ermland) remained under the jurisdiction of its bishop, who from 1508 became the highest provincial dignitary and head of the Prussian *Landesrat*. The Warmian bishopric first depended on the archbishopric of Riga, secularised in 1566, and then continued to be directly overseen by Rome.[13] In consequence, during and after the Reformation, the majority of Warmia's population remained Catholic, while the bishop alone represented the Warmian estates, including the town of Kulm, which, in contrast to the estates of the Royal Prussian palatinates, were not allowed to elect and send their own envoys to the provincial diet.

The peace treaty between Poland and the Teutonic Knights, concluded at Thorn in 1466, confirmed the privileges granted in 1454. In compensation for their great losses during the Thirteen Years War, the major cities were given villages and landed property outside their city walls which provided their treasuries with important new income from taxes, milling rights, local markets, brewery privileges and other sources.[14] Similarly, rich landowners from old and famous Prussian families who, after 1466, had fled their lands in eastern Prussia, which were still under the Order's control, to settle in Royal Prussia, were compensated by the Polish king with lands and offices. But even this could not completely eradicate their lingering resentment against the Polish monarchy for letting slip the opportunity of destroying the Teutonic state once and for all.

In 1467, the Polish diet in Piotrków sanctioned the new structures of the Prussian *Landesrat*, now including three palatines (of Pomerania, Chełmno, Malbork), three castellans (Kulm, Elbing, Danzig), three chamberlains, one for each palatinate, and two representatives from each of the three main cities, Thorn, Danzig and Elbing. Every new palatine's appointment had to be unanimously confirmed by the remaining members of the diet. From 1526, the palatines summoned the district dietines, sent out tax decrees which needed the consent of the rest of the Prussian estates, mobilised the levy in wartime, and headed the palatine and country courts, with powers of jurisdiction over the nobility.[15] All three palatines also held starosties (leases on royal lands, from which they received their remuneration).[16] Royal Prussia soon came to be dominated by a political elite: almost half of all Prussian palatinates between 1454 and 1772 were drawn from the twenty Prussian noble families which produced at least three members who achieved senatorial rank in the Prussian provincial diet. The Działyński family

[12] Marian Biskup et al. (general eds.), *Historia Pomorza*, vol. II/1: '1464/66–1648/57', ed. Gerard Labuda (Poznań: Wydawnictwo Poznańskie, 1976), p. 201; and Bär, *Behördenverfassung*, p. 36.

[13] Aloizy Szorc, *Dominium Warmińskie 1243–1772. Przywileje, prawo chełmińskie na tle ustroju Warmii* (Olsztyn: Wydawnictwo Pojezierze, 1990), p. 23; Christiansen, *The Northern Crusades*, pp. 123–4; 142; 159.

[14] Andrzej Klonder, 'Szlachta a Królewszczyzny Prus Królewskich za Stefana Batorego (1576–1586)', *Zapiski Historyczne* 52, no. 3 (1987), 78.

[15] Wacław Odyniec, *Dzieje Prus Królewskich 1454–1772* (Warsaw: PWN, 1972), pp. 29–30.

[16] Bär, *Behördenverfassung*, p. 35.

provided sixteen Prussian senators, eleven of whom were palatinates, the Czapski family fifteen, six of whom were castellans, four palatines, and the Konopacki family followed with ten senatorial members, three of whom occupied Royal Prussian bishoprics.[17]

The three castellans in Prussia, whose tasks were mainly to give military support to the palatines and to raise the Prussian noble levy in time of war, were also granted royal lands for their subsistence. The office of chamberlain was created only in 1478 and had no judicial and administrative role, but they held a seat in the council as Prussian senators and received profits from landed property. Royal Prussia also had a separate treasurer who was appointed by the king and collected the taxes agreed upon by the whole Prussian Diet during its two annual sessions held on the feast days of St Stanisław (8 May) and St Michael (30 September) in Marienburg and Graudenz.[18] Most other officials, after the Polish pattern, held royal sinecures attached to functions which had become purely honorary, like the cup-bearer, the carver, the sword-bearer and the ensign. The ambition of the Prussian *Landesrat* to maintain as high a degree of judicial and political self-government as possible resulted in its election of all aldermen and members of the district and municipal assessorial courts, while the city courts elected or co-opted their members from among the urban political elite represented in the city councils. The mass of the nobility was excluded from these procedures until the early sixteenth century, which demonstrates the powerful role of the *Landesrat*, the senatorial offices, and the representatives from the three major cities before the 1526 reforms which established a 'lower chamber' in the Prussian Diet.[19]

As the extensive landed estates administered by the Teutonic Knights had been seized by the Polish king, 50.9 per cent of the land in Royal Prussia was now made up of royal estates, comprising 17 royal towns and 264 villages, which could be distributed to noble office-holders, or to the major Prussian cities as *królewszczyzna* (royal land in the hand of a leaseholder or starosta). This compares with 33 per cent in Little Poland, 15 per cent in Great Poland, and 14 per cent in Mazovia.[20] Of the three Prussian palatinates, Pomerania with nineteen starosties and a large number

[17] Jerzy Dygdała and Krzysztof Mikulski, 'Zmiany w elicie władzy Prus Królewskich w XV–XVIII wieku', in Jerzy Dygdała and Krzysztof Mikulski (eds.), *Szlachta i ziemiaństwo na Pomorzu w dobie nowożytnej XVI–XX wieku, Materiały sympozjum w Toruniu 9 IV 1992* (Toruń: TNT, 1993), pp. 10–16.

[18] Jan Gerlach, 'Grudziądz miejscem obrad sejmiku generalnego Prus Królewskich (1454–1772)', *Rocznik Grudziądzki* (1963), 15.

[19] Jolanta Essmanowska-Dworzaczkowa, 'Ruch szlachecki w Prusach Królewskich w I połowie XVI wieku' (unpublished doctoral dissertation, Poznań University, 1951), p. 8; see also Zbigniew Naworski, *Sejmik Generalny Prus Królewskich 1569–1772. Organizacja i funkcjonowanie na tle systemu zgromadzeń stanowych prowincji* (Toruń: UMK, 1992), p. 43.

[20] A. Mączak, in *Historia Pomorza*, II/1, p. 201; and Zielińska, according to Antoni Mączak's figures, ibid., p. 88. Bömelburg shows that in 1771, four Royal Prussian starostas still paid more than 10,000 złp *kwarta* taxes, which put them among the seven richest starostas in Great Poland and Royal Prussia; Bömelburg, *Zwischen polnischer Ständegesellschaft*, pp. 137–8; see also Klonder, 'Szlachta a królewszczyzny Prus Królewskich', p. 77.

of prosperous towns was richer than Chełmno with fourteen, and Malbork with seven starosties. Pomerania was not only the largest but also the most populous palatinate, with about 150,000 inhabitants in the late sixteenth century.[21] Increasingly, in the seventeenth century, the wealthiest starosties tended to go to a group of senatorial families consisting mainly of newcomers from Poland or Lithuania, whose appointment was opposed by the local Prussian nobility.[22]

Nevertheless, no closed caste or class of landowning magnates emerged. Analyses show the high decree of fluctuation and instability of the Royal Prussian landholding families – a pattern typical for the Polish-Lithuanian nobility as a whole[23] – with merely eight Royal Prussian families more or less continuously holding starosties and royal landed estates between the late fifteenth and the end of the seventeenth century.[24] The lesser senatorial offices often served as stepping-stones to higher office in Prussia or Poland, but career patterns were far from predictable. In the incorporation act the Polish king had assured the Prussian estates that only natives would be appointed to royal offices in the province. This privilege was violated almost immediately, however, and very few native Prussians obtained the bishoprics of Warmia and Chełmno. Instead, from the sixteenth century, Polish kings promoted native Poles to these offices which provided their holders with considerable income and political influence. This was but one of many disputes which emerged from the very outset. Despite the spirited defence by the *Landesrat* of its right of self-government, the abolition of the Prussian governorship in 1467, the royal refusal to establish a separate Prussian appeal court and the conflict with the king about the appointment of the Warmian bishop in 1470 only increased Prussian resistance to 'Polish interference'.[25] In 1472, the *Landesrat* presented a programme which demanded the observance of the privileges of 1454, above all of the *ius indigenatus*, the return of Prussian offices and lands granted to Polish appointees and the restoration of the governor. In 1485, the confederated Prussian estates challenged the king by refusing their oath of allegiance until he fulfilled his promises. It was only during the reign of Casimir's successors, Jan Olbracht and Alexander, that tensions eased somewhat. In 1506, as a concession to Prussian demands, king Alexander created a separate treasury which was directly subordinated to the Polish king alone, and

[21] Chełmno had 95,000, and Malbork 55,000, or 26.3 inhabitants per km², making it the most densely populated; Pomerania had 11.4 and Kulm 20.4 inhabitants per km². In the sixteenth century, Royal Prussia contained ca. 298,000 inhabitants, and at the end of the eighteenth century almost 400,000 (20.2 per km²); see Odyniec, *Dzieje Prus Królewskich*, p. 18.

[22] Stefan Ciara, *Senatorowie i dygnitarze koroni w drugiej połowie XVII wieku* (Wrocław: Ossolineum, 1990), p. 82.

[23] Robert I. Frost, 'The Nobility of Poland-Lithuania', 1569–1795', in Scott, Hamish M. (ed.), *The European Nobilities in the Seventeenth and Eighteenth Centuries*, vol. II: *Northern, Central and Eastern Europe* (London and New York: Longman, 1995), pp. 209–13.

[24] *Historia Pomorza*, p. 204; Dygdała and Mikulski, 'Zmiany w elicie', 19–29.

[25] Janusz Małłek, 'Verfassung, Verwaltung, Recht und Militär im Königlichen Preußen', in Ernst Opgenoorth (general ed.), *Handbuch der Geschichte Ost- und Westpreußens*, 3 vols., vol. II/1: 'Von der Teilung bis zum Schwedisch-Polnischen Krieg, 1466–1655' (Lüneburg: Verlag Nordostdeutsches Kulturwerk, 1994), pp. 52–5.

which enhanced the Prussian estates, pride in their self-government and their independence from Polish and Lithuanian fiscal needs.

At the core of the conflict was the nature of the relationship between Poland and Royal Prussia. According to the Prussian estates, they had concluded a union with the person of the Polish king by guarding their control over 'internal affairs'. The incorporation act, however, which was signed not only by Casimir Jagiellończyk but also by several Polish senators, bishops and representatives of the city of Cracow, speaks of Prussia joining the *regnum*, granting the provincial nobility the same privileges as the Polish noble estates. As Karol Górski and Janusz Małłek have argued, it then would have made little sense for the Prussians, faced with the wrath and military might of the Teutonic Order in 1454, to conclude a union exclusively with the king, and not with the military and political apparatus behind him, unless they had a completely unrealistic view of the Polish monarchy and constitution. For the new relationship with Poland was based as much on a vision of the importance of the estates in limiting the power of the ruler, as on a desire for protection against the ruler: it was unlikely that the Prussians would exchange the despotism of the Order for the despotism of a foreign ruler. But in the emerging Renaissance state, the Polish szlachta had successfully demanded a share in legislation and the conduct of public affairs, such as the distribution of offices and the decision over war and peace, and the right of protection against the arbitrary exercise of power by the king, the royal council and the king's entourage.[26] The formation of a strong corporate structure, in which the szlachta, representing the *res publica*, complemented the authority of the crown given to the king to administer, was well under way in the early fifteenth century.

The electoral principle had emerged as early as the fourteenth century, due to the practice of partible inheritance by the ruling Piast dynasty and to their extinction after 1370. As Polish Renaissance writers presupposed the monarchy's limitation by a social contract between the ruler and the 'political nation', the szlachta, it is not surprising that Poland was particularly receptive to the political ideas which accompanied the conciliarist movement in Europe. The Polish nobility eagerly absorbed Marsilius of Padua's argument against the justification of the divine right of kings, and in favour of electoral monarchy and government by council. The new Academy of Cracow, founded in 1364, was a centre of conciliarist thinking, profoundly influencing the fundamental principle of the government of Poland: rulers receive their legitimacy by delegation from the people and the communicative nature of sovereign power.[27] At the same time, however, Aris-

---

[26] Henryk Litwin, 'W poszukiwaniu rodowodu demokracji szlacheckiej. Polska myśl polityczna w piśmiennictwie XV i XVI w.', in Sucheni-Grabowska, A. and Żaryn, M. (eds.), *Między monarchą a demokracją. Studia z dziejów Polski XV–XVIII wieku* (Warsaw: Wyd. Sejmowe, 1994), pp. 23–5; Jerzy Wyrozumski, 'Geneza senatu w Polsce', *Senat w Polsce. Dzieje i teraźniejszość. Sesja naukowa, Kraków 25–26 maja 1993* (Warsaw: Kancelaria Senatu RP. Biuro Informacyjne, 1993), p. 29.

[27] Quentin Skinner, *The Foundations of Modern Political Thought*, vol. II: *The Age of Reformation* (Cambridge University Press, 1978; 6th edn, 1996), p. 123.

totelian political philosophy dominated Poland's constitutionalist literature: the mixture of the three best forms of government, monarchy, aristocracy and polity, was considered by far the most suitable and successful model for the multinational and multireligious Rzeczpospolita, in stark contrast to the political ideology associated with the 'new monarchies' of the fifteenth and sixteenth centuries, such as Aragon-Castile, France, the Habsburg monarchy under Maximilian I, and England after the War of the Roses.

Constitutionalist ideas did not remain mere abstractions, but gained increasingly concrete definition: despite the regular succession of the Jagiellonian kings until the death of the childless Sigismund August in 1572, the Polish nobility possessed a de facto election agreement with its monarchy.[28] The privileges obtained by the Polish szlachta at Nieszawa, in 1454, which tied the royal demand for the levée-en-masse to the consent of local noble dietines, and which gave the szlachta influence on the election of judges, were important milestones on the way to the Polish parliamentary system. In 1493, a bicameral diet with a senate council as upper house, and a lower house, the chamber of envoys (*izba poselska*) representing each local dietine, gathered for the first time in Piotrków. From 1505, 'nihil novi' – nothing new – could be legislated without the mutual consent of the senate and the chamber of envoys. The legal norms of the Polish kingdom clearly reflected not the monarchs', but the nobility's political aspirations, as well as those of the church and, to some extent, of the cities and the countryside.[29]

Since the introduction of bicameralism, the parliamentary structure and the limitation of the powers of the monarch by the rule of law had formed the core of the Polish constitutional ideal. During the mid-sixteenth century, Andrzej Frycz Modrzewski, a political writer and supporter of the Reformation in Poland, emphasised that a strong Polish monarchy, albeit limited and controlled by the Diet, might advance the cause of social reform and shield political and religious peace in Poland through tolerance and internal consensus against the attack of 'papal tyranny'. Significantly, the wars against the Teutonic Order, whose regime influential writers such as Paweł Włodkowic condemned as tyrannical, contributed much to the formulation of a constitutional theory of szlachta sovereignty.[30] Włodkowic's thesis that all free men had the right to resist tyrannical power found its reflection in Casimir Jagiellończyk's justification of the incorporation act of 1454: Prussia had been illegally taken from Poland, and its citizens had every right to return to the crown after their ordeal at the hands of the Teutonic Knights. Lawyers and scholars from Cracow University even propounded the view that such

---

[28] Gottfried Schramm, 'Polen, Böhmen, Ungarn: Übernationale Gemeinsamkeiten in der politischen Kultur des späten Mittelalters und der frühen Neuzeit', in Bahlcke, J., Bömelburg, H.-J. and Kersken, N.(eds.), *Ständefreiheit und Staatsgestaltung in Ostmitteleuropa. Übernationale Gemeinsamkeiten in der politischen Kultur vom 16.–18. Jahrhundert* (Leipzig: Universitätsverlag, 1996), pp. 29–30.

[29] Anna Sucheni-Grabowska, 'Społeczność szlachecka a państwo', *Polska w epoce Odrodzenia* (Warsaw: Wiedza Powszechna, 1986), pp. 19–20.

[30] Litwin, 'W poszukiwaniu', p. 21.

an act was nothing exceptional: 'It happens almost daily that kings and rulers are rejected for their violence and injustice, while new rulers are accepted.'[31] For the Prussians, just as for the Sicilians who in the thirteenth century broke the tyrannical power of their Anjou rulers, or the Dutch who repudiated Philip II in the 1580s, the uprising against a tyrant was legitimised by divine and common law.

By virtue of shared political ideals and parliamentary traditions, the incorporation of Prussia therefore united two similar political cultures. The strong defence of Prussian privileges, as laid down in 1454, did not stem from an anti-Polish, separatist spirit, but from embracing the same corporate values and belief in the power of self-government and the rule of law as the Polish nobility.[32] As in other parts of the Commonwealth, Royal Prussian nobles considered themselves the 'political nation', but the Prussian nobility could not interfere in the self-government of the cities as easily as could starostas in Poland in the affairs of Polish towns.[33] In Royal Prussia, enclaves of noble property within the cities (*jurydiki*), which in Poland and Lithuania contributed decisively to the growing domination of the nobility over the urban population, were prohibited. Despite a permanent conflict of interests, which intensified during the seventeenth and eighteenth centuries, the legal barriers between urban and noble self-government, economic interests and jurisdiction remained more effectively in place in Royal Prussia. The estates, and in particular the cities, were aware that it was their specific historical tradition of 'German law', their medieval Kulm charters and the special relationship with the crown since the rebellion of 1454, that had created strong roots of decentralised policy-making.[34] It was in this legal and economic sense – and not in the sense of nineteenth-century ethnic nationalism – that the burghers were proud of their 'German legacy'. The cities were usually joined by the richer and middling szlachta in the defence of their traditions of self-government and decentralised power structures, reflected in the rights and privileges granted to them by the Teutonic Knights as well as by the Polish kings since 1454/66.

### THE UNION OF LUBLIN

The creation of a lower chamber of envoys to complement the Royal Prussian *Landesrat* decisively changed the position of this body at the beginning of the sixteenth century. It was transformed into a general diet (*Landtag*), modelled on the Polish Sejm.[35] The *Constitutiones Sigismundi*, decreed by Sigismund I in 1526,

---

[31] Ibid., p. 25, quoting Jakub z Szadka, jurist in Cracow, in 1464.
[32] Józef Gierowski, 'Szlachecki samorząd województw i ziem w XVI–XVIII w.', *Acta Universitatis Wratislaviensis* 945, Historia LXVI (1988), 154.
[33] Daniel Stone, 'The End of Medieval Particularism: Polish Cities and the Diet, 1764–89', *Canadian-Slavonic Papers* 20 (1978), 194–207; also Bogucka and Samsonowicz, *Dzieje miast*, pp. 324–5.
[34] Gierowski, 'Szlachecki samorząd', p. 158.
[35] Janusz Małłek, 'Bikameralismus in Ordenspreußen, Königlich-Preußen und Herzogtum Preußen vom 15. bis zum 18. Jahrhundert', in Blom, H. W., Blockmans, W. P. and de Schlepper, H. (eds.),

institutionalised the bicameral system: the Prussian diet was to meet biannually, preceded and followed by regular dietines in the three Prussian palatinates. The new power which the szlachta acquired through these local dietines to confirm the decisions of the general diet has been interpreted as a successful restriction of the oligarchy of the senate chamber and its small circle of councillors. As the poorer Prussian nobility learned from their Polish counterparts in the central Sejm, the former unity and harmony between the szlachta, the noble members of the senate (the former *Landesrat*) and the cities suffered.[36]

To what extent the unanimity of the Prussian estates was undermined by this development was demonstrated in the 1560s, when the powerful 'execution movement' spilt across the borders of the province. The Polish szlachta's demand for the 'execution of the laws' (*executio legum*) and the restoration of revenues from alienated royal lands to the king's treasury (*executio bonorum*) was directed against the power of leaseholders of royal lands whose economic base often provided them with political influence over a provincial client network and ultimately a seat in the senate council.[37] The execution question was linked with another demand: the parliamentary union of Poland with Lithuania and Prussia, which, so the szlachta envoys hoped, would lead to a more equal distribution of tax burdens and the complete legal and political assimilation of all parts of the Polish-Lithuanian state. As the royal share of land in Royal Prussia was particularly large, the temptation for the king to alienate it in return for special services and favours was great. The grievances of the lower Prussian nobility and the towns against the thirty-five Prussian starostas, some of whom infringed shamelessly upon noble and urban brewery rights and quarrelled over the use of lakes and forests, were notorious.[38] Although Royal Prussian nobles generally opposed the idea of a closer union with Poland, their representatives in the chamber of envoys pressed for support of the execution movement, against the unanimous resistance of the members of the Prussian senate council. During sessions of the Polish Sejm in 1562 and 1563, delegates from both Prussian chambers were invited to join the parliamentary debate when the concept of Prussian self-government, the cherished *causae notabiles*, came under strong fire from the Poles. Should the Prussians abstain and

*Bicameralisme tweekamerstelsel vroeger en nu handelingen van de internationale conferentie ter gelegenheid van hel 175-jarie bestaan van de eerste Kamer der Staaten-Generaal in de Nederlanden* (The Hague: SDU, 1992), p. 178.

[36] Witold Szczuczko, 'Izba niższa generalnego Prus Królewskich 1548–1562', in Nowak, Zenon (ed.), *W kręgu stanowych i kulturalnych przeobrażeń Europy Północnej w XIV–XVIII wieku* (Toruń: UMK, 1988), p. 138; Gerlach, 'Grudziądz miejscem obrad', pp. 16–18; and Janusz Małłek, in *Handbuch der Geschichte Ost- und Westpreußens*, pp. 61–2.

[37] Edward Opaliński, 'Die Funktionen regionaler Ämter im Machtsystem der polnischen Adelsrepublik in der zweiten Hälfte des 16. und in der ersten Hälfte des 17. Jahrhunderts. Das Beispiel der Woiwodschaften Łęczyca und Sieradz', in Bahlcke, Bömelburg and Kersten (eds.), *Ständefreiheit und Staatsgestaltung*, pp. 75–80.

[38] Witold Szczuczko, *Sejmy koronne 1562–1564 a ruch egzekucyjny w Prusach Królewskich* (Toruń: UMK, 1994), p. 18.

defend their special status or opt for participation and shared obligations, side by side with their Polish and Lithuanian brothers? The decision was more or less taken for them. With the support of the Polish szlachta at the Lublin Sejm in 1569, King Sigismund August decided to incorporate the Royal Prussian parliament into the Polish Sejm. The majority of the lower nobility continued to insist on the validity of the privilege of 1454 and refused to take their seats among the Polish szlachta in the Sejm of 1569, but the Prussian senators started yielding to royal pressure. They were convinced, they later argued, of the duty to obey their king by entering the Polish senate. The offices of the palatines and castellans, as well as the two bishops of Warmia and Chełmno, now played a double role, as Prussian provincial councillors, or *Landesräte*, and as Polish senators, or *Reichsräte*. Noble envoys, elected by the Prussian general diet, were henceforth represented in the chamber of envoys of the Polish Sejm, where they could defend the interests of the Prussian nobility.[39]

Since the eighteenth century, historians have repeatedly claimed that this union, which merged parts of the Prussian Diet with the Polish Sejm, decisively diminished or even destroyed the self-government and the special privileges of the province.[40] The transformation of the Prussian Diet into a regular Polish-style *ante-* and *post-comitialis*, meeting before and after the sessions of the Polish-Lithuanian Sejm and summoned by the king, certainly meant a great change to the country's political traditions and to the nature of its constitution, but it did not abolish them. Indeed, Royal Prussia remained the only province in the Polish crown lands where a bicameral structure (of a senate and a chamber of envoys) survived on a provincial level until the end of the Commonwealth, and where cities remained part of the corporate political culture, despite the wish of the lower nobility everywhere in the Commonwealth to enhance local powers of self-control to the detriment of central legislative bodies.[41] From the second half of the seventeenth century, the palatine and district dietines were held independently of the Prussian Diet, which enhanced the internal decentralisation of the country. This trend was also reflected in the growing numbers of Prussian envoys, elected by the Prussian Diet or travelling independently and without mandate, who participated in the Polish Sejm from the 1660s, until the Sejm of 1764 limited their number. In contrast, the number of Polish and Lithuanian noble envoys was restricted to two per palatinate.

The incorporation of the Prussian senators and szlachta into the Polish Sejm first provoked considerable disorientation and disunity among the Prussian nobles. When challenged by the cities during the 1572 Prussian Diet as to why the Prussian

---

[39] Naworksi, *Sejmik Generalny*, p. 46; see also APGd Nucleus Lengnicha 300.29/237–8 (Index).
[40] Gottfried Lengnich, *Geschichte der Lande Preußen*, vol. II, p. 369; see chapter 9 below.
[41] Henryk Olszewski, 'Ustrój polityczny Rzeczypospolitej', in Tazbir, Janusz (ed.), *Polska XVII wiek* (Warsaw: PWN, 1974), pp. 88–93; Andrzej Kamiński, 'The *Szlachta* of the Polish-Lithuanian Commonwealth', in Banac, Ivo and Bushkovitch, Paul (eds.), *The Nobility in Russia and Eastern Europe* (New Haven: Yale Consortium, 1983), pp. 35–8; Małłek, 'Bikameralismus', pp. 175–87.

senators had surrendered to the new union, the palatine of Chełmno defended himself and his peers:

> As the estates (*Lande*) do not remember that they ever defected from the old union [of 1454], and always defended their ancient liberties, it is obvious that the new union was forced upon them, so that they had to accept it against their better judgement. It worries the councillors (*Räte*) from the countryside to see that the cities separated themselves from the other councillors and the lesser nobility, and sought dispensation from the union, which the representatives from the countryside never supported. They only gave their oath because they respected the late king [Sigismund August] . . . The only councillor clearly intent on staying with the previous, unaltered state of union was the palatine of Marienburg.[42]

Why did the Prussian nobility accept the union? Historians have yet to give a satisfactory answer to this problem. Most interpretations rely on the schematic idea of a fundamental hostility between the Prussian 'oligarchy' (i.e. the senate, including the three major cities) and the lower szlachta.[43] This view of clear-cut social and political divisions between the upper and the lower chambers in the Prussian diet, however, conflicts with ample evidence of szlachta willingness to back decisions and activities of their senators who represented Prussian interests in the Polish Sejm, before and after 1569.[44] The diet protocols in the Gdańsk archives suggest that the influence of a few strong personalities among the Prussian nobility in both chambers was decisive. One of them was Jan Kostka, castellan of Danzig in 1572, who argued in favour of political realism: 'The Polish senators would never allow the Prussians to form a separate state, once they had incorporated and joined them with the crown . . . It was not obvious why they would desire such a thing anyway.'[45]

Despite the accepted wisdom that diverging economic interests split the szlachta and the representatives of the towns and cities, the protocols also reveal that szlachta support sometimes extended to the major Prussian cities. The estates in both chambers demonstrated solidarity in the face of subsequent attempts by the king and the Sejm to impose new customs duties on Danzig and the whole province, or to submit the cities' independent jurisdiction to noble or royal courts in Poland.[46] Thus Zbigniew Naworski might be closest to the truth in stressing that the Prussian estates oscillated between a sense of duty to the king, the support of a closer union and the defence of privileges confirmed in the incorporation act.[47] Any resistance was subsequently overcome by the king's single-mindedness, peer pressure from the Polish nobility and a lack of unanimity among the Prussians them-

---

[42] Lengnich, *Geschichte der Lande Preußen*, vol. II, p. 411.

[43] Szczuczko, *Sejmy koronne*, pp. 179–84.

[44] In several instances, the lower szlachta backed the senate in conflicts with Poland over the independence of the Prussian treasury; Stanisław Achremczyk, *Życie polityczne Prus Królewskich w latach 1696–1772*, Rozprawy i Materiały OBN im. Kętrzyńskiego (Olsztyn: PAN, 1991), pp. 188–9.

[45] Lengnich, *Geschichte der Lande Preußen*, vol. III, p. 48.

[46] 'Laudum Mariaeburgense' (8 July 1671), 'Urkunden und Lauda betr[effend] die Immunität der preußischen Städte, 1626–1742', APT Kat. II, VII.26, pp. 142–6.

[47] Naworski, *Sejmik Generalny*, p. 47.

selves. The sense of loss regarding the former unity was greatest among the cities. In 1572, they complained that considerably fewer senators and szlachta attended the biannual Prussian diets than in the past; by avoiding the general Diet, envoys went directly from the exclusively noble palatinate dietines to the Polish diet. The palatine of Chełmno, Jan Działyński, agreed with the city representatives: 'that things are not as they ought to be . . . one feels that the councillors are not as conscientious as they once were, as some of them try to curry favour with the court. I alone want to stand by the country [Royal Prussia] and freely speak my mind.'[48]

Although the three major Royal Prussian cities had refused to join the central Sejm in Lublin, they still felt it necessary to send observers to the Polish Sejm, and the secretary of the city of Danzig produced detailed reports and protocols of the diet sessions.[49] Well-versed in lobbying techniques, the Prussian cities tried to influence the king mainly through private audiences, or even relied on the noble representatives of Royal Prussia and their good will to defend urban needs and interests. Abstention had its political advantages: this strategy saved the most powerful among the cities (in particular Danzig) from pressure to agree to taxation imposed by the Sejm and enhanced their special status. After 1648, they did not even appear any longer at royal elections, though they insisted that they retain the right to participate in the election of their king. Trying to manipulate political decisions behind the scenes seemed both convenient and more effective.

The obvious disunity of the Prussian estates, created by the union of 1569, left deep scars on political life in the province and exposed the central problem that hampered the Royal Prussian-Polish relationship for the following two centuries: the choice between direct participation in the Commonwealth's policies, and the preservation of Royal Prussia's separate realm of law and self-government. Later chapters will try to explain why self-government and the sense of being different was so vital to the Prussian cities, and, to some extent, also to many Prussian noblemen. The definition of their separate identity, which the Prussians had formulated during the fifteenth century, clearly took quite a battering in 1569, and their self-esteem suffered. Old identities came under attack and new ones were tested.[50] Prussian nobles and burghers recast their roles in the new Polish-Lithuanian Commonwealth, until the reforms of 1791 effectively abolished the separate constitution of Royal Prussia. What is most important, however, is that the union of 1569 did not herald the end of the Prussian Diet; it remained an instrument protecting Prussian legal traditions. Two of the most important among these traditions were the *ius indigenatus* and Kulm law.

---

[48] Lengnich, *Geschichte der Lande Preußen*, vol. III, p. 6.
[49] For the activities of the city secretaries of Danzig and Thorn (called 'residents') in Warsaw, see Kazimierz Maliszewski, 'Mieszczańskie formy i metody komunikacji społecznej w wielkich miastach Prus Królewskich w XVII–XVIII wieku', *Zapiski Historyczne* 57, no. 4 (1992), 39–62; and Walter Recke, 'Der Danziger Hof in Warschau und seine Bewohner', *Mitteilungen des Westpreußischen Geschichtsvereins* 24 (1925), 17–40.
[50] Ringmar, *Identity, Interest and Action*, p. 83.

## THE *IUS INDIGENATUS*

Nothing else, I suppose, do the Prussians hold against me than the fact that I am not a native of their country; I come, in fact, from Mazovia and Poland, and my descent is partly from Germany.[51]

These were the words of Marcin Kromer, whom the Prussian estates rejected as the royal nominee for the post of administrator of the chapter of Warmia in 1570, and then as candidate for the bishopric of Warmia, vacated after the death in 1579 of Cardinal Hosius – the first non-native Prussian bishop to have presided over this see.[52] The election proceeded under royal and papal pressure, and Kromer became head of the Prussian estates, after the Prussian diet bestowed upon him the title of *indigena*, against the opposition of several senators and some envoys of the szlachta and the major cities.[53]

The *ius indigenatus* (*indygenat*, *Indigenat*) was one of the fundamental privileges which predated Polish rule, but which Casimir Jagiellończyk had confirmed in 1454. It was formulated as the exclusive right to have only native Prussians nominated as officeholders in the province.[54] This privilege, widespread in Poland and in Europe generally, was conferred by descent from parents who were natives of the country or province, in contrast to foreigners, *alienigenae*, who were born outside or were of foreign parents. In 1562 the palatine of Chełmno Jan Działyński, speaking for the nobility, chose a slightly different definition: '(those) who came to Prussia to establish their homes here, must observe and defend the Prussian liberties'.[55] Thus acceptance of a country's constitution and customary rights offered an alternative to birth as a means of acquiring a political identity, although it was dependent upon recognition by existing citizens. Access to the *ius indigenatus* meant citizenship and membership in the political nation and the privileged legal and social status which that represented.[56]

The holder of the highest office in the Royal Prussian diet, the bishop of Warmia, was responsible for summoning the estates when there was an interregnum after the death or demise of the Polish king; therefore it seemed vital to the Prussian nobles

---

[51] Wojciech Kętrzyński, 'Martin Cromers Rede über das preußische Indigenat', *Altpreußische Monatsschrift NS* 17 (1880), 349.

[52] Aeneas Sylvius Piccolomini (later Pope Pius II) had been appointed bishop of Warmia by Calixtus III, but against the will of the Warmian chapter; he never actually conducted the affairs of the bishopric over which he officially presided from 1457 to 1458; Stanisław Achremczyk, Roman Marchwiński and Jerzy Przeracki (eds.), *Poczet Biskupów Warmińskich*, Biblioteka Olsztyńska 23 (Olsztyn: Instytut im. Wojciecha Kętrzyńskiego, 1994), pp. 105–19.

[53] Lengnich, *Geschichte der Lande Preußen*, vol. II, p. 412, and vol. III, pp. 4, 10–11.

[54] *Krótkie o Indygenacie Prześwietney Prowincyi Pruskiey obiaśnienie* (n.p., 1739), folio 2v.

[55] Stanisław Salmonowicz, 'Idea federacyjna i samorządowa w dawnej Rzeczypospolitej', in *Pamiętnik XIII Powszechnego Zjazdu Historyków Polskich, Poznań 6–9 września 1984 roku*, part II: 'Sprawozdania i sympozjów' (Wrocław, Warsaw, Cracow: Ossolineum, 1988), p. 63.

[56] Sławomir Gawlas, 'Stan badań nad polską świadomością narodową w średniowieczu', in *Państwo, naród, stany i świadomości wieków średnich. Pamięci Benedykta Zientary, 1929–1983* (Warsaw: PWN, 1990), p. 193.

and burghers that a man with such power over them ought to be one of them, who knew and respected their laws and immunities. Kromer's difficulty was that he had neither Prussian parents, nor a reputation for cherishing Royal Prussia's special constitution. In 1570, a note sent by Warmian nobles to their Polish brothers in the Sejm protested against the appointment of the Pole and *alienigena* Martin Kromer to the post of administrator of the Warmian bishopric: 'The nobility in Warmia [is] oppressed by the confiscation of their estates without reason, frightened by mandates and . . . penalties and summons to deprive them of their property. The Poles [doing all this] call themselves our brothers, but nobody remembers any brotherly demonstration of sympathy from them.'[57]

In response, Kromer claimed that the union of 1569 had united Prussia and Poland into one body. As a result, he continued, Poles and Prussians, as brothers, now had the same rights and entitlements to be appointed to each others' dignities and benefices. His argument that Prussians did not count in Poland as foreigners (*alienigeni* or *extranei*) was frequently used by the Polish side in future debates in the diets.[58] Although Prussian nobles started to acquire non-Prussian offices and lands from 1575, with the Kostka family taking the lead,[59] there was little real mutuality. Until the end of the Commonwealth, considerably more non-Prussians received dignities in Prussia than vice-versa, and ironically, this was precisely Kromer's argument in favour of his promotion in Prussia: that other non-Prussians had held offices in the province before him.[60]

In contrast to the Royal Prussian version, the Polish concept of *indigena* had little national connotation, but designated social status, and was practically synonymous with a *terrigena*, someone with the status of a landowning nobleman. *Terrigena* developed among the nobility as a distinct expression for the land-owning szlachta, usually exclusive of burghers or poor nobles without land, although several land-owning burghers from Danzig, Marienburg and Cracow had been accepted as Polish *indigenae*.[61] Zbigniew Naworski has observed that the concept of *terrigena* had acquired a more limited meaning; in the fifteenth century, it more broadly defined an inhabitant of a distinct land and region, without social connotations; by the seventeenth century, however, it was restricted to landed noblemen in the third generation born in the province.[62] These differences in meaning contributed to the sharp conflicts which arose over the issue of the distribution of Prussian offices and

[57] Lengnich, *Geschichte der Lande Preußen*, vol. II, p. 413.
[58] Kętrzyński, 'Martin Cromers Rede', 349–50.
[59] Richard Jacobi, 'Thorn, Elbing, Danzig und die polnischen Königswahlen 1573–75', *Mitteilungen des Copernicus-Vereins* 15 (1907), 44.
[60] Krzysztof Mikulski (ed.), *Urzędnicy Prus Królewskich XV–XVIII wieku* (Wrocław: Ossolineum, 1990), p. 32; for Kromer's claim, see Kętrzyński, 'Martin Cromers Rede', pp. 349 and 352.
[61] On foreigners who became Polish *indigenae*, see Zygmunt Wdowiszewski, 'Regesty Przywilejów Indygenatu w Polsce, 1519–1793', *Materiały do Biografii, Genealogii i Heraldyki Polski* V (1971), 8–78.
[62] Achremczyk, *Życie*, p. 269; Zbigniew Naworski, 'Indygenat w Prusach Królewskich 1454–1772', *Czasopismo Prawno-Historyczne* 35 (1983), 34.

lands to Poles: although the same vocabulary was applied, it had different implications. The expression of *terrigena* was rarely, if ever, used by the Prussian nobility, who continued to defend the Prussian rights of the *indigena* in their political dialogue with the king and the Polish nobility.[63]

The debate over foreigners receiving profitable offices in Royal Prussia was not resolved. The *ius indigenatus* remained, more than any other privilege, the foundation of what Prussian nobles understood as Prussian liberty. In 1537, the protocol of the General Diet of Prussia noted that the repeated attempts by the king to abolish it were regarded as 'the worst of all injustices committed against the lands and estates of our province. Everybody recognises that after the abolition of this privilege [*ius indigenatus*] . . . in the future, there would be practically nothing left of all the other rights we had . . . It is, indeed, the source of the whole Prussian liberty.'[64] Even after the union of 1569, the Polish concept of one general *ius indigenatus* for the whole Commonwealth did not catch on in Prussia. On the contrary, the Prussian estates were alarmed by the Polish tendency to override and devalue provincial privileges; indeed, the 1569 Lublin Sejm had abolished the Lithuanian *ius indigenatus* altogether.[65] Prussian treatises regularly stressed legal parallels with Lithuania, whose laws, like those of Prussia, ought to be respected by the Poles: 'The union with Lithuania was concluded *salva omnia jura* . . . It follows that Lithuanians and Prussians should not be forced against their will to accept Sejm decisions, in order to preserve the liberty of each nation, for the common good.'[66]

By the 1580s, however, many nobles, attempting to keep up appearances, had tacitly accepted that newcomers from Poland and Lithuania would be given the title *indigena* if they settled in Royal Prussia, acquired land and assumed their offices in the spirit of the province's liberties and interests.[67] In the seventeenth century, voices were raised against this practice, suggesting that it was the Prussians themselves who should be blamed for failing to defend their most central privilege: 'The crown-Poles took our leaseholds, starosties, castellanies and even palatinates in Prussia, and we still insist on the royal assurance that this does not touch our rights! But during our diets, we offer them the first places, admit them to our honours and shamelessly make them our in-laws.'[68] Nevertheless, it was recently entitled and assimilated *indigenae*, who, like converts, were often the

[63] *Indigena* was regularly used in Prussian debates and instructions to the local dietines; e.g. Jan Werden, 'Indigenat Ziemi Pruskiej przez Jana Werda podkomorzego pomorskiego nowskiego starostę, odpis z druku' (1634/1647), Ossol. 1562.

[64] 'Sejmik Generalny, Toruń, 8.5.1537', in Karol Górski and Janusz Małłek (eds.), *Prusy Królewskie i Prusy Książęce w XV i XVI wieku*, vol. I: *1466–1548, wybór tekstów* (Toruń: UMK 1971), p. 64.

[65] Naworski, 'Indygenat', 36.

[66] 'Zavadius Vapulans seu Refutatio Tractatus super advertentiam defectum Imperii Sarmatici quatenus concernit Civitatem Gedanensem', (1676), APGd, Bibl. Archivi 300.R, Tq 25, p. 9.

[67] Ibid., p. 92.

[68] 'Głos wolny', in Ochmann, *Pisma Polityczne*, p. 106; see also the protocols of the 1652 Diet, APGd, Recesy 300.29, no. 136, pp. 107ff.

fiercest defenders of their newly-gained privilege, trying to bar other newcomers to Prussia from receiving crown lands.[69] In 1696, the Prussian *ius indigenatus* was still a central part of the political programme of the Royal Prussian nobility: 'If the Prussian Indygenat is no longer upheld and no longer considered important, then all other rights and royal privileges no longer apply.'[70]

The Prussian cities shared this sense of indignation over the abuse of the privilege. Their dilemma was that the definition of the *ius indigenatus* not only differed between Poland and Royal Prussia, but was contested even within their province. As with the Polish use of *terrigena* in the seventeenth century, the term *indigena Prussiae* lost its general meaning of 'native Prussian' and became synonymous with a landed nobleman of Royal Prussian origin.[71] This development had serious consequences for the idea of citizenship and the issue of burgher participation in the Prussian political nation, defined by the nobility more and more exclusively as a nation of noble *indigenae*. The focus on the nobility was increasingly accepted by landowning burghers of the major Prussian cities, such as Michael Behm von Behmfeldt, an ennobled Danzig burgher and councillor. He defined *indigena* as somebody 'who was born in this palatinate or land, and owns hereditary lands'.[72] He shared this view with the Prussian nobleman who wanted to restrict the status of all *indigenae* to the landowning nobility, 'because anyone who does not have landed property, as the law prescribes, is not a citizen, and if he is not a citizen, what kind of *indigena* can that be?'[73] The conflict over status between ennobled patricians, like Behmfeldt, and the szlachta was evident in the fight for precedence in the voting order in the Prussian Diet, where the three major cities insisted on casting their votes before the szlachta envoys. Not all burghers, however, owned land, and most would not agree with Behmfeldt's attitude: the majority of the burghers continued to adhere to the earlier interpretation of the *ius indigenatus* as a right of birth and origin, and not of landownership. The landless nobility probably also disagreed with the principle of landownership as a requirement of the *ius indigenatus*, but their opinion was neither asked nor recorded.[74]

Since knowledge of the German language was recognised until 1570 as a condition for being an *indigena*, and the original Prussian privileges were written in German and preserved in the city archives, some historians have emphasised the great influence of the national identity of 'German burghers' on this fundamental

---

[69] Examples in Naworski, 'Indygenat', pp. 49, 54.

[70] Adam Bajerski, *Z Dotrzymanego Indygenatu Pruskiego dobro pospolite z niedotrzymanego uszczerbek y Ruina Prowincyi, przez Indigenę Pruskiego światu wywiedziona przydana Juris Correcti inter Fratrem & Sorores de Successione defensio* (n.p., 1696), folio B2.

[71] Teresa Borawska, 'Der Begriff des Indigenats im Streit um ein Zunftaufnahmegesuch in Allenstein 1523', *Zeitschrift für Geschichte und Altertumskunde des Ermlands* 43 (1985), 8.

[72] Michael Behm von Behmfeldt, *De Indigenatu Sincera Collatio Jurium et Privilegiorum Poloniae et Prussiae Regiae ad sapentia Statuum Disidia mente bona, concordiae gratia scripta* ([Danzig], 1669), p. 1.

[73] Bajerski, *Z Dotrzymanego Indygenatu*, folios E3v.–E4.

[74] Klonder, 'Szlachta a królewszczyzny', pp. 78, 87.

law.[75] The above examples show, however, that the Royal Prussian nobility, among whom many were not German-speaking, was intensely concerned with the preservation of the *ius indigenatus*. When, for pragmatic reasons, Latin and Polish replaced German as the language of *Landtag* debates in the late sixteenth century, the protests of several urban representatives found no support among the nobility. Language was no longer a criterion for defining an *indigena*: whereas there were German burghers from outside Prussia who were denied the *ius indigenatus*, there is no known case of a non-German speaker who was denied the status of *indigena* if he was a native of Royal Prussia and fulfilled all other conditions for citizenship, such as legal birth and the ownership of property.

The Polish-Prussian debate continued to be a source of trouble. During the 1682 dietine in Marienburg, the Cujavian bishop Jan Gembicki commented, not without flattery, that any citizen of Royal Prussia regarded the *ius indigenatus* as his most valuable 'klejnot pruski' (Prussian jewel).[76] In 1648, the burghers asserted the equal status of burghers and nobles who had acquired or inherited the province's *ius indigenatus* – an argument used to defend the cities' right to buy and own land.[77] Frequently, nobles and burghers made common cause in the Prussian diet for the defence of this privilege.[78] In 1676 a Danzig burgher stressed that 'the nobles and the burghers, the whole province of Prussia and all its members, reserved this right for themselves, which the king had repeatedly confirmed'. The cities were keen on granting the right to purchase landed estates in the city's vicinity only to those who had been born in the city and were 'bene meriti'.[79] The burgrave of Danzig, von Werden, justified the separate Prussian *ius indigenatus* with the argument that Royal Prussia was economically the most important province of the crown: 'the nerve-centre of the whole republic' and 'the pupil and antemurale of the sea'. Bajerski blamed the decline of urban prosperity on *alienigenae*, such as Polish or Lithuanian starostas, who had no patriotic interest in investing in the long-term development of their Prussian leaseholds. Any Prussian-born burgher was considered a better citizen than a Polish appointee. In 1652 the palatine of Chełmno, Jan Ignacy Bąkowski, rejected the nomination of Polish *alienigenae*, because they deprived Prussia of its income by taking money out of the country. This issue was so hotly contested during the Sejm held in Warsaw in the March of 1654, that the envoys departed without coming to a conclusion and had to schedule a second Sejm in the same year.[80] The right of natives to obtain offices in their province was therefore

[75] Naworski, 'Indygenat', p. 41; Michał Cieślewicz, 'Pare uwag o indygenacie pruskim', *Zeszyty Naukowe Wydziału Humanistycznego Uniwersytetu Gdańskiego*, Historia 3 (1974), 21.
[76] Achremczyk, *Życie*, pp. 279–80.
[77] Konopczyński, 'Prusy Królewskie w unii', p. 128.
[78] Achremczyk, *Życie*, p. 274; Naworski, 'Indygenat', p. 52.
[79] 'Zavadius Vapulans', APGd, Bibl. Archivi 300.R, Tq 25, pp. 7, 35–6: 'ut quis in Prussia genitus sit, sive sit Nobilis, sive Civilis stratus homo'.
[80] Werden, 'Ziemi Pruskiej', p. 85; Bajerski, *Z Dotrzymanego Indygenatu*, folios C3–C3v.; and APGd, Recesy 300.29, no. 136, 5d–e, folios 24bff, and 300.29, nos. 140–1, folios 129–32b, 147–50.

vital for the common good and prosperity of the whole province, and it was the responsibility of all estates to maintain Royal Prussia as their country with its distinct laws.

During the later seventeenth and eighteenth century, when the appointment of *alienigenae* to starosties and the profitable ecclesiastical offices in Royal Prussia became routine practice, the defence of this right assumed the character of a political ritual in Royal Prussia. Instructions issued by the local dietines to their envoys contained with predictable regularity clauses dedicated to the defence of the *ius indigenatus*.[81] Royal Prussia won repeated victories over the appointment policy of various kings, and several prominent nobles had to resign from their promised nomination after prolonged Prussian resistance, as in 1675, when the Prussian diet refused the title of *indigena* to the castellan of Poznań, Krzysztof Grzymułtowski, who had to give up all hope of becoming starosta of Sztum (Stuhm).[82] The same thing happened to Andrzej Przyjemski with regard to the castellany of Chełmno in 1662, and the Prussian *indigena* Komorski was rejected as standard-bearer of Malbork in the same year, because he was not *possessionatus*. The most famous case was the rejection of chancellor Jerzy Ossoliński as starosta in Puck (Putzig), which the influential Działyński family had previously held. The debate was resolved by compromise; Ossoliński received Strassburg instead of Puck. Until the mid-eighteenth century, most senatorial offices, except for the two bishoprics, remained in the hands of *indigenae*, while some of the most profitable starosties changed owners mainly among foreigners, the majority of whom received the status of *indigena* post-facto from the Prussian diet.[83]

A particular twist to the *ius indigenatus* was its validity in both parts of Prussia, which emphasised the former unity of the country's identity. With the voluntary submission of the estates of Prussia to the Polish king in 1454, the privilege became valid in the undivided province. After the demise of the Teutonic Order in the sixteenth century, a Prussian born in Ducal Prussia was naturally an *indigena*. The common past and the continuing sovereignty of the Polish king over Ducal Prussia justified this view: in 1548, the Warmian representative von Knobelsdorff confirmed the right of a nobleman from Sambia in Ducal Prussia to be appointed to offices in Royal Prussia, because 'he was born under a prince who is the vassal of our king, and our king is not just the ruler over one part, but over the whole of Prussia'.[84] By 1600, although the legal and political situation had not fundamentally changed, the Royal Prussian estates prohibited the acquisition of lands in their province by noblemen from Ducal Prussia, and the tradition of shared citizenship came to its end. The increasingly hostile light in which the

[81] For example, in 1669, APT Kat. II, VII.33, pp. 1764, 1960; see also Naworski, 'Indygenat', p. 50.
[82] Ciara, *Senatorowie*, pp. 83–4.
[83] Ibid., p. 272.
[84] Franz Hipler, 'Die Ermländische Bischofswahl vom Jahre 1549', *Zeitschrift für Geschichte und Altertumskunde des Ermlands* 11 (1897), 84.

political system of Ducal Prussia was viewed by a growing group among the Prussian estates therefore had legal repercussions for the relationship between the two provinces.[85]

These conflicts show that the debate about the *ius indigenatus* was not only about the distribution of sinecures and economic competition with nobles from other provinces. The Royal Prussian estates defended their privilege against the threat that old laws might no longer be honoured – '*pacta nulla sunt*' – which would ultimately question the basis of Prussia's membership in the Commonwealth, the incorporation privilege of 1454. In one form or another, Prussian nobles as well as burghers constantly returned to this argument, in diets and treatises, in pamphlets and histories. As Behm von Behmfeldt observed: 'The Prussians see themselves excluded from their own fatherland's benefices by the courtiers (*aulicis*) of Poland . . . As those foreign dignitaries do not know their laws and privileges, as *non-possessionati* in Prussia, they also do not suffer for the defence of (Prussian) castles and for the good government of their offices.'[86]

The *ius indigenatus* was the very basis of the political nation of Royal Prussia, defined by the distinctiveness of traditions and customs, which foreigners could acquire: many burghers from Silesia, Brandenburg and other parts of the Empire came to Royal Prussia and became true Prussian burghers. But like foreign noblemen, they were suspected of not being able to share the same sense of urgency in the promotion of the common good and interests of Prussia as a fellow *indigena*. When the bishop of Cracow, Maciejowski, demanded that a Prussian nobleman should adopt Polish customs since the Prussians accepted the Polish crown, the Warmian delegate von Knobelsdorff replied sharply: 'It is nevertheless more convenient that bad customs are replaced by good ones, and not the opposite. Your domination shows that ours are better, therefore, the worse habits of the Poles must yield. We therefore do not recognise you as our masters, but only the one . . . that is the king, our protector and lord.'[87]

The debate about the *ius indigenatus* was continued in Prussia, with a massive output of treatises during the eighteenth century.[88] The *ius indigenatus* was a central instrument of identity and self-definition for Prussian burghers and nobles alike. It was upheld as a sacrosanct right to control the province's offices and lands, a right contested by the Teutonic Order, and now frequently encroached upon by the Polish crown and Sejm, to whom the Prussians had entrusted their protection and future. The *ius indigenatus* continued to be confirmed by the Polish kings, but the same kings carried on violating it. Nothing symbolises better the ambiguity of the

---

[85] Naworski, 'Indygenat', p. 42, and Salmonowicz, 'Prusy Królewskie i Książęce', p. 70.
[86] Behm, *De Indigenatu*, p. 4.
[87] Hipler, 'Die Ermländische Bischofswahl', p. 83.
[88] For example, Andreas Schott, *Tractatio Juris Publici de Indigenatu Polonorum ex jure publico Polonico deducta* (Danzig: G. M. Knoch, 1738), and the discussion of the privilege in the Prussian periodicals of the eighteenth century such as *Das Gelahrte Preußen* or *Erleutertes Preußen*, e.g. 'Vom Glück der Pommern in Preußen', *Erleutertes Preußen* 4 (Königsberg: Hallervorden Erben, 1728), pp. 384ff.

Polish-Prussian relationship. Likewise, no other issue succeeded so well in evoking the old spirit of unity among burghers and nobles, the political estates of Royal Prussia.

## THE DEBATE ABOUT KULM LAW

In contrast to the *ius indigenatus*, Kulm law was closely associated with the Teutonic past of the province and the German colonisation of the country. The validity of this law code, known since the Middle Ages, was also recognised and confirmed by the Polish king in 1454 as one of the pillars of Prussian self-government. Down to the mid-sixteenth century, it had seen several new editions and translations from the Latin original, which was burnt in 1233 and replaced in 1251 with a new document by the Teutonic Order. In a society so conscious of customary laws and legal traditions, the interest in the Kulm law code (*Kulmer Handfeste*) was great. Its basis was a mixture of Flemish, Saxon-Magdeburg and, by the sixteenth century, also Polish customary law, though the origins of these various traditions are difficult to trace.[89] Although the purpose of Kulm law was originally the foundation – or 'location' – of villages and towns, the nobility also submitted to its jurisdiction, which from 1521 was administered by the Prussian Diet as the highest court of appeal in the country. In 1585, however, the Prussian lower chamber decided to accept the newly-created Polish crown tribunal in Piotrków as their appeal court instead. Ten years on, the Prussian szlachta created their own noble law code, after several failed attempts by the diet to formulate a general reform of the Prussian law code which would have been comparable to the Lithuanian statute of 1588. In Royal Prussia, the nobles chose to diverge from the common constitution and created the so-called *korektura pruska*, a noble law-code which was rejected by the Prussian cities.[90] The reason usually given for this separation is the changing interests of the nobility after the end of the Order's rule over Prussia, when land became more readily available through royal leases or by purchase. Kulm law, with its hereditary partition of land and property, continued to suit the burghers, but not the nobles, whose lands diminished so much in size through division among their wives and children that poverty became a real threat to their descendants. In particular, the rule that women had equal inheritance rights and could demand half their husbands' property – a tradition of Flemish origin and suited to an urban environment – was strongly opposed by the Prussian szlachta.

---

[89] Manfred Wermter, 'Die Bildung des Danziger Stadtterritoriums in den politischen Zielvorstellungen des Rates der Stadt Danzig im späten Mittelalter und der frühen Neuzeit', Arnold, Udo (ed.), *Ordensherrschaft, Stände und Stadtpolitik* (Lüneburg: Nordostdeutsches Kulturwerk, 1985), pp. 81–124; Zbigniew Zdrójkowski, *Zarys dziejów prawa chełmińskiego 1233–1862* (Torun: UMK, 1983).

[90] Zdrójkowski, *Zarys dziejów prawa*; Achremczyk, *Życie*, pp. 242–4; Marian Borzestowski, 'Sprawa uchwalenia korektury pruskiej w obradach sejmiku generalnego Prus Królewskich 1580–1599', in Zdrójkowski, Zbigniew (ed.), *Księga Pamiątkowa*, vol. II (Toruń: UMK, 1988), pp. 235–70.

In 1572, urban representatives rejected the claim by the castellan of Danzig, Jan Kostka, that after the union of Lublin Kulm law was no longer of any importance for the province as a whole but merely valuable as a legal framework for local urban settlements. The burghers in the Prussian diet defended the continuity of their legal tradition, denying that after the merger with the Polish crown Prussian law had become obscure and only 'existing in people's imagination': instead 'it could be found at all places in many hundreds of copies'.[91] As the Teutonic period became more remote, some doubts crept into the minds even of burghers. Seventeenth- and eighteenth-century authors, in search of the medieval, pre-Polish origins of the code, scrambled for hard evidence; a commentator who collected constitutions of the smaller Prussian cities admitted to the silence of many sources: 'antiquis Scriptoribus hac de re fere silentibus'.[92]

As Kulm law had been granted to the province by the Teutonic Order, it was long associated with the German origin and past of its inhabitants. German historians, particularly before 1945, capitalised on this connection to German legal traditions: Edward Carstenn wrote that Royal Prussia 'fought for its independence, and therefore its Germanness . . . because the inhabitants thought and acted in a German way'.[93] Overlooking the fact that most Polish royal cities had been founded on Kulm law,[94] even Polish historians have emphasised the split between the nobility and the cities in Royal Prussia as a sign that the burghers remained 'German' while the szlachta adopted Polish laws and traditions; the diversion from Kulm law and the common jurisdiction in royal courts were often quoted as the most obvious signs of such 'Polonisation'.[95] Few analyses have taken into account that, although the nobility rejected inconvenient parts of its own Kulm law tradition, the Prussian szlachta always opposed a complete assimilation to Polish legal conventions. Debates in the Prussian Diet, as well as dietine instructions, prove that Prussian nobles did not simply want to adopt Polish status and customs; several envoys refused to vote for the reforms and insisted on the creation of a separate Prussian tribunal, an argument backed by the cities, and later unsuccessfully revived by the Patriotic Party in the eighteenth century.[96] If 'Polonisation' had really been a general aim of the nobility in Royal Prussia, why did they not simply accept Polish law in the first place? Why did they continue to instruct their noble envoys that 'long-cherished customs are our law and the key to the interpretation of our laws, privileges, liberties and immunities'?[97] Why did the Prussian nobles

---

[91] Lengnich, *Geschichte der Lande Preußen*, vol. III, p. 20.

[92] *Privilegium Civitatum Minorum Prussiae Occidentalis commentariolo Ill[ustratur], praemittitur de civitatibus minoribus introd[uctio] historica* (Danzig: Knoch, 1739), preface.

[93] Carstenn, 'Die preußischen Stände', p. 80.

[94] Zdrójkowski shows in a rough estimate that about 224 cities in Poland-Lithuania, not including Ukraine, were founded on Kulm law between 1233 and 1701; Zdrójkowski, *Zarys dziejów*, p. 70.

[95] Kazimierz Slósarczyk, 'Sprawa zespolenia z Koroną za Jagiellonów, 1454–1572', *Roczniki Historyczne* 3 (1927), 107–9; Salmonowicz, 'Prusy Królewskie w ustroju', p. 53.

[96] Lengnich, *Geschichte der Lande Preußen*, vol. III, p. 451; see chapter 9 below.

[97] Konopczyński, 'Prusy Królewskie w unii', p. 123.

continue to underline the distinct character of their constitution by consciously identifying themselves with the status of the Lithuanian nation within the Commonwealth – a place which neither the Polish Sejm nor the court would concede to them? Vice-chancellor Jerzy Ossoliński, for example, rejected the common cause between Lithuanians and Prussians: 'I am surprised to see that the [Prussian] province . . . wants to regard itself equal to Lithuania.'[98]

Political and historical treatises by burghers, on the other hand, usually stress that the legal sources that fed their urban constitutions did not exclusively originate in German law, but also stemmed from the privileges received from the Polish kings and Polish legal traditions.[99] There were indeed few remnants of pre-Polish times. The Act of Incorporation of 1454 was interpreted as a contract between the Polish Crown and the free representatives of the old Kulm-law cities in Prussia, with the goal not only of preserving ancient privileges, but of extending them under the Polish crown: 'The union with Poland has not cancelled the customs and advantages of our country but strengthened and confirmed them instead.'[100] Laws and freedoms were diligently recorded on page after page in Prussian broadsheets, periodicals, handwritten and printed newspapers.[101] Central to the burghers' argument against change were neither the German origins of the laws, nor their sanction by the Teutonic Knights, but their importance for Prussian self-government, for example the free election of judges and magistrates from among their midst, and other liberties which the Teutonic Knights had tried to curb. The privilege of holding diets and local assemblies features prominently in these texts.[102] They conceal, however, that the right to assemble in dietines had not been part of Kulm law and had not existed during Teutonic rule over Prussia: such an admission might have undermined the legendary antiquity and 'eternal' validity of Prussian privileges. Thus ancient laws were usually unspecified, and the unnamed author in Hanow's *Preußische Sammlung* of 1747–9 admitted quite frankly: 'One cannot deny

---

[98] 'Excerpta Conventualia Terrarum Prussiae et quidem in anterioribus Notabiliora nobil[is] Gregorii Hesii quondam Syndici Thoruniensis; in subsequentibus vero Praestantiora nobiliss[imi] Simonis Schultzii Secret[arii] post Pro-Consulis ibidem meritissimi contentia, 1422–1655', Bibl. PAN Gd., Rosenberg Bibliothek Uph. fol. 145, p. 296.

[99] Edmund Cieślak, 'Przywileje Gdańska z okresu wojny 13-letnej na tle przywilejów niektórych miast hanzeatyckich', *Czasopismo Prawno-Historyczne* 6, no. 1 (1954), 61–122; Karol Górski, 'Z dziejow ustroju Pomorza', *Rocznik Gdański* 7–8 (1935); G. Lengnich, *Staats-Recht des Polnischen Preußens aus dem Lateinischen übersetzt von G. Künhold* (Danzig: Schreiber, 1760), folio A5v.

[100] Johann George Elsner (Thorunensis), *Einige Historische Anmerckungen von der Bürgermeisterlichen Würde in Thorn, als der Herr Anton Giering in ordentliche Rat-Küre 1738 zu derselben wie auch praesidierenden Ampte erhoben wurde* (Thorn: Nicolai, 1738), folio B2.

[101] Maliszewski, 'Mieszczańskie formy i metody', pp. 39–61 and passim; *Continuirtes Gelehrtes Preußen* I (Thorn: Nicolai, 1725), p. 182.

[102] [Christoph Hanow (ed.)], *Preußische Sammlung* 3, part 10 (Danzig: Schreiber, 1750), p. 603; Hartknoch, *Privilegia quaedam Prussica notis et animadversionibus necessariis illustrata opera et studio C. Hartknoch*, appendix to Christoph Hartknoch (ed.), *Petri de Dusburg Ordinis Teutonici Sacerdotis Chronicon Prussiae, cum Anonymi cujusdam Continuatione, aliisque Antiquitatibus Prussicis C[hristoph] Hartknoch e MSS codicibus recensuit notisque illustravit* (Frankfurt and Leipzig: Hallervordi, 1679), p. 455.

that in ancient times many privileges were not written down in constitutions . . . But they remain nevertheless unwritten rights and customs which had legal power among the Germans.'[103]

Taking advantage of the obscure origin of their laws, some Prussian historians, such as Georg Peter Schultz, bluntly denied the Teutonic Knights any creative role in the evolution of Kulm law. Kulm law, he emphasised, contained mainly customary laws and was compiled in imitation of Magdeburg law by the Prussians themselves: 'As the judges in Kulm did not have their own written laws, and the Order did not create any, but in most cases observed German law from Magdeburg, which did not exist in written form . . . they wrote to the Scabinos Magdeburg-enses and to scholars. What they wrote in reply they happily accepted and applied.'[104] Some historians entirely ignored the German-Teutonic past of the Prussian settlers and their laws. In 1657, the Danzig burgher and brewer Constantin Schröder wrote that 'everything the city of Danzig has acquired flowed from the generosity of the most gracious Polish kings'. The source and fountainhead of Danzig's liberties was the Polish monarchy, and the city possessed all its beneficial laws and privileges thanks to the incorporation of 1454. It seems, however, that this was one step too far for the historically-minded city fathers of Danzig who took offence at the exclusivity of Schröder's view of the origin of Prussian legal traditions and prohibited the printing of his treatise.[105] Critics of Schröder's work who point at factual mistakes overlook the fact that Schröder had no access to the city's archives: his compilation of Danzig laws was therefore a pioneering work which reflected the ambivalence and scarcity of reliable legal sources generally available to Danzig burghers even of prominent position.[106]

With the exception of Schröder, who possibly wanted to flatter his paymaster, the Polish king, most writers did not completely ignore the German roots of Royal Prussia's urban settlements: burgomaster Elsner from Thorn referred to the colonisation of the province by German nobles and burghers who imported their native laws.[107] Even here, however, the association of the Kulm law code with the Teutonic Order elicited little enthusiasm, and Elsner gave most credit to the Prussian estates' own achievements. Missing records and unwritten customary law encouraged a flexible interpretation of the past and invited myth-making: Jan Kostka's version of the Kulm code as a 'local law' for a handful of towns, Schröder's royalist interpretation and burgomaster Elsner's learned discourse on Prussia's

[103] Hanow, *Preußische Sammlung* 3, p. 644.
[104] G. P. Schultz, 'Variae Observationes de Prussia Polonica', APT Kat. II, VIII.46, p. 45.
[105] Stanisław Matysik, 'Elias Konstantyn Schröder. Gdański prawnik i sekretarz królewski z XVII wieku. Życie i dzieło', *Czasopismo Prawno-Historyczne* 6, no. 1 (1954), 153–75.
[106] His main opponent was Gottfried Lengnich, whose own compilation *Jus Publicum Dantiscanum*, was only printed in 1900 by W[ilhelm] Pierson (Quellen und Darstellungen zur Geschichte West-preußens 1, 1900), pp. 3–4, owing to objections by the city council against the publication of such *arcana* (secrets).
[107] Elsner, *Historische Anmerckungen*, folio B.

colonisation by German settlers – these different versions reflect the use of history for the purpose of justifying present political claims.

It was much easier for the urban magistrates than for the nobles to outline their political programme on the basis of Kulm law, which was favourable to their economic and legal interests. The Royal Prussian nobility was easily tempted not only by the availability of Polish royal leaseholds and offices, but also by the feeling that they ought to accept the reciprocity of rights and duties that increased with their integration into the political body and nation of the Commonwealth. Jan Kostka made this clear at an early stage of the debate, in 1573, when he denied that the Prussian nobility could have the best of both worlds. Protection by the Polish crown, he argued, had its price: taxes, contributions, the *levée-en-masse* in support of their Polish brothers, and the abolition of the exclusive Prussian *ius indigenatus*. In response, the burgomasters of the major cities insisted sharply that reciprocity was fulfilled by the mere act of incorporation in 1454: 'in this alone consisted the subjection of the Prussians' – on its own a major advantage for Poland.[108] Unlike the *ius indigenatus*, Kulm law had become associated more and more with the special role that the cities played in the province of Royal Prussia. The burghers had tried to defend the unity of the noble and the burgher estates on the basis of this law code. It was meant to secure the survival of the specifically Prussian character of their constitution and their way of life, the prosperity of the cities and the whole province: their laws, customs and liberties (*prawa, zwyczaje y wolności Pruskie*) were truly Prussian attributes, for which, they thought, their neighbours envied them, because they differed from those of the crown Poles.[109] The cities' sense of historical and political superiority, and their unwillingness to concede amendments on several practical economic matters, drove the nobles to establish their own law code. The question remains how the burghers changed and adapted to their role in the political life of the province and the Commonwealth, in their endeavour to maintain a common Prussian national identity, despite growing friction and conflicts with the king and the nobility.

[108] Lengnich, *Geschichte der Lande Preußen*, vol. III, p. 17.
[109] Bajerski, *Z Dotrzymanego Indygenatu*, folio E3v.

# 3

# Royal Prussia and urban life in the Polish-Lithuanian Commonwealth

The City of Dantzigk is in the province of Pomerellia, reckoned under the Crown of Poland, reckoned also in Prussia. . . . in the Yunckerhoff are certaine orders having a Free Brotherhood or company of the principall off the City, admitting through Friendshippe whome they thinke good. These att some daies in the yeare hold Frolicke Feasts, where is lusty Chear, good wyne and beere, musicke of various sorts . . . all with Civill Mirth. The Order and Attendance more than Burgameisterlike, the Servitours with garlands on their heads . . . as the drummers in Holland and these parts use. These Feasts might well beecom the entertayne off an Embassador or a Prince for order, state and plenty. (Peter Mundy)[1]

The Artushof in Danzig, here described by the English traveller Peter Mundy who passed through the city in 1640, served as the political and ceremonial meeting place for the St George merchant brotherhood, whose members in Teutonic times had martially excelled in crusades against the Baltic pagan tribes. At the turn of the fifteenth century, the merchants of Danzig, most of German or Flemish origin, had secured dominant positions in the city's economy and in the council. These medieval connotations of knighthood changed their meaning, however, in the same measure as the alienation between the burghers and their Teutonic masters intensified, before Danzig switched allegiance to the Polish crown and shouldered the main burden of the war against the Order. The new identity, forged by the relationship to Poland, was reflected in the iconography of public buildings, such as the town hall and the Artushof: frescos, painted by a Dutch artist in 1605, depict battle scenes of Danzig burghers fighting side-by-side with Polish and Lithuanian troops against the Teutonic Order. An allegorical arch adorns the town hall ceiling, symbolising the union of Danzig with the Commonwealth. Under the Polish eagle, protected by a divine hand, Danzig merchants and Polish nobles shake hands, confirming commercial contracts which allowed the city to prosper.

There is no doubt that the union helped Danzig's prosperity, as the city gained a monopoly over most trade from and to Poland, specialising in rye and wood, which

---

[1] Peter Mundy, *The Travels of Peter Mundy in Europe and Asia, 1608–1667* (Cambridge University Press, 1907), p. 209.

was shipped down the Vistula river. Since the Middle Ages, Danzig had also been a transit port for goods from Hungary, Lithuania, where Danzig merchants had established bases in Wilno (Vilnius) and Kowno (Kaunas) in 1400, and other Baltic towns, such as Livonian Riga and Reval. It had long-standing trading relations with England, the Netherlands, Sweden, and Russia via Königsberg.[2] As the old Hanseatic network, centred in Lübeck, disintegrated, the Dutch and West European ports gained importance for Danzig's market. Export, however, relied heavily on the supply from the Polish hinterland, which explains to some extent Danzig's pro-Polish stance in the conflicts with the Teutonic Order during the fifteenth century. It was only with the economic depression caused by the Polish-Swedish wars in the 1620s and 1650s that Danzig's strong position as a Baltic trading port was undermined, favouring new contenders such as Königsberg and Riga. An additional negative factor for all three major cities of Royal Prussia were the high trade tariffs set by the Polish crown, and supported by the Polish-Lithuanian Diet. In contrast, German towns on the Baltic and the North Sea had received more favourable tariff conditions from the emperor, a fact frequently deplored in merchants' gravamina: 'The Roman Emperor secures great prosperity in his lands by keeping the tariffs low, and, unlike the crown of Poland, he attracts much trade in his lands, so that between Breslau and Hamburg there are no custom duties.'[3] Considering that more than half of Danzig's ships engaged in grain trade with Western Europe in the first half of the seventeenth century, however, one has to take such lamentations with a pinch of salt.

Thorn and Elbing, the other two major cities of Royal Prussia who had traditionally sent representatives to the *Landesrat*, usually lived in Danzig's political and economic shadow. All three, however, shared the consciousness that even after the Union of Lublin they maintained a powerful voice not only in Prussian but also in Commonwealth politics. Michael Müller, who has extensively analysed the cooperation and conflicts between the Royal Prussian cities and the noble estates, has pointed out that from the end of the sixteenth century urban politicians started to press for a closer integration into the parliamentary system. Their goal, however, was to maintain indirect influence on, rather than direct participation in, Polish parliamentary procedures.[4] Behind their pretended aloofness and their insistence on discussing vital urban affairs in separate audiences with the Polish king loomed their economic power, which – at least in the case of Danzig – was efficiently exploited in all negotiations with the Commonwealth, well into the eighteenth century. Nevertheless, the eagerness of the cities to participate fully in parliamentary decision-making in their own provincial diet remained intense throughout the

---

[2] Artur Attman, *The Russian and Polish Markets in International Trade, 1500–1650* (Göteborg: Publications of the Institute of Economic History of Gothenburg University, 1973), pp. 56–66.
[3] Letter, 5 July 1669, 'Missiva der Stadt Danzig', APGd, Missiva 300.27, no. 80, p. 60.
[4] Michael G. Müller, 'Wielkie miasta Prus Królewskich wobec parlamentaryzmu polskiego po Unii Lubelskiej', *Czasopismo Prawno-Historyczne* 45 (1993), 257–8.

sixteenth and seventeenth centuries. As the Prussian szlachta increasingly tried to intimidate the smaller cities in the chamber of envoys, the three major Prussian cities felt increasingly alarmed. They were proud of the traditional urban–noble cooperation in the Prussian diet and tended to look down on burghers elsewhere in the Polish-Lithuanian Commonwealth, most of whom were not represented in the local dietines and had very little impact on the Polish Sejm.

In this they were not alone. Writers across Western Europe condemned Poland for the condition of its cities. John Barclay, although he had never been to Poland, noted in his *Icon Animorum* of 1617 that the Poles were a 'tribe born to ferocity and licence and do not know how to govern themselves'.[5] As a result, Poland's cities suffered from political anarchy, since the nobility not only looked down on peasants, but on all commoners. Towards the end of the seventeenth century, Bernard Connor, who had briefly been John Sobieski's court physician, noted the absence of cities and divided the Polish nation into

two sorts of people, the Gentry or Freeborn Subjects, who are hardly a tenth part of the Kingdom, and the Vassals, who are no better than Slaves to the Gentry, for they have no Benefit of the Laws, can buy no Estates, nor Enjoy Property, no more than our Negroes in the West-Indies can.[6]

The literature of *descriptio gentium* promoted such stereotypes in Poland-Lithuania itself. In 1630, Maciej Sarbiewski commented self-critically on the Polish nobility: 'they do not give their freedoms and honours to plebeians'.[7] The picture of the Polish nobility despising commoners, oppressing the peasantry and undermining the prosperity of cities was fed during the seventeenth century in Germany by the Brandenburg court historiographer Samuel Pufendorf (1632–94): 'Whoever in the Polish nation is not a nobleman, is regarded a peasant, and the burghers in the cities have a bad reputation.' Even more sweeping statements came from Hermann Conring (1606–1681), professor of law at the university of Helmstedt, who emphasised the miserable condition of all non-nobles in Poland.[8] The anti-noble bias of many Polish twentieth-century historians, especially of the Warsaw school, and of Marxist scholars after 1945, further reinforced the stereotype of the anti-urban noble Commonwealth.[9]

---

[5] *Icon Animorum Editio Indice, Capitum, Rerum & verbum, auctior* (Frankfurt: C. Hermsdorff, 1675), p. 93.

[6] Bernard Connor, *The History of Poland in Several Letters to Persons of Quality* (London: D. Brown and A. Roper, 1698) vol. II, pp. 4–5.

[7] Stanisław Kot, 'Descriptio Gentium Poetów Polskich XVII wieku', in *Polska złotego wieku a Europa*, ed. Henryk Barycz (Warsaw: PIW, 1987), p. 848.

[8] Samuel Pufendorf, *Einleitung zu der Historie der vornehmbsten Staaten so itziger Zeit in Europa sich befinden*, I (Frankfurt: Merian, 1682), p. 685; Hermann Conring, *Cyriacus Thrasymachus Andreae Nicanori amico suo S.P.D.* (Helmstedt: Henningus Mullerus, 1655), p. 17.

[9] See remarks by Gershon David Hundert, *The Jews in a Polish Private Town. The Case of Opatów in the Eighteenth Century* (Baltimore and London: Johns Hopkins University Press, 1992), p. xv; Maria Bogucka, 'Towns of East Central Europe from the Fourteenth to the Seventeenth Century', in Mączak, Antoni, Samsonowicz, Henryk and Burke, Peter (eds.), *East Central Europe in Transition*

## Urban life in the Polish-Lithuanian Commonwealth

Literature on the 'decline' of the Polish cities is extensive. Yet it was not just in Poland-Lithuania that cities faced a decline in power and influence in this period, or that nobles expressed contempt for urban culture. The threat to urban liberties from expanding princely powers was at least as serious elsewhere in Europe. 'Walled peasants' was the nickname given to the burghers of Osnabrück by noble envoys of the duke of Braunschweig-Lüneburg in 1647, when they defended their old right of jurisdiction in the city-court.[10] In France, tax riots in Lyon in 1632 against royal tax collectors, and the republican movement of the burghers of Bordeaux during the Fronde in 1648–50, involved the confrontation of urban and noble parties.[11] And the bishop of Münster, Christoph Bernhard Galen, earned his reputation as 'bombing Bernhard' in 1660, when he subjected his city to heavy shelling and transformed the once autonomous Münster into a mighty fortress.[12]

From a Royal Prussian perspective, however, the closest and most shocking case of a city suffering from the repression of its old freedoms was the example of Königsberg. Once part of the rebellious Prussian *Landesrat* in 1454, the city had fallen under Teutonic rule again in 1466, and in 1525 it became the capital of Ducal Prussia under the Hohenzollern dynasty. When Frederick William, the Great Elector, gained sovereignty over the duchy in 1657, his policy towards his estates, and particularly Königsberg, became more aggressive.[13] An alderman, Hieronymus Roth, turned to the Polish king with a plea for assistance against the Elector of Brandenburg in 1661. A member of the anti-Electoral opposition among the nobility and burghers, Roth complained that their duke's sovereignty had left them 'with merely a shadow of the ancient happiness that our forefathers enjoyed on the basis of their liberties'.[14] At the same time, the burghers of Königsberg sent letters to Warsaw expressing their great desire to 'become Polish subjects once

(Cambridge University Press, 1985), pp. 97–108; and Stanisław Salmonowicz, 'Prusy Królewskie i Książęce jako terytoria styku dwuch kultur, XVI–XVIII w.', in Czubiński, Antoni and Kulak, Zbigniew (eds.), *Śląsk i Pomorze w stosunkach polsko-niemieckich od XVI do XVIII w. XIV Konferencja Wspólnej Komisji Podręcznikowej PRL-RFN Historyków. 9.–14. VI. 1981 r.* (Poznań: Instytut Zachodni PTPN, 1987), p. 74.

[10] Heinrich Schmidt, 'Zur Vorstellungswelt deutscher Städte im 17. Jahrhundert', in Wegener, Werner (ed.), *Festschrift für K.G. Hugelmann zum 80. Geburtstag*, 2 vols, vol. II (Aalen: Scientia, 1959), p. 515.

[11] Christopher Friedrichs, *The Early Modern City, 1450–1750* (London and New York: Longman, 1995) pp. 307–8, 313–14.

[12] Georg Hebbelmann, *Münster zur Zeit Christoph Bernhard von Galens (1650–1678)*, Westfalen im Bild, Historische Ereignisse in Westfalen 5 (Münster: Landschaftsverband Westfalen-Lippe, 1992), pp. 5–6.

[13] Gerhard von Glinski, *Die Königsberger Kaufmannschaft des 17. und 18. Jahrhunderts*, Wissenschaftliche Beiträge zur Geschichte und Landeskunde Ost- und Mitteleuropas 70 (Marburg: Herder-Institut, 1964); Gerd Heinrich (ed.), *Ein sonderbares Licht in Teutschland. Beiträge zur Geschichte des Großen Kurfürsten von Brandenburg 1640–1688*, Zeitschrift für Historische Forschung, supplement 8 (Berlin: Duncker and Humblot, 1990).

[14] Reinhard Adam, 'Der Grosse Kurfürst und die Stände des Herzogtums Preussen nach dem Frieden von Oliwa', in *Acta Prussica. Abhandlungen zur Geschichte Ost- und Westpreußens, Festschrift zum 75. Geburtstag von Fritz Gause*, Beihefte zum Jahrbuch der Albertus-Universität 29 (Würzburg: Holzner, 1968), p. 187; and Ernst Wichert, 'Die politischen Stände Preußens, ihre Bildung und Entwicklung bis zum Ausgang des 16. Jahrhunderts', *Altpreußische Monatsschrift* 5 (1868), 447.

more, as we had been in the past'.[15] During a personal conversation with one of the Elector's closest ministers, Otto von Schwerin, Roth expressed his distrust of authority unchecked by laws and the close control by its citizens and subjects: 'the Elector's rule made us miserable, now he wants to subject us to slavery'.[16] Taxes were no longer subject to approval by the estates, custom tolls were raised against the will of the Königsberg merchants and collected not for the benefit of the city but of the ducal treasury; municipal offices and duties were taken over by the ducal bureaucracy; sumptuary legislation was decreed by the ducal governor, not by the city council. All these major and minor trespasses on municipal self-government embittered the urban magistrates against their newly sovereign duke and confirmed them in their view that the loss of Polish overlordship delivered them directly into the arbitrary power of the Elector.[17] In 1674, Frederick William forced Königsberg once more into submission by threatening a full-scale bombardment in order to obtain excise taxes he had demanded for the Dutch war in 1673, after joining the European coalition against Louis XIV. When the three cities of Königsberg refused to pay, the ducal governor in Prussia, Ernst Croy, besieged the city with 3,700 troops, forcing the burghers to pay not only the excise but also the costs of military occupation of 20,000 Talers. After this incident, Ducal Prussian city representatives lost their impact on the political institutions of the country, a development against which the three big Royal Prussian cities felt protected by their own constitution and their privileges.[18] It may well have struck the Ducal Prussian cities as paradoxical that it was under the rule of a German dynasty that their Kulm and German constitutions steadily lost their legal force, while the three major Prussian cities under the Polish crown retained these traditions and kept them alive.[19]

Nevertheless, the awareness of the extent of powerlessness of the Polish cities, despite legally valid documents signed and sealed by their monarch, constantly frightened the burghers of Royal Prussia. The fact that in 1662, despite Danzig's rescue efforts, the minor cities of Royal Prussia lost their seats in the Prussian Diet greatly contributed to the burghers' obsession with the defence and exercise of their privileges.[20] The harassment of the small cities by elements of the Prussian

[15] Johann G. Droysen, *Geschichte der preußischen Politik*, vol. III: *Der Staat des Großen Kurfürsten* (Leipzig: Veit, 1872), p. 194.

[16] Janusz Małłek, 'Eine andersartige Lösung. Absolutistischer Staatsstreich in Preußen im Jahre 1663', *Parliaments, Estates and Representation* 10, no. 2 (1990), 182; also Otto Nugel, 'Der Schöppenmeister Hieronymus Roth', *Forschungen zur Brandenburgisch-Preußischen Geschichte* 14 (1901), 413.

[17] Fritz Gause, *Geschichte der Stadt Königsberg* (Cologne, Vienna, Graz: Böhlau, 1965–72), vol. II, pp. 506–19.

[18] Stanisław Salmonowicz, 'O roli i formach reprezentacji stanów w państwie brandenbursko-pruskim doby absolutyzmu', *Czasopismo Prawno-Historyczne* 37 (1985), 165.

[19] Danzig expressed this paradox in 'Zavadius Vapulans', APGd, Bibl. Archivi 300.R, Tq 25, p. 18; see also Hans Roos, 'Das Ständewesen in Polen (1505–1772)', in Gerhard, Dietrich (ed.), *Ständische Vertretungen in Europa im 17. und 18. Jahrhundert* (Göttingen: Vandenhoeck and Ruprecht, 1969), p. 346.

[20] Bogucka and Samsonowicz, *Dzieje miast*, p. 323.

szlachta had started as early as in the fifteenth century. Nobles often exploited the fact that original documents of privileges had perished during wars and natural disasters, and towns were unable to prove their immunities on paper.[21] Hence, magistrates never missed an opportunity to point out the different legal and historical developments which distinguished Polish cities from their Royal Prussian counterparts. The Thorn historian Christoph Hartknoch explained that 'one has only to consider the Kulm law code to understand that this country of Prussia was much happier than any other'. The source of this happiness was the freedom of the burgher estate to convene in the Prussian Diet side by side with the nobility: 'Thorn, Elbing and Dantzig send their representatives to the provincial diets, where they have their seat above the lower nobility (*Ritterstand*), such as no city in the whole Polish kingdom.'[22]

By royal decree, Prussian cities and burghers were expressly exempted from the constitution of Piotrków (of 1496), which had excluded non-nobles from the right to buy and own land in Poland and had forced many wealthy Polish burghers to sell their lands.[23] No wonder, therefore, that the Prussian burghers were acutely aware of their privileged position in the Commonwealth: 'the cities in Royal Prussia are beyond doubt in a much better condition than they were previously under the Teutonic Order, and than the Polish cities are even now'. The first reason was 'the freedom of the Prussian burghers in the large and small cities to buy and own *bona terrestria* or landed estates'.[24] Agreeing with urban opinion, the Prussian senator Ignacy Bąkowski, palatine of Chełmno, in 1651 defended the greater political and economic freedoms of the Prussian cities in the Prussian diet: 'We cannot permit that in any way our Prussian cities would become equal to their Polish counterparts.'[25] The special position of the Royal Prussian cities was clearly recognised by Polish authors, such as the historian Marcin Kromer: 'the condition of the simple people is much better in Prussia than in the rest of Poland, as they use laws in common with the nobles. They are excluded neither from the ownership of land nor from offices and honours.'[26] The country's prosperity and well-being depended on the fact that nobles and burghers lived in harmony, an ideal that distinguished the Prussians from the rest of the Polish-Lithuanian provinces and the source of their self-perception as a society with a superior social, political and economic structure.

[21] Andrzej Wyrobisz, 'Zatargi mieszczan ze starostami soleckimi w XVI, XVII i XVIII wieku', *Małopolskie Studia Historyczne* 12 (1969), 365–76.

[22] Christoph Hartknoch, *Alt-und Neues Preußen oder preußischer Historien zwei Theile mit sonderbarem Fleiß zusammengetragen durch M. Christophorum Hartknoch des Thornischen Gymnasii Professorem* (Danzig: Johann Schreiber, 1684), vol. II, pp. 624, 632, 633, 641.

[23] Tomasz Opas, 'Z problemu awansu społecznego mieszczan w XVII–XVIII w.', *Przegląd Historyczny* 65, no. 3 (1974), 468.

[24] Hartknoch, *Alt-und Neues Preußen*, vol. II, p. 641.

[25] Achremczyk, *Życie*, p. 70.

[26] Marcin Kromer, *Polska czyli o położeniu, ludności, obyczajach, urzędach i sprawach publicznych Królewstwa Polskiego księgi dwie*, ed. Roman Marchwiński (Olsztyn: Pojezierze, 1977), p. 171.

# The Other Prussia

During the sixteenth and early seventeenth centuries, about 30 per cent of all cities and towns in the Commonwealth had royal privileges and most were endowed with Magdeburg and Kulm law, while about 70 per cent belonged to private owners, without traditions of self-government. Despite royal immunities, sealed and confirmed, very few cities could send representatives to the Sejm. During the sixteenth and seventeenth centuries, Cracow, Wilno and Lwów had been entitled to send delegates to all Sejm sessions, but they were denied voting rights by the nobility, despite repeated royal support.[27] Warsaw and Poznań were granted the right to send delegates to election and convocation diets alone.[28] Lublin gained limited rights to be represented during royal elections after 1677, and a general right to sit in the Polish Sejm from 1703, but never exercised it. Kamieniec Podolski was admitted to election and coronation diets after 1670 for its role in the Turkish wars, but never used its privilege. Most cities relied on petitions relating to urban affairs and – similarly to the imperial cities in the Holy Roman Empire before the constitutional changes implemented by the Peace of Westphalia in 1648 – merely assumed observer status during diet sessions. As they were generally denied voting rights, few cities even sent deputies to royal elections, and the cities represented in general or convocation diets never engaged in debate.[29]

The contrast between the theoretical confirmation of political rights for Polish cities by royal privilege on the one hand and the political reality on the other was drastically highlighted by Sebastian Petrycy in the early seventeenth century, when he compared the Polish royal cities to a donkey:

> To his surprise the donkey was invited to the wedding, and he looked forward to the fine food, but when he arrived, he was ordered to the kitchen to carry wood and water. In the same way, some of our cities go to the Sejm, but they sit far away, ready to listen to what they are ordered to do.[30]

In contrast to the three major royal cities in Prussia, Cracow, Wilno and Lwów, the three cities theoretically privileged to send representatives to general Sejm sessions, were considered part of the noble estate. It was not urban virtues, therefore, but

---

[27] Janina Bieniarzówna, *Mieszczaństwo Krakowskie XVII wieku* (Cracow: Wydawnictwo Literackie, 1969), pp. 133ff; Jan Ptaśnik, *Miasta i mieszczaństwo w dawnej Polsce* (Warsaw: Państwowy Instytut Wydawniczy, 1949), p. 229; Bogucka and Samsonowicz, *Dzieje miast*, p. 322. Cracow had the right of representation from 1505, Wilno from 1568 and Lwów fom 1658, as a reward for its resistance to the Swedish invaders.

[28] See for extensive treatment of Polish cities' privileges, Ptaśnik, *Miasta*; Jan Riabinin, *Rada Miasta Lublina* (Lublin: TPNL, 1935); Janina Bieniarzówna and Jan M. Małecki (eds.), *Dzieje Krakowa. Kraków w wiekach XVI–XVIII*, vol. II (Cracow: Wydawnictwo Literackie, 1984); Jan Dobrzański and Jerzy Kłoczowski (eds.), *Dzieje Lublina* (Lublin: Wydawnictwo Lubelskie, 1965); Bogucka and Samsonowicz, *Dzieje miast*; Bieniarzówna, *Mieszczaństwo Krakowskie*; and Marian Biskup, 'Rola miast', 87ff.

[29] Ptaśnik, *Miasta*, pp. 216–40.

[30] Ibid., pp. 230–31.

their corporate status of nobility which justified their elevation over other cities. This seems an important difference to the position of the Royal Prussian cities, represented in the Prussian diet not as a noble corporate estate but as genuine cities. In this respect, the Prussian burghers followed the example of their neighbours in the Empire, where cities did not wish to deny their urban traditions and interests. Instead of 'noble blood', urban immunities and freedoms were the basis of their political identity.[31]

The debate about the weakness of Polish urban society and the alleged 'ruralisation' even of the Prussian cities touches the fundamental issue of the difference between countryside and town, and the nature of a city.[32] Although medieval and early modern cities liked to uphold the fiction of being autonomous legal and social bodies, ramparts and walls were not impermeable. In the early modern period, there was never a clear division of labour between town and countryside.[33] Neither was landownership and interest in agrarian questions a sign of impoverishment and of the 'agrarianisation' of the city. After all, it was the richest members of the town elites who purchased land and made a living from it. Even merchants complemented their own profits from trade with income from landed estates, rents, brewery rights and monopolies on the sale of spirits. They relied on local production and markets, especially during the later seventeenth and eighteenth centuries, when Danzig's overseas trade volume suffered from war and increased competition.[34] It was the suburbs, built on the cities' patrimonial lands, which experienced their most rapid growth in that period. They prospered not only from overseas trade but from local and regional exchange to an extent that has often been underestimated.

Most patricians leased land on a limited contract, for several decades, or for their lifetime. Hence it was relatively difficult for them to build up landed patrician dynasties over several generations. Very few families maintained landed property over a prolonged period of several generations.[35] From the mid-sixteenth century, the Giese family had bought several villages and leased royal lands and offices far away from Danzig, but the Gieses remained active in the council until the main branch of their family died out in 1687. One of the few burgomasters of Danzig to

[31] Schmidt, 'Zur Vorstellungswelt', p. 514.
[32] As an example for the decline thesis and 'ruralisation' of the Prussian cities, see Bogucka and Samsonowicz, *Dzieje miast*, pp. 549–50; and Salmonowicz, 'Prusy Królewskie i Książęce', p. 74; similarly, Francis L. Carsten, *Geschichte der preußischen Junker* (Frankfurt: Suhrkamp, 1988), p. 29; see the convincing social and economic arguments against this thesis by William Dwight van Horn, 'Suburban Development, Rural Exchange and the Manorial Economy in Royal Prussia, 1570–1700', (Ph.D. diss., Columbia University, 1987), p. 183, and by Mikulski and Dygdała, 'Zmiany w elicie', pp. 28–9.
[33] Heide Gerstenberger, 'Was ist eine Stadt?', in Groth, Andrzej (ed.), *Zwei Hansestädte Bremen und Danzig im Laufe der Jahrhunderte* (Gdańsk: Marpress, 1994), p. 15.
[34] Michael North, 'The export trade of Royal Prussia and Ducal Prussia, 1550–1650', in Heeres, W. G. et al. (eds.), *From Dunkirk to Danzig. Shipping Trade in the North Sea and the Baltic, 1350–1850* (Hilversum: Verloren Publishers, 1988), pp. 383–90.
[35] John Muhl, 'Danziger Bürgergeschlechter im ländlichen Besitz', *Zeitschrift des Westpreußischen Geschichtsvereins* 71 (1934), 89ff.

leave urban office was Jan von Werden, who had become one of Royal Prussia's largest landowners in the sixteenth century. He was ennobled by Sigismund I and, exceptionally, was shunned by his fellow patricians, because he was known to maltreat his peasants. Like Werden, several patrician families received a noble title, often after service as burgomasters, royal secretaries and royal burgraves. But while in the seventeenth century Polish towns and burghers had to give up their landed estates under pressure from their starosta or neighbouring noble owners, the Royal Prussian cities – in their function as corporate landowners – actually increased the extent of their properties: in 1570 the three main cities in Royal Prussia owned 1,514 km² or 172 villages (8 per cent of landed estates), but by 1772 they had 292 villages (31.5 per cent) in the province.[36]

It is remarkable how few of these landowners left the cities and turned their back on urban political office. Among the top sixteen property-owners in the seventeenth century, the most prominent examples were the Danzig families of von der Linde, Brandes, Giese, Zierenberg, Kerschenstein, Norchmann, Wieder and Schmieden, who maintained their seats in the council, while the following families opted out of burgher life, or died out: Bartsch von Demuth, Schachmann, Wichmann, von Jaski-Köhne, Schrader, von Gehema, von Bodeck. Landownership, however, was not necessarily linked to ennoblement. The city council could also lease its corporately owned land to individuals, which was often resented by the rest of the citizenry.[37] In this way, a considerable number of noble proprietors entered city life and acquired urban property, often by advantageous marriages between noble sons and burgher daughters, and, less frequently, of noble women to burghers.[38] Despite owning property outside the city walls, the overwhelming majority chose to have their residence in the city. Gottfried von Peschwitz, a university-trained lawyer and councillor in the Danzig government, who owned land and accepted nobility, remained a staunch defender of the city's privileges and, in the 1660s, wrote an influential treatise scolding the Prussian and Polish nobility for abusing their peasants; he even defended the right of the city to harbour and protect peasants who escaped the heavy burdens and abuse inflicted by their landlords.[39]

If, therefore, Prussian patricians eagerly asserted their membership of the political nation, they did not do so because they wanted to mimic Polish nobles. If they acquired lands like the nobility, it was not a sign that the cities were losing

---

[36] Opas, 'Z problemu', p. 468; and Marian Biskup, 'Über die Rolle und Bedeutung des Großgrundbesitzes der großen Städte von Königlich Preußen im 16. und 17. Jahrhundert', in *Problemy razvitiia feodalizma i kapitalizma w stranach Baltiki*, Conference Proceedings, 14.–17. March 1972 (Tartu: Tartu Ülikool, 1972), pp. 263–5.

[37] Muhl, 'Danzigs Bürgergeschlechter', pp. 89–100; and Cieślak, *Walki*, pp. 29–40.

[38] Włodzimierz Dworzaczek, 'Przenikanie szlachty do stanu mieszczańskiego w Wielkopolsce w XVI i XVII wieku', *Przegląd Historyczny* 47, no. 4 (1956), 656–84.

[39] 'Godofredi de Peschwitz Dissertatio Theologico-Iuridico-Historica von Vindicir-Abforderung der verlauffenen Bauren undt Untertanen und deren Praescription' (n.d.), APGd, Bibl. Archivi 300.R, T 14, pp. 503–5, 510–12.

their urban character in Royal Prussia, but to consolidate their status in the town hierarchy by demonstrating their wealth and civic pride. The evidence suggests that the noble and burgher estates were never rigidly closed social groups, an impression fostered in early modern political literature by many nobles themselves who liked to emphasise the distinctiveness of their status.[40] In contrast to the praise of the 'wholesome' noble life and 'virtuous' country existence, the city was seen as a 'Babylon', corrupted by sin, hypocrisy and luxury.[41] Such treatises were often aimed as moral admonitions at absentee noble landlords who lived in cities and engaged in court politics or – against the noble code – conducted commerce themselves, and were therefore condemned by their more humble, country-based brothers. Such views flourished among the Polish szlachta from the sixteenth century, when Jan Zamoyski's opinion on cities summed up noble apprehensions about city life:

In Western Europe real cities prosper because the burgher estate has many rights there. But because their happiness is the result of the violation of noble privileges and freedom, I prefer not to have [cities] at such a price. The happiness of the people cannot be measured on the basis of handicrafts, or by walls and great buildings, of which we have no shortage anyway.[42]

The core of this theory was that burghers, due to the non-noble character of their professions, trades and crafts, could not be citizens of the political nation of the Sarmatian Commonwealth. One of the most widely read tracts of the seventeenth century, which stressed the exclusivity of noble-Sarmatian citizenship, was the anonymous 1671 eulogy of the Commonwealth, *Domina Palatii – Regina Libertas*. It described the king as the head, the senators as the teeth, the szlachta as the main body with the free vote at its heart, and the commoners as legs and feet, on which the body stands. Stanisław Orzechowski, a sixteenth-century writer and Ruthenian nobleman, maintained that only nobles had all three qualities of true Sarmatian citizens: freedom, truthfulness and faith. The peasants had no freedom, the merchants and burghers no truthfulness, and other commoners very often pursued unworthy activities.[43]

Despite Starowolski's attempt in his genealogy of the 124 leading Sarmatian warriors and writers to turn the definition of Sarmatian nobility into a concept of merit and personal distinction in the service of the Commonwealth, with no regard for noble blood, the political and cultural identity attached to the Sarmatian myth of origin by the majority of the Polish szlachta was aimed at excluding all com-

---

[40] Stanisław Gierszewski, *Obywatele miast Polski przedrozbiorowej* (Warsaw: PWN, 1973), p. 81 and the last chapter in Dwight van Horn, 'Suburban Development'.
[41] Dwight van Horn, 'Suburban Development', pp. 396–9.
[42] Quoted in Ryszard Szczygiel, 'Udział magnaterii w urbanizacji ziem Polskich w XVI wieku', *Acta Universitatis Wrocłaviensis* 945, Historia 66 (1988), 256.
[43] Stanisław Grodziski, 'Obywatelstwo w szlacheckiej Rzeczypospolitej', *Zeszyty Naukowe Uniwersytetu Jagiellońskiego* 67, Prace Prawnicze, no. 12 (1963), 48.

moners from the virtues associated with the Sarmatians, and consequently from full political citizenship.[44] If the values of Sarmatian ideology, however, were so central to nobles' self-definition, as most Polish historians have emphasised,[45] why was the concept so sparingly used in the private discourse of the nobility? Most Polish political and historical authors of the seventeenth and eighteenth centuries did not use the expression 'Sarmatian'. One of the most famous noble diaries of the seventeenth century, Jan Pasek's Memoirs, never as much as mentioned the concept of Sarmatian citizenship. And Starowolski's Sarmatian heroes mainly addressed a European and non-Polish public, of which the places of publication, such as Cologne and Danzig, are some indication.[46] Why did he admit Sarmatians with a non-noble background, such as the leader of the Zaporozhian Cossacks, Piotr Sahajdaczny, the son of a burgher from Sieradz in Great Poland, or Stanisław Hosius, also from burgher stock? Starowolski's vision reflected an ideal of the Commonwealth as a multi-national community of citizens, which included deserving commoners. It did not find much favour with his fellow Polish noblemen. Starowolski did score highly with the Prussian burghers, however, who felt encouraged to identify with the political nation of the Commonwealth and its civic values. If there was a place for Cossacks and commoners in Starowolski's definition of Sarmatian citizenship, there was also a place for the Prussian burghers.

Royal Prussia's outstanding wealth of political and constitutional literature on the nature and aims of citizenship was fed by two sources: the burghers' high motivation to maintain their status as citizens both of the province and the Commonwealth, and of an urban community, modelled on and sharing the constitutional values of the larger state. Prussian burghers may have been critical of the conditions in the cities of the Commonwealth, but they were in no doubt that Poland-Lithuania was a more favourable environment for the preservation of their liberties than some neighbouring states. Although Royal Prussian burghers feared being relegated to the status of Polish burghers, they were well aware that there were worse options than being a royal city in the Polish-Lithuanian Commonwealth.

CIVIC IDEALS AND THE WELL-ORDERED URBAN COMMUNITY

There are two kinds of children. There are those of a slave-like disposition who do not like hard work and have no inclination towards guiding the republic; the others are the urban and

---

[44] Czesław Hernas, *Barok* (Warsaw: PWN, 1980), pp. 455, 468–9; on Starowolski, see Andrzej S. Kamiński, 'Imponderabilia społeczeństwa obywatelskiego Rzeczypospolitej Wielu Narodów', to be published with the proceedings of the conference 'Rzeczpospolita wielu narodów i jej tradycje', Instytut Historii Uniwersytetu Jagiellońskiego, Cracow 15–17 September 1997. I am grateful to Prof. Kamiński for allowing me to read his text in its unpublished form.

[45] For example Janusz Tazbir, 'Sarmatyzacja katolicyzmu', *Studia Staropolskie* 29 (1970), and his 'Ksenofobia w Polsce XVI i XVII wieku', in *Arianie i katolicy* (Warsaw: PWN, 1970).

[46] *Simonis Starovolscii Sarmatiae bellatores* (Colonia, 1631).

free-spirited who by nature seek the most interesting matters to judge and explore for themselves.[47]

Despite Polish noble prejudice against the urban professions and commercial values, the nobility and the burgher elites of Royal Prussia shared an idea of what comprised the citizen's practical and public duties. The most influential political movements of early modern Europe, namely neostoicism and natural law teaching, reached the Commonwealth from the North West via the old trading routes which for centuries had connected Royal Prussia with the Netherlands. Danzig's contacts with the Netherlands had never been purely commercial; apart from the lively trade with grain and other bulk products, the Prussian patriciate also entered a lively intellectual and cultural exchange with the Dutch. Jan Harasimowicz has emphasised the Dutch character of much of Danzig's and other Prussian cities' art and architecture, which developed independently from the Italian influences – the '*Welsch* manner' – on Cracow under the Jagiellonians. Buildings and paintings by Dutch and Flemish artists dominated the cityscape of 'the most Netherlandish of all Baltic cities'.[48]

The same is true for political ideas. Neostoic thinkers such as Justus Lipsius formulated the concept of civic society that could be easily harmonised with the constitutional ideals of a Commonwealth balanced between liberty and royal power, a well-ordered government, obedience to a justly governing authority limited by fundamental laws, and the conviction that a successfully administered body politic must be geared towards justice and the common good.[49] These ideas reached beyond Royal Prussia's borders and did not pass unnoticed among the Commonwealth's szlachta. Although Gerhard Oestreich associated neostoic political theory mainly with the rising absolute monarchies of the Holy Roman Empire, in particular Protestant Brandenburg-Prussia, Polish Catholicism was no obstacle. In fact, the transmission of the neostoic movement to Poland was usually supported by the Jesuit Order. The case of Poland-Lithuania seems to confirm the thesis of Heinz Schilling and Michael Müller that there was no link between one particular constitution or form of government and one particular confessional church or denomination. Calvinism was not a particularly fertile ground for republicanism, as the example of Brandenburg shows after 1613; nor did Lu-

---

[47] Sebastian Petrycy z Pilzna in 1605, paraphrasing Aristotle (*Politics*, 1254. a17–b16), in Jan Harasimowicz (ed.), *Sztuka miast i mieszczaństwa XV–XVIII wieku w Europie Środkowowschodniej* (Warsaw: PWN, 1990), p. 9.

[48] Jan Harasimowicz, 'Bürgerliche und höfische Kunstrepräsentation in Krakau und Danzig', in Engel, Evamaria, Lambrecht, Karen and Nogossek, Hanna (eds.), *Metropolen im Wandel. Zentralität in Ostmitteleuropa an der Wende vom Mittelalter zur Neuzeit* (Berlin: Akademie-Verlag, 1995), p. 99; Teresa Grzybowska, *Artyści i Patrycjusze Gdańska* (Warsaw: DIG, 1996), p. 11; also Juliette Roding, 'Dutch Architects in Danzig and the Southern Baltic in the 16th and 17th Centuries', *Tijdschrift voor Skandinavistiek* 16, no. 2 (1995), 223–34.

[49] Gerhard Oestreich, 'Political Neostoicism', in *Neostoicism and the Early Modern State*, ed. Brigitta Oestreich and H. Koenigsberger (Cambridge University Press, 1982), pp. 57–75.

therans or Catholics have more authoritarian features, as the rebellious tendencies of the Lutheran urban population of many Hanseatic and free imperial cities – often in opposition to Calvinist magistracies – have demonstrated.[50] Edward Gibbon's verdict of the 'irregular tendency of the popish towards liberty, and the unnatural inclination of the Protestant towards slavery' cannot be applied to Poland-Lithuania.

One of the earliest translations of Lipsius's treatise *De Constantia* appeared in 1595 in Polish in Cracow. The Polish and Lithuanian students eagerly absorbed Lipsius's teaching during their studies abroad and at home, while Lipsian works became an obligatory element in many nobles' private libraries. The Dutch thinker gained particular popularity among the moderate constitutionalists, who equally rejected radical republican ideas and absolute monarchy. In 1589 Jan Zamoyski pushed for more efficient parliamentary procedures on the basis of Lipsius's proposals for an orderly government, and in 1607 Jan Ostroróg, palatine of Poznań, attacked the excessive decentralisation of political life in the *sejmiki*. Both, however, were opposed to measures which would have given more control to the monarch.[51] Maria Pryshlak has shown that during the mid-seventeenth century, in response to the Polish-Swedish crisis, senatorial political writers such as Łukasz Opaliński and Andrzej Maksimilian Fredro continued to be steeped in neostoic ideas and the doctrine of the *forma mixta*, reflected in the works of Lipsius, from which they frequently quoted.[52] Lipsius remained popular because, in contrast to Machiavelli, whose image of the shrewd prince was inspired by the metaphor of the fox and the lion, the Dutch neostoicist advocated a moral body politic based on the rule of law.

A Catholic nobleman with landed estates near Thorn echoed the Polish senators' neostoic search for a better Commonwealth. His suggestions, not unlike those of his neighbours in the towns, aimed at improving the citizens' sense of duty and at a closer involvement in the pursuit of the common good, much along Lipsian lines. In the instructions to the 1654 Prussian dietine in Kowalewo, he appealed to the nobles and cities of Prussia to raise higher taxes, and to the clergy to contribute to the crown treasury: things would be better in the republic

if particularly the gentlemen from the clergy put their love of the fatherland and support for the army before their liberties . . . and the *czopowe* and the *accise* duties were paid by our Prussians to the crown treasury, and if these payments went like other ordinary provisions to

[50] Heinz Schilling, *Civic Calvinism in North-West Germany and the Netherlands*, special issue of *Sixteenth-Century Journal*, vol. 17: *Essays and Studies* (Missouri: Sixteenth-Century Journal Publishers, 1991); *Die Reformation in Deutschland und Europa. Interpretationen und Debatten*, Sonderband des Archivs für Reformationsgeschichte 1 (1993), esp. 591–613.

[51] Maria O. Pryshlak, 'The Well-Ordered State in the Political Philosophy of the Polish Aristocracy' (Ph.D. diss., Columbia University, 1984), chapter 3; on Zamoyski, see Stanisław Kot, 'Hugo Grotius a Polska w 300-lecia dzieła o prawie wojny i pokoju', in *Reformacja w Polsce* (1926), 3–4.

[52] Maria O. Pryshlak, 'Forma Mixta as a Political Ideal of a Polish Magnate: Łukasz Opaliński's Rozmowa Plebana z Ziemianinem', *Polish Review* 26 (1981), 26–42; see also Gottfried Schramm, 'Staatseinheit und Regionalismus in Polen-Litauen (15.–17. Jahrhundert)', *Forschungen für Osteuropäische Geschichte* 11 (1966), 12–14.

our Republic, or if, for the greater good and efficiency of the Republic all the palatines agreed among themselves to pay their taxes *ducta proportione* directly for the [upkeep of the] army.[53]

Thus Oestreich's judgement that 'the general tenor of [Lipsius's] teaching is bourgeois . . . its principles – strict performance of duty, inspection of conscience, constant work and equality of legal status for all – had little to do with the old world of the European nobility', is too restrictive and cannot be readily applied to Poland-Lithuania.[54] The connection between the Lipsian neostoic movement and the ideology of Hohenzollern central power is, therefore, not as 'natural' as Oestreich considered it to be. Despite some Polish criticism of Lipsius's strong emphasis on monarchical authority, Lipsian ideals were more compatible with the central European *Ständestaat* and monarchy limited by law, than with the Hohenzollern motto *necessitas non habet legem* (necessity knows no laws).[55] In consequence, Lipsian ideas entered Royal Prussia via Polish constitutionalist theory, and not via Berlin or Königsberg. Fredro and Opaliński belong among those Polish writers most frequently quoted in Royal Prussian political treatises. Magistrates and scholars also observed the developments in the Netherlands directly. At the Gymnasium in Thorn, Ernst König supervised a series of dissertations on civil law and political theory which reflected the latest teaching of natural law and neostoic approaches to the idea of good government. Of Western Pomeranian origin, and after university studies in Jena, Leipzig and the Netherlands, König had specialised in natural law. The ideas of Samuel Pufendorf, who was still alive in 1675 when one of König's students published a dissertation on the *Origins of Civil Laws*, feature prominently in his works. König argued in truly Lipsian style for a strong and just authority over citizens who enter a contract with their ruler on the basis of natural laws that are binding for both the ruled and the government, in contradiction to the Hobbesian Leviathan-state and its tyrannical nature. Based on immutable and universal laws of nature, the moral laws of human society and an early form of welfare state, the Royal Prussian city-governments clearly modelled their vision of citizenship on Lipsius's blueprint: a Prussian *civitas*, dependent on 'general laws, common and universal to all, which oblige the subjects to obedience'.[56]

Gabriel Nakielski from Marienburg, one of König's students, emphasised that obedient citizens must be rewarded with fair and just government and legislators. The best guarantee against the likely descent of an overbearing ruler or authority into tyranny was the willingness of the whole body of citizens to contribute to the common good: 'Not only one part, but all citizens benefit when there is advantage

---

[53] 'Instrukcja sejmiku Kowalewskiego województwa Chełminskiego 10.1.1654', APT Archiwum Sczanieckich, no. 248, p. 10.

[54] Oestreich, 'Political Neostoicism', p. 68.

[55] See the critique of Oestreich's interpretation of Lipsius by Martin van Gelderen, 'Holland und das Preußentum: Justus Lipsius zwischen Niederländischem Aufstand und Brandenburg-Preußischem Absolutismus', *Zeitschrift für historische Forschung* 23 (1996), 29–56.

[56] *Dissertatio Politica de Legibus Civitatis in genere, quam in Gymnasio Thoruniensi praeside M. Ernesto König subjicit Gabriel Nakielski Mariaeburgensis* (Thorn: Coepselius, 1675), p. 21.

to the whole city and not just to some parts: subjects obey laws out of love, not slavish fear when they venerate good kings rather than fear tyrants.'[57] The right of resistance and disobedience based on natural law were particularly interesting topics for the Prussian burghers whose identity and history depended so strongly on the rebellion of 1454 against the Teutonic Knights. Royal Prussian civic spirit touched upon the principles of urban republicanism, and its rhetoric resembled the anti-Habsburg literature produced in sixteenth-century Dutch cities.[58]

Two central issues, with which Lipsius and Grotius had inspired the Dutch independence movement and heartened the rebels against the seemingly over-whelming Habsburg forces, were military reform and the moral justification of war. As Oestreich emphasised, for the United Netherlands 'war and military life were the basis of (its) independence and at the heart of its sense of nationhood'.[59] Like the late sixteenth century for the Dutch, the seventeenth century in Poland-Lithuania was a period of almost constant warfare (*bellum perpetuum*), arising from the Commonwealth's ever more acute conflicts with its neighbours. For the Prussian cities, this had grave implications when in 1626 and again in 1655 they effectively became the frontline against the Swedish invaders. Many Prussian sources, including the diary of Heinrich Stroband, mayor of Thorn, make this link between the Dutch wars and the threat to Poland-Lithuania's security. Stroband himself was involved in the peace negotiations between the Swedes and the Poles in Königsberg in 1630, where he acted in the service of the castellan of Kulm, Fabian Czema.[60] Royal Prussian interest in the debate about the efficiency of the Polish defence and its constitutional implications was therefore genuine.

In contrast to the Dutch and Royal Prussian city-dwellers, noble Sarmatian warriors would not hide behind fortress walls and urban ramparts. Fredro, as one of the most eloquent champions of szlachta freedoms, stressed the need for the defence of Poland by an improved infantry and cavalry force, instead of improved fortresses and strongholds. Monarchy, he argued, had a tendency to decline into despotism: cities and ramparts enabled despots to strengthen an oppressive regime over their people. Poland, in contrast, was governed by a mixed constitution where monarchy was tempered with aristocracy and democracy.[61] This Polish point of

---

[57] Ibid., pp. 30, 32.

[58] Nicolette Mout, 'Ideales Muster oder erfundene Eigenart. Republikanische Theorien während des niederländischen Aufstands', in Koenigsberger, Helmut G. (ed.), *Republiken und Republikanismus im Europa der frühen Neuzeit*, Schriften des Historischen Kollegs, Kolloquien 2 (Munich: Oldenbourg, 1988), 169–94; Winfried Schulze, 'Estates and the problem of resistance in theory and practice in the sixteenth and seventeenth centuries', in Evans, Robert J. W. and Thomas, Trevor (eds.), *Crown, Church and Estates. Central European Politics in the Sixteenth and Seventeenth Centuries* (London: Macmillan, 1991), p. 167.

[59] Oestreich, 'The Military Renascence', in his *Neostoicism*, p. 76.

[60] APT Kat. II, XII.3, pp. 35–60.

[61] *Militarium ad Harmoniam Togae Accomodatorum* (Amsterdam: Forster, sumptibus Wistenhof, 1668), pp. 180–1; see Robert I. Frost, 'The Polish-Lithuanian Commonwealth and the 'Military Revolution'', in Biskupski, Marian B. and Pula, James S. (eds.), *Poland and Europe: Historical Dimensions. I: Selected Essays from the Fiftieth Anniversary International Congress of the Polish Institute of Arts and*

view, that cities and fortresses were useless as Sarmatians had traditionally defended their country, kingdom and constitution on the battlefield with their own bodies and the noble *levée-en-masse*, was deeply influenced by the model of Sparta, popularised among nobles in the classical curricula of Jesuit colleges, academies and private instruction for the szlachta sons, and taught through the study of Machiavelli's *Discourses*, which had also influenced Lipsius.[62] Hostile to Machiavellian rulership, the Poles embraced the Spartan model, especially since the age of artillery raised more and more doubts about the invincibility of conventional fortresses: 'the Spartans did not even allow their city to have walls, for they wanted the ability of the individual – and no other defence – to protect them'.[63]

Fredro's greatest fear was that with the help of infantry, and in particular mercenary troops, absolute monarchs would easily be able to oppress the freedom of the people; for the aristocratic regime of Poland, Fredro insisted, the cavalry was the more appropriate form of defence. His sense of reality told him, however, that in the mid-seventeenth century, when Swedish forces threatened the very existence of the Polish state, reform was essential.[64] Relying on Lipsian advice, he urged the Commonwealth to undergo a moral and ethical catharsis and adopt classical virtues to order its military affairs. Constancy, self-discipline, courage and good order were also recommended by Lipsius – within fortresses as much as on the open battle-field.[65] Once more, neostoicism held at least as much appeal for monarchists as for constitutionalists.

In contrast to the Polish szlachta, the Prussian cities had inherited fortified cities from their Teutonic rulers and tried to update their defence systems. They entertained a city militia, and the guilds had strictly regulated defensive duties on the walls of their quarters. The idea of a Spartan lifestyle seemed of little appeal to craftsmen, merchants, lawyers and pastors. An essential task in perfecting a well-ordered republic materially and spiritually was to care for the upkeep of fortified walls: Hermann Conring, professor of law at the university of Helmstedt, whose treatises were read and taught by many Prussian burghers, defined a city as 'a place encircled by ramparts, strong and well-stocked with ammunition'. He praised German cities for the successful preservation of their wealth and freedom even after the catastrophe of the Thirty Years War. In contrast, he showed his contempt for the failure of the Polish defence system during the Swedish wars, which, he

---

*Sciences of America*, East European Monographs (New York: Columbia University Press, 1993), pp. 44–5.

[62] Janina Freylichówna, *Ideał Wychowawczy Szlachty Polskiej w XVI i początku XVII wieku* (Warsaw: Nakładem Naukowego Towarzystwa Pedagogicznego, 1938), pp. 64ff; S. Salmonowicz, 'Jesuiten-schulen und Akademische Gymnasien im Königlichen Preußen vom 16. bis zum 18. Jahrhundert', *Zeszyty naukowe wydziału humanistycznego Uniwersytetu Gdańskiego* 15 (1985), 21–2; Oestreich, 'The Military Renascence', p. 78.

[63] Peter Bondanella and Mark Musa (eds.), *The Portable Machiavelli* (London and New York: Penguin Books, 1979), p. 337.

[64] Frost, 'Military Revolution', p. 45.

[65] Oestreich, 'The Military Renascence', p. 79.

argued, had sent John Casimir flying from his kingdom for security in Silesia in 1655. Poland therefore deserved no better than to be conquered by the Swedes, who had become the new protectors of Europe against the barbaric East.[66] Conring simplified a very complex issue: in reality, Polish doubts about the usefulness of fortresses and ramparts in Poland-Lithuania made a lot of sense. The scarcity and lack of fortified cities and towns in Poland-Lithuania made it much more difficult for invading troops to feed themselves off the land, as the Swedes painfully experienced during their invasion of Poland between 1655 and 1660, when only the rich and fortified towns of Royal Prussia and Pomerania could give them long-term shelter. Walls, therefore, were an ambiguous instrument of war. Once Thorn and Elbing had been conquered by the Swedish troops, these two cities suffered Swedish occupation for several years. Only Danzig's walls successfully withstood Swedish attacks.

The Danzig burgomaster and patrician Lucas de Linda (Linde), a convert to Catholicism and a landowner, ennobled by the Polish king, agreed with Conring in defending the advantages of life in walled cities and the habits of a burgher's lifestyle: 'Danzig is not only the strongest rampart and protector of Prussia, but also of the whole of Poland; only a few years ago, it repelled the arms of Sweden, arresting its king's military attack and the progress of his well-equipped army.'[67] Linde's hint at the usefulness of fortified walls for the defence of the Common-wealth against the Swedes during the Deluge left nobody in doubt that he was a burgher who took pride in his fortified, successfully defended city. No Polish bickering about the oppressiveness of 'non-noble' walls could convince the Danzig burghers that it was not their city that had saved the whole republic.

Nevertheless, the Polish-Spartan approach found some support among the Prussian citizenry. Johannes Nemorecki backed the Spartan method of defence in a speech on the constitution of cities, delivered at the Gymnasium in Elbing: 'When the leader of the Spartans, Lycurgus, was asked why Sparta was invincible, he replied that it was not defended by bricks but by men . . . laws and discipline in a city-state are much more effective than ditches and ramparts: nothing protects a city better than the citizens' concord and virtue.'[68] The debate in Prussia continued in 1679, when the nobleman Bogusław von Unruh, from Great Poland, defended a dissertation under König in Thorn. In agreement with Nemorecki's view, he confirmed that 'a city derives strength not from its walls, place and buildings, but

---

[66] *Exercitatio de Urbibus Germanicis D.O.M.A. praeside H[ermanno] Conringio praeceptore ac fautore plurimum honorando ex ejusdem privatis praecipue discursibus concinata publice in Illustr[issima] Academia Julia 1641 defendit Gerardus Bode, Hamburgensis* (Helmstedt: Henning Müller, 1652), folios A1 and Bv; Conring's pro-Swedish treatise had the title *Cyriaci Thrasymachi De Iustitia Armorum Svevicorum in Polonos* (Hamburg: n.pub., 1655).

[67] Lucas de Linda, *Descriptio Orbis et Omnium Rerumpublicarum* (Leiden: Petrus Leffen, 1655), p. 965.

[68] *Orationes problema politicum de praecipuo Civitatum requisito seu Fine ex parte excutientes, ac in Encaenis Gymnasii Elbingensis publice inter alias habitae* (Elbing: Bodenhausen, 1646), folio C2.

from its people'.[69] During times of war and real military threat from outside, however, the Spartan ideology was much less attractive. In 1700, a year after it was occupied by Brandenburg troops, the citizenry of Elbing presented the magistracy with grievances about the bad state of the walls and criticised the unwillingness of the city government to improve it. The defencelessness of the city, the burghers argued, would be interpreted by the king and the Polish nobility as a sign of disloyalty to the republic and certainly be punished. They demonstrated their resolve to stand together 'as one man' and to defend their badly kept walls to the last drop of blood against the enemies of the Commonwealth.[70]

The underlying theme of these debates on the best form of a city and its defence was the nature of citizenship.[71] The German background of so many burgher families in Royal Prussia has led historians to believe that it was the model of German free cities, or imperial cities, and German political culture which influenced the burghers' ambitions and world view.[72] In reference to the Aristotelian and Renaissance tradition, free imperial cities in seventeenth- and eighteenth-century Germany usually called themselves 'republics' to express their identity with the 'common weal' of a free people. Zedler's dictionary of the early eighteenth century defined *respublica* as 'a free people, country, city or community, which recognises either no single ruler or only some kind of limited rule'. A 'city-republic', with its connotations of antiquity, referred to a political body with independent or strong self-governing constitutions. This definition, however, was not universally accepted. In 1641, when the bishop of Bremen accused the Hanseatic city of insolence because she called herself *respublica* in imitation of Venice and the Swiss city-republics, the city fathers responded that they had received the title from the emperor in ancient times. It was a sign of the declining powers of self-government in German cities when, in 1717, the imperial court admonished them not to use the title republic any longer.[73]

---

[69] *Exercitatio Politica de Origine ac Rebus huic necessariis nominatim, territorio et publicis reditibus, praeside M. Ernesto König, Gymn. Thoruniensis Rectore, Boguslaus ab Unruh, eques Polonus respondens* (Thorn: Johannes Coepselius, 1679), folio 1v.

[70] 'Missiva der Stadt Elbing. Klage der Stadt Elbing gegen den Rat (1700)', Rkps. Elbl., APGd, 369.1 no. 228, pp. 2–3.

[71] On the Renaissance citizen, who was at the same time a man-at-arms, see the classic work of Hans Baron, *The Crisis of the Early Italian Renaissance. Civic Humanism and Republican Liberty in an Age of Classicism and Tyranny* (Princeton University Press, 1955), and J. G. A. Pocock, *The Machiavellian Moment. Florentine Political Thought and the Atlantic Republican Tradition* (Princeton University Press, 1975).

[72] Wippermann spoke about a 'German bourgeois feeling of superiority' in his *Der Ordensstaat als Ideologie*, p. 85; Gottfried Schramm emphasized the burghers' distance to Poland on the grounds of their Lutheran religion in his *Der Polnische Adel und die Reformation* (Wiesbaden: Franz Steiner, 1965), p. 121.

[73] Wolfgang Mager, 'Respublica und Bürger: Überlegungen zur Begründung frühneuzeitlicher Verfassungsordnungen', *Der Staat*, supplement 8 (1987): *Res Publica. Bürgerschaft in Stadt und Staat*, pp. 72–4.

Did the Prussian burghers, so keen on the preservation of their immunities and their powers of self-government, follow the proud self-definition of German patricians? They were certainly familiar with the political theory and reality of German free cities, as many burgher sons travelled to Germany for their university studies.[74] The Danzig burgher and syndic Reinhold Curicke directly addressed the question whether Danzig could compare itself in status with the free cities in the Holy Roman Empire, which were only answerable to the emperor himself, but independent of the estates, princes, bishops and other authorities. His answer was cautious. Although he accepted the comparison, he stressed that urban freedom was never licence but the recognition of legal authority. Unlike in the Empire, the Polish king was not the sole authority over the city: using a typical Renaissance metaphor,[75] Curicke described the city as part of the larger body of the republic, with all its members. Had he denied this relationship to the republic, he would have fundamentally questioned Danzig's seat in the Prussian Diet. Therefore, he was eager to emphasise that it was not one particular king, but the whole crown of Poland, the *regnum*, to which the city owed obedience and allegiance.[76]

The loyalty to the crown of Poland included a double duty: the preservation of the royal cities and their economic power for the king and for the good of the whole republic.[77] In his memorandum about the state of Thorn's ramparts in the 1590s, Stroband argued that the common good and the laws needed the physical protection of a system of well-functioning fortifications. As a proof of loyalty towards the Polish king and Commonwealth, Thorn had to maintain its walls against the Turkish danger, as *antemurale Christianitatis*, and against the threat of the Teutonic Knights, who continued to claim the property of the Prussian lands. Stroband's reference to the Knights who strove to 'subject us again to the slavery of their black cross' consciously invoked the heroic past which had forged the union between city and republic: '*in antiqua unione Regni Poloniae*, under the protection of our king and lord'.[78]

For Ernst König, the republic was the whole 'body of civil society under one government', such as the Holy Roman Empire, France or Poland-Lithuania, and provided a spiritual mould, whereas a city (*civitas* or *urbs*) was merely one material part or form of society. In other words, Danzig, Thorn and Elbing were members of a larger body politic and society, the Polish-Lithuanian Commonwealth, which

---

[74] Between 1575 and 1772, ninety-five students from Royal Prussian towns studied in Helmstedt; Marian Pawlak, *Studia uniwersyteckie młodzieży z Prus Królewskich w XVI–XVIII wieku* (Toruń: UMK, 1988), annexe, table 4; Michael Stolleis (ed.), *Hermann Conring 1606–1681*, Historische Forschungen 23 (Berlin: Duncker und Humblot, 1983).

[75] Ringmar, *Identity*, p. 153.

[76] Reinhold Curicke, *Der Stadt Dantzig Historische Beschreibung* (1645), (Amsterdam and Danzig: Johann und Gillis Janssons von Waesberge, 1687), pp. 75–7.

[77] Johannes Schultz [Szulecki], *Tractatus historico-politicus de Polonia nunquam tributaria* (Danzig: Rhetii Haeredes, 1694).

[78] APT Kat. II, II.12, Stroband, pp. 9v–14.

gave them a spiritual and material form.[79] This approach was not uncommon in European political theory: Jean Bodin's *République* was translated into English as 'commonweal', and Bodin regarded France too as a realm composed of many distinct territories and political units, increasingly forged together – more or less successfully – by the crown. In contrast to France, however, in Poland-Lithuania it was the szlachta who led the initiative towards a more unitary state. Unlike the city fathers in the towns of the Holy Roman Empire, who ultimately looked to monarchical or imperial authority but not classical republicanism, the cities of Royal Prussia felt comfortable with the republican elements of Polish-Lithuanian constitutional theory.[80] It was with growing suspicion, however, that they watched the development towards greater national uniformity and – among their own Prussian lower nobility – towards republican extremism, which increasingly threatened to undermine the nature of the contract by which they had entered the Commonwealth.

It was not only the threat to their immunities and political self-government which underlined the similarities with the situation of German imperial cities. As in Germany, Royal Prussian magistrates routinely faced challenges from their own subjects, who demanded greater participation in the running of urban affairs. In Royal Prussian cities, the 'third estate' (*Dritte Ordnung*) played an exceptionally strong role in the city's political decision-making.[81] The council appointed the 'third estate' from among the commercial and professional groups, especially the merchant and craft guilds of the cities (*verfaßte Bürgerschaft*). This institution dated from the early sixteenth century, when quarrels had broken out between the council and the citizenry over religious and political grievances during the Lutheran Reformation. Despite royal protection for Catholic city councils, the *Dritte Ordnung* successfully obtained participatory rights when Lutherans took over the urban government.[82] In contrast to Royal Prussia, the influence of guilds suffered in many German imperial towns, including Nördlingen, where in 1552 the guilds were abolished and the corporate character of representative bodies in the city government was replaced by a looser and more individual political participation of the citizenry.[83]

In the course of the seventeenth and eighteenth centuries, the citizenry periodically strengthened its position after the interference by the Polish kings in urban

---

[79] König, *Exercitatio Politica de Cive*, p. 2, paragr. I/8.
[80] See Wilfred Nippel, 'Bürgerideal und Oligarchie', in Koenigsberger, *Republiken und Republikanismus*, pp. 1–18, where it is argued that participatory democracy in German cities had little in common with classic republicanism, which dominated the political language in the Royal Prussian cities; also Schilling, 'Gab es im späten Mittelalter', pp. 119–20.
[81] Heinrich Kramm, 'Streiflichter auf die Oberschichten der mitteldeutschen Städte im Übergang vom Mittelalter zur Neuzeit. Zur Frage des Patriziats', in Rössler, Hellmuth (ed.), *Deutsches Patriziat 1430–1740*, Büdinger Vorträge 1965 (Limburg (Lahn): L. A. Starke, 1968), pp. 125–56.
[82] Maria Bogucka, 'Walki społeczne w Gdańsku w XVI wieku', in Labuda, Gerard (ed.), *Szkice z Dziejów Pomorza* (Warsaw: PWN, 1958), pp. 399ff.
[83] Christopher F. Friedrichs, *Urban Society in an Age of War: Nördlingen 1580–1720* (Princeton University Press, 1979), p. 12.

confrontations between the magistrates and the third estate in the latter's favour, which led to a temporary weakening of the ruling elites and their bodies, the assessorial court and the council. Although similar developments also occurred in the Empire's free cities, where the emperor intervened in the internal affairs of the citizenry and the council, the power of the Polish kings over their royal cities and their willingness to get involved far exceeded the imperial activities.[84] Unlike imperial cities, whose monopoly of power, or *jus territorii et superioritatis*, was acknowledged in the Westphalian Peace of 1648, the Royal Prussian cities were not allowed to appoint their own first burgomasters and presidents (burgraves). Instead they were nominated by the Polish king, who after 1523/25 also confirmed the city councils of Thorn, Danzig and Elbing. In contrast to the Polish-Lithuanian Commonwealth, German free cities usually followed the motto 'town law breaks state law', which not even Danzig with all its economic power sought to adopt against royal decrees.[85] Despite the three cities' internal constitutions, drawn up on the basis of customary law by the cities themselves and called *Willküren* as in Germany, the three major Royal Prussian cities could not claim such a right. The opinion of some German historians that Danzig, Thorn and Elbing were three 'independent city-states' has no legal or historical basis but follows the myth which the city-fathers nurtured in the late eighteenth century under the threat of the two partitioning powers, Russia and the kingdom of Prussia.[86]

The powers attached to citizenship were also a central issue that concerned the internal fabric of the Royal Prussian cities. Until the seventeenth century, Danzig distinguished between two main categories, the *Großbürgerrecht*, given to all politically active members and to the (mostly richer) merchants, and the *Kleinbürgerrecht* for certain categories of craftsmen, sailors, watermen and other labourers.[87] Citizens born in a Hanseatic city, or whose parents were from such a city, were entitled to possess either of these two burgher rights. Thus the city-fathers, who defended the *ius indigenatus* in the Prussian senate, made exceptions when it came to their own commercial obligations as members in an international organisation, the Hanseatic League. Burghers from all over the Northern, Baltic Hanseatic areas, from the German lands, Livonia and even from Flanders, were accepted by the Danzigers as members of a supra-territorial, international trading community. The right to be elected to urban office as Prussian *indigena* then came with a perman-

---

[84] Asch shows the tendency of the emperor to avoid direct involvement as an arbiter; instead he sent mediators to appease the quarrelling parties in Lübeck; Jürgen Asch, *Rat und Bürgerschaft in Lübeck 1598–1669. Die verfassungsrechtlichen Auseinandersetzungen im 17. Jahrhundert und ihre sozialen Hintergründe*, Veröffentlichungen zur Geschichte der Hansestadt Lübeck 17 (Lübeck: Verlag Max Schmidt-Römhild, 1961), pp. 151, 162–3.

[85] 'State law' has to be understood here as the royal privileges which defined and limited the cities' constitution; see Zbgniew Rymaszewski, *Sprawy Gdańskie przed sądami zadwornymi oraz ingerencja królów w gdański wymiar sprawiedliwości XVI–XVIII w.* (Wrocław: Ossolineum, 1985), p. 166.

[86] Stanisław Salmonowicz, 'Das königliche Preußen im öffentlichen Recht der polnisch-litauischen Republik, 1569–1772', *Studia Maritima* 6 (1987), 41–2, 59–60; see chapter 9 below.

[87] 'Wer des Bürgerrechts fähig oder unfähig erachtet wird', Bibl. PAN Gd., 403.

ent settlement and the newcomers' oath of allegiance to the cities' constitutions.[88]

Over the course of the seventeenth century, the distinction between major and minor citizenship came under attack and was finally abolished after prolonged conflicts between the council-government and the third estate or constituted community of the guilds and craftsmen: 'the guilds only wanted to know about one common citizenship, which was introduced anno 1670'.[89] Only labourers could gain a cheaper and less privileged version of citizenship. Contrary to the social processes in the Empire, where historians have recorded many examples of a further polarisation in status between citizens, especially after city oligarchies won representation in the Imperial Diet in 1648, in Royal Prussia the distinctions between the various groups of citizens with burgher rights diminished.[90] How important the debate on citizenship was in reality is demonstrated by the fact that in most Prussian towns and cities the proportion of inhabitants without any burgher rights was as high as 70–75 per cent; it was from among these inhabitants that the *Dritte Ordnung* sometimes sought support, in order to put pressure on the magistrate and increase the chance that their own grievances would be heard. A particularly memorable protest march in 1678 by a Lutheran crowd, directed not only against the Catholic church but also against the privileged settlements of Mennonite traders and craftsmen in the suburbs, ended in the looting and burning of the Carmelite monastery near Danzig.[91]

A common complaint of the merchants and craftsmen of the *Dritte Ordnung* in Thorn, Danzig and Elbing from the sixteenth century was that lawyers and career politicians, the so-called *literati*, had increasingly replaced the merchant patriciate in the city council, leaving no place in the council hierarchy for people from the trades who would have better understood the financial and economic interests of the majority of the active, professional population.[92] Unlike in Germany, however, where the ruling urban oligarchies successfully curbed the influence of the guilds and crafts, in the Prussian cities the conflicts brought slow but steady victories in favour of the *Gewerke*, the craft guilds and the representatives of each quarter (the four main craft guilds) who had a right to sit in the council.[93] The guilds achieved their greatest victory over the city council of Danzig in the eighteenth century,

---

[88] Ibid., sections 1 and 5; Gottfried Lengnich, *Jus publicum Civitatis Gedanensis*, ed. Otto Günther, Quellen und Darstellungen zur Geschichte Westpreußens 1 (Danzig: Th. Bertling, 1900).

[89] 'Wer des Bürgerrechts fähig', Bibl. PAN Gd., 403, p. 289.

[90] Hildebrandt, 'Rat contra Bürgerschaft', 233–7; Asch (*Rat und Bürgerschaft*, p. 33) emphasises the growing alienation between merchant and council families in Lübeck, due to the latter's rise in the 'Junker-Kompagnie' and nobility.

[91] Bogucka and Samsonowicz, *Dzieje miast*, p. 465; Georg Schröder, 'Besuch Johann Sobieskis in Danzig, 1677', APGd, Bibl. Archivi 300.R, no. Vv. q 21, pp. 297–300.

[92] Salka Goldmann, *Danziger Verfassungskämpfe unter polnischer Herrschaft* (Leipzig: Teubner, 1901), p. 35; Schröder, 'Besuch Sobieskis', p. 24; see also 'Discursus de Commerciis Regni Elbingam reducendis', APGd, Rkps. Elbl. 369.1, no. 2910, pp. 6–7, which criticizes nepotism among the city fathers who neglect urban commerce.

[93] Stanisław Herbst, *Toruńskie cechy rzemieślnicze* (Toruń: Nakładem Cechów Toruńskich, 1933), p. 56; Edmund Cieślak, 'Gotfryd Lengnich a walki polityczne w Gdańsku w połowie XVIII wieku', *Ars Historica* 71 (1976), 663–4 and his *Historia Gdańska*, vol. III, pp. 542–78.

when a royal decree sharply limited the powers of the council and secured a fuller participation of the third estate in urban legislation and policy-making.

Little wonder that the political doctrine from which the Prussian burghers most eagerly distanced themselves was Bodin's theory of the citizen-subject. Bodin singled out the political elite, the members of the council, as the only group of citizens designated for political activity. All other burghers were to be second-class citizens: 'The first and highest level of citizenship consists of the participation in the magistrates, in assemblies and public councils, but those who do not enjoy this right have very diminished and limited rights.'[94] In the same measure as there was only space for a single sovereign power in Bodin's state, magistrates would not share authority with the citizenry. Bodin considered immunities merely as customs, protected by tradition and a contract with the sovereign magistrate, who was obliged by conscience and natural law to respect them. Apart from the fact that Bodin never won sympathy for his theory of *rex legibus solutus* in a country which relied not simply on the good will of a ruler, but on the royal election, fundamental laws and parliamentarianism to limit the powers of the monarchy, Bodin's definition of a citizen did not go down well with the Royal Prussian urban elites. Georg Schultz denied that the Prussians ever delegated political decision-making to the diet or the king:

The Prussians do not let themselves be obliged to such obedience [to forcibly pay tribute or taxes] by the Polish diet, but they deliberate as free people at their own general diet about how much money they want to give, and it depends on their friendliness and their good will, and not at all on the decision of the Polish diet.[95]

Basilius Czölner, professor of law in Thorn, and his student from Elbing, Gottfried Zamehl, rejected Bodin's definition and emphasised that a citizen was always a member of society with full rights, no matter how politically active he was, as long as he obeyed the laws and fulfilled his financial, economic and military duties.[96] A basic condition for being granted citizenship was therefore, in good Aristotelian fashion, not only holding an office but the fulfilment of one's civic obligations.[97] It would have been unthinkable for Zamehl to exclude the majority of conscientious, tax-paying citizens with burgher rights from political participation. Only mixed government could therefore be considered beneficial for the preservation of civil society: Bodin's idea of the magistrates' undivided sovereignty was not conducive to stability and the common good.[98]

---

[94] Quoted by König, *Exercitatio Politica de Cive*, paragr. I/3, folio A2.
[95] 'Variae Observationes de Prussia Polonica ab G. P. Schultz P.P.O., hortis publicis Ao. 1712 die 30 Januarii dictatae, excerpit call. Johann Ludwig Kuttig, Thoruniensis', APT Kat. II, VIII.46, p. 37.
[96] Basilius Czölner, *Disputatio Politica de Cive, ejus essentia et proprietatibus etc. quam C.B.D. Humanae Societatis praeside Basilio Czölner, Godofredus Zamelius respondens* (Thorn: Franciscus Schnellboltz, 1648), paragr. 5–18.
[97] König, *Exercitatio Politica de Cive*, paragr. I/2, folio A2.
[98] Czölner, *Disputatio Politica de Cive*, paragr. 18.

Unlike the students of natural law theories propagated in the university lecture-halls of Samuel Pufendorf's Berlin or Hermann Conring's Helmstedt, where Bodin, Lipsius and Grotius were revered as the founding fathers of strong monarchy, Royal Prussian law-students in the Gymnasia of Thorn, Elbing or Danzig were taught that their commonweal was not based on the unconditional obedience and subjection of the citizen to the undivided power of their paternal sovereign, neither within nor outside their city. Indeed, the cities developed a culture of disobedience to illegitimate power, which was deeply rooted in their historical memory of the events of 1454. While the burgomasters and council members of the royal cities continued to protest against the Union of 1569 and boycotted the Sejm thereafter, the citizenry used similar tactics against their own council governments whenever they felt wronged and excluded from the rights that were their due on the basis of the city's ancient constitutions. In both cases, the battle-cry was a reference to the past. Very consciously, urban constitutional writers projected a mirror-image of the Commonwealth's mixed form of government onto their own urban constitutional theory. The authors who most fervently supported Prussian political participation in the Commonwealth also underlined the participatory principles contained in their urban constitutions. Some of the grievances of the *Dritte Ordnung* made outright comparisons between the relationship of the citizenry to the magistrates and that of the city of Danzig to the king and the Commonwealth.[99]

It seems unlikely that in the later seventeenth century German constitutional ideas provided anything but a distant scholarly reference for the burghers in Royal Prussian towns. The increase in central bureaucratic structures and the strengthened domination of territorial rulers over formerly free cities in the Holy Roman Empire was compatible neither with the rhetoric nor with the reality of Royal Prussian urban politics. The consensus about what constituted the perfect citizen generally stressed his natural sociability as a basic virtue of the corporate ideal of the well-functioning city-society. *Non subjicimus* – we will not subject ourselves – was the ritual protestation of the Prussian burghers against any attempt to curtail their ancient rights. Under no circumstances was a citizen (*civis*) to be confounded a subject (*Untertan*): 'What has been defined as a citizen depends on the form of government, and not subjection, as citizen is the name for those who . . . would rather govern than be obedient subjects.'[100]

Despite a very clear definition of citizenship within the city, limited by specific constitutions, conditions and criteria for the purchase of burgher rights, the meaning of being a 'citizen of Royal Prussia' remained contested. Many burghers resented being looked down upon by the nobility, since they believed their cities contributed equally, if not proportionally more, to the common good and the prosperity of the province. In the 1720s, a contribution to the periodical *Das Erleuterte Preußen* speaks about the unique mixture of nations and peoples which

---

[99] Schröder, 'Besuch Sobieskis', p. 22.
[100] Czölner, *Disputatio Politica de cive*, paragr. 20.

formed the basis of the Prussian nation. Almost nobody, the author observed, could call himself a true Prussian, since most had ancestors who had arrived from other provinces in the Holy Roman Empire, Poland or other countries. Therefore, the only common denominator of all Prussians was the 'Band der bürgerlichen Societät', the ties of civic community, of which the nobility was as much as a part the burghers in the cities.[101]

This echoes the historical utopia of a common Prussian citizenship, widely popularised by Christoph Hartknoch, Royal Prussia's foremost seventeenth-century historian: 'When the Teutonic Order started the Prussian War, the nobility did not live in the countryside, as they do now, but in the cities, next to other burghers . . . as in Germany, the nobles originally also lived in the towns.'[102] The feeling of lost harmony, of lost unity and solidarity, when all citizens, whether nobles or burghers, subscribed to the same civic virtues and values, was strong in burgher literature during the seventeenth century and saw a revival in the eighteenth, together with visions of an idealised Prussian past. To answer the important question of why the three major Prussian cities repeatedly asserted and demonstrated their allegiance to this Commonwealth, whose anti-urban record seemed to shock so many West European observers, one must therefore explain the powerful Prussian myths of self-definition and of historical identity.

[101] 'Vom Glück der Pommern in Preußen', *Erleutertes Preußen* 4 (Königsberg: Hallervorden Erben, 1728), p. 384.
[102] Hartknoch, *Alt- und Neues Preußen*, part 1, p. 446.

# 4

# History, myth and historical identity

Every time a society finds itself in crisis it instinctively turns its eyes towards its origins and looks there for a sign. (Octavio Paz)[1]

Since the revival of interest in national origins during the Renaissance, prompted by the rediscovery of Tacitus's history of the pagan tribes which challenged the decaying Roman Empire, history steadily gained respectability as an academic subject at schools and universities. The questioning of philosophical and theological certainties and authorities during the Renaissance and Reformation period engendered an identity crisis, when late medieval Christian societies were confronted with the un-Christian heritage of classical antiquity. Poland-Lithuania was no exception: Italian and German Humanism had reached Cracow, the old Polish capital, even before Bona Sforza (1494–1557), the daughter of Gian Galeazzo, duke of Milan, and Isabella of Aragon, married king Sigismund I in 1518 and brought Italian artists and scholars to the Polish court. A society as steeped in the culture of classical antiquity as that of the Polish-Lithuanian nobility took seriously Cicero's dictum that 'not to know what happened in the past, means ever to remain a child'.[2] Its sense of the past was greatly enhanced by the accumulation of political, legal and economic privileges since the late fourteenth century, which prevented the Polish king from collecting taxes, declaring war or passing any new laws without the nobility's consent. For politically active citizens, the past provided a valuable set of examples and models for future action and political legitimacy, boosting their self-confidence.

The same was true for the citizens of Royal Prussia, who regarded themselves in historical, political and national terms as a distinct group within the Commonwealth. For the burghers in particular, collective historical memory was patriotic scripture: being citizens of the fatherland – the city, the Prussian province or the wider Commonwealth – involved rights as well as responsibilities. History was a

---

[1] Quoted by Harold Berman, *Law and Revolution. The Formation of the Western Legal Tradition* (Cambridge, Mass.: Harvard University Press, 1983), p. 558.
[2] 'Nescire autem, quid antequam natus sis, acciderit; id est semper esse puerum', quoted by the Polish historian Szymon Starowolski, *Simonis Starovolsci Penu Historicum seu de dextra et fructuosa ratione Historians legendi Commentarius* (Venice: Zenarii Haeredes, 1620), p. 19.

crucial instrument for the education and formation of loyal and able citizens, both burgher and noble. Since their incorporation into the Polish kingdom, the Prussian social and political elites had looked to Humanist Cracow and its university, compelled by the need to produce qualified councillors and burgomasters, secretaries and delegates to the Polish Sejm and the Prussian diets. The activities and influence of a large circle of international Humanist scholars at Cracow, many of South-German, Alsatian, Silesian or Hungarian origin, peaked in the 1520s.[3] Between 1493 and 1517, until the Reformation shattered the link, eighty-eight students from Danzig alone studied at the Jagiellonian University in Cracow, but student numbers from Royal Prussia dropped sharply after 1525 as the Prussians created their own, Protestant education system.[4] Urban Latin schools were remodelled into institutions of higher learning; from the middle of the sixteenth century, the three academic Gymnasia in Danzig, Thorn and Elbing transformed Royal Prussia into a centre of classical studies. New curricula combined Protestant theology and the traditional Humanist disciplines of philosophy, poetry, grammar and rhetoric with an emphasis on new subjects such as law, political theory and history.[5] From 1535, the Gymnasium in Elbing flourished under the leadership of the Dutch Humanist Wilhelm Gnapheus, who introduced Melanchthon's educational ideas. Danzig followed in 1558 with the foundation of a Humanist school which, in 1580, received the title of Academic Gymnasium, and became the most prominent Prussian school, particularly in the early 1600s when Barthel Keckermann, the Calvinist natural law thinker, taught there. After the decline in significance of the university of Cracow, a large number of Protestant and even Catholic nobles from all over the Commonwealth sent their children for a solid Humanist education to the Royal Prussian Gymnasia, whose attraction increased markedly until the success of Tridentine Catholicism depleted student numbers in the early seventeenth century.[6]

The Gymnasium in Thorn was reorganised in 1568, around the time when the first Jesuit schools were established in the province. Although the Protestant Gymnasia have been credited with higher educational standards than their rival Jesuit colleges, the school which the Jesuit Order opened in Thorn in 1605 enjoyed growing popularity, not only among the Polish-speaking Catholic population, but also among the families of Protestant craftsmen and day-labourers. The competi-

[3] Jacqueline Glomski, 'Erasmus and Cracow, 1510–1530', *Yearbook of the Erasmus of Rotterdam Society* 17 (1997), 1–18.
[4] Władysław Pniewski, *Język polski w dawnych szkołach gdańskich* (Gdańsk: Towarzystwo Przyjaciół Nauki i Sztuki, 1938), p. 14; Pawlak, *Studia uniwersyteckie*, table 6.
[5] For example the curriculum of 1688, *Catalogus Lectionum et Operarum Publicarum in Athenaeo Gedanensi hoc cursu annuo expendiendarum proposito Januario ineunte* (Danzig: in Atheneo), which offered a course by Joachim Hoppe, history professor in Danzig, on 'Historiam nonnullorum Regnorum publice in Jure Institutiones Juris Civilis & Canonici' (paragr. 2).
[6] Janina Freilichówna, *Ideał wychowawczy Szlachty Polskiej w XVI i XVII wieku* (Warsaw: Nakładem Naukowego Towarzystwa Pedagogicznego, 1938), p. 68; Stanisław Tync, *Dzieje Gimnazjum Toruńskiego*, 2 vols, vol. II: *1600–1660*, Roczniki TNT no. 53 (Toruń: TNT, 1949), pp. 82–3.

tion between the Society of Jesus and the Protestant schools for the hearts and minds of future citizens, especially those of Polish and Lithuanian noble extraction, became fiercer in the late seventeenth century. In 1684 the Thorn Jesuits compiled a curriculum which reveals heavy borrowing from their Protestant counterparts: Latin, Greek, rhetoric, poetry and metaphysics, as well as natural sciences and history. As a result, the Thorn Protestant Gymnasium increased its provision of Polish language classes to avoid alienating Polish-speaking Lutheran or Calvinist families. Thorn had a substantial Protestant Polish-speaking population among all groups of society, as evidenced in 1698 when the guild masters thanked the city council for cutting back the time allotted to sermons and organ-playing in the 'Polish church services for Polish Protestant servant folk', so that they could go back to work sooner rather than later.[7]

Preparation for political activity in the city and the Commonwealth included training in rhetoric and oratorical skills. As Joachim Pastorius, director of the Gymnasium in Elbing from 1651–4 and history professor in Danzig from 1654–67, recommended in his letter to the son of the Danzig burgrave Adrian von der Linde, Cicero's 'robust and accurate style' was best suited for political speeches.[8] The core program of *eruditio historica* included the study of Pliny and Cassiodor, two of the most frequently quoted sources for sixteenth-century Polish and Prussian historians. Knowledge of heraldry, *Kleinodia Polona Libertatis*, for noble students was balanced with the writing of treatises on the usefulness of cities in Poland, designed for the sons of burghers.[9] Following their Order's *Ratio Studiorum* of 1599, the Jesuits in Thorn echoed the patriotic tone of Protestant teaching and similarly stressed the future role of the students as citizens of the Commonwealth, in the diet or city council's public affairs. From the mid-seventeenth century, the Jesuits carried on training their students in law, rhetoric and public speaking, while Protestant curricula started to emphasise theology, literature and mathematics.[10]

Religious differences did not prevent the burghers in the Royal Prussian cities from sharing with the nobility views on the necessity of political education. Georg Wende, rector of the Thorn Gymnasium towards the end of the seventeenth century, compared the tasks fulfilled by city councillors with those of Chinese mandarins, whose high standards of education and their noble descent made them the most suitable for state service. Wende warned that political education for the common good should not be neglected even in schools where theological education

---

[7] Ephraim Praetorius, 'Kirchen-Sachen', KM 130, p. 272.

[8] Pastorius started his career as a Calvinist with Arian sympathies, but ended his life a canon at Frauenburg (Frombork): *Ad nobilium Adolesc[entem] Sigismundum de Linda, Magnifici & Nobili Viri Adriani de Linda Burgrabii & Praeco[n]s[uli] Dant[iscani] Filium Epistola, de recte eloquentia Romanae studio* (Danzig: Georg Rhetii, 1649), p. 327; Lech Mokrzecki, 'Dyrektor Gimnazjum Elbląskiego Joachim Pastorius (1652–1654) i jego poglądy na historię', *Rocznik Elbląski* 4 (1969), 59–83.

[9] 'An expediat Polonis habere civitates munitas, respondetur affirmative' (1684), Ossol. 1552/I, p. 117.

[10] Stanisław Salmonowicz, 'Nauczanie prawa i polityki w Toruńskim Gimnazjum Akademickim od XVI do XVIII wieku', *Czasopismo Prawno-Historyczne* 23 (1991), 53–85.

(Confucianism in China – Lutheranism in Royal Prussia) was generally preferred.[11] History and its great men were used as examples, while the knowledge of past constitutions, governments and kingdoms served as a treasure-trove of models, bad and good, for criticism and imitation.[12] Public-spirited education, intended to fortify urban burghers' pride in their citizen status, was also valued by Michael Mylius, a history professor in Elbing, who in 1642 wrote on the occasion of the death of the royal envoy and palatine of Pernau in Livonia, Count Ernst Dönhoff, of the greatest achievements of the deceased nobleman: '[He] travelled all over Europe's regions and kingdoms, especially those whose languages he easily mastered, and after his return as a great citizen of this body politic he made use of [what he had learned] for the good of the republic.'[13]

Patriotic behaviour was therefore measured by the use made of education for the common good of the state and the province: Dönhoff 'restored peace for God, the king and the people, for holiness, majesty and utility, *publicae salutis summam*'.[14] Personal virtues and qualifications were not an end in themselves, but a means to serve – in Dönhoff's case – the city of Elbing and the Polish-Lithuanian Commonwealth. In 1651, Gottfried Zamehl, from a prominent family of burgomasters and poets laureate in Elbing, whose father had collected the manuscripts of medieval Prussian chronicles, went on a study trip to Western Europe. After his return, he summed up the patriotic purpose of his experience abroad:

We travel to various nations and regions, but meanwhile we do not lose our love for our fatherland, nor shall we ever hold it in contempt; . . . it is not enough to live well abroad, but the motivation for all industrious activities [in foreign countries] is to come back with fame and honour to the fatherland.[15]

The hope that burghers would adopt the ideal of education recommended by the city authorities was also expressed in the appeal by the theology professor and senior pastor of Thorn, Jan Neunachbar, to appoint a local Thorunian or Prussian preacher to a vacant parish in the city: 'not only do locals know the nature of their fatherland, and what is good for it, better than foreigners: but also the citizenry will be encouraged to spend something on their children and educate them for the benefit of the fatherland'.[16]

[11] Lech Mokrzecki, 'Zainteresowanie historyczne Jerzego Wendego, rektora Gimnazjum Akademickiego w Toruniu 1695–1705', in Zdrójkowski, Zbigniew (ed.), *Księga Pamiatkowa 400-lecia Toruńskiego Gimnazjum*, vol. I: *XVI–XVIIIw.*, (Toruń: TNT, 1992), p. 338.

[12] Lech Mokrzecki, *Studium z dziejów nauczania historii*, Wydział nauk społecznych i humanistycznych 46 (Gdańsk: GTN, 1973), pp. 81, 87, 132–3.

[13] Michael Mylius, *Exequiae Ill[ustrissimi] D[omini] D[omini] Magni Ernesti Comitis a Dönhof, Palatini Parnaviensis Torpat[ensis] Praefecti Elb[ingensis]* (Elbing: Bodenhausen, 1642), folio A2.

[14] Ibid., folio A4v.

[15] Gottfried Zamehl, *Studiosus Apodemicus, sive de peregrinationibus studiosorum Discursus Politicus* (Leiden: Jacobi Köhleri, 1651), preface and pp. 77–8.

[16] The appointment was for a pastor's position in the new town of Thorn, in 1671; Praetorius, KM 130, p. 172.

Most historical works in Royal Prussia were written by burghers and disseminated from local printing presses, some of them attached to the schools. Jurisprudence ranked highly among the career choices of the urban elites, who wished to grasp the intricacies of their own constitutions and laws, the traditions of Kulm law and their ancient privileges granted by the Order and the Polish monarchy. But even law was approached from a historical angle. It was not merely historians who were sought, but lawyers who knew history, in the words of Pastorius 'the parent of all sciences'.[17]

Under the influence of the universities of the Empire and other European states, where the teaching of Roman law in the Renaissance had laid the foundations for the rationalist school of natural law, legal training at the Prussian Gymnasia adopted the focus on 'public law'. The academic preparation for public office was inspired and guided by the science of cameralism (*Kameralwissenschaften*) in the German universities of the late seventeenth century such as Jena, Halle, Frankfurt an der Oder, Helmstedt, Heidelberg and Leipzig, where many future burgomasters and councillors of Royal Prussian cities completed their studies.[18] Prussian students and scholars who visited German universities followed the debates about Athenian democracy, the mixed constitution of Sparta and the advantages of aristocracy or monarchy; upon their return to Royal Prussia they applied what they had learnt to their domestic context, focusing on the dangers of tyranny, on the defence of their privileges and immunities inherited from previous generations, on the advantages of the aristocratic and democratic elements in the polity and on the prospects for reform of the practice of government in their own state, the Polish-Lithuanian Commonwealth.[19] German political science (*Staatenkunde*) appealed not only to Royal Prussian students: the idea that laws and constitutions had no power and meaning unless they were backed by true political power in the service of the common good held a strong attraction for seventeenth-century Polish constitutional thinking.[20]

In such an environment, the writing and teaching of history was central to

---

[17] Joachim Pastorius, *Orationes duae quarum prima inauguratis de praeciosis Historiae Autoribus altera de potissimis eiusdem argumentis agit* (Elbing: Corell, 1651–2), folio Ev.

[18] Salmonowicz, 'Nauczanie prawa', 54–6; also Klaus Neumaier, *Jus Publicum. Studium zur barocken Rechtsgelehrsamkeit an der Universität Ingolstadt*, Ludovico Maximilianea Forschungen 6 (Berlin: Duncker and Humblot, 1974), pp. 13–15, and Notker Hammerstein, *Jus and Historie. Ein Beitrag zur Geschichte des historischen Denkens an deutschen Universitäten im späten 17. und im 18. Jahrhundert* (Göttingen: Vandenhoeck and Ruprecht, 1972), pp. 72–6.

[19] Adrian von der Linde, 'Beschreibung der Pohlen Art und Policey' (Bibl. PAN Gd. Nl 27.4, no. 9); David Braun, *De jurium regnandi fundamentalium in Regno Poloniae* (Cologne: Theodor Brabeus, 1722); Andreas Baumgarten, *De majestate principis* (Thorn: Coepselius, 1686); Martin Böhm, *Commentarius de Interregnis in Regno Poloniae* (Thorn: Nicolai, 1733), and numerous dissertations by the students of Hartknoch (see bibliography). On the use of republican concepts in the seventeenth century, see Wilfried Nippel, 'Bürgerideal und Oligarchie. "Klassischer Republikanismus" aus althistorischer Sicht', in Koenigsberger (ed.), *Republiken und Republikanismus*, pp. 17–18.

[20] Hammerstein, *Jus und Historie*, p. 101; similarly, Kazimierz Kocot, *Nauka prawa narodów w Ateneum Gdańskim, 1580–1793*, Seria A, no. 97 (Wrocław: Wrocławskie Towarzystwo Nauk, 1965), p. 105.

75

contemporary political debate, which consciously used the past as an instrument for expressing present political needs. Poland and Royal Prussia were no exception. The Dutch republic used the republican myth of Venice in the same way.[21] The Poles certainly seemed to know their origins. The mythical common descent of all nations of the Polish-Lithuanian Commonwealth from the ancient Sarmatian warrior-heroes, who successfully resisted Roman attempts to conquer them, was fashioned into a statement of the Commonwealth's constitutional and political superiority over West European societies oppressed by absolute royal power. Szymon Starowolski founded his reputation as a patriotic historian early on by collecting a pantheon of Sarmatian heroes, of *bellatores et scriptores*, who included representatives of all nations of the Commonwealth, similar to the gallery of Swedish-Gothic heroes assembled by Johannes Magnus.[22] References to great historical rulers and nations pointed at the imitation of past virtue. As the Goths were to the Swedes, or the Batavians to the Dutch, so were the Sarmatians to the Poles.[23] Roger Mason exposed a very similar process in medieval Scottish mythology and chronicles, expressed politically in the Declaration of Arbroath in 1320, where Sallust's idea of liberty stood godfather.[24] History, applied as a political instrument, forged a community's sense of the past by several means, including a collective name, a myth of origin and descent, a shared history and a specific political culture based on the freedom of its citizens, within a limited territory.[25]

The degree to which thinking was guided by mythical analogies was expressed by the Italian Jesuit Possevino, a widely travelled expert on Poland: 'legends and *fabulae*, as hidden and obscure they may be, are more powerful than poems'. Mythology and miracles were accepted as long as they had a purpose. The Renaissance historian Scaliger confirmed this view: no mythology was created for its own sake, all myths pointed beyond themselves to some political or didactic purpose, helping nations to identify with their own past and to apply historic virtues and values to the improvement of their present situation.[26] Although the Renaissance clearly popularised the genre of national history-writing, Kurt Johan-

---

[21] Eco O. G. Haitsma Mulier, *The Myth of Venice and Dutch Republican Thought in the Seventeenth Century* (Van Gorcum: Assen, 1980), p. 3.

[22] Kurt Johannesson, *The Renaissance of the Goths in Sixteenth-Century Sweden* (Berkeley: University of California Press, 1991), p. 82.

[23] Notable are the chronicles *Batavia* by Hadrianus Junius (Adriaen de Jonghe, 1511–1575) and Cornelius Aurelius' *Divisiekroniek* (1510) on the mythical Batavian king Bato, or the Batavian hero Claudius Civilis, who successfully fought the tyrannical Roman governor of Emperor Nero, Vitellus.

[24] Roger A. Mason, 'Chivalry and Citizenship. Aspects of National Identity in Renaissance Scotland', in Mason, Roger A. and MacDougall, Norman (eds.), *People and Power in Scotland. Essays in Honour of T.C. Smout*, (Edinburgh: John Donald, 1992), p. 51.

[25] Kenneth Schellhase, *Tacitus in Renaissance Political Thought* (Chicago and London: University of Chicago Press, 1976), p. xiii.

[26] Elżbieta Sarnowska-Temeriusz, *Świat mitów i świat znaczeń. Maciej K. Sarbiewski i problemy wiedzy o starożytności* (Warsaw: PAN, 1969), pp. 93–4, 109; see also Johannesson, *Renaissance*, p. 78, and Hans-Werner Goez, 'Die Gegenwart der Vergangenheit im früh- und hochmittelalterlichen Geschichtsbewußtsein', *Historische Zeitschrift* 255 (1992), 66–8.

nesson has stressed that the creation of identity based on myths of the origin of peoples, cities, families or nations was not linked to one specific historical period but corresponded to a general human need to harmonise past and present.[27]

Under the influence of the Humanists, secular history was now commonly structured in *historia locorum, temporum, familiarum et rerum gestarum* – the study of an area or place, of chronological events, of dynastic and national descent, and finally of all events relating to a society and its institutions, the church, schools, governments and magistracies. Jean Bodin's attack on the German theory of *translatio imperii*, the idea of continuity between the ancient Roman Empire and the Holy Roman Empire, sparked renewed interest in other themes of history: *historia humana* (the history of secular society), *historia naturalis* (including the laws of nature), and *historia divina* (on religion and revealed truth).[28] Despite the unpopularity of Bodin's political theory, his historical methodology, focusing on historical *particularia*, suited the Prussian burghers. The historical tradition of cosmography and Sleidanus's theory of the four world monarchies, Babylon (or Egypt), Persia, Greece and Rome, had never put down strong roots in Prussia.[29] Guided by patriotism, national and provincial history was much more popular.

In the sixteenth century Danzig secretary Caspar Schütz had stressed the need for historical education. He regretted that little knowledge of the Prussian past survived, due to ignorance and lack of learning not only among the pagans, but also among the Teutonic Knights. Historians of the following century wanted to remedy this situation.[30] In *De natura et proprietatibus historiae commentarius*, published posthumously in 1613, Keckermann was one of the first Prussians to follow Bodin's history of *particularia*. In contrast to the usual Ciceronian approach, the Danzig professor did not accept rhetoric as the main instrument of history, but considered historical research a branch of philosophy and, more specifically, of logic: 'nobody can write history well who is not a good logician'.[31] Throughout the seventeenth century, the Royal Prussian Gymnasia included Bodin's historical methodology in their curriculum, a fact mentioned in the 1676 lecture notes of the future burgomaster Johann Gottfried Rösner, who attended the lectures of the Thorn historian Ernst König on Bodin's *Historia pragmatica*. Rösner followed Bodin's subdivision of history into new subjects, as recommended by Keckermann:

---

[27] Johannesson, *Renaissance*, p. 83.

[28] Werner Goez, *Translatio Imperii* (Tübingen: Mohr, 1958), p. 365; Johannesson, *Renaissance*, p. 243.

[29] Johann Philippi (Sleidanus), *De quattuor summis imperiis*. On Prussia see Udo Arnold, 'Geschichtsschreibung im Preußenland bis zum Ausgang des 16. Jahrhunderts', *Jahrbuch für die Geschichte Mittel- und Ostdeutschlands* 19 (1970), 83–7.

[30] Caspar Schütz, *Historia Rerum Prussicarum Wahrhaffte und eigentliche Beschreybung* (Danzig: Groß, 1599), preface; Karl Kletke, *Quellenkunde der Geschichte des Preußischen Staates: Die Quellenschriftsteller zur Geschichte des Preußischen Staates*, vol. I (Danzig and Berlin: Schröder, 1858), pp. 73–157; Gottfried Centner, *Gelehrte und Geehrte Thorner* (Thorn: Bergmann, 1763).

[31] Emil Menke-Glückert, *Die Geschichtsschreibung der Reformation und Gegenreformation. Bodin und die Begründung der Geschichtsmethodologie durch Barthel Keckermann* (Leipzig: Hinrichs, 1912), pp. 124–5.

the history of ethics, political economy and history, and ecclesiastical history, as well as the history of scholarship (*prudentia*) and philosophy.[32] These subjects were no longer inferior to Ciceronian rhetoric as they had been in the early sixteenth century. Not only biblical empires, but individual states, nations, peoples and even cities should be looked at from the angle of their universal significance, using the same tools and categories as ecclesiastical or world history in the past.[33] Starowolski echoed this approach in his early seventeenth-century treatise on the utility of history aimed at students at Cracow University: history only makes sense when 'it reflects the deeds and events of all peoples of all times and all areas as in a great mirror'.[34]

Prussian urban historians followed these recommendations. Unlike most histories of German Hanseatic cities in the Empire, Royal Prussian *Particular-Historie* never ignored the larger dimension of the wider commonwealth: 'nam pius est, patriae scribere facta, labor' – it is pious work to write the history of one's fatherland.[35] *Amor patriae*, love of the fatherland, however, never entirely eclipsed the larger context. Walter Hubatsch observed that even sixteenth-century Prussian chronicles of monasteries and small towns never lost sight of the history of the whole Prussian province, in which such chronicles were embedded.[36] This is an important point, as German historians, transfixed by the power of nineteenth-century Prussia, have often argued that Danzig, Thorn and Elbing were in fact 'city-states' which possessed quasi-independence from the Polish-Lithuanian state. The view behind this interpretation was that the Royal Prussian burghers were at odds with a foreign, hostile Polish environment, whose culture they never accepted. A closer look at the historical and political writing of several Prussian burghers, however, reveals, a rather different picture.

Keckermann's idea of a perfect education combined patriotic with cosmopolitan values and suggests that his definition of *patria* did not end on the ramparts of his city. The fatherland, whose history one knew best, was also the place where one developed talents useful for public service and the common good. Such an endeavour made the burgher a precious and honoured member of society – his own local community, as well as human society at large.[37] The writing and teaching of history, especially at grammar school level, were therefore recognised public services for the good of the republic, and not merely an amateur's hobby-horse.

---

[32] Rösner, 'Lectiones publicae habitae in celebri Gymnasio Thoruniensi Ao 1676 et 1677 et 1678', KM 40, R 4° 16, pp. 22–3.

[33] Menke-Glückert, *Geschichtsschreibung*, pp. 130–2.

[34] Starowolski, *Penu Historicum*, p. 4.

[35] Joachim Cureus, *Newe Chronica des Herzogthumbs Ober und Nieder Schlesien Wahrhaffte und grüntliche Beschreibung* (Eißleben: Rätel, 1601), p. ii.

[36] Walter Hubatsch, 'Zur altpreußischen Chronistik des 16. Jahrhunderts', *Archivalische Zeitschrift* (Bayerisches Hauptstaatsarchiv Munich), 50/51 (1955), 429. This idea is best reflected in the German concept of *Landesgeschichte*; see Pankraz Fried, *Probleme und Methoden der Landesgeschichte* (Darmstadt: Wissenschaftliche Buchgesellschaft, 1978).

[37] Keckermann, quoted by Zamehl in *Studiosus Apodemicus*, p. 84.

Two other historians of Royal Prussia in the later seventeenth century, Pastorius and Hartknoch, wrote comprehensive guides to the history of the Polish-Lithuanian state to instil patriotic sentiments and a sense of duty among the young.[38] History-teaching had to focus on the need of young Prussians to acquaint themselves with the history and constitution not only of their cities but also of the Commonwealth. After their travels abroad, their *peregrinatio*, the young returned to the service of their *patria* as the new generation of their cities' political elite. This fatherland was the city, as referred to by fellow Danzigers or Torunians in Samuel Schönwald's travel *album*; but the *patria nostra* could also be the Commonwealth and Poland, whose historical greatness was felt to be at stake in 1655, the year of the Swedish invasion, when Schönwald and other youngsters studied abroad and discussed their anxiety about the fate of their various home provinces. Such diary entries from the 1650s demonstrate the similarity of attitudes of young burghers and nobles towards their Commonwealth, assuring mutual friendship and lamenting the war that was afflicting their common fatherland.[39] Dedication to the *respublica* was the very essence of the Ciceronian idea of the active life, shared by the Polish nobility.

The intellectual life and high educational standards in the Prussian Gymnasia, as well as Keckermann's ideals, inspired one of the Polish szlachta's most outspoken supporters of noble patriotic duty, Andrzej Maksimilian Fredro. In his educational programme of 1666 he voiced the need not only for nobles, but also for Polish burghers to imitate the Prussian cities in regularly sending their sons to foreign countries to learn languages and observe foreign customs, although Fredro did not explore why educational standards were higher in the Prussian Protestant schools. Protestant preachers had to undergo an academic training which included theological studies at a university, while Catholic priests, with the rare exception of those who could afford to go to Rome, or who received an adequate stipend, launched their careers in one of the numerous local seminaries or Jesuit colleges in Poland.[40] In many respects, however, the educational ideals of nobles shared similar requirements and a similar spirit of public duty as the education of the Prussian patriciate. Just as young burghers were prepared for public office, noble education was aimed at active participation in the political structure of the Commonwealth, as deputies to the Sejm, court officials, or even for a post as a senator. What Germany later called *staatsbürgerliche Erziehung* (civic education) was the most important element of the curriculum for a Polish or Lithuanian nobleman. History was central. A young nobleman had to be told of his origins so as to fill him with pride and a

---

[38] Joachim Pastorius, *Florus Poloniae seu Polonicae Historiae Epitome Nova* (Leiden: F. Heger, 1641), and Hartknoch, *Respublica Polonica duobus libris illustrata* (Lipsiae: Hallervorden, 1678).

[39] A similar diary, also from 1655, is Andreas Baumgarten's 'Stammbuch', APT Kat. II, XII.12: 'in this highly unhappy and most afflicted state in which our fatherland finds itself, I sign, Matthias Stanislaus Grodzki, Polish nobleman' (p. 195).

[40] Henryk Barycz, *Andrzej Maksimilian Fredro wobec zagadnień wychowawczych* (Cracow: PAU, 1949), pp. 51–2.

consciousness of the obligations connected with his role as a member of the noble Sarmatian nation.

Thus from the early seventeenth century the Humanist genre of history as *descriptio orbis terrarum* was replaced by a history of nations and fatherlands: the idea that the values of the past had an immediate impact on the present made anachronism a virtue. Changes in the patterns and contents of myths serve therefore as valuable tools for measuring alterations and shifts in a society's political culture. The economic and social crises in the Royal Prussian cities following the Swedish wars of the seventeenth century, the decline of their privileges and the political disappointment felt among the Prussian burghers about the behaviour of the nobility and the Polish king towards them – all this was reflected in the writing of history and in political publications. The period from early Humanism, when myths of origin were invented and first disseminated, to the eighteenth-century Enlightenment, which under the impact of the political and military crisis of the Polish-Lithuanian Commonwealth discarded many old legends, is crucial for the development of historical writing in the Prussian cities. Its citizens never turned away from history; on the contrary, when old myths no longer rang true, new myths had to be developed to account for a change in political attitudes and mentalities.

### TRADITIONS OF HISTORY-WRITING IN POLAND AND PRUSSIA

Despite the hostility of Royal Prussian historians towards the legacy of the Teutonic Order after 1454, chronicles from the Teutonic period still exerted considerable influence on the political and intellectual atmosphere of Royal Prussia and the view burghers and nobles held of their Prussian nation's past. The following three traditions formed the source base for Prussian historiography in the seventeenth and eighteenth centuries: chronicles commissioned and controlled by the Teutonic Order, a separate religious chronicle tradition, and secular provincial history or *Landesgeschichte*, based mainly in the Prussian cities.

In numerous chronicles the Teutonic Knights celebrated their conquest of the Prussian lands as a victory of Christianity over the heathens. Their chronicle tradition found its first and foremost exponent in Peter von Dusburg, whose 1326 history of the Teutonic Order, based on the Order's archival material in Marienburg as well as oral tradition, not only offers a vivid description of the life, wars and political organisation of the Knights, but also attempts to explain pagan Lithuanian and Prussian society and customs to a Christian audience.[41] Preserved in several transcriptions, Dusburg's chronicle held great attraction for historians of the early modern era and was published in 1679 by the Prussian historian Christoph Hartknoch.[42] Until this date, the more popular version of this chronicle was the

---

[41] Steven C. Rowell, *Lithuania Ascending. A Pagan Empire within East-Central Europe, 1295–1345* (Cambridge University Press, 1994), pp. 38–41.

[42] *Petri de Dusburg Ordinis Teutonici Sacerdotis Chronicon Prussiae, cum Anonymi cujusdam Continuatione,*

translation into Latin verse by Nikolaus von Jeroschin, a chaplain with the Teutonic Knights, but not a member of the Order's hierarchy itself, a fact reflected by numerous departures from Dusburg's highly favourable account of the history of the Order. A contemporary of Jeroschin and a parish priest from Deutsch-Eylau, Johann von Posilge, left a chronicle of Prussia which also demonstrated its independence from the panegyrical school promoted by the Grand Masters of the Teutonic Order. Posilge, who was not an immigrant from Germany but a native Prussian from nearby Marienburg,[43] exerted great influence on later historians hostile to the Teutonic Order. In general, however, the majority of the Order chronicles presented a positive picture of the knights' activities in the *Ordensland*.[44] After 1454, a secular branch of chronicle-writing emerged among laymen and clergy with an interest in the pagan and Teutonic past, albeit from an anti-Order point of view. This third tradition was located in Königsberg, the capital of Ducal Prussia after the secularisation of the Order in 1525, and in the three main Royal Prussian cities, who had headed the opposition movement against the Teutonic Knights alongside the Prussian nobility. The Prussian burghers, who started to compile the history of their cities and province, continued using the Grand Masters' chronicles alongside anti-Teutonic traditions, which had the greatest impact on the chroniclers of Danzig.[45] Foreign sources, including the histories of the Livonian Order, German medieval chronicles, and ancient sources before and during the time of the migrations in Europe, were also consulted, especially on the pagan past. One of the most influential post-Reformation sources was Simon Grunau's strongly anti-Teutonic *Prussian Chronicle*.[46] This work sparked controversy from the time of its composition in the early sixteenth century. The Teutonic Order, and subsequently historians from Ducal Prussia and Germany, accused its author, a Dominican from Tolkemit, not only of being uninformed and highly selective in his use of sources, but of maliciously distorting the history of the Order, dwelling on local customs and inventing sources that never existed. Grunau also attacked the Reformation, especially in the cities of Thorn and Danzig, and has therefore frequently been called anti-German. Remarks against 'die Deutzschen', however, are exclusively directed against the Teutonic Knights or against Lutheranism, not against Germans as a nation.[47] It was precisely these features and the admittedly anti-Teutonic bias that made it popular reading among contemporaries to whom the account was

*aliisque Antiquitatibus Prussicis C[hristoph] Hartknoch e MSS codicibus recensuit notisque illustravit* (Frankfurt and Leipzig: Hallervordi, 1679; 2nd edn, Jena: Nisius, 1679); see Max Töppen, *Geschichte der preußischen Historiographie von Dusburg bis auf Schütz* (Berlin: Verlag Wilhelm Hertz, 1853), p. 9.

43 Arnold, 'Geschichtsschreibung', p. 83.

44 Hubatsch, 'Zur altpreußischen Chronistik', pp. 420–62, and 'Deutschordenschroniken im Weichselland', *Ostdeutsche Monatshefte* 22 (1956), 713–18.

45 Arnold, 'Geschichtsschreibung', p. 79.

46 Simon Grunau, 'Preußische Chronik', in *Die preußischen Geschichtsschreiber des 16. und 17. Jahrhunderts*, vols. I–III (Leipzig: Duncker und Humblot, 1876–1896).

47 David Braun, *De Scriptorum Poloniae et Prussiae Historicorum, Politicorum & J[uris] C[onsul]torum* (Elbing: Bannehr, 1723), p. 247; Wippermann, *Der Ordensstaat*, p. 76.

accessible in manuscript form. It was not printed until the nineteenth century, but was frequently copied. In the eighteenth century, the canon of Heilsberg Adalbert Heide expressed his preference for Grunau, because 'Schütz, Dusburg and Jeroschin did not oppose the Teutonic Knights strongly enough'.[48] Modern German historians, however, have not only shown little tolerance for Grunau's work, but have given little thought to the meaning of his much-criticised stories.

Although Grunau rejected the un-Christian, sinful heathens, his fantastical legends convey a more positive picture of the life and character of the Prussian tribes than of the Teutonic Knights, who are described as cruel and malicious. Overall, the image of the brutish pagan Prussians, in whose condemnation Aeneas Sylvius Piccolomini had delighted in his influential chronicle of the Slavs in the fifteenth century, little by little began to change. Genuine interest in Prussian ancestry gradually replaced the horror felt towards non-Christian customs and idolatry. In 1584, Caspar Hennenberger described in great detail the pagans' gruesome life-style, their sacrifices of human beings to their gods, their fierceness in war and their brutishness, but continued with Helmoldus' reference to their talents, their patience and their friendliness towards anyone who was well-disposed towards them.[49]

Caspar Schütz, the first historian who systematically used the protocols of the Prussian estates before and after 1454, was critical of Grunau's fantastical stories and myths about the Prussians.[50] His own details of Prussian customs and superstition, however, are surprisingly rich for somebody who rejected all *fabulas*. His emphasis on the kindness and hospitality of the pagan forefathers, who were, according to Helmoldus, 'men with numerous favourable natural dispositions, full of humanity and by necessity patient', once more paints a positive picture. For the Order Schütz had only disgust and contempt. The pagans were 'in their majority almost completely wiped out by the hand of the Order', and the Teutonic Knights continued to ravage the country even after the forcible conversion: the knights raped and killed wives, children and servants, abused the courts and hampered justice, and let people rot in their prisons, while the emperor unjustly favoured the Order.[51]

Polish historiographical influences had already grown stronger during the alliance of Poles and Prussians in the last wars against the Teutonic Knights.[52] From

---

[48] Heide, 'Archiwum Vetus et Novum Ecclesiae Heilsbergensis ex variis Historiae Prussicae Scriptoribus', ADWO H.37, p.8.
[49] *Kurze und wahrhafftige Beschreibung des Landes zu Preußen* (Königsberg: Georg Osterbergern, 1584), pp. 19f. Similarly, Murinius's Polish chronicle, *Kronika albo krótkie z kronik rozmaitych zebranie spraw* (1582), ed. K. W. Wójcicki, Biblioteka starożytna pisarzy polskich 4 (Warsaw: n.pub., 1844), p. 10; there is also a new edition, ed. Zenon Nowak, Kronika Mistrzów Pruskich (Olsztyn: Wydawnictwo Pojezierze, 1989).
[50] Schütz, *Historia*, continued from 1525 to 1598 by David Chytraeus.
[51] Schütz quotes approvingly from the speech of von Baysen, the governor of Prussia, against the Teutonic Knights during the rebellion of 1454 (edition of 1599, pp. 199–199v).
[52] For example the work of Jan Długosz and Wincent Kadlubko, and from the early sixteenth century,

the time of Grunau and Schütz, Prussian chronicles started to depict the Teutonic Order in dark colours as the main foe of the cities and as a collective tyrant, composed of a power-hungry German immigrant nobility which was interested only in destroying the liberties of the country and its political elites: the Prussian Georg Kunheim, for example, wrote in his early sixteenth-century history of the Teutonic Order, 'Franconian, Swabian and Bavarian folk do no good to Prussian land'.[53] Another anti-Teutonic chronicle in Danzig, the *Ebert-Ferber-Buch*, named not after its author, but after the Danzig burgomasters in whose ownership it was discovered, continued to influence Prussian history until the later seventeenth century.[54] Historians in the Royal Prussian cities accurately caught the spirit of bitterness and rebellion which dominated the war against the Order. The fact that the eastern parts of Prussia were retained by the Knights in 1466 did not escape wry comment. The handwritten marginal notes by a sixteenth-century reader of the chronicle of Johann Lindau of Danzig, which recounts the recapture of Königsberg by the Teutonic Order, indignantly exclaim: 'Yes dear Königsberg, if you had just allowed it, you could now be as free as a bird . . . but you gave [the Order] a friendly kiss of Judas.'[55]

The 1520s, which saw the final victory of Poland and Royal Prussia over the Teutonic Knights and resulted in the secularisation of the Order by its last Grand Master, Albrecht of Hohenzollern, were an especially productive period for historiography in both Royal Prussia and in the newly established Duchy, from 1525 a vassal state under the Polish crown. Despite the political separation, early sixteenth-century chronicles reveal that both parts of Prussia remained intellectually very close. Grunau in Elbing and Oliwa, Hennenberger in Königsberg, and Schütz in Danzig – the three main chroniclers of the sixteenth century – all based their accounts of their pagan ancestors largely on one source: Erasmus Stella. The latter, who continued to exert a great influence on Prussian history-writing for the next 200 years, was no native Prussian. As burgomaster of Zwickau in Saxony, he was only linked to Prussia by his friendship with the bishop of Pomesania and the early sixteenth-century Grand Master of the Order Friedrich, duke of Saxony and count of Thüringen. Lacking access to the rich manuscript archives and chronicles in the possession of the Order and subsequently of the libraries in Königsberg, Danzig, Elbing and Thorn, Stella was the first historian to base his research on the Prussian past almost exclusively on the literary and historical sources of antiquity.[56] He

---

Maciej Miechowita's work on Sarmatia, *De Duabus Sarmatiis Asiana et Europaeana* (Cracow: Vietor, 1517); see Tadeusz Ulewicz, *Sarmacja. Studium z Problematyki słowianskiej w XV i XVI wieku* (Cracow: Biblioteka Studium Słowianskiego U.J., 1950), pp. 53ff.

[53] 'Franken, Schwaben, Baierart, dem Lande Preußen nicht gut ward'; Töppen, *Geschichte*, p. 102.

[54] Udo Arnold, *Studien zur preußischen Historiographie des 16. Jahrhunderts* (Bonn Bad-Godesberg: Wissenschaftliches Archiv, 1967), p. 99 and Kletke, *Quellenkunde*, pp. 93–4.

[55] Töppen, *Geschichte*, p. 100.

[56] *Erasmi Stellae Libonothani De Borussiae Antiquitatibus libri duo* (Basel: Johannes Frobenius, 1518); Arnold, *Studien*, p. 118.

added a new element to Prussian historiography: his chronicle aimed at a comprehensive history of the province (*Landesgeschichte*) in the context of a world history
of *res gestae* from biblical times, through the age of the four world empires and the
migrations, and ending in his own period. In contrast to Humanist cosmographies,
history in the sixteenth and seventeenth centuries was expected to be nationally
focused and complete. What could not be known had to be invented.[57]

Stella examined the ancestry and lifestyle of the ancient Pruzzi, many of whom,
according to Dusburg, 'had remained in the country'.[58] Stella's *De Borussiae
Antiquitatibus libri duo*, took ample evidence from a combination of several contradictory historical sources, such as Herodotus, Jordanes and Ptolemy, Tacitus, Pliny
and Helmoldus, Aeneas Sylvius, Strabo and Otto Frisingensis. Although he did not
invent the derivation of the ancestry of the Prussians from the Ulmigeri – so called
by Jordanes – or Culmigeri (with etymological reference to the Prussian heartland
of Kulm), he was an early and powerful propagator of this thesis. Thus he filled the
much lamented historiographical gap between the origin of all European nations
from Noah's son Japheth, a common feature of Humanist historiography,[59] and the
discovery of the Pruzzi by the first Christian missionaries of the ninth and tenth
centuries. The 'dark age' of the migrations, known at the time only from very rare
sources, was now enlivened with the mythology of the Prussian descent from king
Waidewutus and his brother Prutenus. This king had three sons (later inflated to
seven, then twelve in Grunau), who represented the Prussian provinces. As
Prussians and Lithuanians were said to be brothers, Stella included one son with
the name Litalanus, leader of the Alani, who broke away from the 'common mother
*Borussia*' to found his own country and people in Lithuania.[60] The idea that the
Baltic peoples, including Lithuanians, Livonians, Samogitians (from Żmudź) and
Prussians, were all one nation (*una gens*), had already been a commonplace in
Dusburg's work in the fourteenth century.

According to Stella, the ancient Prussians were a branch of the Sarmatian tribes
described by Tacitus (Venedi, Daci, Alani). They had come to the lands east of the
Vistula and the Baltic shore as immigrants and mixed with the remnants of the
Gothic peoples.[61] Impressed by Tacitus's description of the ancient Germanic
tribes, who had no fortified houses, lived simply and worshipped nature, Stella

---

[57] Sonia Brough, *The Goths and the Concept of Gothic in Germany from 1500 to 1750. Culture, Language
and Architecture*, Mikrokosmos 17 (Frankfurt, Bern, New York: Peter Lang, 1985), p. 56.

[58] Hartknoch quotes Dusburg in *Altes- und Neues Preußen*, preface.

[59] Benedykt Zientara, 'Świadomość narodowa w Europie Zachodniej w średniowieczu. Powstanie i
mechanizmy zjawiska', in Gieysztor, A. and Gawlas, S. (eds.), *Państwo, Naród, Stany w Świadomości
Wieków Średnich, Pamięciu B. Zientary 1929–1983* (Warsaw: PWN, 1990), pp. 11–26; also Paul
Joachimsen, *Geschichtsauffassung und Geschichtsschreibung in Deutschland unter dem Einfluß des Humanismus*, vol. I (Leipzig, Berlin: Teubner, 1910), and Ulewicz, *Sarmacja*, pp. 25–6.

[60] The other two sons were Pomesanus and Galingius, the two other old Prussian territorial names. The
remaining regions in Prussia were then named after the grandsons of Waidewutus and Prutenus:
Warmia, Natangia, Sudavia, etc.; Stella, *De Borussiae*, chapter II and pp. 29–30.

[61] Ibid., pp. 24–5.

attached the same attributes to the Baltic Prussians. The Saxon historian belonged to a generation of German scholars who had reacted to the Italian shunning of the Gothic-Germanic barbarians with a counter-attack: Tacitus was their weapon and proof that the Germans were not just cruel barbarians but possessed piety and a communal spirit, strength in war and nobility by merit. Rejecting the sophistication of high Roman culture as decadent, the 'noble barbarians' were part of the Humanist cult of ancestor-worship which Stella introduced to Prussia.[62] Significantly, neither Stella nor his imitators in Prussia integrated the Prussians into Germanic culture, but into the Sarmatian world.

### THE GOTHIC MYTH

Gothic mythology in Poland-Lithuania received a boost not only from Germany but also from Sweden, where it was even more powerfully propagated by the Magnus brothers, who used the history of the Goths by Jordanes to confirm the association of the Swedes with the Gothic tradition. The myth had expanded by the late sixteenth century, when Sigismund III, from the senior branch of the Swedish Vasa dynasty, was elected to the Polish throne. Hartknoch reports that from this time the Poles thought the Goths were in fact of Sarmatian origin like themselves. According to Hartknoch, this theory gained particular significance in 1622, when Adam Macovius, legate of the Polish king Sigismund III, was sent to the Spanish court in order to inquire about any remaining Gothic monuments and sources from which the Sarmatian-Gothic relationship could be deduced. Paweł Piasecki, Sigismund's court historian, was employed on a similar mission.[63] The Gothic-Sarmatian myth was also meant to facilitate the task of Jesuits sent to Sweden from Poland in order to make proselytes among opponents of King Charles IX, Sigismund's uncle, who – in Polish opinion – had usurped the Swedish throne. Persecution of his opponents caused an exodus of about 400 Swedish Catholic emigrés to Poland, where the Jesuit college in Braniewo (Braunsberg) became the favourite place of education for young Swedish Catholics. Some of them found a cruel end after their return to Sweden under the rule of Gustav Adolf, while others joined the Polish court and fed the Sarmatian-Gothic myth with panegyrics to the Vasa king on the Polish throne.[64]

An appreciation of the foundations of Prussian mythology is vital for an understanding of the further development of Prussian historical identity. The most significant feature was not the fact that the Prussians invented their specific version

---

[62] According to Rowell, Dusburg had already used the example of the pagan Lithuanian 'noble savages' to criticise the Roman church; Rowell, *Lithuania*, pp. 39–40; also Johannesson, *Renaissance*, p. 87.

[63] Hartknoch emphasized that there were Swedes 'who at the court of king Sigismund were not men of little learning'; *De Originibus Gentium Prussicarum Dissertatio III* (Königsberg: Reusner, 1679), p. 45.

[64] For example, Johannes Messenius, *Genealogia Sigismundi Tertii* (1608); see Oskar Garstein, *Rome and the Counter-Reformation in Scandinavia. Jesuit Education Strategy 1553–1622* (Leiden: Brill, 1992), pp. xxiv, xliif.

of the past, but what was absent from it: the German element. There was no attempt to construct a bridge to the Holy Roman Empire, nor to the Germanic past of Tacitus's vision of *Germania* which was so valuable for German Lutheran reformers and Humanists.[65] Despite the clear recollection by Prussian burghers that most of their families originated from Germany, they not only signed an act of political and administrative incorporation with the Polish crown in 1454; they also founded a historical association with the Poles, as their historiographical tradition had to find a new home in a Sarmatian environment. The result, the creation of a highly adaptable and complex mythology which combined the Gothic-Germanic with the Sarmatian-Polish traditions, suited the political needs of the Prussian nobles as well as the townspeople.

The main source for Gothic history was the adaptation by Jordanes, bishop of Ravenna, of Cassiodorus's twelve books on the history of the Goths from 551 and their victories in Italy under Theodoric's rule. The great warrior genealogy of the Goths had gained fame from the legend that the god Mars had been born among them, while several other Gothic heroes supposedly descended from Hercules.[66] The strong emphasis on military skills and prowess, however, was not the only characteristic which endeared the Goths to later European historiography and national literature, most aptly expressed in baroque Germany in Lohenstein's and Gryphius's anti-French *Arminius* dramas. It was what Jordanes had written about the deep religiosity, the wisdom and the honest simplicity of their lifestyle, which made them superior to the 'corrupt Romans' who were identified in seventeenth-century Germany with the French enemy. In the forefront of the pro-Gothic literature that began to flourish in Europe during the Renaissance and the baroque periods were the Swedes, who exploited Jordanes's extravagant claim that Scanzia, the Gothic homeland, was the cradle of all nations: 'quasi officina gentium, aut certe velut vagina nationum'.[67]

The popularity of Gothic mythology reached its first climax during the Swedish Reformation in the debate between the Catholic Magnus brothers, the Lutheran Vasa dynasty and its court historians, each side trying to establish its politically and religiously correct descent from their Gothic forefathers.[68] With the Reformation victorious, the independent Gothic heritage changed its connotations. As the Lutheran confessionalisation of the country progressed, the dynasty's historical legitimacy and power had to be asserted against rival aristocrats and a suspicious rural population. To overcome the internal and external reluctance to recognise

---

[65] Else-Lilly Etter, *Tacitus in der Geistesgeschichte des 16. und 17. Jahrhunderts* (Basel and Stuttgart: von Helbing and Lichtenhahn, 1966).

[66] Brough, *The Goths*, p. 21.

[67] 'Chronica Iordani Episcopi Ravennatis civitatis, de origine ac vocabulis Gentis Gothorum edita ad Castalium, sumptaque ex auctoribus', in *Variarum libri XII & Chronicon ad Theodoricum Regem* (Lyon: J. Chouet, 1595), chapter 13.

[68] Brough, *The Goths*, p. 24 and Johannesson, *Renaissance*, pp. 78–87 and 126–7.

Vasa monarchical rule, a Protestant version of the Gothic myth proved highly useful. It was no coincidence that Johannes Magnus's Latin *History of All Goths and Vandals* of 1554 was published in Swedish in 1611, the year when Gustav II Adolf became king of Sweden. The book not only provided the justification for a long genealogy of Vasa kings whose names were attached to high numerators of dubious validity, including Erik XIV and Charles IX, but enabled Gustav Adolf to identify with the expansionist designs of the mythical Gothic king Berik, who united his people behind him and conquered the Baltic regions.[69] Although strict Lutheranism rejected chiliastic ideas, seventeenth-century Pietism carried deterministic notions into Sweden. Gustav Adolf's sobriquet, the 'Lion of the North', was taken directly from the four books of Ezra, prophesying the coming of the end of the world in the time of the fourth world monarchy, the time of eternal peace.[70] This image of the Swedish Lutheran saviour-liberator, aptly promoted by the Swedes during their involvement in the Thirty Years War but barely believed in the cities of Prussia targeted by Gustav Adolf's armies after 1626, struck a chord similar to the last-emperor ideology of Joachim of Fiore and other chiliastic thinkers.

It was not just Sweden which was affected by the Gothic myth, which travelled in the baggage of the invading Swedish armies that spread Swedish domination across the Baltic after 1621. In particular Livonia, conquered by Sweden in the 1620s and Pomerania, which was partitioned in 1648 at the peace of Westphalia between Sweden and Brandenburg, became outposts of Gothic mythology. Jordanes's theory that the Goths came from Scandinavia and settled on the mainland, subjugated the Germanic Vandals and drove a conquering path eastward into the territories of the Scyths and Sarmatians, was eagerly picked up by Swedish historians but just as strenuously rejected by Polish and Prussian authors.

As Erasmus Stella had done for Prussian history, so the German chronicler Albert Krantz, who was influenced by Tacitus and the new 1515 edition of Jordanes, effectively rehabilitated the Goths in Germany. His *Vandalia*, published in 1518, became the German historiographical credo of the century. This work considered the barbaric Germanic peoples to be the root of all Gothic-Germanic and Slavonic nations, descending from Noah as a big family of *gentes* who all originated from continental Europe. For Krantz, the Gothic-Germanic Vandals and Slavonic-Sarmatian Venedi were the same people. Krantz based his idea of Germanic Vandal-Goth unity on the old idea of a universal German monarchy – the fourth and last empire according to the biblical prophecies. This monarchy was based on *'communis ditio* (power or law) *a Germania'*, which implies that German law (Magdeburg and Lübeck law) spread widely in central and east central Europe. This legal concept, rather than culture or language – 'from the river Don to the

87

Rhine, there are many different languages' – was central to Krantz's definition of Germanic-Vandal hegemony.[71]

Stella published too early on Prussia to adopt any of these new theories concerning the Goths, but they proved highly influential in Poland. The most intriguing document is the history written by the Alsatian Humanist Jodocus Ludwik Decius, a Habsburg diplomat at the court of Sigismund I, who tried to prove the common descent of Poles and Germanic Vandals, making the German king Tuisco the ruler of both the Poles and the Germans over an empire which stretched from the Don to the Rhine. He interpreted the wars between both peoples as a conflict between equal brother-nations, whose sense of honour did not aim at one-sided domination; they fought 'for the dignity of political power and the freedom to rule . . . and not to eliminate each other's cultures and languages'.[72] Few Polish and Lithuanian writers sympathised with this line of interpretation. In open defiance of this Gothic-Slavic myth of cohabitation and friendship, Jan Długosz traced the Prussians back to the Romans, the ancient enemies of the Germanic and barbarian Goths, while historians of Lithuania, like Augustin Rotundus, increased the Lithuanians' fame by assigning them a descent from Roman senatorial families, to the extent that the Latin language became an integral part of the cultural identity of the szlachta of the Grand Duchy of Lithuania.[73] With the chances of the Polish Vasas regaining the Swedish throne steadily diminishing, the Gothic mythology receded and the Sarmatian ideology gained ground, particularly during the Polish-Swedish wars from 1600 to 1660.

Starowolski repudiated Decius's harmonising approach and fiercely rebutted condescending German criticism of the Commonwealth's military power and political constitution. He wrote in his *Declamatio contra obtrectatores Poloniae* in 1631 that it was not the Goths or Vandals, but the Sarmatians who had dominated Europe for centuries. In a Europe that barely took Swedish power seriously until the early seventeenth century the Swedes had formulated their own myth of Gothic greatness against all odds and found unexpected ideological support from German writers after the success of their arms in the Thirty Years War, while Polish prestige had suffered from the Swedish invasion. In a counterattack against the Tübingen professor Thomas Lansius, Starowolski therefore placed the Sarmatians as rulers over Asia, Europe and Africa. With undisguised sarcasm he asked how anyone could nowadays call those powerful tribes 'non-militaristic, cowardly and ignorant of the art of war.'[74]

---

[71] Albertus Krantz, *Vandalia* (Cologne: L. Soter alias Heil et Socii, 1519), prooemium; see also Ulewicz, *Sarmacja*, p. 134.     [72] Ulewicz, *Sarmacja*, pp. 71–3.

[73] Maria Baryczowa, 'Augustyn Rotundus Mieleski – pierwszy historyk a apologeta Litwy', in *Z dziejów Polskiej kultury umysłowej w XVI i XVII wieku* (Cracow and Warsaw: PAN, 1976), and Jerzy Ochmański, 'The national idea in Lithuania from the 16th to the first half of the 19th century: The problem of cultural-linguistic differentiation', *Harvard Ukrainian Studies* 10 (1986), 304.

[74] 'Mowa przeciw oczczercom Polski', in *Wybór z pism*, Biblioteka Narodowa seria I, no. 272 (Wrocław: Zakład Ossolińskich, 1991), p. 187.

### THE SARMATIAN COUNTER-MYTH

The Sarmatian mythological reversal turned out to be powerful. Ulewicz discovered a copy of Schedel's *Chronicon* in the Jagiellonian University Library bearing the marginal remark by a sixteenth-century hand that the Bavarians, as a Slavonic-Sarmatian people ('because their name derives from *boyars*'), were part of a Slavic realm stretching as far as the Rhine.[75] But early modern Polish authors were not content with merely turning the Gothic theory on its head. It was easy enough to replace the Goths with the Sarmatians as the great family of nations between the Don and the Vistula, Oder or Rhine – wherever the taste for expansion found its limits. The Sarmatian myth, however, was not an ad-hoc invention to counter Gothic-German or Swedish historical theories accompanying diplomatic or military warfare, but had deep roots, like Gothic mythology, in ancient and medieval chronicle literature.[76]

In the fifteenth and sixteenth centuries, on the basis of works by Herodotus, Juvenal, Ptolemy, Pomponius Mela and the Anonymous Gaul, the Sarmatians were identified in early Humanist sources as Slavonic tribes which had migrated from the Balkans or Asia Minor.[77] By the second half of the sixteenth century, the historical canon of the great Slavic-Sarmatian family which included the Poles and their brothers, the Czechs, Ruthenians, Lithuanians, Mazovians, Prussians, Pomeranians, and even the Croats and the Dalmatians, was firmly established. The ground had been laid by the Polish histories of Kadłubek, bishop of Cracow, and Jan Długosz (1475), and by Maciej Miechowita's history of Sarmatia (1521) and the works of his followers.

Długosz placed greatest emphasis on the biblical formulation of the Sarmatians; the story of Babylon and the descent of the Sarmatians from Japheth, who lived in Pannonia and the Carpathian mountains, continued to influence most chronicles over the following two centuries.[78] The legendary founder of the Polish nation was Lech, which explained why many foreigners called the Poles Lechitae. Maciej Miechowita's main merit was to transfer the notion of a faraway country called Sarmatia to Poland-Lithuania and to give it a fixed place on the central European map. His concept of a European and an Asian Sarmatia estab-

[75] Ulewicz, *Sarmacja*, p. 78.
[76] Ulewicz, *Sarmacja*, p. 17; Stanisław Cynarski, 'Sarmatyzm – ideologia i styl życia', in Tazbir, Janusz (ed.), *Polska XVII wieku. Państwo, społeczenstwo, kultura* (Warsaw: Wiedza Powszechna, 1974), pp. 269–95; Tadeusz Mańkowski, *Genealogia Sarmatyzmu Polskiego* (Warsaw: PWN, 1946); Wiesław Müller, 'Epoka baroku i sarmatyzmu', in Kłoczowski, Jerzy (ed.), *Uniwersalizm i swoistość kultury polskiej*, vol. I (Lublin: KUL, 1989), pp. 217–40.
[77] Ulewicz, *Sarmacja*, pp. 4–6.
[78] Stanisław Cynarski, 'Uwagi nad problemem recepcji Historii Jana Długosza w Polsce XVI i XVII wieku', in *Dlugossiana – Studia historyczne w pięcsetlecie śmierci Jana Długosza* (Cracow, Warsaw: PWN, 1980), pp. 281–90, esp. p. 286; Urszula Borkowska, 'Uniwersalizm i regionalizm w Rocznikach Jana Długosza', in *Uniwersalizm i regionalizm w kronikarstwie Europy Środkowo-Wschodniej* (Lublin: Instytut Europy Środkowo-Wschodniej, 1996), pp. 7–26 (with English summary).

lished great-power status for the Poles' mythical homeland and their historical identity, overcoming – as the Germans did with the help of Tacitus – the stigma of obscurity and barbarity. Still a vague concept during the first half of the sixteenth century, by the first interregnum in 1572–3 the Sarmatian theory was already influencing the Polish-Lithuanian nobility's political agenda. The expressions *Polonus, Poloni* were frequently replaced by *Sarmata, Sarmatae*. Outside Poland, foreigners started to acknowledge the identity of the Sarmatian Poles, like Melanchthon in his 1558 letter *De origine gentis Henetae, Polonicae seu Sarmaticae.*

The culture of Sarmatism has usually been accused of breeding xenophobia, narrow-minded chauvinism or plain expansionism. The development of a Polish-Sarmatian superiority-complex has been blamed for the decline or even collapse of Polish culture during the seventeenth and eighteenth centuries.[79] One of the voices considered representative of this megalomania belonged to the republican writer Stanisław Orzechowski, himself of Ruthenian origin and a convert to Catholicism from Protestantism: 'Let it be known that Lithuania cannot be equal to the Polish crown, nor can any Lithuanian, be he the most important and famous, equal the most lowly Pole – Lithuanian-born, you spend your life under the yoke – but I, as a Pole, like an eagle unbound under my king, fly freely.'[80]

Although Polish and Sarmatian have frequently been used synonymously, the question is how other nations within the Commonwealth dealt with this ideology. If Orzechowski excluded the Lithuanians – officially the second nation in the republic – from the Sarmatian concept, then what degradation was in store for the Prussians? Not all Polish writers, however, agreed with Orzechowski. Aware of the discrepancies between social reality and the Sarmatian noble utopia, the Warmian bishop Marcin Kromer, like Starowolski, rejected the socially exclusive version of the Sarmatian myth, preferring to use it as a geographical demarcation between the ancestral tribes. According to Kromer, Sarmatians already lived between the Oder and the Don when Tacitus was taking great pains to decide whether the tribes between the Oder and the Vistula were Germanic or Slavonic-Sarmatian.[81] Forgiving Tacitus for his ignorance, Kromer drew a sharp line between the Germanic tribes and the Slavonic peoples at the Vistula river: the Sarmatian Slavs, settling east of it, descended from a different branch of Noah's large family, and therefore had no historical or cultural link with the Germanic Vandals or other Germanic tribes.[82] Kromer also turned Jordanes's account of the Gothic immigration from

[79] Cynarski, 'Sarmatyzm', p. 277; Tazbir, 'Ksenofobia w Polsce', passim; and Salmonowicz, 'Prusy Królewskie i Książęce', p. 71.

[80] Stanisław Orzechowski, *Quincunx* (Cracow: Łasarz Andrysowicz, 1564), quoted by Cynarski, 'Sarmatyzm', p. 275.

[81] Tacitus, *De Germania*, XLVI.

[82] *Poloniae sive de situ, populis, moribus, magistratibus et respublica regni Poloniae libri duo* (1575), ed. Wiktor Czermak (Cracow: Gebethner i Wolff, 1901), p. 11; see also Kromer, *De origine et rebus gestis*, p. 2.

Scandinavia on its head: it was not the Germanic Goths, who, according to Tacitus, were autochthonous peoples, but the Sarmatians who came from the North. With this reinterpretation he reconciled the Sarmatian origin with the Swedish descent of the Vasa dynasty on the Polish throne and set an agenda which was respected not only by historians for two centuries to come, but also by the contemporary political establishment, as was first demonstrated in the official recognition he received as Poland's foremost historian by the Sejm.

Whether because of his commoner background or his involvement in Royal Prussian political life, Kromer exerted great influence on urban Prussian historiography, and his Sarmatian theories gained general recognition in Royal Prussia. Although he was appointed bishop of Warmia against the wishes of the majority of the Prussian estates, who rejected him as an *alienigena*[83] and as an outspoken supporter of the heavily contested incorporation of the Royal Prussian diet into the ranks of the Polish Sejm in 1569, Prussian burgher historians frequently and affirmatively referred to his work. Throughout the seventeenth century, he was approvingly quoted as one of the best and most reliable historians and Polish sources, while Joachim Pastorius recommended his *Polonia* in a manual for the education of young noblemen as the most essential Polish history textbook.[84] Even foreign authors who were highly critical of the Polish point of view and the Sarmatian mythology, such as Hermann Conring and the Saxon professor Samuel Schurtzfleisch, knew and quoted the Warmian bishop. As a Royal Prussian senator, Kromer knew that the Prussian nobility would never have consented to being called Poles, but that as nobles they accepted the Sarmatian myth and the political privileges connected with it, the diets and noble courts, the free election of the king, and the mixed form of government. This was possible because the Sarmatian mythology was not one uniform, stereotypical concept, even though it was sometimes used to cover up the extreme differences that distinguished noblemen from each other in the multinational Commonwealth.

### SARMATIA'S BORDERS: THE POMERANIAN–PRUSSIAN DIVIDE

In the political environment of the sixteenth and seventeenth centuries, the myth of the Gothic-Sarmatian family of nations must have appeared an ideal compromise which equally reflected both the older German identity of the Prussian estates and their new allegiance to the Sarmatian world. Indeed, Matthaeus Praetorius, a historian from Memel (1630–1704) who left the Duchy of Prussia to convert to Catholicism, constructed a suitable Gothic-Slavic identity for Prussia on the basis of the similarities between the Gothic, old Prussian and Slavonic languages. His Sarmatian Goths included the Bohemians, the Mecklenburgers, Cashubians, Prus-

---

[83] See chapter 2 above, pp. 34–5.
[84] Braun, *De scriptorum Poloniae*, p. 33; Pastorius, *Palaestra Nobilium*, p. 347.

sians and the Pomeranians. For his work he was rewarded in Poland with the title *historicus Serenissimae Majestatis Regiae.*[85]

Praetorius was the only historian to distinguish between *Germania* and *Teutonia*, a division often assumed but rarely explained by seventeenth-century historians of Germany. *Germania*, according to Praetorius, stretched across all areas and countries between the Vistula, the Oder and the Weser (Visurgis), including many regions where Slavs and Germans had lived together, such as Magdeburg, Brandenburg, Lüneburg and Brunswick, while *Teutonia* was the name for Germany west of the Weser up to the Rhine. This distinction reflects the habit of calling the Knights of the Prussian and Livonian order Teutonic, since they came mainly from upper German or southwest German territories (*Swabia et Allemania*). The heartland of the Sarmato-Goths, however, was in *Germania*, with Prussia and Pomerania in the centre.

What was the purpose of Praetorius's efforts to set clear geographical and historical boundaries? Did he have a political claim in mind? His mythology provides the answer. Referring to the fake stone inscription in honour of Bolesław Chrobry which hailed the Polish king as 'athleta Christi, regnum Slavorum, Gothorum seu Polonorum', Praetorius credited the Polish crown with the power of ruling over the Goths, the Prussians and the Pomeranians, i.e. over *Germania.*[86] He did not go as far as Decius, however, who extended Sarmatian rule to the Rhine. This *Orbis Gothicus* was fiercely contested by historians outside the Commonwealth, who did not pledge their loyalty to the Polish king. The most outspoken opponents of this thesis were Pomeranian historians whose allegiances lay either with the Holy Roman Empire or with the Swedes, who had occupied and successfully retained parts of Pomerania by 1648. Pomeranian historians insisted on the clear distinction between the Germanic Goths or Vandals and the Sarmatian Vends (Wenden, Venedi) who had both settled in Pomerania, although at different times: Germanic Vandals had left these lands before the Slavic Vends invaded them, which meant that the most ancient origins of Pomerania belonged to autochthonous Germanic tribes, the same tribes that Erasmus Stella had discovered in Tacitus.

The endeavours of Praetorius and like-minded Prussian and Polish historians to create a locus for Prussian historical identity in the borderlands between the Slavs and the Teutons, between the Sarmatians and the Goths, found an echo in Micraelius's Pomeranian chronicles. Although Micraelius rejected Polish claims that the Pomeranian territories had rightfully belonged to the Slavs since the time of their mythical Slavic-Vendish king Wissimirus, he accepted that the languages and the nations of Germanic Vandals and Sarmatian immigrants had mixed and

---

[85] *Orbis Gothicus, id est Historica Narratio omnium fere Gothici nominis populorum qua simul Gothicae Sarmaticae acceptam debere et originem* (Oliwa: Textor, 1688), pp. 19ff, 37; Kurt Forstreuter, 'Matthaeus Praetorius', in Krollmann, Christian (ed.), *Altpreußische Biographie*, vol. II (Marburg: Herder-Institut, 1967), p. 517.

[86] Praetorius, *Orbis Gothicus*, p. 100.

assimilated with each other, creating a specific new people and culture in Pomerania.[87] The longing to find an explanation for this past harmony in a historical synthesis between Slavs and Germanic peoples emanates strongly from Micraelius's treatise. At the same time he made clear where the Sarmatian roof ended. In his first and third books on Pomerania, he showed that the Sarmatian-Slavonic immigration was just a phase in Pomerania's history, which passed without leaving deep traces, as the German Saxons returned and reversed the Sarmatian fortunes in the province. Pomerania became German again.

There was even neighbourly hostility felt between Pomeranians and Prussians. The chronicler Matthias Waissel from Ducal Prussia, whose compilation of sixteenth-century sources and ancient literature on the Goths and the Sarmatians contains a useful collection of historical references, pointed to the conflict that arose from the annexation of Pomerelia (Eastern Pomerania) by the Teutonic Knights, a province originally independent of Prussia.[88] Reinhold Curicke from Danzig expressed his pride in his descent from Pomerelia, not from Prussia, and boasted that the Pomerelians were more peaceful and cultured than the savage pagan Prussians, who took so much military persuasion to be converted to Christianity, unlike the Pomerelians, who became Christians more quickly.[89] The clearest reference to this rivalry is made by Egidius van der Mylen, who alludes to the 'hatred which was caused by the oppression inflicted on the neighbouring Vends by the German nation'. According to this author, the nobility of Pomerania was mostly of Saxon-German origin, although some Slavic families remained. Among the Pomeranian chroniclers only Martin Rango adopts a conciliatory tone in referring to the identical origin of Vandals and Vends, who had overcome their hatred for each other by unanimously accepting German (Vandal) culture and language.[90]

Historians in Swedish pay took a different view. Samuel Schurtzfleisch considered the Swedes the 'Greeks of the North', who joined the Germanic battle against Sarmatians (Catholic Poles) and the corrupt Romans (the emperor, the Pope, and the Catholic princes during the Thirty Years War).[91] While recognising the Prussian claim to be a separate nation ('vetus natio, orti sunt ex Slavis'), Schurtz-

---

[87] Johannes Micraelius, *Altes Pommernland, teutsch, wendisch, sächsisch, nebenst Historischer Erzehlung dero in Nähigsten Dreißig Jahren biß auff des letzten Hertzogen Bogislai XIV Todt, in Pommern vorgegangenen Geschichten* (Old Stettin: Georg Rheten, 1640), book I, pp. 16, 140–2, 161; books I and II are respectively dedicated to the Gothic Vandals and the Sarmatian Vends.

[88] Matthias Waissel, *Chronica alter Preußischer, Liffländischer und Curländischer Historien von dem Lande Preussen und seiner Gelegenheit* (Königsberg: Osterbergern, 1599), p. 5.

[89] Reinhold Curicke, *Der Stadt Dantzig Historische Beschreibung* (Amsterdam and Danzig: Johann and Gillis Janssons von Waesberge, 1687), part I, chapter 2; and Micraelius, *Altes Pommerland*, vol. II, p. 241.

[90] Egidii van der Mylen viri Nob[ili], 'Antiqua Pomeranorum Respublica', in Rango, Martin, *Pomerania diplomatica sive de antiquitates Pomeranicae* (Frankfurt: Renisch, 1707) vol. III, p. 80; Rango, Martin, *Diplomata quaedam vetusta Pomeraniae Antiquitates quam maxime illustrantia*, in *Pomerania diplomatica*, p. 14.

[91] Konrad Samuel Schurtzfleisch, *Res Sueo-Gothicas recensebunt Conradus Samuel Schurtzfleisch & Johannes Bering* (Wittenbergae: Schrödteri, 1678), paragr. 2.

fleisch denied this status to the Pomeranians, who descended 'ex Vandalis', from the Germanic Goths. Like Micraelius, Schurtzfleisch agrees that the Pomeranians turned German again after a Slavonic intermezzo; they stopped speaking a Slavonic language after 1404.[92] The fact that the last duke of Pomerania, Bogusław XIV, had died only three years before Micraelius's publication, leaving Pomerania to the fortunes of war, was probably the decisive influence behind this insistence on the German historical link. Micraelius emphasised strongly that the recently extinct Pomeranian dynasty had never had blood relatives among the Polish kings, despite close cultural and linguistic ties with Poland. These Slavic links were now broken, and the Pomeranians had 'rejected the Slavic language entirely, declaring themselves Saxons under the authority of the Holy Roman Empire'.[93] This statement provides the key to Micraelius's idea of the Pomeranian nation. Not part of the Polish-Lithuanian Commonwealth, and no longer under their own dynasty, Pomerania must fall back on the Holy Roman Empire. German traditions returned, and together with them came the political allegiance to the emperor. There was a need, therefore, for the Pomeranians to call themselves German or Saxon again, a condition that did not apply to the Prussians, who were members of the Sarmatian nation under the umbrella of the Polish-Lithuanian Commonwealth and the Polish crown. They had no reason to identify with Germans. Ethnic origins yielded to political allegiance: the Sarmatian roof ended where German imperial power started.

The Pomeranian nobleman van der Mylen was even more explicit: after forsaking its political independence and its past glory with the death of the last hereditary ruler of the Pomeranian dynasty, Pomerania had to suffer renewed subjection to the Saxons and the Empire, as well as partition by Sweden and Brandenburg in 1648.[94] Rejecting Schurtzfleisch's view of Pomerania's purely German character, van der Mylen asserts that the noble families (many of whom were of Slavic origin) and the mixed form of government with its privileges for the estates had once formed the essence of the Pomeranian nation. His description of such a political nation is very reminiscent of the Polish-Sarmatian mythology of noble freedoms, and it comes therefore closest to the idea of the nation that we find among Prussians and other nations (including the Polish) in the Commonwealth.[95]

The core of the disagreement between Pomeranians and Prussians concerned their differing attitude towards the Holy Roman Empire. Pomeranian historians accepted and identified with imperial rule, whereas the Prussians rejected it. While Pomeranians, Brandenburgers, Lusatians, Saxons and other peoples in the Empire divided their national consciousness into a German (and imperial) identity on the

[92] Konrad Samuel Schurtzfleisch, *Dissertatio de origine Pomeranorum* (Wittenberg: Schrödter, 1673), folio A2v–A3; Konrad Samuel Schurtzfleisch and Daniel Tesmarus, *Origines Pomeranicas* (Wittenberg: Schrödter, 1673), pp. 8, 23–4.
[93] Micraelius, *Altes Pommerland*, vol. II, p. 208 and vol. III, p. 305.
[94] Mylen, 'Antiqua', in Rango, *Pomerania diplomatica*, vol. III, p. 84.
[95] Ibid., pp. 238–9.

one hand, and an identification with their own territory (*Landesbewußtsein*) on the other, the Prussians had no reason to assume a German identity.[96] Although they would not deny their ancestors' descent from German families, who had either immigrated or mixed with pagan Prussian families, they, unlike the Pomeranians, identified neither with the German nation nor with the Empire. Instead, in accommodating the Sarmatian myth with their own historical identity, the Prussians accepted Sarmatian citizenship not by becoming Poles but by associating themselves with the constitution and the political system of the Commonwealth. This construction produced a rhetorical tool actively used by Prussian burghers and urban elites in particular in their fight for recognition as fully-privileged citizens under the power of the Polish crown. Historical mythology therefore became the powerful basis of a Prussian burgher vision of Sarmatian history and self-definition, often used to counter their exclusion from citizenship, which the majority of the Polish nobility interpreted against them. Anyone who would listen, particularly other nations represented in the Polish-Lithuanian Commonwealth, received this message: we are Sarmatian Prussians, not subjects but free men and citizens.

[96] Rainer Christoph Schwinges, ' "Primäre" und "sekundäre" Nation, Nationalbewußtsein und sozialer Wandel im mittelalterlichen Böhmen', in Grothusen, Klaus-Detlev and Zernack, Klaus (eds.), *Europa Slavica – Europa Orientalis. Festschrift für Herbert Ludat* (Berlin: Duncker and Humblot, 1980), pp. 490–532.

# 5

# Political identity in the cities of Royal Prussia and the meaning of liberty (1650–1720)

Constat enim & Polonos & Lithuanos Prussosque Sarmatiam quondam Europeam, ut communem matrem coluisse. (Christoph Hartknoch)[1]

If the skilful formulation and adaptation of national and historical myths was so crucial for the sense of identity and international recognition of early modern nations and states, the question remains how the Royal Prussian estates refashioned the Sarmatian myth to suit Prussian political interests. Considering that before 1466 Prussia had been a political entity, it is not surprising that in the mid-seventeenth century historical Prussian identity still extended beyond the borders of the Commonwealth to include the eastern half of the territories of the former Teutonic Order. It is striking, however, that one of the most influential histories of the Polish-Lithuanian Commonwealth itself was written in Königsberg, in Ducal Prussia, where in the early 1670s Christoph Hartknoch, a history teacher, composed his *Respublica Polonica*. By including in his notion of Sarmatia not only Muscovy, Ruś, Livonia, Pomerania, Prussia, Lithuania, Wallachia and Moldavia, but also Silesia, Brandenburg and Lusatia, Hartknoch reached well beyond the geographical limits set by Kromer and Starowolski, who had placed the border on the River Oder. Thus Hartknoch's book is not merely a history of Poland, but represents the maximal definition of mythical Sarmatia. Together with Joachim Pastorius's *Florus Polonicus*, Hartknoch's *Respublica Polonica* was considered the most influential textbook for schools and universities within and outside the Commonwealth.[2]

Following new trends in national and regional history-writing, Hartknoch was the first historian since Stella and Schütz to attempt to trace the whole of Prussian history from the pagan and mythical beginnings to the present in the context of Polish history. He successfully popularised the history of the entire Common-

---

[1] 'It is certain that Poles, Lithuanians and Prussians have venerated the same mother, Sarmatian Europe.' Hartknoch, *Alt- und Neues Preußen*, p. 101.

[2] Mokrzecki, *Studium*, pp. 180–1, 188. Pastorius and Hartknoch conducted a lively intellectual exchange and correspondence on the history of ancient European tribes and nations; *Das Gelahrte Preußen* 1 (1722), 26–8.

wealth, including all its provinces, for a truly European audience. In 1677, disaffected with the university of Königsberg, which was increasingly geared towards the education of civil servants to staff the growing bureaucracy of the Great Elector, Hartknoch moved to Royal Prussia, where he had already built up contacts among the local, highly-educated patriciate, such as the burgomaster of Danzig Adrian von der Linde.[3] In search of ancient Prussian chronicles, he visited the city, where he was also acquainted with Ernst König and the law professor Christian Rosteuscher. König offered him a post at the Gymnasium in Thorn, which he accepted. Until his death in 1687, Hartknoch lived and worked as a history professor in Thorn.

In the preface to his *De Republica Polonica*, which appeared during Hartknoch's first year in Thorn, he wrote: 'I deplore the perversity of those who plainly neglect domestic affairs and deem themselves of much worth when they study remote places of a long-gone past; with the result that they are more lucid about the life of Argos, while being as blind as Tiresias about affairs at home.'[4] In Royal Prussia, Hartknoch's influence was perpetuated by his students, some of whom went on to occupy important administrative offices in town governments not only in their province but also in the Commonwealth.[5] Hence, knowledge of 'their own history' was essential. Hartknoch engaged in the debate about the Polish constitution, which he and his students called 'ours': 'nostri Poloni', 'nostra Polonia', referring to Polish history as 'exemplum domesticum'.[6] Thus at a time when he was still a subject of the Hohenzollern duke of Prussia, Hartknoch identified strongly with the Royal Prussian vision of the Prussian past. He was a champion of the constitutional principles on which the Polish-Lithuanian constitution was built: the mixed form of government, with the king, the senate-aristocracy and the democratic element of the szlachta in an even balance. His advantage over his Polish or Royal Prussian colleagues was that he was well acquainted with the political practice of Ducal Prussia, whose development had not followed the Polish model but the political changes that had occurred in most German states in the post-1648 Empire, where dynastic rulers and centralised bureaucratic state structures had diminished the influence of the noble and burgher estates. Hartknoch therefore approached constitutional questions from a comparative perspective, being better able than most Prussians to contrast the theory and practice of the mixed constitution and its absolutist counterpart.

[3] 'Observationes in Viri D[omini] Samuelis Schurtzfleischii Res Prussorum auctore M. C. Hartknoch P.P ad V[irem] Ill[ustrissimum] et Magn[um] D[ominum] Adrianum von der Linde, capit[aneum] Mirachov[iensem] et praeco[nsulem] Gedan[ensem]', Bibl. PAN Gd., 2460, folio 326b; on Linde, see *Polski Słownik Biograficzny* (Cracow: PAN), vol. XVII, p. 353.

[4] *De Republica Polonica* (1698), preface.

[5] For example Gottfried Rösner, one of the burgomasters who was executed in 1724, and Johann Georg Diesseldorff, history professor at the Danzig Gymnasium from 1697, then burgomaster and 'protoscholarch' from 1710. The latter showed great interest in politics, history, and natural and public law, especially Pufendorf; Mokrzecki, *Studium*, pp. 188–9.

[6] For example, *Disputatio Politica De Incrementis et Decrementis Rerumpublicarum respondens Georg Friedrich a Kalnein* (Königsberg: Reusner, 1673), folio D2v.

Fuelled by King John Casimir's plans to reform the Polish constitution and to introduce an election *vivente rege* in the late 1650s, Hartknoch's political treatises concentrated on the nature and power of kingship. Naturally, the discussion reached back into the sixteenth century, particularly to the introduction of the elective monarchy by all members of the nobility (*viritim*) and the Henrician Articles of 1573. Hartknoch showed that although hereditary succession had been a custom of the Jagiellonian monarchy, it was abandoned in favour of the first truly free election when the *Articuli Henriciani* started to oblige every king to swear a constitutional oath confirming noble privileges and the laws of the realm. Defending this arrangement against John Casimir's designs to revive election *vivente rege*, Hartknoch fully agreed with the Polish constitutionalists' defence of free election.[7] Hartknoch's treatise on this topic is particularly interesting for its reference to the work of Jan Sachs, a burgher from Great Poland and secretary of Thorn, who in the 1660s mounted a powerful defence against the attack launched on Poland by her old foe Hermann Conring.[8] Sachs, who followed Keckermann's political and philosophical ideas on mixed government, turned to the debate on the royal election and the question of how much power ought to be given to the Polish king. Foreign writers, such as Conring, habitually ridiculed the Polish king and his loss of power to the nobility. Sachs rejected this judgement, stressing that the Polish monarch was far from being a powerless puppet controlled by a lawless nobility. Pointing at the Dutch example, to which the Prussian burghers could relate very well, Sachs exposed the drawbacks of a republic without any royal authority: 'Those [like the Dutch] who praise their freedom under an aristocratic regime have but a false and imagined liberty, as they hide their own tyranny under their populist and aristocratic coat, like the Batavi who bragged behind their pipe-smoke of illusory freedom.'[9]

Dutch liberty was unhealthy because it resulted from an unbalanced government. Agreeing with Polish constitutionalists, Sachs insisted that the Polish monarch ought to maintain his prerogatives to stem the tide of the uncontrolled democracy of the szlachta, as well as the power of the aristocracy, the senate. Hartknoch fully accepted this point and agreed with Jan Sachs and Łukasz Opaliński that 'the Poles bestow upon their kings the greatest honours and rightly pride themselves on the fact that kings were more loved in Poland than anywhere else', while in dynasties, such as France or England, kings had to fear for their life. Even republican writers, such as the castellan of Wiślica Andreas z Pilczy Koryciński, who was critical of the 'natural tendency of kings to become tyrants' and

---

[7] *Exercitationum Academicarum de Regno Poloniae prima, quam amplissimo philosophorum ordine consentiente in Ill[ustrissima] Pregelana praeside M[agistri] Christophoro Hartknoch* (Königsberg: Reusner, 1680), p. 7.

[8] Jan Sachs [Franciscus Marinius Polonus], *De scopo Reipublicae Poloniae contra Conringium* (Breslau: Jacobi Treschneri Bibliopolae, 1665); [Hermann Conring], *Cyriaci Thrasymachi De Iustitia armorum Svevicorum in Polonos* (Hamburg: n.pub., 1655); see chapter 3, above, pp. 61–2.

[9] Sachs, *De scopo*, p. 35.

was one of Hartknoch's favourite sources, did not deny the necessity of having a crowned head of state: 'it is noble and dignified to have a king in the state'.[10] The king was particularly precious as the source of all offices and privileges distributed to the citizens and the (royal) cities, where Hartknoch and Sachs lived and worked.

It was not only the monarchy but also the strength of the lower nobility, competing for influence in the local dietines, which gave Hartknoch and Sachs food for thought. Hartknoch used the authority of Polish sources – the works of Starowolski – to warn the Polish nobility against the threat from an oppressed peasantry,[11] and repeatedly referred to his favourite social critic, Aaron Alexander Olizarovius, who not only defended the importance of prosperous cities but condemned the situation of the Polish serfs. Once free *kmetones*, they were now subject 'to servitude and arbitrary regulations contravening divine, natural and international law'.[12] A certain hostility against the average nobleman (or rather his stereotype), who organised rebellions, neglected the state treasury and maltreated his peasants, is also reflected in Hartknoch's main work. He condemned Polish law, under which the penalty for a nobleman who killed a serf was the payment of a fine – a custom that was repeatedly attacked as an act of barbarism by foreign writers. In contrast, Hartknoch praised the Prussian legal system, based on Kulm or Magdeburg law, under which murderers were tried according to natural and divine law and received their just punishment, no matter what their social rank.[13]

Despite this criticism, the image of a peaceful and freedom-loving Poland as an island amidst a sea of war and unrest, especially during the Thirty Years War, aptly promoted by Opaliński in 1648, still had its effect. Hartknoch extolled how Poland, unlike other states, had extended its borders in the past not through conquest and colonies but by peacefully integrating foreigners, who were adopted as equal citizens, in great contrast to the behaviour of the Austrians in Switzerland and the Spanish in the Netherlands, who only antagonised their conquered provinces.[14] This interpretation bears a great similarity to that propagated by the Danzig patrician Michael Behm von Behmfeld, who wrote in 1669 that the Polish kingdom had grown together by 'acquisition or incorporation of several provinces and bodies politic in one free common fatherland'.[15] But Hartknoch also cautioned against granting overwhelming powers to the aristocracy which dominated the crown council and the senate in the Sejm. Exploring the advantages and drawbacks of the aristocratic form of government, Hartknoch supported the criticism of several

---

[10] Hartknoch, *Respublica Polonica*, refers to Łukasz Opaliński on p. 880; Koryciński, *Perspectiva Politica Regno Poloniae Elaborata per quam, quid & qualiter Regibus prospiciendum sit* (Danzig: Förster, 1652), p.100.
[11] Hartknoch, *De Incrementis*, folio D2v.
[12] Olizarovius, *De Politica Hominum Societate libri tres* (Danzig: Förster, 1651), p. 153; see Hartknoch's very similar argument in *Respublica Polonica*, p. 879.
[13] *Respublica Polonica*, p. 609.
[14] Hartknoch, *De Incrementis*, folio E2–E2v.
[15] Behm, *De Indigenatu*, p. 2.

# The Other Prussia

Polish writers who rejected the Venetian model. Krzysztof Warszewicki opposed the Venetian system for its lack of monarchical power, while Stanisław Orzechowski, in response to the Venetian commiserations about the 'poor king of Poland', praised his monarch as 'the most powerful king, not for his gold, but for his people'.[16] Similarly, Fredro contrasted the Polish monarch with the Venetian Doge, who was merely a salaried first senator rather than a genuine prince, while the Polish king maintained his authority with the support of the senate, the nobility and a constitution that gave every citizen the freedom to look after the common good, instead of oppressing him in fear and slavery.[17] Hartknoch agreed, asserting that the Polish king commanded much greater power than the Venetian Doge, who 'cannot exercise any of his powers on the basis of royal ancestral laws'.[18] Constitutionalists like Sachs also found little to recommend in the Venetian model:

Unlike in Venice, our Polish king has not just the title of majesty, but possesses the real majesty and reverence of the kingdom, while the (Venetian) council is composed of rich nobles and patricians . . . there are many who consider the Venetian republic not a republic, but a pure aristocracy, which cannot be said about our commonwealth.[19]

This last distinction is particularly important: unable effectively to temper monarchy on their own, aristocrats needed the help of the third form of government, the republican or democratic element, to curb absolute royal power, its vanity and the pernicious threat to freedom it posed.[20] In all political treatises, Hartknoch and his students reveal their support for limited monarchy, cautioning against ambitious kings and licentious masses alike. The preservation of the controlling function of a strong senate to 'protect the laws and privileges of the reign' meant that every citizen could live in a 'libera Respublica qualis est Polonia'.[21] Thus Hartknoch fully backed Fredro's famous image of the Polish *forma mixta*:

Above all stands the senate as highest mediator, who tolerates neither the use of absolute power against liberty, nor the licence of the nobility against the king, but who is the guardian who reconciles and watches that neither liberty nor absolute power ever gain the upper hand, but that balance be maintained as with a pair of scales, so that all powers are equal, and *libertas* does not encroach upon *majestas*, nor *majestas* destroy our *libertas*.[22]

---

[16] Stanisław Kot, 'Wenecja w oczach Polaków na przestreni dziejów', in *Polska złotego wieku a Europa*, ed. Henryk Barycz (Warsaw: PWI, 1987), p. 311; also Haitsma Mulier, *The Myth of Venice*, passim.

[17] *Scriptorum Seu Togae et Belli Notationum Fragmenta* (Danzig: Förster, 1660), pp. 249, 254, 187.

[18] *Respublica Polonica*, p. 873.

[19] Sachs, *De Scopo*, pp. 42–3.

[20] *Disputatio Politica de Majestatis Regiae Impedimentis, sive apparentibus, sive veris. Quam adspirante Divino Numine et consentiente ampl[itudine] Facultate Philosophiae, in illi Albertina, praeses M. Chr. Hartknoch, et respond[ens] Jacobus Tydaeus Memela Prutenus* (Königsberg: Reusneri, 1674), folio B2v.

[21] *Respublica Polonica*, p. 437.

[22] Fredro, *Scriptorum seu Togae*, pp. 248–9. For a summary of the ideas on the *forma mixta* in seventeenth-century Polish thought, see Andrzej S. Kamiński, 'The Polish-Lithuanian Commonwealth and its Citizens', in Potichnyj, Peter J. (ed.), *Poland and Ukraine. Past and Present* (Edmonton and Toronto: The Canadian Institute of Ukrainian Studies, 1980), pp. 32–57; and his *Republic versus*

Hartknoch even found common ground with Fredro's defence of the *liberum veto*. His opposition to the 'turbulent noble deputies' in the lower chamber,[23] however, markedly distinguished the burgher from Polish szlachta opinion, whose criticism of the role of the aristocratic senate made itself felt particularly strongly in Poland after the Swedish Deluge. The Mazovian nobleman Jan Pasek, who himself fought in the Swedish wars for the Polish king, expressed his disgust for senators who neglect their duties in favour of accumulating power for themselves: 'More likely, I'd sooner uncover stepfathers *inter patres patriae, quorum machinationes* [among the fathers of the fatherland, whose intrigues] have enfeebled the Commonwealth and brought it to the extreme of destitution. We need to seek no further than the Swedish war for proof of . . . how much havoc was wreaked upon the country! And who paved the way? *Mala consilia ordinis intermedii* [The bad advice of the senate].'[24] Hartknoch disagreed with this assessment and emphasised the extent to which diet procedures were hampered because noble deputies in the lower chamber ended their assemblies in confusion ('*in turbas et tumultus*'). Nevertheless, he did not adopt Conring's view on the weaknesses of the Polish parliamentary system, as such disturbances, he assured, were rare occasions, and 'the king, with his senators, later holds *post-comitialia*' during which 'they try to remedy everything which concerns the public good'.[25] The ideal *forma mixta*, provided it worked, catered for everything a well-ordered state could wish for. Hartknoch firmly agreed with Koryciński, who not only condemned tyrannical or oligarchic excesses ('*habuit finem Aristoligarchia Polona*'), but also recalled the dangers of democracy: 'the common people is like a monster with multiple heads, hence its judgement is unstable, varied, unreliable and extracts an obnoxiously high price'.[26] In Hartknoch's opinion, the Polish-Lithuanian republic was able to provide a well-ordered state not by virtue of a strong monarchy but by the mixing of three forms of government, which foreigners usually misinterpreted as a 'state in confusion'. He concluded his own treatise with a quote by Koryciński: '[This is] the greatest paradox on which the ancient and the modern writers agree . . .: Poland is ruled by confusion. Happily, though, this confusion has overcome so many wars and dangers and still contributes to the virgin-like glory of this nation (*gentis*).'[27]

This was the theory. Hartknoch was too good a historian, however, to ignore the political reality which framed Polish constitutional ideals. Finding common ground

---

*Autocracy. Poland-Lithuania and Russia 1686–1697* (Cambridge, Mass.: Harvard University Press, 1993), pp. 26–8.

[23] 'Poloniam laborare morbo comitiali', in *Respublica Polonica*, p. 697.

[24] Jan Chryzostom Pasek, *Memoirs of the Polish Baroque. The Writings of Jan Chryzostom Pasek*, ed. and trans. Catherine S. Leach (Berkeley, Los Angeles, London: University of California Press, 1976), pp. 105, 212.

[25] Hartknoch, *Respublica Polonica*, pp. 697–9, a view recently confirmed by Wojciech Kriegseisen, *Sejm Rzeczypospolitej Szlacheckiej (do 1763 roku)* (Warsaw: Wydawnictwo Sejmowe, 1996), pp. 104–25.

[26] Koryciński, *Perspectiva Politica*, p. 9.

[27] Ibid., pp. 103–4, and Hartknoch, *Respublica Polonica*, p. 884.

with Jan Sachs, Hartknoch regretted that in Poland the mixed form of government was not as perfectly realised as it might have been. The predominance of the nobility, which hampered the Venetian republic, also plagued Poland-Lithuania: 'In the Polish kingdom, the people is clearly excluded from the administration of the republic, which expresses itself in the fact that no commoner is admitted among the solicitors or the judges in the noble courts, or in the tribunals of the Polish crown and the Grand Duchy of Lithuania.'[28] Hartknoch and Sachs shared this assessment with Marcin Kromer, who had stressed that 'in Poland the [political] form of monarchy is mixed with an aristocratic regime'.[29] It is not accidental that none of the three authors were nobles by birth. Their definition of the 'plebeian' or democratic element of the *forma mixta* was different from that of many noble writers, who perceived their world as a noble democracy which singled out the nobility in the lower chamber of the diet as the true representatives of the political nation. From a commoner's perspective, however, the mixed form of government would be more perfectly executed if the Polish idea of citizenship was extended to the burghers: 'Except for the nobles, there are among the political estates in Poland also citizens who live in cities and towns, and those who are called *kmetones* (free peasants) in the villages and the countryside.'[30] Whereas Polish writers see the *vox populi* as a multitude in which 'there is no reason, no council and no power of judgement', Hartknoch separates burghers from free peasants and unfree peasants, and also distinguishes various kinds of commoners according to criteria of legal status and property. Thus Hartknoch's idea of citizenship was not restricted to the szlachta and the burghers, but included the free peasantry.

Royal Prussia, following a greater and truer tradition of liberty than Poland, was therefore closer to realising the ideal form of the mixed constitution which brought freedom and happiness to mankind. Not only did nobles and burghers sit side by side in the Prussian Diet, but until the end of the previous century, Hartknoch emphasised, they had even shared the bench in the tribunals – the Prussian courts founded on Kulm and Magdeburg law – until the nobles decided to join the Polish crown tribunal in Piotrków and to formulate their own revision of the law.[31] This criticism of Polish political reality and the praise Hartknoch had in store for the Royal Prussian constitution enabled him to reinvigorate the separate Prussian sense of national identity, which had survived in the province since the events of 1454–66. The essential ingredient of his formula, however, was the political myth of Prussia.

---

[28] Hartknoch, *Respublica Polonica*, pp. 869–71, 878; Sachs, *De Scopo*, pp. 40–1.
[29] Quoted in Sachs, *De Scopo*, p. 444.
[30] The quote appears only in the earlier edition of Hartknoch's *Respublica Polonica* (1678), p. 245, which makes one wonder whether his later editions were geared more towards a Polish noble readership than towards his circles in Königsberg and Thorn.
[31] Hartknoch, *Respublica Polonica*, p. 879.

## THE POLITICAL MYTH OF PRUSSIA

The Prussian people was born to freedom and 'never suffered a ruler among them'. This was the characterisation so dear to Hartknoch and his fellow historians in the three Prussian cities of Thorn, Danzig and Elbing. Like his favourite Polish historian Krzysztof Warszewicki,[32] Hartknoch attributed the historical development of a country's political institutions to its national character and the customs of its people. To study these traditions, he roamed the Prussian and Cashubian countryside looking for information on the ancient Lithuanian and Prussian tribes, their language, pagan idolatry and customs. With Matthias Praetorius, he travelled the Baltic coast to collect amber in the fashion of the ancient Pruzzi.[33] During this decade, he published several works which made him famous among a German-speaking public, and which appealed predominantly to an audience of burghers in the towns and cities.[34]

The great propensity of the Prussian forefathers to preserve their freedoms more effectively than the Poles and other peoples in the Commonwealth, with whom they shared their inherent love of freedom, distinguished them from other nations. What was unique among the Vends, Sarmatians and Slavs was not so much their personal lifestyle but their political habits: 'the Slavic nations were not ruled by any one man, but they lived in an ancient plebeian and communal freedom, and they decided all more or less important matters in common council'.[35] Hartknoch's conclusions followed promptly. The oldest inhabitants of Prussia, the Sarmatian Vends, likewise lived in a *respublica popularis*, a 'popular republic',[36] and the form of this government was built on the consensus of the whole people: '[This is] a regime which is not only in the hands of one king or the most noble families in the country, but in the hands of the whole people.'[37] The emphasis is on continuity. When the Sarmatian Vends mixed with the Germanic Goths and Vandals, they kept their ancient democracy. This government was shared by all nations that had their origin in Sarmatia, such as Poles, Prussians, Lithuanians, Curonians, Samogitians, Livonians, Czechs, and many more. Hartknoch closely identified the Prussians with this Sarmatian community under one republican umbrella, giving the Sarmatians credit for creating the political culture whose freedoms the Prussians then and now enjoyed. While rejecting Jordanes's contention that Scanzia was the *vagina nationum*,[38] Hartknoch did not hesitate to construct a similar myth for his Sarmatian Prussians: 'It is proven that one European Sarmatia, as one common

---

[32] Warszewicki, *De optimo statu*, p. 32.
[33] 'Christoph Hartknochs eigenhändige Nachricht von M. Matthaei Praetorii Aemulation gegen ihn und seine Schriften ex M[anu]sc[ripto]', *Erleutertes Preußen* 1 (1724), 115.
[34] For example *Alt- und Neues Preussen* (Frankfurt and Leipzig: Hallervorden, 1684) and *Preußische Kirchen-Historia* (Frankfurt and Leipzig: Simon Beckstein, 1686).
[35] Hartknoch, *Alt- und Neues Preußen*, p. 232.
[36] Hartknoch, *De Republica Veterum Prussorum* (Königsberg: Reich, 1676), p. 397.
[37] Hartknoch, *Alt- und Neues Preußen*, p. 232.
[38] Hartknoch, *De Originibus Gentium Prussicarum*, p. 61.

mother, nurtured the Poles and the Lithuanians and the Prussians.'[39] Hence Poles, Lithuanians and Prussians were brother nations of one common descent. The castellan of Elbing, Stanisław Działyński, expressed the same thought when he spoke about the Commonwealth as the 'mother' of the Prussian nobility.[40] But what force had created distinct nations and governments among the Sarmatians? What made Poles Poles and Prussians Prussians?

The Gothic example gives a clue: like the Sarmatians, the Goths had originally been 'used to liberty', blessed with kings who exercised their power 'not absolutely, but in a very limited way'. Those Goths, however, who left Sarmatia and emigrated to Scandinavia, were forced under the yoke of tyranny when they merged with the Swedes.[41] In this passage Hartknoch demonstrates beautifully the mixing of his political agenda with historical mythology. The Swedes, who had brought war and misery to Poland and Prussia during the seventeenth century, were tyrants even in the mythical past. They spoiled freedom, forced an end to democratic government and changed the nature of whole nations and their political identity. The Swedes could even turn freedom-loving Sarmatians into subjugated Swedo-Goths. The parallels with Micraelius's definition of historical and political borders between the Pomeranians who identified with Germany in the Holy Roman Empire, and the Sarmatian Prussians in the Commonwealth who rejected an imperial German identity, are striking. Political cultures divided nations which had emerged from the same mythical origins but now formed new nations, whose identity was dependent on the nature of the political government that ruled them.

Democratic assemblies, however, were not per se a passport to freedom. As a good constitutionalist, Hartknoch saw no obstacle to accepting the myth of Waidewutus, the Prussian king who ruled so wisely, like a 'king bee' in his beehive. It is significant that Hartknoch modified the Polish image of the queen bee, who has no sting with which to exercise real power.[42] Jan Sachs, who borrowed ideas from Juan Mariana (1536–1623), the Spanish Jesuit monarchomach and supporter of popular sovereignty, also used the metaphor in his description of the Polish political system.[43] And Matthias Waissel, the sixteenth-century Prussian historian whose work Hartknoch knew well, referred to Waidewutus as the 'king bee', praising his role as legislator and his civilising effect on the Prussians.[44] In a different political context, this tradition existed in Ducal Prussian political literature, where the 'king bee' was an allegory for a wise legislator and the source of law, popularised with the spreading of cameralist ideas of the well-ordered state. Whatever the exact provenance of Hartknoch's views, his idea of monarchy was rule 'by healthy laws' under elected kings (*electi non nati*) – in clear distinction from

[39] *Alt- und Neues Preußen*, p. 101.
[40] Małłek, 'Sonderbewußtsein', p. 57.
[41] Hartknoch, *Alt- und Neues Preußen*, p. 234.
[42] Ibid., p. 236; for the meaning in a Polish context, see Kamiński, 'The Szlachta', p. 19.
[43] Sachs, *De Scopo*, p. 33.
[44] Waissel, *Chronica*, p. 12.

the hereditary succession in the neighbouring duchy of Prussia under the Hohenzollern dynasty: in Hartknoch's history of Prussia, mythical Waidewutus himself was an elected lawgiver.

There are obvious similarities between the historical myths Hartknoch attached to Polish and to Prussian history. Like the Polish Lechus, Waidewutus divided his Prussian kingdom among twelve successors (his sons), creating an aristocratic government. According to Praetorius and Waissel, the youngest son became the founder of Lithuania, indicating the brotherhood between the Prussians and Lithuanians, or perhaps even the Prussian origins of the Lithuanians.[45] This situation endured after the Goths had left Prussia, until the arrival of the Teutonic Knights. Eventually, however, the lack of a king contributed to the pagan Prussians' military defeat, because each territorial unit or palatinate fought the Knights on their own, without a central organisation. It is impossible not to discover some sympathy in Hartknoch's writing for the ancient Prussian tribes and their heroic struggle against the Order. It would have been hard for contemporary Royal Prussians to overlook some striking parallels: lack of unity was also what plagued the Royal Prussians in the sixteenth and seventeenth centuries; as a result, their privileges diminished and the central role of the Prussian diet was threatened by the increasing decentralisation of decision-making in the Prussian palatinates.

What distinguished the mythical origins of Prussia from the mythical Polish monarchy? If Hartknoch failed to mention formerly legendary Polish kings, such as Popiel or Krakus in Poland, it was not for the lack of historical evidence – he did not have any for Waidewutus either – but because they would have seriously damaged his picture of the 'popular republic'. It was for the same reason that he broke with the Waidewutus saga in his later life. In a letter to Adrian von der Linde, the Danzig burgrave, he strongly criticised the Saxon historian Samuel Schurtzfleisch for his thesis that the ancient Prussians had owed tribute to the Emperor. Hartknoch asserted to the contrary that the Prussians, as an independent people, had elected their own native leaders from the time when they were first mentioned in a source of the tenth century.[46] No dynasty had ruled the Prussian state, 'the nobility was subject to nobody', and when they needed to put together an army for their defence, they commissioned one military leader by election. Hartknoch agreed once more with Helmoldus's description of ancient Prussian liberty: 'The Prussians will not suffer a lord among them.'[47]

This tradition clearly distinguished the Prussians from the rest of the Sarmatians. With the abandoning of the Waidewutus saga, there was now no Prussian counterpart to the Polish Lechus or the Bohemian Czech. Moreover, as one of the many nations of the Sarmatian Commonwealth, the Prussians had preserved a more perfectly mixed state of government, with a strong plebeian, democratic

---

[45] Hartknoch, *Alt- und Neues Preußen*, p. 237.
[46] 'Observationes', Bibl. PAN Gd., 2460, adl. 3266, folio 326b.
[47] Ibid., folios 327–8.

element. Theodor Schieder, who tried to account for Hartknoch's criticism of the Polish system of mixed government by suggesting that the Prussian historian wanted to 'shake up the thesis of the *forma mixta*', errs in his conclusion. Hartknoch was by no means a supporter of strong monarchy, as Schieder suspected, but a more consistent adherent of the *forma mixta* than his Polish counterparts.[48] Neither the Venetian nor the Spartan model could suit Hartknoch, and even the Poles could not live up to the ideal Prussian version of the truly mixed constitution.

Hartknoch was not the only writer to reject the legend of Waidewutus and to elevate Prussian-Sarmatian political culture above the Polish version. Thomas Clagius (Klage), a contemporary Prussian from Polish Warmia, was a Jesuit of peasant or artisan stock. His education and career led him, like Hartknoch, to Lithuania, to Wilno, where he developed a great interest in Sarmatian history. He later became principal of the Jesuit Gymnasium at Braunsberg, where so many Swedish Catholics had imbibed Sarmatian culture, and where he wrote his main religious work *De Linda Mariana*, which Hartknoch knew.[49] Clagius traced back the Sarmatian genealogy and followed Miechowita's definition of European Sarmatia containing many peoples and nations 'greatly diverse in customs, but all by origin from [Sarmatia]'.[50] Few writers on Sarmatia, Poland and Prussia were overlooked by Clagius. Despite his attacks on the unbelievable legends of other historians, he carried on with his own mythology of Prussian Sarmatia, just as Hartknoch did. Clagius once more depicted Sarmatia as an umbrella for various nations: 'The Sarmatian name is not attached to one particular nation, but is common to many.' The author extended the number and geographic spread of the Sarmatians greatly and in agreement with Praetorius's Sarmato-Gothic mythology formulated an expansionist Sarmatian myth which embraced not only the Slavic nations, but also the Germans and the Swedes, the Lithuanians and the Tartars. Practically the whole of central Europe, including the Burgundians and Lombards, originated in the East, in Scythia, which he divided into *Germania* and *Sarmatia*, a concept he borrowed from Jordanes.[51] Prussia's main virtue was that it was the richest and most fertile province among the Lithuanian and Polish lands, and the happiest of all. Without modesty Clagius asserted that Prussia could easily compete with the cities of Batavia (the Netherlands) and other nations, whose ports it provided with grain and other goods. Therefore, Prussia was the jewel of the whole Sarmatian realm and 'the parent and nurturer also of foreign peoples'. Not only the economic lifeline, but a crossroads of many nations, 'a nurturing mother . . . in the

---

[48] Theodor Schieder, *Deutscher Geist und ständische Freiheit im Weichselland. Politische Ideen und politisches Schriftum in Westpreußen von der Lubliner Union bis zu den polnischen Teilungen, 1569–1772/93* (Danzig: Gräfe und Unzer, 1940), p. 43.

[49] Little known is his manuscript 'Sarmatia sive de Originibus et Antiquitatibus primorum in Sarmatia Europaea populorum Dissertatio Latinae de Prussia Historiae apparatus et libri I' (1662), Bibl. PAN Kór., 152.

[50] Ibid., p. 9.

[51] Ibid., pp. 12–13, 117.

centre of Europa', Prussia bore many nations, like a fertile '*vagina nationum*', the function ancient Scandinavia had fulfilled for Jordanes's Sweden. By virtue of being a valuable political and economic entity, Prussia was equal to Poland, Lithuania and Livonia as a distinct nation and a province with fixed boundaries.[52]

The special position of Prussia as a member of the Sarmatian world clearly conferred a special role upon its non-noble citizens. Burgher values of trade and industriousness were Prussia's main assets: Clagius, from a commoner background, also recognised this. It was not the Hanseatic, Teutonic or German past, however, but the Sarmatian mythology which formed the focus of this economic identity. Although the Teutonic Knights had founded most cities, civilised the pagans and granted ample freedoms and privileges on the basis of the Magdeburg and Kulm law,[53] their rule became corrupt. Prussian freedoms and economic prosperity were not the result of the grace and clemency of the Teutonic Knights, but of a mythical, democratic golden age, and were preserved in their own enduring Prussian tradition of liberty.

The transition to Polish rule did not significantly alter the identity of the Prussians as free people, in charge of their own affairs, laws and customs. The concern of Prussian historians with the pagan religion, the ancient customs and the ancient Prussian language – not a Slavic but a Baltic tongue – was therefore highly relevant. The need for original unity and harmony existed even here: the language of the Sarmatians was later divided into Prussian, Lithuanian and Polish.[54] History was both the essence and an instrument of Prussian identity. Royal Prussian burgher historians could not, however, ignore the fact that Prussian customs and traditions were not sacrosanct to their brothers, the Poles and Lithuanians. After 1466, Hartknoch wrote, many noble families adopted a Polish lifestyle and even changed their names into Polish-sounding ones: 'As each country orients its customs towards the customs of its ruler, so too did the Prussian nobility, by adopting Polish customs, dress and language.' But the Prussian burghers lived in the towns of Royal Prussia, where 'the Germans still predominate', while 'few German noble families are left in Royal Prussia'.[55] What happened to the Prussians? Did Polish and Teutonic invasions irretrievably destroy those traditions, leaving only Hartknoch's nostalgia for a better, golden past?

If this was the verdict, it would seem harsh, considering how much effort Hartknoch put into the analysis of the ancient Prussian nation and its political constitution. Could the German traditions, originally imported by the Teutonic Knights and subsequent immigrants, live side by side with the Sarmatian legacy? It is worth remembering how important it was for Hartknoch that the cities were a place where burghers and nobles had once lived in harmony. There, Prussians and

---

[52] Ibid., pp. 270, 272–4, 279–80.
[53] Hartknoch, *Alt- und Neues Preußen*, pp. 623–4.
[54] Ibid., pp. 443–4, 101.
[55] Ibid., pp. 452–3.

'foreigners' from Poland, Lithuania and Germany melted into the Prussian nation. It was in the cities that the ancient laws and liberties were best preserved. The burghers of Prussia, who resisted change most obstinately, were the guardians of Prussian national identity. Urban citizens had played the central role in 1454, when they gained their extensive privileges as a reward for their loyalty to the Polish king. Instead of losing their privilege-based identity, the Prussian cities had even increased their freedoms under the Polish crown, their new source of privilege. Their particular concept of citizenship, their diet, and their more genuinely mixed form of government, which included non-nobles, elevated the Prussian Sarmatians over their Polish brothers. With a parliament that allowed commoners and nobles to participate in the political nation, they were the better Sarmatians. As the old unity of the estates was under threat, and as pressure from the Polish king and the Sejm to give up Prussia's special privileges and immunities increased in the late seventeenth century, Prussian writers not only added their voices to Poland's constitutional reform movement; they also started to defend an image of Prussian political and historical superiority with an energy that ultimately proved detrimental to the unity of the state they had so desired to preserve.

### THE IDEA OF LIBERTY

Poland numbered among Europe's monarchies, but the citizens of the Polish-Lithuanian Commonwealth, who possessed full active and passive political rights, had no doubt that pure monarchies were prisons in which no liberty could flourish. A monarch's rule was always enforced by power and ruthless cunning, and therefore by nature detrimental to free citizenship and the individual responsibility of the *civis activus*. Aristotelianism and classical republicanism, with the mixed form of government at its heart, was popular among Spanish, French and Italian Jesuits such as Francisco Suarez (1548–1617), Robert Bellarmine (1542–1611) and Antonio Possevino (1534–1611), and reached Poland quickly with the growing influence of Jesuit colleges during the sixteenth and early seventeenth centuries.[56] The inclination of Catholics, Calvinists, Lutherans, Anabaptists and Antitrinitarians alike to accept these principles of citizenship as defined in the classical *polis*[57] shows that in the sixteenth century many nobles considered religion a personal matter, not connected with a particular form of government. Hence, it was not surprising that the Prussian burghers easily crossed confessional boundaries to adhere to the same principle of liberty and citizenship. Problems started when the reality of social, political and religious life produced rival claims, and competing liberties started to encroach upon each other. Then, precise definitions and limita-

---

[56] Skinner, *The Foundations of Modern Political Thought*, vol. II, pp. 135–48.
[57] Helmut G. Koenigsberger, 'Schlußbetrachtung. Republiken und Republikanismus im Europa der frühen Neuzeit aus historischer Sicht', in Koenigsberger (ed.), *Republiken und Republikanismus*, p. 285.

tions of urban and noble citizenship, of religious loyalties and of political and economic living space had to be found. Liberty – both 'to' and 'from' – was at the heart of the burghers' political discourse and their identity. But what are the conditions of citizenship? What are the liberties of action free citizens possess?

For burghers depending on trade, crafts and commerce, freedom was naturally associated with urban prosperity. The inscription which dominated the council chamber of the Thorn town hall declared: 'From peace comes liberty . . . good flows from peaceful cities, in which virtue flourishes: integrity is of great advantage, justice is glorious, faith is honourable, so pray that God will give the kingdom and the city peace and security.' This motto pointed to the eternal theme of liberty within a well-ordered public realm living in peace under good laws.[58] The good government of the city, 'gute policey', was the ideal of burghers and council-members alike, who wanted to stem the tide of licence to which many thought the Polish-Lithuanian Commonwealth had succumbed through the corruption of a part of its political elite. The greatest threat to this liberty was the weakening of the rule of law and the lack of a strong senate, which, by balancing the three elements of the mixed constitution, had in the past ensured just government. But now the Prussians feared that with the 'powerful and quarrelling factions of great lords, their unlimited power, arbitrarily breaking our liberty, prostrating and uprooting our royal majesty and the authority of the senate, the whole republic will end in confusion and pernicious anarchy'.[59]

In Royal Prussia the sharpening of political and social conflict was rooted in the divergence of interests of nobles and burghers. The theme of Sarmatian liberty runs like a thread through the political and historical writing of the Prussian burghers, who defended their special status as privileged estates of the province, distinct from the Polish-Lithuanian republic. The Prussian nobility, on the other hand, attached great importance to their active participation in the political struc-ture of the Commonwealth and the shaping of its constitution. These two elements have usually been regarded as contradictory. Was Hartknoch's Sarmatian mother a different parent to the Prussian burghers than to the nobles? Did the fact that burghers claimed other privileges than nobles and used laws different from the *ius terrestre* of the nobility suggest a different idea and practice of liberty? In the political language of their writings, Prussian burghers made an important distinc-tion between liberties in the plural and liberty in the singular.[60] In the plural form, the expression was used in the meaning of 'rights and privileges', often of very limited scope, in the context of property rights, taxation, and the regulation of

---

[58] Simon Schultz, 'Tagebuch', APT Kat. II, XIII.25, p. 212; for the concept of the 'well-ordered' police state and the meaning of 'gute policey', see Marc Raeff, *The Well-Ordered Police State. Social and Institutional Change through Law in the Germanies and Russia, 1600–1800* (New Haven and London: Yale University Press, 1983).

[59] Georg Schröder, 'Notabiliora (1692–1699)', APGd, Bibl. Archivi 300.R, no. Ll, 47, p. 29.

[60] Gerald Strauss, *Law, Resistance and the State. The Opposition to Roman Law in Reformation Germany* (Princeton University Press, 1986), p. 117.

beer-brewing and trade. These liberties, identified in contracts, decrees and immunities bestowed by the king upon the city authorities, had been accumulated over centuries. There was no difference in the principal understanding of the meaning of such liberties between nobles and burghers, between Royal Prussia and Poland. For example, for the brewers in Thorn, to be 'free people' meant to be exempt from the excise which the magistrates had imposed on them in the aftermath of the Swedish wars of the 1650s, and which hurt the prosperity of their trade, particularly since the Jesuits had continued to import cheaper (non-taxed) beer into the city. The excise, in their view, violated their ancient status of freedom, guaranteed to them under the constitution of their city after the end of Teutonic rule.[61]

Another example illuminates the use of 'liberties' in the plural. One of the many rights of the Thorn city council and its burgomasters was the right to appoint their own council members during the annual *Ratsküre*, 'which has been the custom since times immemorial, not only in Thorn, but also in Elbing and Dantzig, and as it is still happening in these two cities nowadays'.[62] As Gerald Strauss has noted with regard to the German free cities, written evidence for such 'immemorial customs' did not always exist. In the Holy Roman Empire after 1648, several cities attempted to win recognition as *Immediatstädte*, municipal bodies directly and exclusively subject to the emperor's jurisdiction. To legitimise their claim, Erfurt, Osnabrück, Münster and Minden invented a series of ancient privileges and documents, and did not even stop at forgery. Their goal was to gain independence from episcopal rule by the bishoprics to which they belonged.[63] As in Prussia, pagan origins were evoked to prove the antiquity of their freedoms.

The liberties which the king had yielded to the Prussian province and its cities required repeated application and confirmation and constant vigilance. Old laws were fragile: they were 'lost when not used'. After the occupation of Pomerania by the Swedes, for example, the Pomeranian estates not only insisted on keeping their old laws and privileges as 'fundamental law', but defined all new legislation as part of their ancient fundamental law code, a practice to which the Swedish crown objected on the grounds that 'laws that have been eroded over time and become obsolete, must be abolished'. The Danzig councillor Reinhold Curicke wrote in 1670 that the confirmation of privileges 'gives the privilege its true existence: without it, the privilege is nothing but a mute and dead letter'.[64] After the incorporation of the Prussian diet into the Polish Sejm in 1569, the assertion of the province's liberties and the right to self-government (regarding *omnes causae*

---

[61] Simon Schultz, 'Tagebuch', APT Kat. II, XIII.25, pp. 170–71.

[62] Ibid., p. 166. The failure of the council in 1675 to appoint all four burgomasters was felt to be a threat to good order – and freedom.

[63] Schmidt, 'Zur politischen Vorstellungswelt', pp. 501ff.

[64] Strauss, *Law, Resistance*, p. 110; Pär-Erik Back, *Herzog und Landschaft* (Lund: C. W. K. Gleerup, 1955), p. 169; Curicke, *Commentarius Iuridico-Historico-Politicus de Privilegiis* (Danzig: Förster, 1670), p. 203.

*notabiles*) was of central importance. Danzig, which had, together with a part of the Prussian szlachta, supported the Habsburg candidature to the throne in 1575, had even been ready to go to war for the reaffirmation of its liberties, which king Stefan Batory refused to grant before the city had sworn its oath of allegiance. Danzig made its oath conditional on the removal of the statute of the Karnkowski commission of 1569/70, which had restricted the political powers of the city council.[65] The split between nobility and cities over the application of Kulm law increased the dangers of an erosion of the 'old laws', particularly those privileges which predated the period of Polish rule over Prussia.

Providing documentary proof of customary law and its application was vital to arguments between Prussians and Poles in the Sejm, as well as in the Prussian Diet, between the Prussian nobility and the Prussian cities, the latter rejecting a closer association with Polish laws and customs. The need to stem the erosion of customary laws by producing written proof inspired more and more lawyers to compile law collections as protection against the ravages of time and desuetude. The great numbers of such collections, still evident in the archives today, and the constant reiteration of important decrees by which Royal Prussia had gathered and maintained rights and liberties since the rule of Casimir Jagiellończyk is a manifestation of this spirit. The significance of sealed documentary evidence of ancient privileges is also stressed in iconography. Reinhold Curicke's treatise on privileges is adorned with the allegory of liberty, depicted as a bird escaping its cage thanks to a sealed parchment in its beak: a woman with a burgher's hat who releases the bird from its state of captivity represents the city of Danzig.[66]

Curicke defined privileges as 'private rights', not general laws, which by their nature contribute to the common good and prosperity of the whole body politic. *Libertas* and privilege (*consuetudo, beneficium, praemium, praerogativa*) were used interchangeably as the source of the general *salus publica*. Curicke, knowing the power of historical references, consciously evaluated the success or failure of political constitutions by quoting from works on the Goths, the Romans, and the Dutch and their prosperous cities, which flourished by virtue of privileges. He warned against the French model, where venality of offices undermined the principle of merit, the very nature of just privileges. Curicke rejected standardisation and centralisation, praising the great variety of local particular rights and social prerogatives; inequality was a virtue. The great range of specific *'jura, libertates, privilegia et immunitates Regni'* of all the provinces and cities of the Commonwealth ensured that the whole republic was happy and prosperous.[67] The romantic nineteenth-century idea that social and political life in early modern towns and

---

[65] Roman Lutman, 'Położenie prawno-polityczne Gdańska w dawnej Polsce', *Rocznik Gdański* 1 (1927), 72; Karol Olejnik, *Stefan Batory* (Warsaw: PWN, 1988), pp. 74ff.

[66] Curicke, *Commentarius*, title page; see jacket illustration.

[67] Ibid., p. 206. For Curicke, a Calvinist, one of the most central privileges for the cities was religious toleration.

cities was ruled by some kind of 'primeval egalitarianism' or communism is therefore absurd.

Nevertheless, liberties could become a liability, endangering the peace of the commonweal when abused. Curicke saw republics as unstable bodies and an easy prey to factional infighting; thus freedoms had the character of a double-edged sword, being 'easily the origin of discord and disturbances'. Any government, Curicke wrote in perfectly Aristotelian manner, can in turn become corrupt when it falls into irresponsible hands, when 'tyrants replace their legally ruling bodies'. In a contract with its citizens, a sound monarchy recognises the force of law as superior and thereby restricts its own authority.[68] This, however, required almost impossible self-restraint and virtues rare in a monarch. Thus the burghers of Royal Prussia shared the Polish constitutionalists' concern for the protection of the rule of law against the abuse of freedoms and privileges: 'There is a greater probability that not liberty, but licence will be victorious, which poisons all human affairs, which curses all things divine, and in which there is no end to litigation, slander, sedition and civil war.'[69] It was the same Scylla of *absolutum dominium* and the Charybdis of democratic *licentia* that Hartknoch had perceived as the dual peril to mixed government. Similarly, Curicke championed the aristocratic values of a strong council government in the cities of Royal Prussia. He condemned the 1606–9 Zebrzydowski rokosz as an example of noble licence that led to civil war. The greatest danger to freedom was the lawlessness of the rule of the mob: '*legibus soluta multitudo*'. Curicke had experience of the licence of the masses in his own city. The relentlessness of the city elites in guarding urban liberties was sometimes turned against them. As the third estate of Danzig sought to restrict council powers in favour of greater participatory rights, the rebellious leadership of several Danzig craftsmen insisted on the continuing validity of the Karnkowski statute of 1570, which had increased the influence of the third estate on urban legislation to the detriment of the city council, despite its formal abrogation by Batory in 1585.[70]

Differences in the notion and interpretation of liberties therefore divided various political and social groups within the cities of Royal Prussia themselves. At a time of harsh conflicts, between the citizenry and the council of Danzig in 1674–8, the king sent a commission to the city which on behalf of the guilds and the representatives of the third estate demanded to see all original documents which had granted political and juridical prerogatives to the city government since the 1450s.[71] The gravamina of 1674 submitted by the Danzig craft guilds (*Gewerke*) to the Polish king complained not only about the financial irregularities and the nepotism of the council elite, but also that 'the council does not communicate to us the privileges, rights and decrees useful to this city . . .; thus we lack many documents to support

[68] Ibid., p. 175.
[69] Ibid., p. 266.
[70] *Historia Gdańska*, vol. II, pp. 298–306; Cieślak, *Walki*, pp. 18ff.
[71] Schröder, 'Tagebuch', APGd, Bibl. Archivi 300.R, Vv.q 21, pp. 61–2.

our cause because the secretaries do not want to give us extracts, for the sheer respect they have for the council'.[72]

The content, meaning and even the existence of the fundamental *jura et libertates* were constantly open to debate. The Danzig council sought to buy the king's favour and the renewed confirmation of the city's immunities 'to protect the city against all decrees that could threaten its religious and political liberties',[73] while the third estate, led by the shoemaker Christian Meyer during the 1670s, appealed directly to the king to increase the participation of guild members in policy-making and legislation. In contrast to the Empire, where an appeal to the emperor usually triggered the dispatch of a commission of inquiry composed of imperial councillors and princes from other imperial territories to reconcile the conflicting parties, the Polish king responded to the plea by the Danzig guilds by visiting the city personally. When both parties discovered that John Sobieski was seeking to gain personal advantage from the conflict which divided their city, the pro-royal protesters failed to keep the support of the masses of the enfranchised citizenry.[74] The royal intervention revitalised the consensus on the meaning of the city's liberties. John Sobieski's demand for the inclusion of an equal number of Catholics and Protestants on the council and among the guild representatives of the city was rejected as contrary to the ancient freedoms of all three urban estates.[75] Rallying to the support of the guild masters from the four Danzig quarters, the council was able to fend off royal demands. The urban negotiators regarded any breach of customary laws and liberties with great suspicion and rejected all novelties on the grounds that they would 'hurt the common good', incurring 'disturbance and many perils'. Historical consciousness – the hint at the longevity of traditions dating from Teutonic times – was always part of this consensus on the principle of liberties.[76]

The issues at stake were therefore not only petty rights and local customs. Here, liberties meant more than royally sanctioned privileges; liberties which constituted a whole way of life turned into liberty – in the singular. Prussian burghers shared with the nobility the idea of liberty as a bulwark against tyranny (whether exercised within the city or from outside), and the preservation of their self-governing bodies, such as the council, the third estate or the dietines on a provincial level. The principle of mutual recognition of freedoms and rights also found its expression on a more theoretical level, such as in the contract theories expounded at the Thorn Gymnasium by Ernst König, who taught his students to reject Hobbes's idea of unquestioned obedience to the Leviathan. Instead, König underlined the republican elements in Grotius's natural law theory, limiting the power and authority of a government in favour of the supreme rule of rational laws.[77]

---

[72] Ibid., p. 21.   [73] Ibid., p. 55.
[74] Gotthilf Löschin, *Geschichte Danzigs* (Danzig: Albertinische Buch- und Kunsthandlung, 1823), vol. II, p. 37.   [75] Schröder, 'Tagebuch', pp. 98–100.
[76] Mokrzecki, *W kręgu*, p. 132.
[77] *Diatribe Politica de Majestate quam suprema majestate favente, in Gymnasio Thoruniense, praeside M. Ernesto König, subjicit Henricus Fibing, Svidnicio Silesius* (Thorn: Coepselius, 1671), paragr. XVI.

The Prussian cities asserted their wish to be as politically and economically self-sufficient as the nobility. They could identify with the republicanism of some country squires, with their ideal of the autarkic, wholesome rural lifestyle, and their criticism of the court culture of the noble 'drones' who no longer knew how to 'live by the sweat of their brows'.[78] This was the autonomy of the hard-working and useful member of society, who abstained from leasing his lands or leaving them in the hands of administrators while living in the luxury of Warsaw, and instead represented his legitimate political aspirations in the local dietine, the embodiment of political virtue and Sarmatian freedom. Noble handbooks on the orderly running of agricultural households during the sixteenth and seventeenth centuries did not emphasise activities in the Sejm, but those in the local dietines.[79] In much the same spirit, the major and minor Prussian cities focused on their role in the Prussian provincial diets rather than the Polish Sejm, where in 1569 they had refused to take their seats in the chamber of envoys. The freedom of local representation in the Prussian Diet, where the Royal Prussian cities participated alongside the nobility, was the fulcrum of the liberties and national identity of the burghers. This political achievement was historically defined and legitimised by the events of 1454. Curicke's gloating that the Prussians rid themselves of the yoke of the Teutonic Order, as '*Belgii ab Hispanis*', could not have passed unnoticed for its very current political message. It was meant as a warning to the Polish nobility and the king to refrain from haughtiness towards them: violations of Prussian privileges by the Poles and a breach of faith could cause the ending of the mutual contract between rulers and ruled, king and subjects.[80] There was a strong emphasis on the right of resistance, as the safeguarding of Prussian privileges and their state of liberty were the precondition of their political loyalty. If need be, the burghers would not hesitate to defend their liberty against the very source of their freedoms, the king and crown of Poland itself. This had nothing to do with popular sovereignty. As a conscientious member of the Danzig patriciate Curicke cautioned that no 'citizen from among the masses, nor any private citizen' was allowed to exercise such an act of disobedience: 'it is in the nature of the multitude either to serve in humility or to rule in insolence'.[81] Resistance was not an individual right, just as privileges were of a corporate nature, not the freedoms of individual persons. Borrowing from the political theory of Polish constitutionalists, he saw the relationship between *plebs* and *senate* as being similar to that between *corpus* and *anima* – the former had to obey the latter.

This was the great dilemma which marked the attitude of the Prussian burghers towards the Polish-Lithuanian Commonwealth: on the one hand they did not suffer any interference from their king and republic; on the other hand, they loved the principles of the Commonwealth's constitution, precisely because they allowed them that freedom. The spirit and structure of Polish political institutions found

---

[78] Dwight Van Horn, 'Suburban Development', pp. 397–8.    [79] Ibid., p. 396.
[80] Curicke, *Commentarius*, p. 239.    [81] Ibid., p. 261.

direct reflection in the way Royal Prussian burghers described their own governmental bodies and the ideal of the mixed constitution in their own province and in their cities.[82] Consequently, Curicke attributed to liberty a more abstract meaning. Freedoms help to safeguard liberty as such, by preventing the oppression of communities and individuals alike. Sir John Elliott has observed that from the eighteenth century rebellions that used the language of liberty became more sophisticated: what happened was 'the transformation of liberties into liberty'.[83] Where there was a strong influence of natural law teaching, such as in the Prussian Gymnasia, however, this process predates the eighteenth century. Liberty of contradiction – liberty to speak out – was essential for the politically mature and active Prussian citizen, whether burgher or noble: 'Liberty, however, consists of saying what you want, so that you may say it without fear.'[84] Curicke summed up the meaning of the Prussian burghers' and citizens' freedom with a quotation from Sallust: 'It is better to live in dangerous liberty than perish in quiet servitude.'[85]

Yet liberty involved risk. This idea was also expressed in a treatise, posthumously published in 1733, by the Thorn professor Martin Böhm who laid particular stress on the significance of the royal election: the freedom gained by an electoral monarchy outweighed the dangers connected with the interregnum, the period without a crowned head between the death of one king and the coronation of the next. Böhm eagerly confirmed the continued right of the Prussian cities to participate in this election, although ever since 1648 the cities had preferred not to appear on the election field.[86] For Böhm the crucial question was not the nature of past liberties and their glittering ideal, but whether such privileges were still valid. It was not as important that the Prussians were free people in 1454, as that these liberties were still guaranteed and effective in 1700; few authors stated this concern with such emphasis: 'It is not enough to live in the past, to sulk over lost liberties and a picture of great glory, we must be a free nation [in the present].' Although ancient customs and laws very much reflect the 'spirit of a nation', only daily reality could put these customs to the test.[87]

The question of legitimate resistance against rulers who disregarded the ancient and present liberties of Prussia was also addressed by Johannes Schultz from Graudenz, who was ennobled by the king around 1697.[88] In his treatise *Tractatus*

---

[82] Ibid., pp. 262–3.
[83] John Elliott, 'Revolution and Continuity', p. 130.
[84] 'Diarium Electionis, Wahl-Reichstag 1697', APT Kat. II, VI.20, p. 248.
[85] Curicke, *Commentarius*, p. 173.
[86] Martin Böhm, *Commentarius de Interregnis in Regno Poloniae a M[artino] Böhmio, professore Gymnasii Thoruniensis, concinnatus nunc e M[anuscrip]to editus ac quibusdam addimentis auctus* (Thorn: Nicolai, 1733), p. 313.
[87] Böhm, *Commentarius de Interregnis*, preface.
[88] H. Grajewski, *Jan Schultz-Szulecki i jego Tractatus historico-politicus de Polonia nunquam tributaria* (Łódź: Towarzystwo Przyjaciół Nauk, 1964), p. 53. Schultz was not tempted by the noble lifestyle; he preferred becoming the rector of the university in Frankfurt (Oder) in 1703, rather than settle on landed estates; Mokrzecki, *W kręgu*, p. 171.

*historico–politicus de Polonia nunquam tributaria*, the act of resistance against the
Teutonic Knights is accorded greatest significance. Schultz argued on the basis of
natural law that liberty was not the freedom from tribute per se, but from tribute
which was enforced on subjects without their consent or the agreement of their
representative bodies. The only acceptable way of paying tribute was therefore in
the form of a voluntary donation.[89] Schultz contrasted the Teutonic Knights' illegal
use of force with the benign rule of law under the Polish king, who was not a
*dominus*, but a *pater patriae*.[90] The thirteenth-century conquest and imposition of
tribute, undertaken by the Teutonic Order contrary to Kulm law, broke international contracts and presented an act of aggression against Poland.[91]

Under the political circumstances of the 1690s, when Schultz composed this
treatise, the commemoration of this historical act of resistance carried a double
connotation in Prussia: what had liberated the Prussians from oppression in the
past was a legitimate action which could be repeated if present or future injustice
necessitated it.[92] The topic which occupied much of the sessions in the Prussian
diet and in the Sejm during the last decade of the seventeenth century was the
amount of contribution and taxation to be given to the Polish crown during the
Turkish wars. The privileges of the province theoretically prohibited the king from
demanding regular taxation if it was not unanimously agreed by the Prussian Diet.
Schultz stressed that the Prussian cities, as a result of compromise, paid a voluntary
contribution to the crown. In contrast, the szlachta deputies followed the Polish
model of consenting not only to a poll tax, but also to regular customs duties to be
collected from Danzig.[93] The violation of one of the Prussian burghers' liberties –
freedom from arbitrary taxation – was perceived as an attack on Liberty itself.
Towards the end of the seventeenth century, then, the Prussian past was increasingly instrumentalised. To writers like Böhm and Schultz, it was not the lawlessness of the Teutonic regime which was an urgent matter of concern, but the
behaviour of the present government towards the Royal Prussian cities. This form
of public discourse, which turned to history in search of support for a present
political argument, was not peculiar to Royal Prussian political culture: Benedict
Anderson has observed the same principle in historical utopias, which are usually
aimed at criticising existing societies and governments.[94]

Prussian constitutionalist writers did not have to look to a distant fairy-tale world,
however, to collect convincing models and examples for their defence of the right of
resistance: the fate of the Dutch republic and its struggle for freedom against the

[89] Johannes Schultz [Szulecki], *Disputationis Juris Publici de Polonia nunquam Tributaria quam praeside
Joanni Schultzio publice submittitur a Henrico Fredero* (Danzig: Haeredes Rhetii, 1694), p. 8.
[90] Mokrzecki, *Studium*, p. 186, quoting from Schultz-Szulecki's panegyrical *Serenissimo Domino Joanni
III Poloniarum Regi* (Danzig: Rhetii Haeredes, 1694).
[91] J. Schultz, *Tractatus historico–politicus de Polonia nunquam tributaria*, 10 parts (Danzig: Rhetii
Haeredes, 1694), treatise no. IX, paragr. 1, 4–6.    [92] Ibid., paragr. 7, p. 275.
[93] Achremczyk, *Życie*, pp. 284–6.
[94] Anderson, *Imagined Communities*, p. 69.

Spanish Habsburgs, which had also inspired Hartknoch and Sachs, were *loci communes* in the historical and political narratives of seventeenth-century treatises. This interest in the Netherlands was fuelled by the frequent study trips to Dutch universities by Prussian burghers, such as Nathaniel Schröder in about 1660.[95] The notebooks of burgomaster Stroband in Thorn contain lectures by the Leiden Calvinist philosopher and theologian Marcus Boxhorn on the revolt of the Dutch and the Portuguese rebellion against Spain.[96] Stroband diligently recorded Boxhorn's discussion of the 'just desertion' by the Portuguese from the Spanish king, who 'ruled through oppression' and the 'extirpation of liberty', and compared this example to the conflicts between Spain and the Netherlands. The frustration with absolute monarchy of the *proceres*, the senators and grandees among the nobility, as well as the oppression of the *populus* with heavy contributions were, according to Stroband's notes, what led to the defection from Spanish domination.[97]

Despite Hartknoch's warning to beware of unbalanced oligarchy, the Dutch model of the well-ordered 'city-republics' held many charms for the burghers of Prussia. The parallel with the Prussians' own resistance against the Teutonic Order was not lost on contemporaries. For many Prussian burghers, it was a means to express their loyalty to the Commonwealth – but again, a loyalty that was made conditional upon the validity and preservation of Prussia's old laws and privileges for the cities. The popularity of Grotius's teaching on international and positive law among the educated burgher elite, documented in Stroband's notebook, was no doubt fed by the Dutchman's defence of the freedom of the seas and free trade, while his views on the necessity of a strong central government barely found mention. Economic treatises by Prussian merchants admired the longevity of the economic and political strength of the Dutch cities, caused by their low tariff policies; in the words of the Danzig merchant and burgher Johann Köstner: 'The Dutch, whose power lies in trade . . . have much lower tariffs in their well-ordered provinces.'[98] Thus liberties in the plural, in the meaning of concrete economic freedoms based on positive law and sealed privileges, and Liberty in the singular, defined as liberty from political oppression, in the terms of classical republicanism and natural law teaching, were hard to separate.

From the late seventeenth century, the burghers' concern with the extent of their own power and their relationship to their monarch focused more specifically on the

---

[95] 'Reisebeschreibung [Georg Schröders] von Dantzig nach Holland und Engelland', Bibl. PAN Gd., 925. Gottfried Zamehl also praises Dutch burgher pride and wealth, in 'Studiosus Apodemicus', pp. 24–5.

[96] Heinrich Stroband, 'Clarissimi D[omi]ni Marcii Zverii Boxhornij Disputationes Politicae A. 1645 Lugd. Batavorum', in '1. Politische Abhandlungen, 2. Verfassung der Niederländischen Generalstaaten, 3. Gedenkbuch des Bürgermeisters H. Stroband III, 1600–1657', APT Kat. II, XII.3; for another example see Nemorecki and Aramus, *Orationes*, Oratio I, folio B2v.

[97] Stroband, 'Boxhornij Disputationes', pp. 6–7.

[98] Johann Köstner, 'Von der Abnahme des Handels in Dantzig', Bibl. PAN Gd., 538, p. 14.

nature of the mutual contract which the historic events of 1454 and 1466 had established. Time and again, they reminded their king that their accession to the crown of Poland had been a voluntary act, based on the proper 'consensus between rulers and ruled', without which civil society could not exist.[99] The threat to such a pact frequently came from human nature, which made a ruler strive for more and more power: '[the ruler] imposes more and more burdens on his subjects, until he adopts the name of an absolute monarch'.[100] The panacea was what the Pomeranian author Johannes Pommeresch called *Bürgerverträge*, contracts regulating the powers of the various estates and orders within the city and their relationship to the ruler. Such contracts limited monarchy by 'certain fundamental laws', or *Willküren*, which the cities of Royal Prussia valued as highly as the szlachta of the republic valued the *pacta conventa* and the right to form confederations and to convene dietines.[101] The demand of the szlachta that the king must comply to the *pacta conventa* found a parallel in the demand of the burghers, addressed to the whole of the republic and the king, to respect their fundamental urban privileges. In the face of such evidence, the thesis of the Royal Prussian cities' aloofness from political argument and the assertion that 'the separatist constitution after 1569 suited the three major cities, as they were uninterested in the general constitution of the republic', are clearly false.[102]

The Polish and the Prussian burghers' notions of liberty did, however, clash over the question of authority: who was to recognise the special constitutions of the Prussian cities? In the eyes of many Polish noblemen, the freedoms of the Royal Prussian province were tarnished by the encouragement they gave to burghers to participate in the political nation. Compared to the freedom of the Polish knight and nobleman, the freedoms of any other nation appeared poor: this was the tenor of an anonymous 1680 pamphlet comparing the freedoms of Poland and Lithuania with those of 'neighbouring duchies and especially the German Empire and the realm of Polish Prussia'. As most Polish writers were well acquainted with the constitution of the Holy Roman Empire and other European states, followed political events and observed the role of the Commonwealth in European politics, they stated their political superiority with some conviction: 'there are more fundamental liberties in Poland – every nobleman can go to the dietine and to the Sejm'.[103] Treatises like this sounded alarm bells in Royal Prussia. Georg Austen,

---

[99] *Theses politicas De Majestate Principis Limitata, praeside M. Joh[ann] Sartorius, Gymn[asii] Thor[uniensi] PP ad ventilandum proponis Antonio Baumgarten, Thoruniensis 1686, den 31. Jan[uar]* (Thorn: Beck, 1686), chapter 1; also Schultz *Tractatus*, IX, paragr. 13, pp. 291–2.

[100] Sartorius, *Theses politicas*, chapter 3.

[101] *Discursus juridico-politicus de summo in civitatibus Imperio quem aeterni numinis gratia aspirante Johannis Pomereschi* (Greifswald: Jegeri, 1654); on fundamental laws and *Bürgerverträge* in Swedish Pomerania, se Pär-Erik Back, *Herzog und Landschaft*, pp. 150–61.

[102] Bogucka and Samsonowicz, *Dzieje miast*, p. 326; Cieślak also summarizes this view in 'Miejsce Gdańska w Rzeczypospolitej szlacheckiej. Zarys problematyki', in Trzoska, J. (ed.), *Strefa Bałtycka w XVI–XVIII w. Polityka – Społeczeństwo – Gospodarka* (Gdańsk: Marpress, 1993), p. 38.

[103] 'Comparatio wolności Polskiey y Litewskiey z wolnością postronnych Xiążąt udzielnych et mi-

whose late-seventeenth-century diaries contain many mock verses, allegorical and polemical pieces in Latin, German and Polish, made note of a hymn to freedom, 'To the country of Prussia': 'Liberty' (in the singular) is a 'ring which binds the souls of men with no end', and whose 'unity preserves the cities'. Liberty is a 'bride' Prussia must 'protect against robbers'.[104] The background to this piece in Austen's *silva rerum* are events in Thorn during the 1680s. The struggle of the Protestants in the city against the vociferous Catholic bishop of Kulm, Kazimierz Opaliński, climaxed in 1688, a year after Hartknoch's death, when Lutherans demonstrated against a *Corpus Christi* procession through the centre of Thorn. The city was sentenced by the Sejm (and the king) to pay indemnities to the bishop, who himself was reprimanded, however, for his actions against the burghers. In the context of this conflict, Austen's verses caution that the 'tyranny' of the Teutonic Knights might repeat itself under a second Catholic tyranny – the foreign clergy sent from Poland: Opaliński was a Pole and not a Prussian *indigena*. It seems, however, that it was not so much the fact that he was a Catholic, but that he was a haughty nobleman taking arbitrary action against the city which upset the burghers: 'Force before Law: they accuse us, but we have been faulted; we are being beaten, but they ask for our punishment; unlawful justice . . . because he is a Pole and free lord; he refuses to be bound by law.'[105] This affair painfully revealed the extent to which the once powerful voice of the Prussian magistrates had lost its weight not only in their province, but also their own city. The rhetorical consensus between the Prussian burghers and the noble understanding of the virtues of Sarmatian liberty was showing some strains in times of religious and political crisis. As soon as concrete grievances emerged, the cities took precautions against their 'Polish bridegroom', who might turn out to be the thief of their liberty instead.

Significantly, the Prussian burghers made no references to some of the most radical attempts by European city-states to establish republican or democratic polities, such as the comunero rebellion in Castile in the late fifteenth century, or the revolution of the citizenry in the city of Emden, which was directed against the territorial ruler of Frisia.[106] It is likely that the Prussians considered such acts dangerously extreme. Stroband, for example, stressed that the anti-Spanish Portuguese uprising, which he admired, was not aimed at establishing a purely

anowicie rzeszy Niemieckiey et Polonoborusse, A. 1680', Bibl. PAN Kór., 384, adl. 25, pp. 51, 55; Kazimierz Maliszewski, 'Kształtowanie się stereotypu Niemca i obrazu krajów niemieckich w potocznej świadomości sarmackiej od XVI do połowy XVIII wieku', in Wajda, Kazimierz (ed.), *Polacy i Niemcy. Z badań nad kształtowaniem heterostereotypów etnicznych* (Toruń: Adam Marszałek, 1991), p. 35.

[104] 'Georg Austen Thorun[iensis] Boruss[us] continuata vero per P[etrus] Düsterwald, Encomia, Vituperata, Stylo lapidari scripta, Epigrammata Collectanea quavis studio hic inserta', APT Kat. II, XIV.71, pp. 54–5.

[105] Ibid., p. 55; see also Stanisław Salmonowicz, 'Życie religijne luteranów toruńskich w XVII–XVIII w.', *Odrodzenie i Reformacja w Polsce* 34 (1989), 115–30.

[106] Koenigsberger, 'Schlußbetrachtung', in Koenigsberger (ed.), *Republiken und Republikanismus*, pp. 296–8.

republican government. There is no doubt, however, that the Prussian burghers shared in the European-wide understanding of Aristotelian constitutionalism, with its reliance upon civic virtue and upon liberties and liberty – in the plural and the singular. Despite their gloomy rhetoric, the burghers were aware of the fact that their situation in a commonwealth built on the principles of *forma mixta* improved their chances of maintaining their privileges. They only had to look beyond the borders of the Commonwealth to find many states, more or less well-ordered and prosperous, whose burghers and nobles no longer enjoyed the liberty they cherished so much. Merchants, brewers, master craftsmen, clerics, burgomasters and lawyers – despite the great variety of their duties in the service of the common good and of their professional interests – shared an important feature: they were immensely pragmatic and practical people. Their political theories and principles were not formulated in an ivory tower, but against the background of political and economic conflicts, and all too often in the light of their experience with early modern warfare, currency devaluation, occupation by armies and plagues. It is to this context of provincial and urban *Realpolitik* that we shall now turn. The Cossack uprisings (1648–54) and the wars with Muscovy and Sweden (1654–60) not only stretched Polish-Lithuanian defence capacity to its utmost limits, but also severely tested the loyalty of the various nations and provinces to the Polish crown. The 'Deluge' of 1655 proved particularly costly to the palatinates and the cities of Royal Prussia, which faced massive attack by the Swedish army and became a major war theatre for five years. The following chapters seek to analyse the changing attitudes of the Prussian urban elites towards these events. Burghers in the Royal Prussian province were as keen and interested in following the political debates, reforms, decisions and military events in the rest of the Commonwealth as the noble deputies sent from Royal Prussia to the Sejm to represent the interests of their province. Observers from the cities actively engaged in political debates in the Prussian Diet, while their urban perspective was put forward in a barrage of treatises and pamphlets produced on their cities' printing presses. Prussian publications, diet instructions, private letters and diaries commented extensively on battles, defeats and victories. What impact did the social and political crises of the seventeenth-century Commonwealth have on the Royal Prussian burghers' historical myths and constitutional ideas, and to what extent did the state's political and economic decline lay the foundations for the alienation which marked the relationship between the Prussian burghers and the crown in the eighteenth century?

# 6

# Loyalty in times of war

War had been a constant reality for the provinces of Poland-Lithuania since the devastating wars against the Teutonic Knights in the fifteenth and early sixteenth centuries. After the Livonian wars in the sixteenth century, and the almost permanent threat of Muscovites, Tartars and Turks to the Commonwealth's eastern and south-eastern borders, the Swedes invaded Poland in the 1620s. The first province to feel the impact, Royal Prussia, proved, however, a tough training ground for the Swedish armies: the two cities they had been most eager to occupy, Thorn and Danzig, staunchly defended themselves and kept their gates closed to Swedish troops. In the naval battle of Oliwa in 1627, the Swedish fleet blockading Danzig was defeated and two Swedish ships were sunk; in June 1629, Gustav Adolf was defeated at Honigfelde, near Marienwerder (Kwidzyn). Some lessons were learned: in 1637, Władysław IV established a separate artillery corps and the army was restructured. The *kwarta* tax, first established in the 1560s to guarantee some continuity in funding the army, was now levied at double the rate to expand Polish-Lithuanian forces more easily in wartime.

Yet nothing prepared the Commonwealth and Royal Prussia for the conflicts of the second half of the seventeenth century, which historians ever since have considered a turning point in the fortunes of this large composite state: the Cossack revolt which triggered the Muscovite invasion of 1654, and the Swedish Deluge of 1655–60, which precipitated Poland-Lithuania's military and political collapse, although the Commonwealth rallied after 1656. The first deprived the Commonwealth of the majority of its Cossack troops, which had been a vital component in its armies, and the second established Sweden, Muscovy and – to some extent – Hohenzollern Prussia as major players in East Central Europe, spelling the end of Poland-Lithuania's 'golden century' and diminishing its international prestige.

## THE PRUSSIAN BURGHERS AND THE COSSACK REBELLION

During the first half of the seventeenth century, and despite the first Polish-Swedish war, Poland was praised, at home and abroad, as an oasis of peace and calm, in sharp contrast to the horrors of the Thirty Years War that was raging across its Western borders.[1] Baltic trade and the prosperity of the Royal Prussian towns, especially of Danzig, reached a peak in the first four decades of the seventeenth century. In 1648, however, when the Peace of Westphalia drew a line under the decades of fighting in the Holy Roman Empire, the outbreak of the Cossack rebellion under Bohdan Khmelnytskyi heralded the end of Poland's image as a stable power.[2] Historians, pointing at the significance of the Muscovite invasion and the Swedish Deluge, have blamed much of the subsequent decline of the Commonwealth on those elements among the Cossacks who sought the protection of the Muscovite Tsar in the treaty of Pereiaslav in 1654, and who subsequently opposed compromise with the republic and the Polish king.[3]

Although the Cossack war did not directly touch the province – apart from the resulting additional tax burdens and a general anxiety over the fate of the Common-wealth – it greatly attracted the attention of the Prussian burghers. Diaries, *silva rerum*, periodicals and historical treatises, even history lectures at Prussian schools, time and again return to the debate about the Cossacks, their character, their military actions, their political claims and the right or wrong of their aspirations. The conclusions which the Prussian writers in the cities drew from the Cossack problem reveal much about their own political goals and self-image within the Commonwealth.

Cossack society and military organisations were extremely complex in their structures and their social, national, religious and political composition.[4] After the incorporation in 1569 of the Ukrainian palatinates into the kingdom of Poland, and particularly after the Union at Brest in 1595, by which a part of the Orthodox episcopal hierarchy of the Commonwealth accepted the union with Rome while maintaining the Orthodox liturgy, Polish presence and the influence of szlachta political values and culture grew substantially among the Ruthenian nobility – a process similar to that occurring among the nobility of Royal Prussia. The leaders of the Ruthenian Orthodox nobility, as well as the Orthodox Cossack leadership, rejected the church union, conscious of the fact that through their religion they occupied a special place in the Commonwealth which, alongside that of the

---

[1] Łukasz Opaliński, *Obrona Polski (Polonia Defensa contra Joannem Barclaium)* (Danzig: Förster, 1648); Johann K. Baron von Blomberg, an English agent of Livonian origin, observed in 1698 that Poland's age of greatness ended on the death of Władysław IV; *An Account of Livonia, a Journey from Livonia to Holland in 1698, sent in letters to London* (London: Buck, 1701), p. 217.

[2] Aleksander Brückner, *Dzieje Kultury Polskiej*, 4 vols. (Cracow: Nakład Krakowskiej Spółki Wydaw-niczej, 1930; reprint Warsaw: Wiedza Powszechna, 1991), vol. II, p. 377.

[3] Andrzej S. Kamiński, 'The Polish-Lithuanian Commonwealth and Its Citizens', in Banac, Ivo and Bushkovitch, Paul (eds.), *Poland and Ukraine. Past and Present* (Edmonton and Toronto: The Canadian Institute of Ukrainian Studies, 1980), p. 49; Frank Sysyn, *Between Poland and the Ukraine. The Dilemma of Adam Kysil, 1600–1653* (Cambridge, Mass.: Harvard University Press, 1985), p. 3; Frost, *After the Deluge*, p. 157.

[4] Kamiński, 'The Polish-Lithuanian Commonwealth', p. 44; for a good analysis of the composition of the Zaporozhian Cossacks see Carsten Kumke, *Führer und Geführte bei den Zaporoger Kosaken*, Forschun-gen zur osteuropäischen Geschichte, Osteuropa-Institut an der FUB, Historische Veröffentlichungen no. 49 (Berlin: Duncker und Humblot, 1993), p. 16.

Protestants, had been recognised during the Confederation of Warsaw in 1573. Even Polish writers acknowledged that political friction was often caused by religious tension between various groups of citizens of the Commonwealth. Fredro, for example, followed the recommendation of Justus Lipsius, who advised rulers to foster only one denomination and faith in a state: 'The multiplicity of religions in a kingdom is not useful. The main reason for the war between us and the Cossacks is the difference of the Ruthenian religion.'[5]

Nevertheless, despite the tendency of modern Ukrainian nationalist historiography to mix up religious and political issues and to represent 'Polonisation' in an exclusively negative light, wide circles among the Cossack leadership – regardless of religion – adopted and cultivated the political ideals of the Polish-Lithuanian Commonwealth, including its elective monarchy, its parliamentarianism and the wide-ranging privileges it granted to the nobility. In the first instance, the Union of Brest had not been forced upon the population of Ukraine by Rome, but was pushed by several Ruthenian bishops. It soon proved a failure. Uniate bishops were not welcome in the Crown Senate, and many Ruthenians preferred conversion to Roman Catholicism to the Uniate church. Although religion was important to generate support for the Cossack cause among the Orthodox Ruthenian population, the motives for the Cossack revolt were not primarily religious, but were rooted in the political and social contempt felt by Polish nobles towards the Zaporozhian Cossacks, and their failure to gain recognition as equal brothers of the Poles. From the late sixteenth century, the polarisation between the privileged Cossack nobility and the non-nobles among the Cossacks, who remained excluded from the liberty which king and Commonwealth granted the Polish-Lithuanian nobility, had repeatedly triggered a series of revolts and unrest. Those who had attained noble status, on the other hand, did not always profit from political integration, as many were denied full enjoyment of their privileges by being absorbed into the client networks of powerful Ruthenian landowners such as the Koniecpolskis and Wiśniowieckis.[6]

There is a parallel between Cossack disaffection over their exclusion and the unsuccessful struggle for ever more access to noble liberties in Poland-Lithuania, and the status of the Prussian burghers, who also felt that they were de facto denied full enjoyment of the rights which their own constitutions theoretically granted them since they had joined the Polish crown in 1454. Instead, they often experienced the resentment of both the Prussian and the Polish nobility in the Sejm, who envied the Royal Prussian burghers for their wealth while looking down on or even excluding less significant towns as 'common peasantry'. This conflicting definition of citizenship found expression in a remark by the palatine of Chełmno, Piotr Działyński: 'Cobblers, porters and other commoners are free to go to church, but they cannot have a part in noble assemblies: it is enough that the major cities have their seat among the senators [of the Prussian Diet].' Prussian Diet protocols

---

[5] Fredro, *Scriptorum Seu Togae*, p. 298.     [6] Kumke, *Führer und Geführte*, pp. 49–50.

minuted several instances when the cities were denied the vote on 'affairs which are only of concern to the nobility'.[7] The Polish and Prussian nobility wrongly suspected the Royal Prussian cities of too great a sympathy for strong monarchical power, just as the republicans among the Polish-Lithuanian szlachta were terrified about Khmelnytskyi's appeal to the Polish king to 'assume absolute authority in order to implement justice'.[8]

The Prussian burgher elite understood very well the aspirations of other groups within the Commonwealth that strove for the exercise of similar autonomous rights. It is indicative that the city councils and the nobility in the senate of the Royal Prussian diet mutually closed ranks when Polish noble tribunals questioned not only the validity of separate law codes in the cities (Kulm law), but also the distinctiveness of laws used by the Royal Prussian nobility.[9] Like the Prussian burghers, the Cossack political and military leadership, the *starshyna* of the Zaporozhian Host, gave the running of its own affairs priority over other considerations, despite its tasks of representing the crown and enforcing royal authority on the Cossack mercenary armies. For individual Cossack bands, organised in a decentralised network, service to the king was just one of the tasks they fulfilled and for which they wished to be rewarded. Stressing the Cossacks' merits for the Commonwealth, hetman Kulaha-Petrazhyckyi wrote to Jarema Wiśniowiecki in 1632 that 'we Cossacks have always bared our necks and given our lives for the inviolability of our fatherland'.[10] But Cossack discontent about the size of the register, established by Stefan Batory to keep them available for military service on the royal pay-roll, had risen steadily during the 1630s, when Cossack raids against Ruthenian landowners and Tartars alike destabilised the border areas of the Ukraine.

This raises the question of identity. Both the Prussian burghers and those Cossacks who were not of noble origin identified not with the Polish nation as such, but with the political concept of active citizenship. For Adam Kysil, himself a Ruthenian noble, the 'gentlemen of the Ruthenian nation' (in which he included at least part of the Cossack leadership), originated from 'one font of the Holy Spirit, in this metropolis of the Rus Principality', and were 'of one nation, of one people'. Under the circumstances of the Cossack rebellion and the treaty of Pereiaslav, however, he regretted that this nation was 'not one, thus we are torn asunder and so decline'.[11] Prussian historians in the seventeenth and eighteenth centuries shared

---

[7] Lengnich, *Geschichte der Lande Preußen*, vol. VII, p. 129; and vol. IX, p. 12.

[8] Kamiński, 'The Polish-Lithuanian Commonwealth', p. 44.

[9] 'Verteidigung der Gerichtsbarkeit der preußischen Städte gegen Versuche, diese abhängig von Adelsgerichten zu machen', APT Kat. II, VII.26, esp. p. 126 (1618); p. 135 (1621), and p. 142 (1671). Nobles supported the cities against the summon of Arians before Polish tribunals. There was also a unanimous protest of the Prussian estates against general custom tolls in 1671 (p. 144), and, in 1677, an appeal by the nobility to respect Prussian noble law (p. 155).

[10] Kumke, *Führer und Geführte*, pp. 64–5 and 228–9.

[11] Frank Sysyn, 'Ukrainian-Polish Relations in the Seventeenth Century: The Role of National Consciousness and National Conflict in the Khmelnytsky Movement', in *Poland and Ukraine*, p. 75.

this sentiment with regard to their own nation. Cossacks and Prussians alike were aware that not only their religion, but also their language, and above all their history, were connected with a different world, separate from Polish noble culture.

The Teutonic past, the Holy Roman Empire and the German language on the one hand, and the Orthodox community or the Uniate church and the Ruthenian language on the other hand, complicated the search for identity, particularly in the Cossack case, as this background was much less established, less homogeneous and institutionalised than the urban world of Royal Prussia. The Prussians had produced a great number of historical treatises confirming a past identification with non-Polish traditions, which did not prevent them from being loyal citizens in the present. On the Cossack side, there were indications that the split between registered Cossacks and those living in non-registered bands could be bridged by their continued awareness of their common cultural origin, as for example when Pavlyuk, the Cossack rebel leader of 1637, appealed to his 'registered brothers' to return to life in the Zaporozhian settlements on the steppe.[12] As the Prussian burghers idealised the urban community, the Cossacks idealised a way of life, customs and laws associated with the environment of the Sich. Just as Kulm law and the duties of citizens in a self-governing city were central to the identity of the Prussian burgher elite, Cossack identity was formed by being a soldier and part of the Host.

The crucial question for both communities was therefore to what extent they could integrate and reconcile their own identity with belonging to the Commonwealth. As we have seen, the Prussian burgher elites did accept this republic and its crown as 'our fatherland', despite the sharp conflicts and hardships they experienced in the seventeenth and eighteenth centuries in common with other citizens of the Rzeczpospolita. A dominant group among the Cossacks did not, and separated themselves to accept the rule and 'protection' of the Tsar in 1654. True to their traditions, the Cossacks even then were far from a tight-knit group or nation, despite the many attempts by their own leadership at forging one. Although Cossack registers were kept in more orderly fashion after 1625, a Zaporozhian army never came into being. Whether registered or not, the Cossacks continued to belong to loosely formed bands. The attempt to create a regular militia was undermined by the inconsistent policies of the Polish authorities, who never succeeded in disciplining or controlling the internal structures and relationships of the Host. Neither the institutionalisation of the *hetmanshchyna*, the military command, at Zboriv in 1649, nor the rebellion under Khmelnytskyi created a centralised power structure.[13]

Cossacks who did retain an attachment to the ideals of the Polish-Lithuanian Commonwealth and who, appalled by the authoritarian ways of the tsar, tried to patch up a compromise with the crown at Hadiach (Hadziacz) in 1658, failed to rally their brothers, who no longer shared the basic idea that the Commonwealth

---

[12] Kumke, *Führer und Geführte*, p. 67.    [13] Ibid., pp. 174–6 and pp. 480–2.

was founded on a liberty that was beneficial to them. It is also possible that Ruthenian political traditions, in contrast to the traditions of urban republican ideology in Royal Prussia, were less likely to foster loyalty towards a republic and constitution as opposed to a monarch and a real person, such as the tsar.[14] In contrast to Cossack attitudes, the faith of the Prussian burghers in the value of the common liberty – a 'jewel' not to be surrendered to the exclusivity of the noble view of the nation – survived in the Royal Prussian towns and remained the strongest basis for their identification with the Commonwealth.

Royal Prussian interest in the fate of the Cossacks was also triggered by the burghers' indignation at Cossack treason and rebellion against the common father-land, and Khmelnytskyi's acceptance of Muscovite rule. The concern of the educated burghers with Cossackdom was far from being of a merely antiquarian nature. Joachim Pastorius taught the history of the Cossack wars at the Gymnasium in Elbing, where his work, *Bellum Scythico-Cosacicum*, was part of the school curriculum.[15] Knowledge of the Cossacks was spread in periodicals and pamphlets, accessible to wider circles of urban society than just the council elite, the professors of the Gymnasium and the clergy. The burghers closely followed the ebb and flow of the military campaigns and took a lively interest in the Union of Hadiach. The most important Cossack contributions to the debate, such as the speeches of Jurii Nemyrych to the diet in Warsaw during the Hadiach negotiations, were translated into German and published.[16]

Jurii Nemyrych, who became one of the central spokesmen for a separate Ruthenian identity, had studied at the Arian Academy in Raków and at Leiden university, where some of the Calvinists among the Prussian elite of the late sixteenth and early seventeenth centuries had also acquired their higher academic degrees. Nemyrych was married to the Calvinist Elżbieta Izabella Słupecka, a relative of the Leszczyński family from Great Poland, and attracted the burghers' attention as a spokesman for religious dissidents among the nobility.[17] His defence of religious and political rights for the Arian szlachta ('free citizens in a free republic') echoed the defence of religious freedom in the Protestant city councils of Royal Prussia. Their 'respublica libera' was their city, and their burghers were 'free citizens', although they did not exercise mutual toleration towards their Catholic neighbours, or towards Arians or Polish Brethren. During the 1650s, Nemyrych

---

[14] Helli Koenigsberger has pointed out the problems republics have in attracting loyalty without commanding the authority of strong kingship; 'Republicanism, monarchism and liberty', *Royal and Republican Sovereignty*, pp. 50–1.

[15] Mokrzecki, 'Dyrektor Gimnazjum', p. 75.

[16] *Reden des Georgius Niemierycz, Abgesandter der Zaporovvischen Kozaken vom Großfürstenthumb Reußlandt (13. April 1659) und Stefan Niemieryczen Obr[isten] über der Reuterey, Comm[andant] des Schlosses Krakau und Abgesandter, nach Außländischer Art dienendem Polnischen Kriegs-Heer* (n.p., 1659), in KM E 4° 465, adl. 3.

[17] In 1639–44, Nemyrych defended the Danzig Arians against the city council. The most direct contact between him and the city was the Arian burgher Daniel Zwicker, whom he commissioned in 1650 to draw a map of Polesie; Mokrzecki, *Studium z dziejów*, p. 122; *PSB*, vol. XXII, 811–13.

led a general levy against the Cossacks and Muscovites while trying to regain territories in the East, where he owned – like many of his fellow Ruthenian noblemen – extensive estates. Despite being forced to escape from Khmelnytskyi's troops himself, he became a spokesman for a general amnesty for the Cossack rebels.

Against the background of the shared search for an identity, one of Nemyrych's projects held particular attraction for the Prussian burghers: in his negotiations with the Ruthenian Cossack leader Ivan Vyhovskyi, successor to Khmelnytskyi, Nemyrych was the leading proponent of a project to create a Grand Duchy of Ruś, which was to include the Cossack lands. The Ruthenians were to be represented in the Sejm by their own representatives, and the palatine of Kiev as well as Orthodox bishops were to receive a seat in the Senate. Nemyrych's proposals were based on a view of the Commonwealth as a free association of several nations. The Royal Prussian burghers not only shared this multinational concept of the Commonwealth, but also worked towards a wider definition of citizenship. Nemyrych's plan to give Ruthenian identity political representation and the Prussian burghers' identification with the Commonwealth had in common the claim to full membership in Poland-Lithuania's political system, including Cossacks and non-nobles. The Poles and Lithuanians would be joined by two more nations: Ruthenians and Prussians.[18] Their political language was similar. Both referred to their favourite models of the Netherlands and Switzerland to demonstrate how a confederation was to work.

With his younger brother Stefan, Jurii Nemyrych formulated a speech which he delivered during the April Sejm of 1659, and which appeared in German translation in three editions. It represented the cause of those Cossacks who sought reconciliation with the Commonwealth and the king, and who were aware, like the Prussian burghers, that the Commonwealth alone, of all the states in East Central Europe, could provide the liberties they so jealously defended against centralised government. Full of regret for having served the Muscovites, they returned all the wiser from their experience: 'For several years, we have served this cold monarchy [Muscovy]. It was fatal to look for better government in a foreign land.'[19] As the representative of 'all the Zaporozhian armies and of the entire Ruthenian Nation', Nemyrych implored the king to be a lord over free peoples and nations, so that they could return to the 'crown of Poland as our fatherland and mother':

This is the most special feature of the government of Your Honourable Royal Majesty, that it is known all over the world for its liberty, and thus is similar to divine government . . . but as there is no liberty in the whole world equal to that which can be found in the crown of Poland, we have been born and educated in liberty, ready to risk our lives for it . . . only if our equality as brothers is observed, will other nations imitate our example and bow to Your

---

[18] Sysyn, 'Ukrainian-Polish Relations', p. 63.
[19] *Reden von Niemierycz*, adl. 3.

Majesty's throne to embrace this invaluable jewel . . . thus returns the prodigal son to his father, and the lost sheep return to their watchful shepherd.[20]

It was too late for repentance, for the Commonwealth as much as for the prodigal son. The conciliatory party was defeated by the pro-Muscovite faction, and the crown lost one of its most powerful military instruments. The principal difference between the Royal Prussian burghers and the Cossacks was that the former did not voluntarily abandon the Commonwealth during its existence, even if the fortunes of war did not always make them heroic defenders of their 'mother', the republic, and the king. In contrast to the rebellious Cossacks, however, the Prussian cities in the seventeenth century avoided swearing allegiance to a foreign ruler, except under the duress of occupation, as did Elbing during both Swedish wars and Thorn during the second Northern War. Thus the citizenry of Danzig and Thorn in particular, proud of remaining loyal to the Polish crown even under attack from the Swedes, passed harsh judgement on the Cossack rebels.

During the early 1650s Royal Prussian accounts of the Cossack wars concentrate on three points: the nature and origin of the Cossacks, their relation to the Commonwealth and the causes of their rebellion. Aaron Blivernitz, Lutheran minister to the Polish-speaking community at the church of St George in Thorn, endeavoured to explain why the Cossacks had plunged the Commonwealth into such turmoil.[21] The work starts in a dark mood, very different from earlier historians' articulate and self-confident praise of Poland's ability to safeguard peace and harmony within a war-stricken Europe. Blivernitz deplores the 'terrible war' which had struck Poland after a period of prosperity and calm, while the rest of Europe was embroiled in warfare. He blames it all on the 'barbaric nature' of the Cossacks, who, instead of fulfilling their duties by guarding the freedoms and respecting the public good of the fatherland, involved the whole republic in a murderous struggle. Significantly, Blivernitz repeatedly referred to this conflict as a civil war, whose main players were the 'Cosaci', one of the many nations (*gentes*) that composed the fatherland, the Polish-Lithuanian Commonwealth.[22] For Blivernitz, the Cossacks were not identical with the Ruthenian nation as a whole; rather, they consisted mainly of an ill-behaved rabble and robbing bands.

Deploring the most unjust and devastating nature of civil war, Blivernitz tried to find the causes of this conflict. In reference to the *starshyna*, the elders of the Cossack Host, the author confirmed that the Cossacks, just like Poles or Prussians, had previously participated in the same political culture that valued the freedoms of the Polish szlachta as the central achievement of their political existence. He

---

[20] Ibid.
[21] Aaron Blivernitz, *Dissertatio juridico-politica de Cosacis an satius sit ad finiendum bellum Poloniae civile, rebelles Cosacos Morte prosequi, eosque funditus exstirpare, An vero Arte & perpetuis induciis cum eisdem pacisci ab Aarone Blivernitzio* (Lissa: n.pub, [1653], in Bibl. PAN Gd., Nl 104, adl. 28).
[22] Ibid., folio B.

recognised the tradition of liberty which the elite of the Ruthenian and Cossack nobility shared with the nobility of the other nations of the Commonwealth.[23] The 'Cossack nation of Khmelnytskyi', a splinter-group that descended into violence and revolt, therefore, no longer had anything in common with the political nations of the Commonwealth. As the Cossacks had once been members of the republic, Blivernitz disagreed with the view of Stanisław Albrecht Radziwiłł who saw them as the 'hair that grows on the body of the Commonwealth', which, when grown too long, can be cut.[24] It was this attitude which the Cossacks, especially those not listed on the Commonwealth's payroll, resented so strongly. In contrast, Blivernitz, despite his strong criticism of the Cossack rebellions, granted them a rightful place among the many sons of the republic, as long as they carried out their duties, for which they should be rewarded. By rejecting their role of law-abiding citizens, and by refusing to promote the common cause of liberty, Blivernitz comments, the rebel Cossacks destroyed it; instead of protecting the fatherland, they exposed it to deadly danger. The author associates Khmelnytskyi, whom he considers the root of all evil, with Spartacus, the demagogue who supported the tyranny of the masses, and with the Roman rebel and traitor Sergius Catilina, who in 62 BC plotted to become a tyrant himself: 'Like Catilina [Khmelnytskyi was] the origin of all rebellion, the demagogue, o tempora, o mores! . . . during the incursions of barbarian tribes! Not only do we fight against friends and neighbours in civil wars, but even against our beloved fatherland do we raise our violent hands.'[25]

Reflecting on whether to negotiate with such 'barbarians' or to strike them with terrible punishment, Blivernitz contemplates that the Cossack problem was just part of a more general malaise afflicting the Commonwealth: a dizziness after having tasted too much freedom, the 'sweet wine of peace, freedom and leisure (*otium*)'. As a remedy, Blivernitz recommends the sobriety of ancient liberties and rights, the 'ancient status' restored, an amnesty for the rebels, and the restoration of harmony among the estates. Whoever refused to take his part in this well-ordered society, however, and did not obey its laws, would not belong to a human community. Therefore, where amnesties and good will failed to restore unity, force would have to step in, as 'it is better that the Cossacks perish than we and our good laws'.[26] This was the verdict: the Cossacks, by their own actions, had set themselves apart as enemies of the common fatherland and traitors to their common mother Sarmatia. In reference to the Prussian past, Blivernitz compares the Cossacks to the Teutonic Knights, who were also tempted by greed and power, and were subsequently ejected from Prussia. This fate, he warns, would also befall the Cossacks because of their disregard for common liberties. Had the pagan Prussian ancestors invested their energies, labours and riches better, they might have created a

---

[23] Sysyn, 'Ukrainian-Polish Relations', p. 63.
[24] Hernas, *Barok*, p. 341.
[25] Blivernitz, *Dissertatio juridico-politica*, folio B2v.
[26] Ibid., folio C2.

different government of their own; but as it was, they had wasted their efforts on the 'criminal and pernicious' Teutonic Order.[27] In a similar way, the Cossacks were to be held responsible for the evil actions of their leader Khmelnytskyi.

When discussing such fundamental matters as the survival of the republic and its defence against those who infringed upon its liberties, the Prussian burgher elite of the mid-seventeenth century closed ranks with the central ideal of the Sarmatian political nation: the constitution of an elected monarchy supported by a body of self-governing local assemblies. Such a concept of virtue nobody could infringe with impunity. In his treatise on the *ius indigenatus*, Behm von Behmfeldt formulated this central virtue of the Sarmatian republic: an elected monarch and its republican constitution could not oppress the nations and peoples that joined by their own free will. Therefore, the Cossacks' deeds against a free commonwealth could not have sprung from justice and just grievances, but from perfidy and maliciousness. In 1669, the year Behm composed his treatise, the Cossack leadership had repeatedly demonstrated their desire to break away from the republic; but even after the abortive attempt to achieve a compromise at Hadiach in 1658, Behm still hoped that

under the new star of a benign king who would serve in true faith the cause of Liberty, the Ruthenian and Cossack realms that were severed and separated [from the republic] could be pacified, and by a non-bloody victory good citizens could be created once more out of enemies . . . just as the Prussians, through a sea of blood, were saved from the yoke of the Teutonic Knights.[28]

The harmonious relationship between the Commonwealth and its constituent nations was therefore at the heart of the Prussian burghers' concern, fifteen years after the Cossacks' defection, and two years after the truce of Andrusovo, which assigned left-bank Ukraine and Kiev to Muscovy. Despite his condemnation of the rebellious Cossacks, Behm drew a slightly different conclusion from the example of Cossack disobedience and treason. Once more, the parallel with the rebellious Prussians and the Teutonic yoke was stressed; but Behm did not blame the Cossacks alone for disregarding (like the Teutonic Knights) the common code of liberty and virtue. It was the Polish magistrates (*Aulici et Clerici*) who were responsible, who ruled the Cossacks 'by denying them their ancient freedoms and privileges', just as the Spanish ruled the Dutch by 'subjecting them all to one rule and law: [but they were] jealous of their special privileges and laws of government'. Behm's hint that the Prussian *ius indigenatus* had also been violated many times by the Polish king and his *Aulici et Clerici* is all too clear. He even complains in the next paragraph against the *invidia* and greed of the Poles.[29] In his personal diary he is even blunter, blaming the whole misery of the Cossack, Muscovite and Swedish wars on the malign spirit of the 'Jesuits, Jews and starostas', who put unbearable

[27] Ibid., folio Dv.    [28] Behm, *De Indigenatu*, pp. 2–3.    [29] Ibid., pp. 3–5.

pressures on the Cossacks.[30] Behm's wish that the Cossacks might be reconciled with a reformed Commonwealth that observes its own ideal of granting freedom to its member nations is complemented by his hope that the Prussians might still be restored to the enjoyment of their full laws and immunities, as in the 'former golden age'. The vision held by many Poles of the Commonwealth as a melting pot of many nations' languages and religions, whose diverse conditions must be coerced by one law, moulded and moderated into 'one society',[31] was therefore unacceptable to the Danziger Michael Behm.

The Cossack wars remained a popular topic among Prussian burghers. In 1684, thirty years after the Muscovite invasion which initiated the years of the Muscovite and Swedish deluge, Gottfried Weis, a Lutheran minister in Thorn and a contemporary of Blivernitz and Hartknoch, composed another study of the Cossacks. The focus of his analysis was, however, more historical and aimed at characterising their habits, traditions and origins.[32] Cossacks in the stricter sense, Weis points out, were the inhabitants of the regions on the lower Dnieper and Don rivers, organised in societies and hordes, among whom the Zaporozhian Cossacks were the most prominent. Like Blivernitz and Behm before him, the author seems to have been acutely aware of a peculiar Cossack identity and lifestyle, as he continued to describe their customs and character as 'inhabitants of river deltas', with a 'tendency towards banditry and sedition'.[33] Weis's careful historical work on the origins of the Cossacks demonstrates how Prussian burghers were willing to apply their sense of history as well as their own methods of researching their Prussian origins to the analysis of the history of other peoples in the Commonwealth. In contrast to Blivernitz, Weis emphasised the heterogeneity of the Cossacks rather than their status as a political or national entity. Nevertheless, he still recognised that they were bound together by the 'jealous protection of their liberty and even more of their licence', which was so 'typical of people who tried to advance from a low status in society'.[34] This pejorative connotation of liberty differs considerably from Blivernitz's and Behm's hopeful conclusions that the majority of the Cossacks might be reconciled with the crown and resume a lawful existence in the free Commonwealth.

It is indicative of the growing alienation between Royal Prussian burghers and the Polish crown that stronger sympathy for the Cossack cause only began to emerge in Prussian political and historical writings of the late seventeenth and early eighteenth centuries. The shift appears in the works of Weis and Böhm as early as

---

[30] Michael Behm, 'Diarium et relatio historica gestorum circa Gedanum et alibi in Poloniae durante nupero bello svecico', Bibl. PAN Gd., 755, p. 16.

[31] Konstanty Grzybowski, *Teoria reprezentacji w Polsce epoki odrodzenia* (Warsaw: PWN, 1959), p. 272.

[32] Peter Iaenichius (ed.), *Meletemata Thoruniensia seu Dissertationes varii Argumenti ad historiam maxime Polonicam et Prussicam spectantes*, 4 vols. (Thorn: Johann Nicolai, 1726) vol. II, pp. 149–87; esp. pp. 153–4.

[33] Gottfried Weis, 'Dissertatio de Cosacis', in *Meletemata Thoruniensia*, vol. II, ed. Petrus Iaenichius (Thorn: Johann Nicolai, 1726), pp. 157–9.

[34] Ibid., p. 159.

in the 1680s: both focus not only on the Cossacks' malign nature, but also on the blame deserved by the Poles for their treatment of the Cossacks. Böhm criticised the Poles for enlisting more Cossacks than they were able to finance and support. Thus the Cossacks had some justification for their rebellion, as the Commonwealth had merely given them rights in order to gain their short-term military support. As soon as their services were no longer needed, however, the Poles denied them active citizenship.[35] Böhm, a Prussian burgher who felt protective of the privileges of his city and his province, easily understood why the Cossacks felt betrayed and abused. Gottfried Weis judged the Cossacks reckless and tough fighters, 'in military strength superior to every other nation', an example to the Poles who used them for training their own youth in warfare. For the exploitation of their skills, however, they gained no permanent political, legal or economic status. Although Weis regarded the Cossacks as a disobedient mob, 'collected from the lowest people',[36] he ultimately blamed the Poles for not having disciplined them better. By their incompetent and selfish treatment of the Cossacks, the Poles were no less guilty in causing trouble than the rebels themselves.

Only in the later eighteenth century did Prussian burghers turn their anger more directly against Polish and Catholic domination and sympathise with the Cossack cause. Most seventeenth-century writers from Royal Prussia, however, categorically condemned the role the Cossacks played after 1648. They stressed that there were many disrespectable and politically unfit elements among the Cossacks, incapable of responsible citizenship. The burghers rejected the image which the Cossack leadership tried to convey of themselves as liberators of the Sarmatian-Ruthenian and Orthodox people from Polish, Catholic bondage.[37] Although the Prussian burghers were equally interested in creating their own Prusso–Sarmatian mythology, they never used their historical ideology as a call for armed rebellion against the Polish king and the republic. They were Prussian burghers, not 'a people in bondage', and they certainly had no need for an autocrat. The Prussians' condemnation of the Ruthenian burghers who joined in the rebellions, especially after 1648,[38] is easily explained by their feelings of superiority and pride because of their institutions of self-government, their Kulm law and their representation in the Prussian Diet. But times were becoming tougher. Loyalty, harmony and pride in being citizens of the Commonwealth and the Polish crown underwent another trial when in 1655 the Swedes invaded Royal Prussia once more.

### THE 'SWEDISH DELUGE' AND THE ROYAL PRUSSIAN CITIES

The loss in 1654 of the highly effective Cossack troops could not have come at a worse time. Despite the treaty of Pereiaslav, the Muscovites invaded Lithuania,

---

[35] Böhm, *Commentarius de Interregnis*, p. 46; p. 158.
[36] Weis in *Meletemata*, pp. 184–5.   [37] Sysyn, 'Ukrainian-Polish Relations', p. 71.
[38] Ibid., p. 72; Kumke, *Führer und Geführte* (pp. 32–40, 59, 68), on 'Bürger-Kosaken'.

seeking permanent access to the Baltic, as they had done under Ivan the Terrible. Sweden, recently released from the Thirty Years War, could not view the threat of a Muscovite victory with equanimity. John Casimir's refusal to renounce his claim to the Swedish throne, however, made a Polish-Swedish alliance impossible. Exploiting the Commonwealth's precarious situation, in July 1655 Sweden took most of Royal Prussia and Poland within a few months. In Poland, the *levée en masse* under Krzysztof Opaliński surrendered to the Swedes at Ujście as early as July, and the palatinates of Poznań and Kalisz were declared Swedish protectorates. In August 1655, parts of the Lithuanian nobility, under the leadership of Janusz Radziwiłł, signed a treaty at Kiejdany subjecting the Grand Duchy to Swedish rule and abjuring his allegiance to the Polish crown. While the Cossacks had accepted the tsar as the new protector of their liberties and the Great Polish and the Lithuanian nobility signed alliances with the Swedes, the majority of the Prussian cities declared their loyalty to the Polish king, as long as their firepower and their bulwarks would allow. Thorn and Elbing, however, were occupied by the Swedes at the end of 1655: Thorn was forced to hand over the keys on 5 December, Elbing exactly a week later.[39] Danzig was left a rock in the hostile sea.

Not even the Swedes could have foreseen how rapidly the Commonwealth would collapse under the combined blows from the East and the North. As during the first Swedish wars in the 1620s, the prime goal of Swedish conquest was to gain a stronghold on the Baltic shore of the Commonwealth. From the outset, therefore, Royal Prussia was the main target of Charles X Gustav's campaign. The Swedish king, who had succeeded Queen Christina on the throne in 1654, obviously agreed with Stanisław Albrecht Radziwiłł, who, in the 1630s, had called Royal Prussia 'the throat and neck of the Commonwealth': nobody 'voluntarily has his own throat cut'. This attitude was shared by John Casimir during negotiations with the Swedes early in 1656; the Polish king rejected any suggestion of exchanging Cracow and Thorn for Elbing and Marienburg.[40] But in 1655, it soon became obvious to the distressed Prussian burghers that the Polish nobility was ignoring such advice not only in responding too slowly to the Swedish threat, but in allowing the enemy to cut the Prussian throat by surrendering to the enemy and recognising the new monarch as its protector.

Danzig stood firm, rejecting all offers of neutrality, flattery and favours, such as the confirmation of their privileges by the Swedish king.[41] Danzig not only refused any compromise with the Swedish invaders, but also together with Thorn and Elbing

[39] Jacob Heinrich Zernecke, *Historiae Thoruniensis naufragae tabulae oder Kern der Thornischen Chronicke* (Thorn: Lauzer, 1711), p. 283; Gierszewski, *Elbląg*, p. 147.

[40] Wacław Sobieski, *Der Kampf um die Ostsee*, Schriften des Baltischen Instituts 5, Serie Balticum, ed. Józef Borowik (Leipzig: Markert und Petters, 1933), p. 157; Frost, *After the Deluge*, pp. 76–7.

[41] Wacław Sobieski, 'Za kim opowiadzały się Prusy Królewskie w roku 1655?', in *Pamiętnik V Zjazdu Historyków Polskich w Warszawie, 28.11 – 4.12. 1930* (Lwów: Polskie Towarzystwo Historyczne, 1930), p. 300; Rudolf Damus, 'Der erste nordische Krieg bis zur Schlacht bei Warschau. Aus Danziger Quellen', *Zeitschrift des Westpreußischen Geschichtsvereins* 12 (1884), 25.

(before the Swedish occupation of both cities), refused all cooperation with the Elector of Brandenburg for fear that he might 'avancer la diminution de leur liberté'. They felt that most articles of this alliance would have been 'more for the advantage of the Elector than of the Polish king'.[42] The thesis that the loyalty of Danzig was due to its economic and trade interests continued to predominate in German and partly also in Polish historiography until well into the twentieth century.[43] The memories, still fresh, of the high Swedish tolls levied on the Prussian ports between 1629 and 1635 might explain the refusal by Danzig to exchange Polish for Swedish sovereignty; yet they do not explain Danzig's rejection of neutrality status, proposed for economic reasons by the Dutch, who were later to come to the city's aid by breaking the Swedish blockade in 1656.[44] A purely economic explanation also fails to clarify why Danzig actively resisted Charles Gustav's armies, which cost the city several times the equivalent of the Polish king's pre-war budget: the debts incurred burdened the urban economy well into the eighteenth century.[45]

One of the keys to an understanding of why Danzig refused to desert John Casimir was the city's relationship to Brandenburg-Prussia and the Great Elector, whose strategy was aimed at freeing himself from the vassal status that bound him to the Polish crown. Samuel Pufendorf confirms this intention in his biography of Frederick William: 'The Elector tried to make as much (political) profit from this war as possible.'[46] Although the majority of the Royal Prussian nobility, gathering around the Pomeranian Wejher family, desperately defended their last military strongholds against the Swedish enemy, in December 1655 the Prussian nobles consented to the treaty of Rinsk with Frederick William, which guaranteed them Brandenburg military support against the Swedes on the condition that they garrisoned their main fortresses and towns with Brandenburg troops. The city attracted much criticism from the Prussian nobility for its refusal to join this alliance.[47] Jacob Wejher even suspected unjustly that Danzig had negotiated neutrality with the Swedes: in his words, Danzig had ruined 'the last chance to save the fatherland'.[48] The city defended its reluctance to sign the treaty on the grounds of its empty treasury, its

---

[42] Sobieski, 'Za kim', pp. 297–8; J. R. Godlewski and W. Odyniec, *Pomorze Gdańskie. Koncepcje obrony i militarnego wykonania od wieku XIII do roku 1939* (Warsaw: Wydawnictwo Ministerstwa Obrony Narodowej, 1982), p. 155.

[43] For example, Karl Hans Fuchs, *Danzig im ersten nordischen Krieg, 1. Abschnitt, 1655/6* (Danzig: A. Müller, 1935); Władysław Czapliński, 'Gdańsk Miasto Wierne', *Wiadomości Literackie* 16, no. 31–32 (1939), 9.

[44] Damus, 'Der erste nordische', p. 10. When the Dutch offered to mediate between the city and Sweden, Danzig rejected this suggestion and emphasised its historical links with Poland; see Guernsey Jones, *The Diplomatic Relations between Cromwell and Charles X Gustavus of Sweden*, inaugural dissertation (Lincoln, Nebraska: State Journal Co., 1897); and Frost, *After the Deluge*, p. 71.

[45] Cieślak, *Historia Gdańska*, vol. III, pp. 51–6.

[46] *De Rebus Gestis Friderici Wilhelmi Magni, Electoris Brandenburgici Commentariorum libri novendecim*, 2nd edn (Leipzig and Berlin: Jeremias Schrey et haeredes H.J. Meyeri, 1733), p. 191.

[47] Lengnich, *Geschichte der Lande Preußen*, vol. VII, pp. 138–9.

[48] Janina Łaska, 'Stosunek Gdańska do Elektora Brandenburskiego w początkowym okresie "potopu" Szwedzkiego', *Rocznik Gdański* 27 (1968), 18.

inability to pay Brandenburg garrisons, the usefulness of organising its own urban defence system, and the warning that Frederick William was much more interested in his own gains than in the defence of the royal Polish province.

There was some gratification for Danzig at the news that in January 1656 the Elector, faced with the threat of a Swedish invasion of his duchy, signed the treaty of Königsberg with Charles X, who promised to observe the duchy's neutrality in exchange for Frederick William's recognition of Swedish suzerainty. Danzig's anger about the Elector's policies flared again after the treaty of Labiau of 20 November 1656, by which Charles X recognised Hohenzollern sovereignty over the duchy. Through a treaty with George II Rakoczi of Transylvania, signed in December 1656 at Radnot, Sweden rallied diplomatic support for its plan to partition the Commonwealth between Brandenburg, Transylvania, the Cossacks and Sweden: the Elector was to take Great Poland, while Sweden would receive Royal Prussia.[49] What was widely perceived in Royal Prussia as Frederick William's 'act of betrayal' of his rightful lord and master, the king of Poland, gave Danzig a moral victory. The council, in unison with the two other major cities, insisted that alliance with the Elector of Brandenburg had always threatened the city's liberties. The Prussian nobility admitted that they had been duped. The extent to which the Elector himself acknowledged the constancy of the Danzigers is expressed in Frederick William's remark that 'the Catholics in the city are passionate supporters of the Polish king', but that the Lutherans were also on the Polish side, protecting the riches rescued from Catholic churches all over Royal Prussia, situated in areas now occupied by the Swedes. The political motivation of Danzig's loyalty was even recognised by foreigners. De Lumbres, the French ambassador to John Casimir, considered that the reason for such widespread love of the Polish king and the Commonwealth was 'parce que le gouvernement de ce Royaume est beaucoup plus doux que le leur'.[50]

Was Danzig's insistence on paying for its own defence rather than contributing to the maintenance of the crown army really revealing the city's policy of narrow commercial self-interest and political flirtation with separatist ideas, as historians have repeatedly emphasised?[51] The decision of Danzig to refuse assistance even to her sister-cities, Thorn and Elbing, is not exceptional if one takes into account that the 1655 diets in Prussia and in Poland had called on the palatinates to mobilise defence locally, owing to the emptiness of the royal treasury. Following pressure from the king, the city agreed to volunteer contributions on condition that this money would be reinvested for the defence of the Prussian province and the city itself.[52] There was no difference between the attitudes of noble and urban estates:

[49] Damus, 'Der erste nordische', p. 39; Frost, *After the Deluge*, pp. 79, 84–5.
[50] Sobieski, 'Za kim', p. 298, quoting from de Lumbres's correspondence.
[51] Stanisław Grzybowski, *Jan Zamoyski* (Warsaw: PIW, 1994), p. 88; Fuchs, *Danzig*, p. 7; Józef Bułstawa, 'Toruń w okresie potopu szwedzkiego w latach 1655–1660', M.A. diss., UMK Toruń (1957–8), p. 23.
[52] Damus, 'Der erste nordische', pp. 18, 43.

even before the Deluge, in July 1651, the Prussian nobility defended their right to deploy the noble levy only within the borders of Royal Prussia, and it was agreed that Prussian contributions to the crown treasury were no obligation, but a 'brotherly subsidy'. During the Sejm of 1655, the anger directed against the palatine of Smolensk for losing this important border fortress to the Muscovites followed the same principle that defence obligations were the responsibility of the local commanders and palatines in the name of the entire republic. The Prussian diet argued that 'each palatinate should carry its own defence costs'.[53] Decentralised defence mechanisms and war financing were the norm and made great sense in the extensive Commonwealth, with the relative weakness of its central institutions.

The purely economic line of argument above all ignores the political debate accompanying the decisions of Danzig, Thorn and Elbing to remain loyal to the Polish crown. The wording of Danzig's obstinate rejection of all Swedish attempts to cajole it into surrender disproves the view that the city's connection with the Commonwealth was only based on commercial interest. The city council answered Swedish approaches with the assertion that 'the matter might develop as it will, but they would never surrender the loyalty with which they were obliged and bound to the kingdom of Poland'.[54] There was an even blunter reaction to the delegates of the United Provinces who stressed the inconvenience which this war was causing to the Baltic markets. The burgomasters who received the envoys from the Netherlands pointed out

that it was the city's main objective to maintain the present constitution of the city under the royal Polish government; not to yield in the slightest from affirming the loyalty and obedience it owed to the king of Poland, rejecting all generous proposals by the king of Sweden which aim at neutrality; to this it was not only held by its duty but also its interest in trade, which was best guarded under the protection of the king of Poland.[55]

Although the city fathers admitted that commercial motives were involved, the next section of their reply suggests that Danzig had a firm conception of the importance of the Commonwealth's political system for the greater good of their urban lifestyle. Any interference with the city's status quo by a power whose government could 'diminish its liberties', and those of the province, was clearly rejected:

For a better understanding, they pointed to the difference between the Polish and the Swedish governments, as under the former the city would not be burdened by custom duties and taxes except those that they had agreed to, while the king of Sweden, on the contrary,

---

[53] APGd, Nucleus Lengnicha, 300.29 no. 238, vol. 69, pp. 8–12, and vol. 70, pp. 113 f; on Smolensk, see APGd, Recesy 300.29, no. 142, pp. 236, 238.
[54] Pufendorf, *Thaten Carl Gustavs*, vol. I, p. 103.
[55] Lengnich, *Geschichte der Lande*, vol. VII, p. 171.

was known for acting arbitrarily, which would be highly detrimental for commerce and trade. Therefore, anything must be avoided that would evoke the slightest impression of their making concessions to the Swedish king.[56]

The political raison d'être for the Danzig burghers was the preservation of all their privileges which secured their general well-being. The city was fighting for a Commonwealth which guaranteed the liberties of more than just its noble citizens. To emphasise that this was the case, the cities repeatedly demanded a share in the political process: 'On the issue of continuing the anti-Swedish alliance, the Danzigers insisted that the deputies [from this province] should strongly urge the Sejm that they not only be represented at all times, but directly involved in the delegations, to watch over the interests of the cities in all matters which concern them, and not to act without their knowledge, *ex rationibis allegatis.*'[57]

Similar considerations motivated Thorn and Elbing, despite the early surrender of both cities to the Swedes. Although historians of Thorn in retrospect tried to justify the city's capitulation to the Swedes in 1655 by pointing to the enemy's great military power and the opinion that the city could have defended itself without assistance for a mere two weeks,[58] research has shown not only that supplies were adequate for a much longer resistance, but that the resolve of the majority of the city council to withstand a Swedish siege was quite strong. What broke the will to defend the fortress was the insistence of the nobility who had sought refuge in the city with their moveable riches and belongings, and who hoped to preserve their property by surrendering to Charles Gustav. Ironically, one of the first measures of the occupying Swedes in Thorn was to confiscate noble property.

Polish historians have sometimes commented on the 'strange' fact that the Polish szlachta argued for capitulation, while the 'German burghers' insisted on defending their city. This only seems unusual when we apply a nineteenth-century definition of ethnicity, which did not figure in the idea of citizenship and political loyalty nurtured by the Thorn burghers.[59] As in Danzig, political and moral arguments clearly dominated the debate between the council and the nobility in the city, and even historical issues occupied a prominent place. The incorporation of 1454, the act of rebellion against the Teutonic Knights and the subjection to the Polish crown were used to justify vital political decisions. The city fathers repeatedly affirmed that no other king could undermine their allegiance to their rightful master: 'Since they had sworn to be faithful to the kings of Poland *per privilegium incorporationis de Anno 1454*, they wanted to clear their tender conscience and resolve to remain loyal to Your Royal Majesty John Casimir unto death.' Therefore, the city had prepared everything and invested great sums and efforts 'for a

[56] Ibid., pp. 171–2.
[57] APGd, Recesy 300. 29, no. 136, folios 26v–27, 'Marienburg, Ante-Comitialis 5.1.1652'.
[58] Jacob Heinrich Zernecke, *Das bey denen Schwedischen Kriegen Bekriegte Thorn*, 2nd edn (Berlin: A. Haude, 1727), pp. 19, 46.
[59] Buława, 'Toruń w okresie', p. 23.

good resistance and heroic defence'.[60] The Thorn council was acutely aware that to pay Swedish contributions would be at least as costly and devastating as to resist them. Having to choose between the frying pan and the fire, they opted for what was sacrosanct to them: loyalty to their rightful king.

The conflict between the city council of Thorn and the noble refugees soon sharpened. The supporters of capitulation to the Swedes were led by nobles from the palatinate of Brześć-Kujawski, among whom were several followers of the disgraced vice-chancellor and primate Radziejowski, as well as the treasurer of Pomerania, Michał Trczyński. The patricians, contemptuous of the 'traitor Radziejowski', who had arrived with his troops as an ally of the Swedes in the Thorn suburbs, insisted that 'it is not the king who has left the republic, but the republic which has left the king'.[61] But as the prospect of relief from Poland, the Holy Roman Empire or Brandenburg became bleaker every day, the general atmosphere in the city turned in favour of surrender. The Prussian noble senators in the city, in remarkable contrast to the city council's attitude towards the Polish crown, argued that any obligations of loyalty were 'nullified by the flight of John Casimir'. In fact the council swore allegiance to Charles Gustav only after the burghers of Thorn had received false reports of John Casimir's abdication,[62] in order to soothe their conscience.

The idea that parts of the Polish and Lithuanian nobility, but not the Prussian burghers of Danzig, had betrayed their lawful king and crown, was central to the idea portrayed later by Hartknoch and numerous other writers that Royal Prussia's burghers were better Sarmatian citizens of the Commonwealth than the nobility. Danzig's boastful celebration of the city's resistance to Brandenburg and Swedish temptation, making it the only major bastion in the North to have held out against the enemies, reached its peak during and after the peace negotiations at Oliwa in 1660. Already in 1656, a representative of Danzig's third estate, the brewer Elias Schröder von Trewen, had anonymously published an allegorical treatise magnifying Danzig's glorious role in the war and condemning the betrayal of the other two major cities, as well as parts of the nobility to the Swedes. He interpreted a dream concerning a widow (Royal Prussia), whose three daughters (Danzig, Thorn and Elbing) were approached by a match-maker (primate Radziejowski) to be married to a splendid knight (Charles Gustav of Sweden): while the two older sisters fall for the knight, the youngest (Danzig) refuses the match, although her brother (the Prussian nobility) and her mother's brother-in-law (the Elector of Brandenburg) try to talk her into accepting it. Danzig, however, the disobedient youngest daughter, even considers suicide rather than accept wedlock with the Swede.[63] This satire was directed both against parts of the Polish-Lithuanian nobility and against the Elector of Brandenburg, and foreshadowed anti-Hohenzollern political litera-

[60] Zernecke, *Das bekriegte Thorn*, pp. 32–3, 19.     [61] Ibid., p. 33.
[62] Ibid., pp. 32, 49; Dworzaczkowa, 'Panegyricus Carolo Gustavo', p. 98.
[63] 'Preußisches Haanen-Geschrey Anno 1656', Bibl. PAN Gd., 672, pp. 32ff.

ture of a later date. His treatise, Schröder admitted, was intended to 'defend the glory of this city, its loyalty and constancy on the side of His Majesty the king and the crown of Poland, while . . . alluding to the goals and intentions of our enemies'.[64]

The Leitmotif of *libertas*, threatened by both the Swedes and the Elector of Brandenburg, was to be fundamental to all subsequent panegyrical literature produced in Danzig between 1657 and 1660. In 1659, after the reconquest of Thorn by Polish and imperial troops under crown field hetman Jerzy Lubomirski and the general of the Austrian forces, Raimondo Montecuccoli, a satirical verse produced in Danzig accused Thorn of neglecting its duty to preserve the common ancient liberty:

Three cities are in the lands of Prussia/ and they are called the largest/ of whose strength and power Poland's enemies used to shy away/ such is Thorn, strong as a border-fortress/ on which one used to rely/ but as it has recently kept an open door, it lets in all who come before it/ and although Elbing was also very firm/ it nevertheless ceded to flattery./ Only Dantzig is the strongest pillar/ the power and benefactor of Prussia/ . . . the reason is her courage/ which she proved many times/ when she fought for freedom and justice/ despite losing many a soldier./ But it is better to choose death than a dishonourable life.[65]

Behind the florid rhetoric of martyrdom was a serious political concern which had already surfaced during the negotiations with the rest of the Royal Prussian estates before the Rinsk agreement. The fact that Danzig, as well as other Protestant-dominated Royal Prussian cities, were seen – without justification – as easy prey for the Lutheran propaganda of the Swedish aggressor, motivated the city fathers to put particular emphasis on their loyalty to the Commonwealth and the Polish crown. Nineteenth-century nationalist historians like Treitschke and Droysen have made much of the supposed cultural alienation of the Lutheran cities from the Catholic Polish environment. But Lutheranism was not a sufficient motivation for the Prussian burghers to welcome their Swedish co-religionists in their province. Samuel Pufendorf, in his biography of Charles X Gustav, observed that it was the Lutheran ministers who 'made the Swedes hated among the population'.[66] The pastor at St Mary's, Eberhard Müller, spoke openly about the 'present Swedish slavery',[67] and continued to stir public unrest although he had been given several warnings by the Swedish authorities. Far from urging the Danzigers to make common cause with the Lutheran Swedes, the city's pastors put their faith in their age-old immunities, which included the free exercise of their religion, rather than

---

[64] Response by an anonymous author, 'Echo zu dem Preußischen Haanen-Geschrey', Bibl. PAN Gd., 672, folios 156–161v; Otto Günther, 'Zwei Miscellen zur Danziger Buchdrucker- und Literaturgeschichte im 17. Jahrhundert', *Zeitschrift des Westpreußischen Geschichtsvereins* 38 (1898), 158.

[65] Bibl. Czart. 1883, 'Wiersze XVII wieku, Ein heimlich Pasquill darinnen die Dantzker der beyden Städte Thorn und Elbing ihr Wappen durchziehen und ihr eigeneß hochheben', p. 116.

[66] Pufendorf, *Thaten Carl Gustavs*, p. 103.

[67] Ernst Kestner, 'Aus Thorns Schwedenzeit', *Beiträge zur Geschichte der Stadt Thorn* 9 (1882), 207.

switching allegiance to foreign rulers notorious for ignoring the liberties of their own subjects.

The Danzigers' bitterness over the disloyalty of so many members of the Commonwealth also explains their great sympathy for the war hero Lubomirski, who was impeached in 1664 for opposing an election *vivente rege*. In contrast, Radziejowski, former vice chancellor and chief collaborator, had been pardoned, reinstated and appointed ambassador to Turkey.[68] Moreover, anti-Protestant agitation gathered pace after 1655. Behm von Behmfeldt, although himself a convert to Catholicism, formulated his concern about Polish Catholic opinion and attitudes towards Danzig in his diary of 1656. With abhorrence he refers to John Casimir's famous oath at Lwów, which declared the Virgin Mary queen of Poland, de facto denouncing all non-Catholics enemies of the fatherland. He was extremely worried about the Lwów confederates' propaganda, which proclaimed the intention to 'eradicate all heretics, especially the Jews and the Scots, and the Protestants – considered to make common cause with the Swedes – and to kill anyone who does not want to join their confederation'. Behm explained that it was 'only because they worry that Danzig would be so upset about the expulsion of all enemies of the Roman Church, that the king passed a declaration to confirm the city's rights'.[69] Not all was well in the relationship between Danzig, the king and the republic, even after this great test of loyalty.

Public displays of loyalty to the Polish king, before, during or after the Swedish invasion, also had their less spectacular side. Rather than polemics, propaganda and panegyrical literature, it was the less ostentatious actions within urban society which demonstrated the spirit ruling in the cities during the Deluge. In Danzig, during the year 1657, the crime register mentions that the city council condemned a burgher, Heinrich Möller, to three years imprisonment for 'correspondence with the enemy'.[70] In Thorn, the council not only defended the Benedictine nuns whom the Swedes wanted to expel from the city after destroying their convent (although it did not try to prevent the Jesuits being expelled), but also a fisherman, Stanisław Cygan, whom the Swedish commander wanted tried for spying and sending messages to the Polish troops besieging the city in 1658, particularly one addressed to John Casimir.[71] The city council prevented the spy's execution and even secured his release with the argument that he was a simpleton who was not aware of his actions. Even under Swedish occupation, the burghers of Thorn proudly continued to celebrate the annual jubilee of their successful defence against the Swedish general Wrangel in 1629.[72] The assertion by the Swedish commander Bülow that

[68] Lengnich, Geschichte der Lande, vol. VII, preface; APGd., Nucleus Lengnicha 300.38, p. 75; Recesy, vol. 90, p. 41.    [69] Bibl. PAN Gd., Uph. fol. 104, folio 9v.

[70] 'Sententiae Criminales Nobilis Judicii Gedanensis Civitatis Primariae ab anno 1558 usque 1690', APGd., Bibl. Archivi 300.R, U 3, folio 43.

[71] BułTawa, 'Toruń w okresie', p. 43.

[72] Bogusław Dybaś, 'Dzieje wojskowe Torunia', in *Historia Torunia*, vol. II, p. 159.

not even Stockholm was as loyal to the Swedish king as Thorn was between 1655 and 1658 seems to be no more than propaganda, considering the numerous complaints by the same commander about acts of disobedience, the failure to pay contribution to his soldiers by the council and population, and a persistent passive resistance in various areas of urban life.[73]

When in Thorn the Swedish commander complained to the burgomasters that the population was insolent and did not pay their dues or turn up for their guard duties, the presiding burgomaster Johannes Preuß answered that he could not command urban civilians like soldiers. The quartermaster of the Marienquartier, Nicolaus Scholz, boldly stated that 'only the servants still do their duties as night guards . . . the burghers send their excuses, that they are no killers'.[74] In the ordinance of 1658, passed by the Swedes in Thorn to organise a more effective control of the burghers' guard duties, Bülow decreed that 'all foreigners present in the city, *sub certa poena*, have to be registered (with the occupation forces) every evening'.[75] In particular the 'Poles here resident should be expelled from the city'. The council refused to comply with this order, 'for Christian sympathy', and because many of them were needed for work on the landed estates belonging to the city, as well as other tasks. The expulsion would furthermore create great confusion and upset the whole structure of the city, as many newcomers from outside Thorn and the Prussian province were employees of the city and servants of the burgomasters. The council would only consent to expel particular suspect individuals, to be named in each case by the Swedes or other burghers, if they imperilled the peace within the city.[76] It was the Swedish occupation force, not the city council, that mistrusted them and saw 'the Poles' as adversaries.

Elbing had been the only major city in the first Swedish wars of the 1620s to be occupied by the Swedes, which made it one of the most despised cities in the Commonwealth in the eyes of the noble estates.[77] In 1626, the traditional solidarity of the three cities had been seriously breached, as Danzig used Elbing's surrender to the Swedes to gain economic advantages and to deprive its sister-city of the right to be the keeper of the Prussian seal. The propaganda war was supported by a Swedish-financed printing press established in the city.[78] A Lutheran minister from Elbing, Balthasar Voidius, himself only a recent immigrant to the city from Saxony, expressed his pro-Swedish view in a panegyric published in Elbing after

---

[73] Kestner, 'Thorns Schwedenzeit', p. 205.
[74] Ibid., pp. 205, 208. The situation in the city, filled with ailing soldiers who lacked food and other necessities, became so terrible in 1658 that the council demanded that the Swedes surrender.
[75] 'Ordinantz bey der Bürgerschafft betreffende', in 'Acta Consularia', APT Kat. II, II.5, folios 66–67 (26.3.1658).
[76] Ibid., folios 78–78v.
[77] Lengnich, *Geschichte der Lande*, vol. VII, p. 257.
[78] Norbert Drabiński, 'Z dziejów okupacji szwedzkiej Elbląga w latach 1626–1635', *Rocznik Elbląski* 2 (1963), 150–2; and Böhme, *Die schwedische Besetzung*, pp. 21–2.

Gustav Adolf's death in 1633: 'The beautiful cities of the German nation deplore your death, which has deprived them of the powerful patron of their privileges.'[79] But Voidius was not a typical representative of the atmosphere in the city as a whole, where a prolific production of pro- and anti-Swedish polemical treatises and pamphlets ensued. Subsequently, however, this chapter in the city's history caused a lot of embarrassment and regret.

As early as in 1626, the Elbing burgomaster and poet laureate Friedrich Zamehl addressed his personal apology for the city's behaviour to what was obviously a pro-Royal Prussian and Polish audience, and in particular to Danzig, whose satirical literature against her treacherous sisters had done nothing to relieve the Elbingers from their predicament. Zamehl denied that falsehood or any conspiracy had motivated Elbing to open its gates to the Swedes, but mere force, the burning of its suburbs, the killing, violence and the failing strength of the city walls.[80] No help was forthcoming from the Duchy of Prussia, in which the Elbingers had misguidedly put their faith – an important motive for the rejection of the treaty with Brandenburg in 1655, and the burghers were generally demoralised by previous exactions, contributions and plundering by all armies, including Polish forces.[81] This gives at least a hint that the infringement upon the city's liberties and immunities by its own royal protector had weakened the spirit which had connected the city with Poland in previous times.

In 1655, an anonymous author from Elbing explained, if not defended, the city's latest surrender to the Swedes despite letters from the king and Danzig urging it to hold out. The writer of the imaginary 'Dialogue Concerning the Surrender of Elbing to the Swedes in 1655' argues that the Swedes were invited into the city by a handful of traitors against the will of the majority of the population and the city council. He accuses Lutheran Swedish spies among the city's clergy of having whipped up opinion against the more moderate, possibly even Calvinist citizens and ministers, and having turned the general attitude against the (Calvinist) Elector of Brandenburg. Daniel, an imaginary burgher from Danzig, expresses his sympathy but stresses that 'for my Danzigers and all other pro-Polish followers, the Elbingers are still on the black list: they bear a blemish which they will not be able to extinguish so easily'. His equally fictitious friend from Thorn, called Elias, then points at the Polish and Prussian nobility who themselves 'in a majority came crawling for Swedish Slavaguardia [*sic*!]', after waiting in vain for support troops from Poland.[82] Another apologetic pamphlet talks of Elbing's great regret at having

---

[79] Balthasar Voidé, *Erst-Jährliche Klag- und Ehren-Gedechtnis/ des Aller Durchleuchtigsten/ Hochgeborenen Fürsten/ Großmechtigsten Herren/ und glorwürdigsten Heldens von Mitternacht Gustavi Adolphi des anderen* (Elbing: Bodenhausen, 1633).

[80] 'Apologia Elbingensium Civitatis qua docet eadem, quas causas habuerit anno 1626 XV. Julii Sveciae Regi Gustavo Adolpho deditionem urbis suae faciendi, autore Frid[erico] Zamelio Co[nsuli]. Elbing[ensi]', APGd, Rkps. Elbl. 369.1, no. 856, pp. 661–80.    [81] Ibid., pp. 664–5.

[82] 'Ein Gespräch von der Übergabe der Stat [sic] Elbing an die Schweden a[nno] 1655', APGd, Rkps. Elbl. 369.1, no. 856, p. 848.

lost its 'virginity' to the Swedes – unwillingly and as a result of rape and assault: 'Upon reflection one must admit/ that surrender to violence does not bring shame/ who wants to call her a whore who lost her virginity to the force of Bellona [the goddess of war]?'[83] There was also general agreement that Lutheran propaganda was successful in the city, which until recently had been ruled by a city government with many Calvinists on its council.[84] This demonstrates that the vicissitudes of confessional strife complicated the situation further: the decision was not simply of loyalty to the rightful king and crown, but also to one's religion – it was not a choice between Polish Catholics and German Lutherans, but between Prussian Calvinists and Prussian Lutherans.

The pressure under which Elbing, after two defections, found itself, was considerable. Pamphlets all over Poland pronounced the city a traitor of the common cause: 'From a fortress to a prostitute, so changed Elbing, not a member of Prussia, but a scandal, to everyone's amazement and abomination.'[85] For several years after the peace of Oliwa, the city tried to defend its continued presence in the Prussian Diet – paradoxically denied by the same Prussian nobles who had themselves advocated the surrender of Thorn in 1655. As a result of the negotiations and the treaty of Wehlau (Welawa) between the Elector of Brandenburg and John Casimir in September 1657, by which the Elector renewed his military support for the Polish king, Elbing was assigned to Frederick William as a pawn for the sum of 400,000 Talers in order to compensate him for his military expenses in the war against Sweden. The insecurity over Elbing's future as part of the Commonwealth added to Elbing's degradation. There is no reason to doubt, however, that the Elbing patriciate longed for the restoration of its former relationship with the Polish-Lithuanian Commonwealth: the king had forgiven them, they argued in the Prussian Diet, therefore the republic, including the whole of Royal Prussia, must do the same.[86] Only after 1661, during the subsequent debate over the right of the 'traitor-city' to sit 'among patriots', Danzig resumed her defence of Elbing in the Prussian Diet, relying on her increased authority derived from her war record.[87] As events discussed in the following chapter will show, however, Elbing remained politically the weakest of the three major cities after the Second Northern War and could no longer count on the strong solidarity of the Prussian, Polish and Lithuanian estates.

A sign that the cohesion of the Prussian estates was in part successfully restored, however, was the unanimity with which the Prussian senate declined to bear the

---

[83] 'Historische Lieder, mitgeteilt von Max Toeppen', *Zeitschrift des Westpreußischen Geschichtsvereins* 39 (1899), 168.

[84] Ibid., pp. 169–70.

[85] 'Elogium Civitatis Elbingensis de Sueticis Armis detortis A. 1655', Bibl. Czart., Teki Naruszewica, 148, p. 1077.

[86] Jan Gerlach, 'Elbląg – strażnikiem pieczęci Prus Królewskich 1503–1772', *Rocznik Elbląski* 2 (1963), 124–5.

[87] Achremczyk, *Życie*, pp. 84–5; and Lengnich, *Geschichte der Lande*, vol. VII, pp. 278–82.

great tax burden requested by the king for the continuation of the Muscovite and Tartar wars in the 1660s. The main rallying point was the rejection of the poll tax that the Polish Sejm tried to extend to the province of Royal Prussia. Appealing in the Sejm of 1662 to the king to observe their ancient privileges of self-government and voluntary taxation, the Prussian senators and noble deputies declared their solidarity with Danzig's refusal to pay more tax: 'one must not yield one inch from ancient custom in order to pass a tax without the cities' consent'.[88] The treasurer of Pomerania approvingly declared: 'The character of (Royal) Prussian cities is very different from that of Polish cities, because the former have a seat and vote in the Prussian Diet and refuse to give up their customs and privileges, nor do they consent to anything detrimental to their freedoms.'[89] The Pomeranian senator was contradicted by the chancellor of the crown, Mikołaj Prażmowski, who insisted that 'the Danzigers, who had not abandoned the crown during the most dangerous times, would certainly not now refuse to help in such a difficult period'.[90] 'Sarmatian Prussia' had proved to be one of the truest sons of the common fatherland, and the Danzigers had passed the test of loyalty with flying colours. The principle upon which this loyalty relied was the mutual agreement that the city's liberties would not be diminished but maintained or even enhanced; but in exchange, Danzig had to share her wealth and the fruits of her prosperity for the common good of the whole republic.

The perception of this mutuality was the key to the Prussian cities' sense of belonging to the Commonwealth. Conrad Thamnitius, a professional panegyricist, who was commissioned in 1651 to praise Thorn's *constantia* in the first Swedish wars, returned to the question of liberty from a European perspective: even in the most liberal hereditary realm, liberty was doomed to decline. Only under a freely elected king did such liberty persist: 'where the virtues and not the persons follow each other in government'. Thamnitius had confidence that Thorn, as the northern gate to the centre and heart of Poland, would show sufficient virtue and strength to defend the Sarmatian lands (and its freely elected monarchy) against the 'Gothic lion'.[91] When destruction and defeat seem near, loyalty could only be sustained by the virtue of the citizens; lack of constancy and faithfulness, courage and persistence, must therefore be a greater enemy than hostile armies.[92] Loyalty had to face death and martyrdom: it would necessarily enhance the fame and reputation of the city and the province within the whole Commonwealth. Such a parade of virtues followed classical patterns of republican ideology and was strongly influenced by the popular anti-Machiavellian doctrine that the citizens, and not the ruler, were

[88] Quote by the Pomeranian treasurer, Jan Gniński, in Lengnich, ibid., pp. 290–91.
[89] Ibid., p. 291.
[90] Ibid., p. 290.
[91] *De Constantia Thoruniensium in obsidione probata oratio* (Thorn: Karnall, 1651), folio F3-F4. Thorn is depicted as the shield of Poland, which, if Thorn fails to do its duty, must face its enemies bare-breasted (folio P).
[92] Ibid., H4-I.

the true defenders of peace and the common good.[93] A similar pamphlet was produced in 1699 for the city of Konitz (Chojnice), by the Thorn professor Martin Böhm. Praising the traditional persistence of Konitz, first as member of the state of the Teutonic Knights and then under the Polish crown, Böhm stresses the city's uncompromising dedication to the defence of its lords and masters in both cases, even for the price of annihilation.[94]

Although the reality of war diplomacy looked rather different, such serious efforts of political rhetoric indicate that the self-confidence and the internal bonds of the Commonwealth were in need of restoration – particularly in its border provinces. It was the Polish royal secretary and court historian Joachim Pastorius who tackled the task of repairing Thorn's scratched reputation.[95] After the city's reconquest by Polish, Lithuanian and Austrian troops in December 1658, Pastorius appealed to the king to show his most gracious clemency, on the basis of the city's heroic record during the 1620s and its share in the great tradition of liberty.[96] Evoking the glory of Sarmatian courage and military virtue, his treatise on the liberation of Thorn from the Swedes fulfilled several functions, but it was primarily meant as a short analysis of the state of the Commonwealth after the Deluge, as well as an appeal for national reconciliation.

Significantly, Pastorius returned to a topic which had been so close to the hearts and minds of the Prussian burghers before the Swedish invasions: the Cossacks. The author compares the city of Thorn with this other unfaithful element of the crown, showing how a group among the Cossack leadership remorsefully returned, convinced by the force of liberty: 'The best *vinculum* for our subjects' souls is liberty.'[97] Pastorius warned, however, that liberty only worked when exercised with moderation: as the Cossack case showed, excessive liberty was easily perverted into pernicious licence.[98] Unlike the Cossacks, however, Pastorius argued, Thorn was forced by sheer military power to cede to the Swedes, while among its citizens there were many who kept their faith in the Polish king and tried to sabotage the occupation. Thorn, as the first among the Prussian cities, must be trusted again; it must be given back the full range of its former freedoms and privileges, and be recognised as a major centre of Poland's economic prosperity. Pastorius concludes the treatise with an appeal to the king to reinvigorate the virtues of the republic and to provide a stable, protective, but liberal roof over its many nations and free

[93] Koenigsberger, 'Schlußbetrachtung', *Republiken und Republikanismus*, pp. 287–8.

[94] *Q.D.B.V. Constantiam Choineciae ordinis Equitum Teutonicorum Mariano variis bellis robatam sub praesidio D[omini] M[agistri] Martini Böhm, publice exponit Simon A. Poltzin Chonecensis* (Thorn: Nicolai, 1699).

[95] Petrus Titius, the Danzig professor and poet laureate at the Gymnasium, called Joachim Pastorius 'dignissimus olim noster Pastorius'; *Jacobi Augusti Thuani Voluminum Historicorum Recensio* (Danzig: Rhetiana, 1685), p. 25.

[96] J. Pastorius, *In Obsessum a se & feliciter recuperatum Thorunium ingressu* (Thorn: Karnall, 1659), pp. 661–2, 670; see also Frost, *After the Deluge*, pp. 152–67.

[97] Pastorius, *In Obsessum*, p. 696.

[98] Ibid., pp. 682, 697.

citizens, under which the burghers of Thorn, and the province of Royal Prussia, had always found a home.

The cities felt the consequences of the Swedish–Polish war for decades. Trade and commerce recovered only slowly, and the Commonwealth had lost much of its international prestige. The peace of Oliwa, in particular, had changed the balance of power in central Europe and had made Poland-Lithuania politically more dependent on its neighbours. The next chapter will therefore look beyond the Polish-Lithuanian borders to Ducal Prussia, a state whose growing self-confidence gave Royal Prussia reason for increasing concern. Although the historical unity of the Prussian lands was still a matter of interest to historians and politicians on both sides of the divide, the actual political and legislative cooperation between Ducal and Royal Prussia had ceased in the second half of the sixteenth century. Yet it was only in the late seventeenth and early eighteenth centuries that the ambitions of the Hohenzollern dynasty created a different and powerful Prussian identity which seriously challenged the historical and political foundations of Prussia's allegiance to the Commonwealth.

# 7

# Divergence: the construction of rival Prussian identities

The common man cannot grasp the nature of kingship. But through things which touch his senses, especially eyesight, he attains a vague idea of its power. This shows that a luxurious court and its ceremonies are far from superfluous or worthy of reproach. (Christian Wolff)[1]

On 18 January 1701 Frederick III, Elector of Brandenburg (1688–1713), crowned himself and his wife, Sophie Charlotte of Hanover, King and Queen in Prussia. Impressed by the sumptuous coronation festivities in Königsberg, Lord Plantamour, the English envoy to Berlin, described the event in great detail:

The coronation ceremony was conducted in a magnificence that went beyond anything one might have imagined . . . Around ten o'clock, the Elector left his chambers, the sceptre in his hand, and the crown on his head, which he had placed there himself. His royal gown was held by the great chamberlain, the Count of Dhona and the young Count Denhoff . . . Walking ahead [of the Elector] were the first officers of Prussia, the Chancellor with the Seals, the Grand Maître with the Globe and the Burgrave or Supreme Judge with the Sword.[2]

Obviously revelling in the splendour of the festivities, Plantamour's sharp sense of observation still caught the unusual circumstances of this event. Here a prince of the Empire dared to elevate himself above other imperial princes on the ground that parts of his patrimonial territories were situated beyond imperial borders. Having been anointed king by his Calvinist court preacher, as well as a Lutheran minister, in order to please his Lutheran estates and subjects, Frederick found that recognition for his new monarchy was not forthcoming as swiftly as he had wished. How protective he was of his royal status is reflected in Plantamour's comment that

[1] Christian Wolff, quoted in Peter Baumgart, 'Der Hof der Barockzeit als politische Institution', in Buck, August, Kauffmann, Gerhard, Spahr, Blake Lee and Wiedemann, Conrad (eds.), *Europäische Hofkultur im 16. und 17. Jahrhundert. Vorträge und Referate des Wolfenbütteler Arbeitskreises für Renaissanceforschung vom 4.–8. 9. 1979*, Wolfenbütteler Arbeiten zur Barockforschung 8 (Hamburg: Hauswedell, 1981), p. 33.
[2] 'Letters from Lord Plantamour, envoy to Berlin . . . to Blathwayt' (1701), British Library, Egerton Manuscripts 2428, pp. 19–19v.

'from the day of the coronation, one was forced to speak exclusively of "king and queen", of "the royal prince and majesty"; if the word "Elector" escaped anyone's lips, this person was fined one Ducat for the benefit of the poor'.[3] The sermon chosen for the occasion also mirrored Frederick's eagerness to be received in the circle of European monarchs: 'Who honours me, I shall honour in return' certainly alluded to the fact that the king of Poland and the monarchs of Denmark and Britain still refused to recognise the Prussian crown, and that the Emperor himself had only grudgingly consented to this act in return for Brandenburg's political and military support.

What had emboldened the duke of Prussia – whose ancestors had until recently been vassals of the Polish crown – to take this step, which would forever change the nature of Prussia's position in Europe? In 1618, the Polish Sejm had agreed to the transfer of hereditary succession in the Duchy of Prussia to the Brandenburg line of the Hohenzollern dynasty. This decision was the vital precondition for the decisive break between Poland-Lithuania and its fief, in 1657, when Frederick William, Frederick III's father, negotiated the sovereign possession of the Duchy in return for changing sides in the Second Northern War. Although the later success story of the Hohenzollern dynasty in Prussia was by no means a foregone conclusion, even contemporary observers of the treaties of Wehlau and Bromberg could not overlook the great potential which sovereign government in Ducal Prussia offered to an imaginative and determined ruler. Power in Prussia was not only unrestricted by imperial institutions and influence, which still limited Brandenburg's policies more often than has usually been acknowledged;[4] in 1657 ducal government was also liberated from the dependency on a suzerain who in the past had regularly interfered with domestic and foreign policy matters.[5]

Frederick III, frequently maligned as his father's unworthy successor, skilfully exploited the new situation for his dynasty. Acquiring royal status was the latest fashion.[6] Several of Brandenburg's rivals within the Empire obtained foreign crowns or at least the prospect of acquiring one in this period: Frederick August of Saxony was elected king of Poland 1697, and the elector of Bavaria entertained

---

[3] Ibid., p. 13v.
[4] For a revision of the older interpretation of 'absolutism', see Neugebauer, *Politischer Wandel im Osten*, esp. chapters 1–2; Edgar Melton, 'The Prussian Junkers, 1600–1786', in Scott, Hamish M. (ed.), *The European Nobilities in the Seventeenth and Eighteenth Centuries*, 2 vols., vol. II: *Northern, Central and Eastern Europe* (London and New York: Longman, 1995), pp. 71–109; Karin Friedrich, 'Facing Both Ways: New Works on Prussia and Polish-Prussian Relations', *German History* 15 (1997), 256–67.
[5] Barbara Janiszewska-Mincer and Franciszek Mincer, *Rzeczpospolita Polska a Prusy Książęce w latach 1598–1621* (Warsaw: PWN, 1988); Anna Kamińska, *Brandenburg-Prussia and Poland* (Marburg: Herder-Institut, 1983), pp. 9–18; Kazimierz Lepszy, *Prusy Książęce a Polska w latach 1576–1678* (Cieszyn: Drukarnia Dziedzictwa, 1932); Barbara Janiszewska-Mincer, *Stosunki Polsko-Niemieckie w latach 1515–1772* (Bydgoszcz: Wydawnictwo Udzielniale WSP, 1997), pp.147–58.
[6] Christoph H. Gütthern, *Leben und Thaten Herrn Friederichs des Ersten Königes in Preußen, Markgrafen zu Brandenburg, des Heiligen Römischen Reichs Erzkämmerer und Churfürsten* (Breslau: Johann J. Korn, 1750), p. 126; Reinhold Koser, 'Das Jubiläum der preußischen Königskrone', *Hohenzollern-Jahrbuch* 4 (1900), 2ff.

well-founded hopes of acquiring the Spanish crown before his unexpected death in 1699. The 1701 Act of Settlement gave the Hanoverian dynasty real prospect of the British crown. The grand duke of Tuscany assumed the title 'royal highness', as had the duke of Savoy, while the duke of Lorraine nurtured hopes of winning the crown of Armenia.[7] The Hohenzollerns were the only dynasty which did not gain an inherently foreign crown, since Ducal Prussia was considered, if not part of the Empire, at least connected to German historical tradition, culture and language, with a majority of its population originating from the German lands. With hindsight, these circumstances made this hereditary Prussian crown a much more potent threat to other German princes than the occupation of the elective Polish throne by the Elector of Saxony, or the acquisition by the Welfs of the British throne. More important in the context of the two Prussian provinces, however, is the question of Polish-Prussian reactions to the self-coronation and its impact on the relationship between the two parts of Prussia. The first Hohenzollern monarch not only created a royal counterpart to the Polish crown, but the new kingdom was regarded as a serious threat to neighbouring Polish Prussia, as the province was called after 1701, in order to distinguish it from the Prussian monarchy.

The extent of constitutionalist resistance to Hohenzollern political claims in the newly created kingdom itself is difficult to evaluate, since government propaganda came to dominate the academic and public debate after 1701. If in Brandenburg and Pomerania resistance to the bureaucratic reforms of the eighteenth and early nineteenth centuries was more effective than traditionally suspected by the majority of pro-Hohenzollern historians, there is reason to believe that pre-absolutist concepts of estate power also survived in East Prussia, particularly after the influx of Polish ideas from the annexed provinces of West Prussia after the Polish partitions at the end of the eighteenth century.[8] Much more archival work needs to be done on this topic, particularly since it was official policy in the nineteenth century to exclude from publication or even destroy any blatantly anti-Hohenzollern material.[9] This chapter examines to what extent the historical traditions which had linked the two provinces from the time of the common effort against the Teutonic Knights continued to have significance for the Prussian political and academic elites. In the second half of the seventeenth century, the historical unity of the Prussian lands was still a matter of interest to historians on both sides of the

---

[7] Peter Baumgart, 'Die preußische Königskrönung von 1701, das Reich und die europäische Politik', in Hauser, Otto (ed.), *Preußen, Europa und das Reich* (Cologne and Vienna: Böhlau, 1987), p. 68; Baumgart, 'Der Hof der Barockzeit', pp. 25–43; Franz Lüdtke, *Polen und die Erwerbung der preußischen Königswürde durch die Hohenzollern* (Bromberg: Richard Krahl 1912), Part II: Appendix, p. 11. On Savoy, see Robert Oresko, 'The House of Savoy in Search of a Royal Crown in the Seventeenth Century', in Robert Oresko et al. (eds.), *Royal and Republican Sovereignty in Early Modern Europe* (Cambridge University Press, 1997), pp. 272–350.

[8] Neugebauer, *Politischer Wandel*, pp. 21, 65–125; on the impact of the partitions, see Bömelburg, *Zwischen polnischer Ständegesellschaft*, pp. 339–76.

[9] Andrzej Kamieński, *Stany Prus Książęcych wobec rządów Brandenburskich w drugiej połowie XVII wieku* (Olsztyn: OBN im. Wojciecha Kętrzyńskiego, 1995), p. 6; also Sobieski, 'Za kim', p. 297.

divide, but actual political cooperation between Ducal and Royal Prussian nobles and burghers had ceased in the late sixteenth century. To understand the gradual alienation between the two parts of Prussia,[10] it is vital to analyse the reasons which contributed to the formation of two conflicting Prussian political and national identities in the seventeenth and early eighteenth centuries.

### THE STRUGGLE AGAINST *ABSOLUTUM DOMINIUM*

The ending of Ducal Prussian allegiance to the Polish crown sparked a series of conflicts between the two very different political cultures of Royal and Ducal Prussia, especially during the later part of the Great Elector's rule. While the Polish side emphasised the continued right of the Polish king to call himself duke of (the whole of) Prussia even after 1657, on the grounds of the *homagium eventuale* – a clause in the treaty of Wehlau which prescribed a return of Ducal Prussia to Polish overlordship if the house of Hohenzollern were to die out in the direct male line, the Elector of Brandenburg and his supporters stressed Hohenzollern *summa potestas* and his independent *dominium* over the Ducal Prussian lands. Relations between Brandenburg-Prussia and Poland, therefore, remained tense, not least due to the fact that a large body of opinion among the Duchy's noble and urban estates supported the Royal Prussian point of view. Despite complaints of the estates of both parts of Prussia that they had neither agreed to nor participated in the decision to grant Frederick William sovereignty over the duchy, parts of the treaty had been ratified by the Polish Sejm in 1658, although there were plenty of indications that confidence in its terms was quickly eroded by mutual distrust and violations.[11] Particular outrage was caused in Royal Prussia by the clause which promised to the Elector the possession of the city of Elbing unless Poland compensated the Elector financially for the assistance he had rendered the Commonwealth against the Swedes between 1657 and 1660. Additionally, Frederick William gained the East Pomeranian districts of Lauenburg and Bütow (Lębork and Bytów), which had returned to Polish rule as fiefs after the death of duke Bogusław XIV of Pomerania in 1637.[12] In exchange, Ducal Prussia owed the Polish king military support – 1500 infantry and 500 cavalry – during the war against the Swedes and Muscovites, and subsequently for any new war, particularly against the Turks.[13] Neither side, however, fulfilled these obligations satisfactorily (Frederick William was bound by his 1656 neutrality agreement with Muscovy), despite confirmations of the treaties during the Polish Sejms of 1659 and 1661. The starosta of Puck and castellan of

[10] Janusz Małłek, 'Das Königliche Preußen und der Brandenburg-preußische Staat in den Jahren 1525–1772', in *Preußen und Polen*, p. 48.
[11] Albert Waddington, *L'acquisition de la Couronne Royale de Prusse par les Hohenzollern* (Paris: Klincksieck, 1888), pp. 313, 328.
[12] Anna Kamińska-Linderska, 'Lenno Lębork i Bytów na tle stosunków polsko-brandenburskich (1657–1670)', *Studia i Materiały do Dziejów Wielkopolski* 6 (1960), 65–122.
[13] Kamińska, *Brandenburg-Prussia and Poland*, pp. 9–12.

*Divergence: the construction of rival Prussian identities*

Chełmno, Kazimierz Zawadzki, complained that protests by the Royal Prussian senators and deputies against the treaties had not been taken seriously by the king: 'it is obvious that the treaties of Bydgoszcz were made without the consensus of the whole Commonwealth'.[14] As disputes with the Royal Prussian estates arose over tolls and custom tariffs illegally collected by Frederick William on the Vistula,[15] neither side was prepared to yield. Since Elbing had not been handed over to the Elector, he refused to support the Poles in the war against Muscovy, the Cossacks and the Tartars. Instead of promoting neighbourly assistance, the treaties of 1657 stimulated growing resentment between the Commonwealth and the Elector and contributed to a further alienation between the two parts of Prussia.

The most immediate consequence of his newly won independence was the sharpening of the policy of the Great Elector towards his estates, who complained that their ruler had left them 'with merely a shadow of the ancient happiness that our forefathers enjoyed on the basis of their liberties'.[16] These liberties had been formulated in the fundamental law of 1542, the so-called *Regiments-Nottel*, which had fixed the parliamentary structure of the country: the institution of an upper chamber of councillors, burgraves and court officials, and a chamber of the lower nobility, as well as regulations which were also part of the Royal Prussian constitution, such as the *ius indigenatus*.[17] The freedom of action of these parliamentary institutions was markedly restricted from 1657, when grievances were no longer directly sent to the Elector, but had to be addressed to the newly appointed governor of Prussia, Bogusław Radziwiłł, a Lithuanian Calvinist and a prominent collaborator with Sweden during the 1650s. One of the conditions presented by the Ducal Prussian estates during the treaty negotiations at Bydgoszcz had been a Polish pardon for the Lithuanian traitor. His former association with Sweden, however, did not prevent Radziwiłł from having two Königsberg burghers hanged for asking Sweden for assistance against the military occupation of their city by Brandenburg forces.[18] The investiture of a governor was one of the most bitterly contested issues between the Prussian estates and Frederick William, since this governorship violated the guarantee of self-government of the Ducal Prussian

---

[14] *Serenissimo ac Potentissimo Ioanni III Poloniarum Regi orthodoxo Vere repraesentans Speculum Anomalium in Capitis Imperii Sarmatici a Casimiro Zawadzki Castellani Culmensi, Gubernatore Lipinensi* (Warsaw: Schreiber, 1690), folio A4v; the additional clauses concerning Elbing, Lauenburg and Bütow never found the parliamentary approval of the Polish-Lithuanian estates.

[15] The new Vistula tolls, which induced Lithuanian merchants to move the bulk of their trade to Königsberg, hit Danzig's trade with Lithuania; Fritz Gause, *Die Geschichte der Stadt Königsberg in Preußen*, 2 vols. (Cologne and Vienna: Böhlau, 1972), vol. I, p. 518.

[16] Reinhard Adam, 'Der Große Kurfürst und die Stände des Herzogtums Preussen nach dem Frieden von Oliwa', in *Acta Prussica. Abhandlungen zur Geschichte Ost- und Westpreußens, Festschrift zum 75. Geburtstag von Fritz Gause*, Beihefte zum Jahrbuch der Albertus-Universität 29 (Würzburg: Holzner-Verlag, 1968), p. 187; and Ernst Wichert, 'Die politischen Stände Preußens, ihre Bildung und Entwicklung bis zum Ausgang des 16. Jahrhunderts', *Altpreußische Monatsschrift* 5 (1868), 447.

[17] Janusz Małłek, *Ustawa o rządzie (Regimentsnottel) Prus Książęcych z roku 1542* (Toruń: UMK, 1967); Neugebauer, *Politischer Wandel*, p. 36.

[18] Janiszewska-Mincer, *Stosunki Polsko-Niemieckie*, p. 148.

estates in their provincial diet (*Oberräte* and *Landräte*).[19] As reported by Franz von Lisola, the imperial envoy to Poland who negotiated with the Elector of Brandenburg and maintained contacts to the Prussian estates, Frederick William's anti-Polish policy led to great tensions between the ducal government and the estates. Lisola expressed his amazement at the

strong aversion to the Elector in the whole Duchy of Prussia, not just among the Catholics but also among the Lutherans and the common folk . . . they all plan rebellion as soon as possible, mainly because of religion, and because the Elector aims at gaining sovereignty over Prussia, to subject it to the arbitrary power of his ministers from Brandenburg and to abolish all privileges, the Elector joined the Swedish party without the consent of the estates, thereby provoking the revenge and the hatred of the Poles against them.[20]

The replacement of the immediate relationship between the estates and their duke by an appointed intermediary also broke the historical agreements and privileges of 1454/66, the most common point of historical reference of the Prussian estates and the symbol for the 'eternal link' between Prussia and the Polish crown.[21] That the Elector was aware of the pro-Polish atmosphere among his subjects is evident in his remark to Radziwiłł, that he should 'treat the Prussian estates benignly, so they might forget their Polish fodder'.[22] In direct reference to the Royal Prussian historical tradition, representatives from Königsberg and the opposition party in the Ducal Prussian Landtag defended the 'liberty of the Prussians, who, since they had become Christians, were a free people subject to no one'.[23] The estates expressed the same opinion in 1657, in the presence of Frederick William: 'In 1454, the estates subjected themselves voluntarily to the rule of King Casimir and joined the crown of Poland. This country is therefore a member and part of the crown and participates in all its freedoms and rights.'[24] The voluntary subjection of the Prussian estates in 1454 to the Polish crown had therefore remained as sacrosanct to the Ducal Prussian estates as to their Royal Prussian brothers, as a permanent symbol of the common Prussian past and principle of liberty. The odious sover-

---

[19] Janusz Małłek, 'Eine andersartige Lösung. Absolutistischer Staatsstreich in Preußen im Jahre 1663', *Parliaments, Estates and Representation* 10, no. 2 (1990), 181; Jörg Jacoby, *Bogusław Radziwiłł. Der Statthalter des Großen Kurfürsten in Ostpreußen*, Wissenschaftliche Beiträge no. 40 (Marburg: Herder-Institut, 1959).

[20] J. Vota [pseud. for Onno Klopp], *Der Untergang des Ordensstaates und die Entstehung der preußischen Königswürde* (Mainz: Kirchheim, 1911), quoting from Lisola's reports in 1656.

[21] The arguments used by the estates against the institution of a governor on the basis of the privileges of 1454, 1466 and 1525 is described by Egloff von Tippelskirch, *Die Statthalter des Großen Kurfürsten*, Institut für Politik und Internationales Recht der Universität Kiel, Abt. 1/31 (Quackenbrück: Trute, 1937), p. 74.

[22] Jacoby, *Bogusław Radziwiłł*, p. 49.

[23] Adam, 'Der Große Kurfürst', p. 193.

[24] Józef Szwagrzyk, 'Ludność Prus Książęcych wobec traktatu Welawsko-Bydgoskiego, 1657–1660', in Gierowski, Józef A. (ed.), *O naprawę Rzeczypospolitej XVII–XVIII w. Prace ofiarowane Władysławowi Czaplińskiemu w 60 rocznice urodzin* (Warsaw: PWN, 1965), p. 180, quoted from the protocols of the Ducal Prussian Landtag, 8 October, 1657.

eignty of the Elector had severed the links to Poland that had held ducal power in check for the last 150 years, and was cutting off the estates from protection by the Polish crown – even if this protection had recently existed more in theory than in practice.[25]

The result, felt many Ducal Prussian nobles, was slavery. Taxes were no longer subject to approval by the estates, as the *Landkasten*, the right of noble self-taxation, was taken from the Ducal Prussian Diet in 1680. Customs duties were raised against the will of the Königsberg merchants and collected not for their profit but for that of the ducal treasury; municipal offices and duties were taken over by the ducal bureaucracy; teachers in ducal pay were excluded from the right to be citizens of Königsberg; printing presses and other professionals had to apply for licences and privileges to ducal officials instead of the city; sumptuary legislation was decreed by the ducal governor, not by the city council: all these major and minor trespasses on municipal and noble self-government had embittered the estates against their newly sovereign duke and confirmed them in their view that the loss of Polish overlordship delivered them directly into the arbitrary power of the Elector.[26] While he believed that the basis and nature of the relationship had changed with the treaties of Wehlau and Bromberg, the estates rejected any recognition of the new legal situation until 1661, when the Elector elicited an acknowledgement of the treaties of 1657 from his estates; but the stalemate was only resolved when the Elector agreed to recognise traditional immunities, 'as long as they did not infringe upon his sovereignty'.[27]

One that did so was the estates' most cherished privilege: the right to appeal to the Polish king and republic, with which they had often been able to play one ruler off against the other for their own benefit.[28] Consequently, the conflict between the Elector's idea of sovereignty and the political ideal of the estates that a ruler could only expect obedience after he had recognised the privileges and fundamental laws of the realm, continued to cause trouble. In 1661 the Elector expressed his surprise over the 'unusual and unheard-of' demand by the estates that they be freed of their obligation as subjects if he did not respect their immunities and rights.[29] The estates insisted that the idea that oaths and contracts were binding for both rulers and the ruled was not merely a Polish invention, but existed also in Sweden and the Holy Roman Empire. During the coronation ceremonies of the Polish kings, the *pacta conventa* had to be recognised by each new king after 1573: Henri of Valois was

---

[25] Stefania Ochmann, *Sejmy lat 1661–2. Przegrana batalia o reformę ustroju Rzeczypospolitej* (Wrocław: Wydawnictwo Uniwersytetu Wrocławskiego, 1977), shows the lack of interest in Ducal Prussian affairs in the Polish Sejm.

[26] Gause, *Geschichte der Stadt Königsberg*, pp. 506–19.

[27] *Urkunden und Aktenstücke*, vol. XVI, pp. 630ff.

[28] Szwagrzyk, 'Ludność', p. 180; also Małłek, 'Eine andersartige Lösung', 182.

[29] *Urkunden und Aktenstücke*, vol. XVI, pp. 311ff; Hugo Rachel, *Der Große Kurfürst und die ost-preußischen Stände, 1640–88*, Staats- und Sozialwissenschaftliche Forschungen 24, ed. G. Schmoller and M. Sering, part 1 (Leipzig: Duncker und Humblot, 1905).

warned that if he did not recognise the nobles' rights drawn up in the Henrician articles, he could not become king of Poland.[30] In Royal Prussia, the obligation of the king to confirm the *pacta conventa* and the special rights of the cities in the province, remained their 'pupilla libertatis', as the Danzig burgomaster Johann Ernst von der Linde called the szlachta privilege 'nothing concerns us without our consent'.[31] Appealing to these principles, the Ducal Prussian estates demanded an application of the Polish model: 'We not only want to keep our privileges but we want to extend and improve them, as the Poles did when they won their freedoms during the *interregna*.'[32] And in 1661, the Elector's confidant and chancellor, Otto von Schwerin, reported: 'Your Electoral Highness would not believe to what extent the Polish crown is dear to their hearts, and how they all seek their good in this connection, so that they insist on maintaining some recourse to Poland.' In 1670, Schwerin wrote to Frederick William again: 'As long as one generation lives who remembers Polish rule, there will be a source of resistance in Prussia.'[33]

The main source of constitutional conflict between the pro-Polish faction among the Ducal Prussian estates and the Electoral party focused on the role of the ruler and his exercise of power. While pro-Hohenzollern theorists proclaimed the duty of the ruled to believe and trust in the good intentions of the ruler *legibus solutus*, some among the Ducal Prussian estates, including the burghers of Königsberg, defended the principle of fundamental laws restricting the power of central government. The Ducal Prussian estates remained aware of the common act of disobedience against the tyrannical Knights and the incorporation of the whole province of Prussia into the Polish crown: as a sign of protest against the Elector of Brandenburg during the Diet of 1661–3, the estates renewed their oath to the Prussian union, formed in 1440 against the Teutonic Order.[34] Now it was not the Teutonic Order, but the outsider from Berlin who diminished their liberties, while the Polish crown, with whom they had formed 'one body', was their natural home.[35] The belief that they were dealing with a foreign ruler provoked a refusal to finance the Elector's other domains and provinces in the Empire, which had no connection with Prussia but through the dynasty: 'Shall the last drop of blood be wrung from the Prussian nobility, although they have nothing to do with the Holy Roman Empire?'[36]

[30] Henryk Olszewski, 'Ustrój Polityczny Rzeczypospolitej', in Tazbir, Janusz (ed.), *Polska XVII wieku* (Warsaw: PWN, 1969), p. 66.

[31] [Johann Ernst von der Linde], *Gratiani Severini Lipiński ad V[incentum] C[onstantinum] Starodobski Nob[ilem] Pol[onum] Epistola* (Danzig, 1712), p. 24.

[32] Adam Vetulani, *Lenno Pruskie. Od traktatu Krakowskiego do śmierci księcia Albrechta, 1525–1568* (Kraków: Polska Akademia Umjejętności, 1930), p. 86.

[33] Małłek, 'Eine andersartige Lösung', 183; Kazimierz Piwarski, *Dzieje Polityczne Prus Wschodnich, 1621–1772* (Gdynia: Instytut Bałtycki, 1938), p. 68.

[34] Rachel, *Der Große Kurfürst*, p. 32; Kazimierz Piwarski, *Dzieje Prus Wschodnich w czasach nowożytnych* (Gdańsk, Bydgoszcz: Instytut Bałtycki, 1946), p. 59.

[35] Rachel, *Kurfürst*, pp. 18–19.

[36] Ludwig Tümpel, *Die Entstehung des brandenburgisch-preußischen Einheitsstaates im Zeitalter des Absolutismus 1609–1806* (Breslau: Marcus, 1915; repr. Aalen: Scientia, 1965), p. 41.

## Divergence: the construction of rival Prussian identities

What separated the Elector and his advisors from the Prussian opposition was a fundamental difference in the understanding of human nature, the function of government, and its impact on the common good. Since Gerhard Oestreich's analysis of the influence of the neostoic movement on Brandenburg-Prussia, most histories of the Great Elector have stressed the crucial impact of natural law thinking on the formulation of Hohenzollern raison d'état. Frederick William had been a student in Leiden, where he had grown fond of Lipsian political ideas and the concept of the early modern welfare state.[37] Yet one ought to be careful not to contrast, as is often done, this early form of 'enlightened absolutism' with the supposed ignorance and unintellectual provincialism of the Prussian nobility, both in Ducal and Royal Prussia. The estates were thoroughly familiar with natural law and political theory. This was demonstrated by the rebels in the 1661 diet in Königsberg, when they quoted from Grotius to show that government unbound by laws was always detrimental to a country.[38] The vocabularies of political theory in both parts of Prussia often echoed each other closely, although in reality they were often applied towards different ends: while the Ducal Prussian government and bureaucrats promoted an increasingly centralised ducal authority in Ducal Prussia, the diet of Royal Prussia, as well as the opposition in Ducal Prussia, related neostoic values to the mixed form of government and the Polish constitutionalist model.

To overcome the resistance of the lower nobility who continued to aspire to Polish liberties, Frederick William sought to attract a handful of powerful East Prussian Junkers who followed his version of neostoic ideology, many of them converts to Calvinism, which from 1613 had been the religion of the Hohenzollern dynasty. Mixed with Dutch neostoicism, the Calvinist confessionalisation of Brandenburg-Prussia was never greatly successful among the burghers and the lower nobility, but it found a strong following among the duke's political entourage and lent new impetus to the government's administrative, financial and military reforms.[39] In Brandenburg, Veit Ludwig von Seckendorff elaborated the model of a strictly centralised bureaucracy on which the ruler could rely to enhance his authority against the particular interests of the estates, while Eberhard von Danckelmann, the Calvinist educator and subsequent first minister under Frederick III, spoke about the elite of state officials as 'the church militant'.[40] Anxious to preserve their Lutheran religion, the Prussian estates were reluctant to accept new ideas

---

[37] Gerhard Oestreich, 'The Netherlands Movement in Brandenburg-Prussia', in *Neostoicism and the Early Modern State*, pp. 118–31; Gerhard Oestreich, *Strukturprobleme der frühen Neuzeit. Ausgewählte Aufsätze* (Berlin: de Gruyter, 1969), pp. 285ff; Melton, 'The Prussian Junkers', pp. 86–7.

[38] J. Małłek, 'Absoluter Staatsstreich', p. 63.

[39] Sieglinde C. Othmer, *Berlin und die Verbreitung des Naturrechts in Europa. Kultur- und sozialgeschichtliche Studien zu Jean Barbeyrac's Pufendorf-Übersetzung und eine Analyse seiner Leserschaft*, preface by Gerhard Oestreich, Einzelveröffentlichungen der Historischen Kommission zu Berlin no. 30 (Berlin: de Gruyter, 1970); Melton, 'The Prussian Junkers', pp. 89–90.

[40] Oestreich, *Strukturprobleme*, pp. 285, 288.

about the role of the ruler and his central government; they resented the fact that their *pater patriae* ruled them from Berlin, dictating what he considered the common good for Königsberg and the Ducal Prussian nobility. Acting on Seckendorff's advice, Frederick William employed many Huguenots in both his Brandenburg and Prussian administrations, which further alienated the native Lutheran elites. In Ducal Prussia, unlike France during the religious wars, the Netherlands during the Dutch Revolt or the Holy Roman Empire after 1555, it was the Calvinists who represented the institutionalised power of the state, while Lutheranism promoted ideas of resistance.[41]

The difference between the Elector's understanding of neostoic values and that which was applied in Polish Prussia was obvious to contemporaries. Especially during the last three decades of the seventeenth century, historical and political treatises in both Prussian provinces served as instruments in the power struggle between the two different political systems and ideologies. Promoting the idea that the Polish-Lithuanian Commonwealth was a haven of unbridled freedom for the self-willed, greedy nobility, the Great Elector's anti-Polish propaganda has successfully influenced generations of historians. Nevertheless, a hard core of East Prussian nobles and burghers remained unconvinced, knowing that the Polish limited monarchy had not always been a failure. These anti-Hohenzollern voices joined in the chorus defending the Polish constitution and Polish sovereignty over the once united province of Prussia. During the 1660s, a satirical leaflet was found near the Königsberg cathedral in Kneiphof containing the following verses: 'The senators have been bribed/ the noble deputies have not spoken/ the resistance of Königsberg has now been broken/ on small towns they throw bare bones/ No longer for you the pride of noble Prussians/ if you want to become slaves of Brandenburg.'[42] Brandenburg had become a symbol for slavery, oppression and the successful implementation of Hohenzollern rule. In the Commonwealth, Prussian burghers, supported by nobles inside and beyond the Polish-Prussian borders, insisted that the rule of law was the only safeguard against tyranny. In 1669, the year of Michael Wiśniowiecki's election to the Polish throne and of the flight to Warsaw of the Ducal Prussian nobleman Christian Kalckstein to agitate against the Elector, Joachim Pastorius wrote in praise of the Polish constitution: '[Our] kingdom is like a temple and an asylum for the law, and the law holds the sceptre;

---

[41] Andreas Nahama, *Ersatzbürger und Staatsbildung. Zur Zerstörung des Bürgertums in Brandenburg-Preußen* (Frankfurt, New York, Bern: Peter Lang, 1983), pp. 25–30; Quentin Skinner, *The Foundations of Modern Political Thought*, 2 vols. (Cambridge University Press: 1978, 6th edn, 1996), vol. II: *The Age of Reformation*, pp. 318–48. For Huguenot influence on Poland, see Czesław Chowaniec, 'Poglądy polityczne rokoszan 1606–07 wobec doktryn Monarchomachów Francuskich', *Reformacja w Polsce* 11 (1924), 256–66. For a comparison with other Lutheran resistance movements in the Empire, see Heinz Schilling, 'Reformation und Bürgerfreiheit. Emdens Weg zur calvinistischen Stadtrepublik', in Moeller, B. (ed.), *Stadt und Kirche im 16. Jahrhundert* (Gütersloher Verlagshaus, 1978), pp. 128–61.

[42] Otto Nugel, 'Der Schöppenmeister Hieronymus Roth', *Forschungen zur Brandenburgischen und Preußischen Geschichte* 14 (1901), 426.

naked force rules elsewhere . . . But my king is ruled by the law.'[43] Echoing such views, the Ducal Prussian estates adapted Lipsius's idea of the common good to their own interpretation of natural law: the fate of Kalckstein, abducted from Warsaw by Frederick William's agents and executed in Memel, gave good reason to be wary. Grotius's recommendation that 'pacta sunt servanda' served as a vital defence of their increasingly vulnerable position.[44] Religious, political and individual freedoms which had been granted and confirmed by rulers in the past should remain the constitutional basis of the relationship between rulers and ruled. Just as Royal Prussian burghers tended to ignore the 1569 Union of Lublin, which incorporated representatives from the Prussian senate and the chamber of deputies into the Polish Sejm and devalued their powers of self-government, the Ducal Prussian estates pretended that the treaties of 1657–8 had never been signed. They had not been asked and had not agreed: they constituted no mutual contract and therefore held no legally binding force for them. There was no conscious solidarity among the Royal Prussian estates and the Ducal Prussian rebels, but they still used the same political language and adhered to the same traditional principles and understanding of liberty, based on ancient law and an established constitution.

The extent to which Lipsius's teachings concerning prudent statesmanship could be directed against the Elector's absolutist designs was demonstrated by one of Hartknoch's most eloquent students in Königsberg, the young Georg Friedrich von Kalnein, son of the chancellor at the ducal court. In 1673, Kalnein published a treatise on the principles of the well-ordered cameralist state which, at first sight, the electoral government could not but have approved. References to Jean Bodin's formulation of divinely legitimised power fill the introductory chapter. Even the Dutch revolt, a favourite topic of anti-absolutist literature, is shown here entirely in the light of divine providence, instead of the natural right of resistance.[45] Kalnein certainly supported an effective taxation system, a strong military organisation and the freeing of peasants from heavy burdens. So far, young Kalnein must have lived up to the expectations of his father, who had not only signed the execution order of the rebellious Kalckstein,[46] but was renowned for his loyal support of the Elector's efforts to overcome the estates' resistance during the 'Long Diet' of 1661–3. Yet there are several surprising notes in this treatise: like Hartknoch, Kalnein junior identified with the Poles as 'our brothers' and cautioned against sudden changes in legislation. In clearly neostoic terms, he criticised the abolition of well-proven privileges and rights, which could imprudently destabilise a state. He even praised the Polish military for its bravery and refined battle techniques, and adopted a view

---

[43] This panegyric was copied by the professor at the Thorn Gymnasium, Martin Böhm in his 'Elenchus Manuscriptorum', PAN Kracow 1936, folios 49–49v.

[44] G. Oestreich, 'The military renascence', in his *Neostoicism*, p. 80.

[45] *Disputatio Politica De Incrementis et Decrementis Rerumpublicarum respondens Georg Friedrich a Kalnein* (Königsberg: Reusner, 1673), folio A2v.

[46] 'Responsum a Regentibus Prussiae', 10 December 1670, APGd, Bibl. Archivi 300.R, Vv 171, folio 196b, co-signed by Wallenrodt and Tettau.

on defence matters rather similar to that of many Polish writers: money alone was not the *nervus belli*, 'but rather the virtue of our citizens'.[47]

The similarities to numerous political treatises originating from Royal Prussia, directed against the Elector's *absolutum dominium*, are all too clear. One anonymous publication from Thorn most accurately summed up the central disagreement between the Ducal Prussian government and the political culture of the noble and burgher estates.[48] Focusing on the right of free exercise of religion, the author stressed that the moral difference between the governments of Ducal and Royal Prussia was not only the question whether a ruler ruled by law, but whether the fundamental laws of the realm were made by the ruler or by his estates. Does not a ruler whose estates impose *pacta conventa* on him and demand respect for the fundamental laws of the realm run the risk of losing his power and his control over public affairs? For this supporter of the mixed form of government and the Polish constitution, the answer was obvious: 'this need not be feared, as long as there is no confusion between highest and absolute power'. Only those who are so ignorant that they cannot make this distinction will fear fundamental laws.[49] This attitude was incompatible with the Hohenzollern idea of the *suum cuique*: the ruler was to decide over the distribution of reward and punishment – 'to everyone what he deserves'. Frederick William and his successors insisted that the legislator and the ruler must be one person in order to ensure the well-being of the whole realm against the particular interests of the estates. It was in this spirit, for example, that the Elector deprived the nobility in the newly annexed provinces of Lauenburg and Bütow of their ancient rights of self-taxation, despite the vociferous protest of the Royal Prussian and the Polish diets.[50] Thus, despite similarities in the vocabulary, the governing elites of Royal and Ducal Prussia came to rather different conclusions on the location of legislative authority. While Frederick William wrote about his rebellious estates in June 1661, 'it is time that the people's mouths be stuffed',[51] the Danzigers were taught to praise the participatory nature of the mixed form of government: 'the will of the whole city must be represented, and in a mixed republic everything is determined by fundamental laws'.[52]

Royal Prussian political writing fostered a clearly negative picture of absolute power, or *directum dominium*. The most benign monarch's rule was by definition 'absolute' if he did not tolerate the participation of, and the control over legislation by, the estates of the realm. Once more the meaning of liberty was crucial: for Royal

[47] Kalnein, *De Incrementis*, folios D–Dv.
[48] 'Miscellanea Thoruniensia: Politica Specialis Erotemata quaedam statum Poloniae concernantia', APT Kat. II., V.13.
[49] Ibid., pp. 124–5.
[50] Barbara Szymczak, 'Sejmiki Prus Królewskich wobec Księstwa Pruskiego i polityki elektora Fryderyka Wilhelma w latach 1648–1668', *Przegląd Historyczny* 86, no. 2 (1995), 175.
[51] *Urkunden und Aktenstücke*, vol. IX, p. 255.
[52] *Respublica Mixta An sit Irregularis in Inclyto Gedanensium Athenaeo [Johann Christoph] Rosteuscher disquiret publice G[abriel] F[riedrich] Schumann* (Danzig: Rhetius, 1689), p. 10.

Prussian writers, liberty was the right of the citizens to promote the common good by conducting their own affairs, while for the Hohenzollerns and their supporters, the public good demanded that this liberty was more or less relinquished and reserved to the ruler. For the Royal Prussian estates, the diet was responsible for the common good and had always been the 'place to come to for the rescue of the fatherland',[53] not an instrument subject to the will of the ruler.

HISTORICAL IDENTITY AND THE CREATION OF THE PRUSSIAN MONARCHY

The increasingly confident regime of the sovereign electors not only changed Ducal Prussia's political culture, but it also influenced the way history was written. In particular, works which pointed to the common origin of Prussia, and historical treatises which focused on the fact that all Prussians were 'in faithful dependency on the Polish crown', became increasingly rare in the Duchy.[54] Under King Frederick William I (1713–40), works which mentioned the former dependence of Ducal Prussia on the Polish crown would be banned or burned. The representation of the two provinces in historical writing became increasingly divided by the development of different historical myths. The picture of a united Prussia slowly crumbled.

In 1677, the pro–Hohenzollern court historian in Königsberg, Jacob Lydicius, outlining the origin and rise of the house of Hohenzollern as rulers in Prussia, emphasised that Frederick William had enhanced the reputation of his dynasty not only as elector of Brandenburg in his capital Berlin, but as a ruler of 'the Prussians and Sarmatians'.[55] Even Hartknoch, in his main work on the history of Poland, in the chapter *De Prussia* merely outlined the history of Ducal Prussia after the rebellion of 1454, while passing over in silence the fate of Royal Prussia as a province under the Polish crown. Hartknoch wrote this book when he was still employed by the university of Königsberg, which explains the exclusive use of the name of Prussia for the duchy under Hohenzollern rule. In contrast, the work *Alt- und Neues Preußen*, published in Thorn, extensively describes both parts of historic Prussia. In the later decades of the seventeenth century, then, historians in the pay of the Elector of Brandenburg frequently ignored the historical links of Ducal Prussia with the Polish crown. In contrast, Royal Prussian historians continued to cherish the idea of a united province of Prussia, firmly rooted in the common past under the sovereignty of the Polish crown, but at the same time safeguarding its own laws and autonomous traditions. The Warmian writer and lawyer Casimir Gałęzowski, for example, included the major cities of both parts of Prussia in his

---

[53] APGd, Recesy 300.29, no. 157, p. 49.
[54] Philip Jacob Hartmann, *Respublica Prussiae* (Königsberg: Reusner, 1686); repr. in *Acta Borussica* II (1731), pp. 33, 37–8.
[55] *Notitiae Ducatus Prussiae delineatio generalis & specialis, Jacobi Lydicii, Hohensteina-Prussi* (Wittenberg: Mevii, 1677), preface.

mid-seventeenth century description of the province: Thorn, Elbing, Danzig, Königsberg, Kulm, Braunsberg and Marienburg were the main cities of what Gałęzowski called a united *ducatus Prussiae*. He consciously failed to mention the fact that Königsberg and the eastern part of the country were ruled by a duke of the house of Hohenzollern, as if Royal and Ducal Prussia were still one state under the sceptre of the Polish king.[56] Lydicius, however, avoided any association with the Polish crown in his history of Prussia. He had been taught details of historical mythology and the European migrations by his former mentor in Wittenberg, Samuel Schurtzfleisch, a declared adversary of Hartknoch's interpretation of Prussian history and a supporter of the myth of king Waidewutus as a strong and sovereign lawgiver.[57] In contrast to Hartknoch, Lydicius assigned a more important role to one of the ancestral tribes who lived in the Baltic provinces, the Vends, and considered them to be of German origin. As Lydicius stressed, their prowess in fighting the Teutonic Order was only matched by Brandenburg's glorious achievement in securing sovereign rule over the remnants of the Teutonic state.[58]

In Royal Prussia, however, the warlike nature of the Germans was depicted in a very negative light after the Swedish wars. The Elector of Brandenburg and his troops were compared with the hated Teutonic Order.[59] A satirical verse from Elbing addressed to 'Bellona', the goddess of war, implores her to leave Poland and turn either on the Turks or the Germans, who 'have a great zest for war'.[60] The Teutonic Knights remained the common foe of both provinces, whose historians continued to regard them as 'foreign Germans', and historical treatises refuting Conring's claim that Prussia had belonged to the Holy Roman Empire were legion in Königsberg as well as in Danzig. As in Royal Prussia, the great love of the historians of Ducal Prussia for their pagan forefathers, killed and oppressed by the vicious Knights, was more than a sentimental antiquarian fashion. Like Hartknoch's myth of Prussia – shared by his Royal Prussian contemporaries – the pagan past acquired a political function at a crucial moment in Prussia's history, when Elector Frederick III revealed his plan to transform the Duchy of Prussia into a kingdom. Political and historical writing on both sides of the Prusso-Prussian border played the role of a barometer. How was the common Prussian origin moulded into two contrasting versions of a Prussian identity, formed on the one hand by republican traditions and the political culture of the Commonwealth, and on the other hand by the newly created monarchy?

The diplomatic negotiations preceding the coronation of 1701, as well as the debate about Frederick's personal qualities, have been exhaustively scrutinised by

[56] Casimir Gałęzowski, *Iusta memoria spectatae dudum Nobilitatis Civitatum et Civium ducatus Prussiae* (Braunsberg: Weingärtner, 1650), folios Cv–C2.
[57] Lydicius, *Notitiae Ducatus*, dedication and preface; Hartknoch expressed his negative opinion of Schurtzfleisch in his letter 'Observationes in Res Prussorum', Bibl. PAN Gd. 2460, adl. 326b.
[58] Lydicius, *Notitiae Ducatus*, chapter I.
[59] Friedrich Herzberg, 'Chronik der Stadt Elbing, 1668–1704', Bibl. PAN Gd. 1439, p. 758.
[60] Bibl. PAN Gd., NL 100. 8°.

historians.[61] Little interest, however, has been directed towards the impact which the creation of a Prussian kingdom had on historical and political writing and the conscious effort of the Hohenzollerns to overcome the division of Prussia into two nations and political cultures. Waddington, for example, dismissed all historical myth-making as '*argument archéologique*'.[62] The acquisition of the royal crown was, however, a formidable opportunity to lay claim to the myths of the Prussian past and the whole country's historical greatness to enhance the importance of the new kingdom. The son of the Great Elector was a gifted manipulator of historical and political symbolism intended to enhance the reputation of his newly acquired dignity. Historians were given a prominent place in the preparations for the coronation ceremony. Previous efforts to present Ducal Prussia as a separate entity from Royal Prussia, which had dominated pro-Hohenzollern literature since the early seventeenth century, were slowly reversed during the run-up to the coronation. Instead, authors in the pay of the Hohenzollern court began forcefully to re-assert the image of a united Prussia. The intention behind this shift alarmed the political elites of Royal-Polish Prussia, as the transformation of Ducal Prussia into a kingdom was not only the final step towards full independence from the crown of Poland and the common Polish-Prussian past, but it also enhanced the fears of nobles and burghers in the Polish part of Prussia that the new monarchy fostered expansionist designs. Later historians have all too often interpreted the coronation as just another step towards the partitions of Poland. In the nineteenth century, the Prussian nationalist Droysen wrote: 'What had originally been a work of vanity later became a masterpiece of statesmanship.'[63] Yet even without the knowledge of future events, the creation of a *Rex Borussorum* did not seem a good omen for Polish Prussia.

The obstacles facing Frederick III's quest to become king of Prussia were considerable: objections were to be expected not only from Poland-Lithuania and its Prussian province, but also from the emperor and the representatives of the Teutonic Order whose main seat was now in the Swabian town of Mergentheim. Ever since 1525, the remaining members of the Teutonic Knights who refused to accept the secularisation of their order had continued to protest against the 'heretical', illegitimate rule of the house of Hohenzollern in Prussia.[64] The Order insisted that Hohenzollern sovereignty over Prussia, which, as Frederick III asserted, depended on nobody except 'on God and the sovereign duke', was unacceptable to them.[65] Neither Frederick William nor his son, however, intended to

---

[61] Besides Waddington, Baumgart, Lüdtke and Vota, see Heinz Duchhardt, 'Die preußische Königskrönung von 1701', in *Herrscherweihe und Königskrönung im frühneuzeitlichen Europa. Festschrift für E. Kessel* (Wiesbaden: Steiner, 1983), pp. 89–101; and Karl-Ludwig Feckl, *Preußen im Spanischen Erbfolgekrieg* (Frankfurt, Bern, Chichester: Peter Lang, 1979).

[62] Waddington, *L'acquisition de la Couronne*, p. 55; similarly, Wippermann, *Der Ordensstaat*, p. 82.

[63] Baumgart, 'Die preußische Königskrönung', p. 66.    [64] Vota, *Der Untergang*, p. 501.

[65] Theodor Schieder, 'Die preußische Königskrönung von 1700 und die politische Ideengeschichte', in his *Begegnungen mit der Geschichte* (Göttingen: Vandenhoeck und Ruprecht, 1962), p. 186.

break with the emperor or abandon their elevated position in the Holy Roman Empire, where the margraves of Brandenburg belonged to the electoral college of imperial princes. The care which Frederick III took to inform Leopold I of his designs shows that the Empire was still a political entity to be reckoned with. He admitted that it would be unimaginable to gain the crown for Brandenburg, as it was part of the Empire, and still a 'vassal state of the emperor [whose consent] for such a crown I will never get'.[66] But Frederick shrewdly succeeded in winning the emperor's support for the crown in Prussia by exploiting Leopold's need for assistance during the crisis over the Spanish Succession in 1699–1700, as the Habsburgs rallied support against the Bourbons.

Imitating the self-coronation which Charles XII of Sweden had conducted in 1697, Frederick III's self-coronation in 1701, conducted in great baroque splendour, also revealed the changes which had occurred since the constitutional struggles between the Great Elector and his estates during the 1660s. During the 1680s, the cities and the free peasants (*Kölmer*) had been excluded from the Landtag, in which the nobility now felt rather isolated. Since the real political power of the estates had been largely broken, it was much easier for the Hohenzollern rulers to advertise the legitimation of their power by 'the will of the people'. Thus Frederick III's ambassador to Vienna, Bartholdy, told the Emperor's ministers: 'the origin of all government on earth which God has not given directly to his people is *ex populi voluntate* . . . the Elector is therefore a sovereign lord who received his sovereignty and *iura majestatica* by such a contract'.[67] Frederick had indeed been eager to gain formal recognition for his crown from the noble estates by sending one of his most loyal supporters among the East Prussian aristocracy, Christoph von Dohna, to convince them. Dohna returned to Berlin reporting to Frederick his success in winning over the majority of the councillors and the higher nobility, including the burgrave of Königsberg, as well as the college of *Landräte*. It is not clear, however, how reliable this support was, as the estates had refused contribution in 1700 and had protested against the Elector's plans to build new Calvinist churches in the Lutheran duchy.[68] Soon after the coronation, the East Prussian *Landtag* was no more: it was convoked for the last time in 1704.

In reality, the act of self-coronation was not based on the idea of a contract between a ruler and a people, guaranteed by fundamental laws, but was an ostentatious declaration of the divine right of kings. Despite dispensing with the medieval ritual of anointing and crowning the king by the church and the emperor, the Prussian crown was to be given by God alone, without any worldly intermediary, reflecting the priesthood of all believers, headed by the monarch-to-be. This was a bold act, and contemporaries, not least the Prussian king himself, were well aware of its symbolism:

[66] Ibid., p. 187; Waddington, *L'acquisition de la Couronne*, p. 44.
[67] Vota, *Der Untergang*, pp. 548–9.
[68] Waddington, *L'acquisition de la Couronne*, pp. 226–7.

Kings who receive their power from the estates of the realm wear their royal insignia only after being anointed . . . but Your Majesty, whose royalty was not founded on the will of the estates . . . but on the example of the most ancient kings, on its own foundations, did not have to consider such a procedure, as You previously possessed already the full set of Regalia due to Your sovereignty.[69]

Critics of Frederick's style of government and his alleged vanity have later accused him of superficiality, arguing that the coronation was not the demonstration of real power, but the self-delusion of a rather weak, hesitant and vainglorious ruler. King Frederick II, who judged his grandfather 'small in great things and great in small things', should have recognised, however, that contemporaries unequivocally regarded the coronation as a success. Leibniz grasped the power of its symbolism, when he observed that 'the name makes a thing real and complete, the *complementum essentiae*'.[70] It had been Frederick I's explicit goal to establish that his crown was as worthy and dignified as that of any other European monarchy: 'to the end that there be no more difference in title and other honours between his Electoral Highness and other European kings, in particular the kings of Sweden, Denmark and Poland'.[71]

Prussia's neighbours also understood the importance of the act of self-coronation. Besides the Pope and the Teutonic Order, the strongest protests came from the Polish Sejm and the Polish Prussian Diet. Frederick had reckoned with this opposition, hence the caution he applied in negotiations with the Polish king. Making a symbolic concession to the ancient ties to the Polish crown, Frederick called himself 'king in Prussia', not 'king of Prussia'. Nevertheless, a fierce Polish-Lithuanian attack came from Jan Mikołaj Radziwiłł, later palatine of Nowogródek, who ostentatiously addressed a European audience with his condemnation of the new monarchy. He submitted a pamphlet to the Parlement of Paris, calling the coronation a 'felony committed by the Elector of Brandenburg, who turned a vassal state into a kingdom'.[72] From 1701 to the final recognition of the Prussian monarchy by the Sejm in 1764, several diets and dietines of Polish Prussia – as Royal Prussia was now called – and Poland-Lithuania regularly submitted protests, despite the success of Frederick's diplomacy and policy of bribery among influential members of the Senate and wider circles of the nobility.[73] As the diet of May 1701 in Graudenz was disrupted over conflicts between the cities and sections of the nobility on issues of taxation, there is no evidence of any immediate official reactions from the Polish Prussian estates. In the central Sejm, however, the deputies from Great Poland and Łęczyca demanded the immediate expulsion from

---

[69] Baumgart, 'Die preußische Königskrönung', p. 79, quoting from a panegyric by Johann Christian Lünig of 1701.   [70] Ibid., pp. 66, 84.   [71] Ibid., p. 75.
[72] 'Vox Justa et Libera Joannis Ducis Radziwiłł, MDL incisoris protestans atque manifestans contra attentatum jus Regni et Reip[ublicae] Polon[niae] incompetenti Corona et titulo regio a Seren[issimo] Frederico III, Electore Brandenburgico usurpatis', quoted in Waddington, *L'acquisition de la Couronne*, p. 320.
[73] Ibid., pp. 321ff.

Poland of Hoverbeck, the Brandenburg resident, and asked the Polish king to adopt the title *Rex totius Prussiae*, instead of the previous *magnus dux Prussiae*.[74] But Augustus II of Poland and a circle of pro-Brandenburg politicians, such as the bishop of Warmia, Andrzej C. Załuski, had personally recognised Frederick's new royal title. In the fashion of his father, Frederick William, who in 1669 had nurtured plans to acquire the Polish crown by becoming a Catholic, the new king left the bishop in the hope that he would convert to Catholicism. Against such prominent supporters in the Senate Council, the resistance of the Polish szlachta was not effective enough to unite the Commonwealth against Brandenburg. Several dietines even hoped to find an ally in Frederick against increasingly obvious designs by Augustus II to strengthen the Polish monarchy.[75] This, and the growing threat of a Swedish invasion at the start of the Great Northern War, diluted the strength of protesting voices against the creation of Frederick I's kingdom.

In response to attacks from Poland and the Teutonic Order, the new king mobilised historical and literary talents within and beyond the borders of Prussia. In June 1700, Załuski received a letter from Friedrich Werner, another Brandenburg diplomat in Warsaw. Werner had studied history in Königsberg with Hartknoch[76] and enthusiastically reported that he had found proof in old histories of Prussia, such as those of Hennenberger and Stella, as well as in the world history of the Dutch historian Ortelius, that pagan Prussia had been a kingdom under its wise and strong monarch Waidewutus. The same information had reached the court in Berlin, where this piece of evidence was received with great exaltation. Werner thanked Załuski for his support for the creation of the monarchy, which he considered the 'restitution of a title which historically belonged to the Prussian nation'.[77] Royal Prussia was especially alarmed by the Hohenzollern claim to territories which constituted the realm of king Waidewutus, a well-known figure in Prussian historiography and not in the least a new discovery: 'Everything that Waidewutus distributed among his sons and which still bears their names, Your Electoral Highness still possesses, with the exception of Warmia and Kulmerland.'[78]

This definition of Prussia did not mention Malbork and Pomerania, the two other palatinates of Royal Prussia, but it could not have been much more outspoken about the future goals of the new Prussian monarch: Prussia was no longer confined to the duchy of Prussia, but it had regained its historical unity. The Hohenzollern

---

[74] APGd., Recesy 300.29 no. 165, p. 161 (Sejm, 30 May 1701).

[75] Lüdtke, *Polen und die Erwerbung*, p. 14; and Waddington, *L'acquisition de la Couronne*, p. 199.

[76] Under Hartknoch he produced the thesis *Dissertatio Historica de Idolatria et Aliis Superstitionibus ritibus Veterorum Prussorum sub praesidio M. Chr. Hartknochen, Passenheimensis Prussi, publico eruditorum examini submittit Friedericus Wernerus, Regiom[ontis] Prussus* (Königsberg: Reusner, 1675).

[77] Waddington, *L'acquisition de la Couronne*, p. 190; Walter Hubatsch, 'Kreuzritterstaat und Hohenzollernmonarchie. Zur Frage der Fortdauer des Deutschen Ordens in Preußen', in Conze, W. (ed.), *Deutschland und Europa. Festschrift für Hans Rothfels* (Düsseldorf: Droste-Verlag, 1951), p. 196.

[78] Schieder, 'Königskrönung', p. 198.

monarchy, in the fashion of its mythological predecessors, reclaimed the whole ancient kingdom. This confirmed Polish Prussia's worst fears. When in 1699 members of the Polish szlachta, including noblemen from Royal Prussia, had launched a written protest against the occupation of Elbing by Brandenburg troops, they had warned that the Elector aimed at 'the direct domination of the whole of Prussia'.[79] The Royal Prussian burghers were no less concerned. Kazimierz Rubinkowski, postmaster in Thorn, forcefully rejected Hohenzollern pretensions to be *reges Borussorum*, warning that 'the Brandenburger has an uncontrollable appetite for Warmia and Polish Prussia, inventing great claims to these territories'.[80] But Frederick's assurances that his elevation was purely formal and his de facto power had not increased could not allay Polish Prussian fears. The 'découverte excellente' of the ancient king of the Prussians was used by the Berlin court with great skill. Werner explained to Załuski how useful it was in the diplomatic business to convince foreign rulers of Prussia's rightful place among the monarchs of Europe, since the present *Rex Borussorum* could look back on a long tradition. Werner had copied the historical claims and sent them to the Vatican as well as to the French king, 'to prove that Your Electoral Highness did not seek anything new, but only wanted to restore the old dignity, which had a good effect on those who had claimed that a crown was no good unless it was given by the Pope and the Emperor'.[81]

In the Commonwealth, once the news of the coronation had sunk in, a war between pamphleteers ensued. Following Jan Radziwiłł's protest against the creation of the Hohenzollern monarchy, Frederick's confidant Christoph von Dohna replied in an anonymous treatise, defending his sovereign's right to rule the eastern part of Prussia as he pleased. Like Werner, Dohna expressly referred to the historical justification of a Prussian monarchy: 'this Duchy of Prussia, which His Electoral Highness possesses *jure supremi dominii*, had been honoured with the status of royalty for a very long time, as Ortelius and other famous historians have demonstrated'.[82] Dohna, who pretended to write from the perspective of a Polish nobleman, showed his true colours when he justified with references to Bodin and Pufendorf 'the right of a sovereign duke to answer to no one under the sun except God'.[83] A Polish reply was swiftly forthcoming, suspecting that Dohna was anything but a Pole ('I cannot find anything Polish in your writing'), even though it was written in the Polish language. Yet the Polish author showed a measure of self-criticism when he suggested that the Poles had given up the duchy of Prussia too easily, and, if they were not more careful, they risked losing the western part of Prussia to Hohenzollern greed as well.[84] With a tribute to Hartknoch, the Polish author dismissed the legend of the Prussian king Waidewutus and asserted the

---

[79] APGd, Rkps. Elbl. 369.1, no. 326.
[80] Maliszewski, 'Kształtowanie', p. 40.
[81] Schieder, 'Königskrönung', p. 198, and Duchhardt, 'Königskrönung', p. 94.
[82] Lüdtke, *Polen und die Erwerbung*, pp. 17–18 and appendix, p. 10.
[83] Ibid., appendix, p. 10.
[84] Ibid., appendix: 'Responsum patriae amici ad epistolam cuiusdam aulici', pp. 16–17.

republican freedom of the pagan ancestors.[85] This confrontation demonstrates how vital Hartknoch's republican myth of the Prussian ancestry had become in an age when the citizens of the Commonwealth were increasingly scorned for the 'backwardness' of their mixed form of government among the monarchies of Europe. To consolidate his argument, the Polish pamphleteer compares the duke of Prussia to the starosta of Halicz, whose realm had once been a kingdom, but who would never have dreamed of royalty himself: he was much happier as a free citizen of the Commonwealth than he would have been as a vassal king. This attack on the new king in Prussia not only emphasised the fact that the Commonwealth had not consented to his elevation, but also that he was still considered a vassal of the Polish crown.[86]

Soon the Waidewutus myth gained in sophistication under the pens of the new generation of pro-Hohenzollern historians in the kingdom. In 1722 and 1723, rival historical periodicals were set up in Thorn and in Königsberg respectively. In Königsberg, Michael Lilienthal's *Erleutertes Preußen* explained the heroic past of Prussia's Waidewutus and its long monarchical legacy. In Thorn, Georg Peter Schultz edited *Das Gelahrte Preußen* and reprinted extracts from political treatises, such as the defence of the Polish-Lithuanian constitution by Jan Sachs against Hermann Conring's attacks in the 1660s, and works by Hartknoch. Nevertheless, both learned periodicals used the name of Prussia for the united province, competing for the 'most truthful' representation of Prussia's ancient and medieval traditions.[87] At the same time, there were conscious efforts to forge a new sense of dynastic loyalty and identity within Brandenburg-Prussia. It became harder for nobles and cities to resist the self-created image of their new monarch. Nobody expressed better the attraction which the identification with this monarchy must have exerted than the panegyricist Johann von Besser, whose *History of the Coronation of 1701* appeared shortly after the ceremony and was reprinted in 1712. The work set the pace for subsequent appraisals of the creation of the Prussian crown and its meaning for the future of the Hohenzollern dynasty and its people:

> Since once upon a time Prussia was a kingdom . . . it was jealous of its neighbours who were monarchs; its people, like the children of Israel, were moved by the glory of neighbouring kingdoms, wailing 'give us a king so that we can be like others' . . . But all this has been helped by Your Majesty's coronation. Prussia has become not only a royal Prussia, but a kingdom itself.[88]

[85] Ibid., appendix, p. 21.
[86] Schieder, 'Königskrönung', p. 199.
[87] Maria Dunajówna, 'Pierwsze Toruńskie Czasopismo Naukowe w XVIII w., Das Gelehrte Preussen', in Zdrójkowski, Zbigniew (ed.), *Księga Pamiątkowa 400-lecia Toruńskiego Gimnazjum Akademickiego XVI–XVIII wieku* (Toruń: TNT, 1972), p. 246.
[88] Johann von Besser, *Preussische Krönungsgeschichte oder Verlauf der Zeremonien mit welchen der Allerdurchl[auchte] Großm[ächtige] Fürst und Herr Hr. Friderich der Dritte Markgraf und Kurfürst zu Brandenburg die königliche Würde des von ihm gestiffteten Königreichs Preußen angenommen* (Cölln a. d. Spree: Ulrich Liebpert, 1712), p. 3.

## Divergence: the construction of rival Prussian identities

The sense of superiority which resulted from the elevation to royal glory was irresistible for most estates of the former Ducal Prussia, and even for the citizens of the once rebellious Königsberg. The former political admiration for Polish Prussia now turned into a historical and political claim to the western part of the province. Michael Lilienthal deplored the fact that the twelve sons of Waidewutus had split up the pagan kingdom and destroyed its unity and grandeur; but he praised Frederick's service to Prussia: 'Thus, Frederick has restored your glory, and made you as famous as you had been in the past.'[89] The fact that one part of the historic Prussia was under the slowly declining power of Poland, ruled by the Saxon Wettins, seemed an insult to Prussian pride. In the new kingdom, republican treatises on the virtues of the mixed form of government vanished, and Prussia's former obligations and allegiance to the Polish crown were no longer mentioned, despite Frederick's formal assurance that the *homagium eventuale* and the validity of the treaties of 1657 were still in place after the coronation.[90] The Hohenzollern dynasty claimed its full authority over the history of Prussia: 'Everything that has been good for Prussia has come from the house of Brandenburg. Its first duke, Albert [*sic*], freed it from the obscene yoke of the Teutonic Knights, while Frederick William the Great [Elector] liberated it from the double burden of fiefdom and elevated the province to sovereignty.'[91]

Scholars in the former Ducal Prussia also began collecting more and more references to a specifically Prussian identity. They mused about the national character of the native Prussians who, unlike the German immigrants, were never false and deceitful, but open and trustworthy. It was the 'foreigners', such as Bavarians, Swabians and Franconians, and not the 'National-Preußen' who gave the Prussians a bad reputation.[92] A similar piece in the same periodical also plays down the German origin: the Prussians were 'composed of a great melange of foreign nations'. It was due to this mixture, the writer concludes, that 'only a few remain of the original Prussian race (preußische Race)'.[93] It was not Brandenburg, the German part of the Hohenzollern dominions, from which was derived the future name of the state, but Prussia. It was as if, after 1701, the newly founded kingdom of Prussia wanted to rid itself of the stigma of Germanness, as this was associated with the Teutonic past. In 1703, Johann Peter Ludewig, professor at the University of Halle in Brandenburg, answered the protest against the coronation which the Teutonic Grand Master submitted before the Imperial Diet in Regensburg.[94] Ludewig's attack on the Teutonic Knights went much further than the anti-Teutonic writings of Hartknoch or other Royal Prussian historians in the

---

[89] Schieder, 'Königskrönung', p. 200.
[90] Lüdtke, *Polen und die Erwerbung*, appendix: 'Reversalien Friedrichs I von 1701', pp. 7–8.
[91] Besser, *Preußische Krönungsgeschichte*, p. 4.
[92] *Erleutertes Preußen* I, 157–8.    [93] Ibid., IV, 384.
[94] Johann Peter Ludewig, *Verthaidigtes Preußen wider den vermeinten und widerrechtlichen Anspruch des Teutschen Ritter-Ordens und insbesondere dessen an. 1701 auf dem Reichstag zu Regensburg ausgestreutes unbefugtes Gravamen über die Königliche Würde von Preußen* (Mergentheim [Berlin]: n.pub., 1703).

previous century. The author not only exposed the vices of the Knights, but used the historical myths of the Waidewutus saga against the Teutonic Order's claim on Prussia:

Prussia was a sovereign kingdom and not subject to other rulers, and Helmoldus wrote that the Prussians were a freedom-loving people, which never accepted the yoke of foreign domination . . . and the Prussian nation, which extended far into Poland and Lithuania, chose from among their noblemen one with the name Waidewutus and made him king over Prussia.[95]

This paragraph contains the boldest assertion of the newly created dynastic Prussian national identity so far. Not only was the Hohenzollern king well within his rights to follow the Prussian example of Waidewutus by reconstructing his kingdom, but Frederick I was now considered a son of the freedom-loving, sovereign Prussian nation. Frederick had become a truly Prussian king: 'The Prussians, [the councillors of Königsberg] said, not only were the luckiest among the nations to have a king, but one by the grace of God: a king from among their brothers, since His Majesty was born within the Prussian borders and in the city of Königsberg, and therefore belongs to us.'[96] The act of instrumentalising historical myths in the service of diplomacy was more than a symbolic gesture; it had concrete political results. It initiated a new monarchy in Europe and a new dynastic and national Prussian identity which was potentially expansive, as it laid claim to territories outside the duchy's former political borders. The old unity of Prussia, whose loss had been deplored by the Royal Prussian historians, suddenly gained a new significance. The historiographical traditions in the two provinces of Prussia changed drastically after the coronation of 1701. How seriously the rival contenders for the 'politically correct' Prussian past took the myth of Prussia's royal descent is demonstrated by the fact that the Waidewutus controversy became the subject of parliamentary debate. A report by the resident of Thorn in Warsaw from the Polish Sejm in January 1701 recorded that

the ministers [of the Elector of Brandenburg] speak confidently about the ancient kings of Prussia, such as Pruteno and his brother Waidewuto; but there are much stronger reasons *in contrarium* to prove that Waidewutus and his twelve sons are pure inventions, and . . . there is greater probability that there never was a king among the Prussians, but that they lived in republics. Meanwhile, present circumstances seem to favour the Elector's rule over Prussia, as during the past Swedish war [of 1655–1660], when he obtained the *absolutum dominium* in Prussia and profited from those fateful events.[97]

Polish Prussian historians and politicians reacted against this Hohenzollern usurpation of the common Prussian past by asserting the province's separate traditions, distancing themselves from the previously popular idea of Prussian unity. A typical

---

[95] Ibid., p. 6.    [96] Besser, *Preußische Krönungsgeschichte*, p. 62.
[97] APT Kat. II, VI.23, 'Berichte vom Reichstag zu Warschau, Jan.–Oct. 1701', pp. 9–10.

response came from Philipp von Schröter, a councillor in Elbing, who asserted that the western part of the old Prussian lands belonged to the Polish-Lithuanian Commonwealth in the same way as Lithuania: as it surpasses the kingdom of Prussia in prosperity and the beauty of its cities and countryside, it 'is justified to carry the Grand Ducal title'. The legitimate owner of the title, of course, was the Polish king who had been grand duke of Lithuania, Prussia and Ruś since the fifteenth century.[98] The more the new monarch in neighbouring Brandenburg-Prussia emphasised the sovereign nature of his power, the more the burghers and nobles in Polish Prussia stressed their special privileges and immunities, maintained and confirmed over centuries by the Polish king. David Braun, the burgrave of Marienburg, pointed to the 'consent of the Prussian estates on which the Polish king was dependent, as he himself did not possess any sovereign right to coin money in Prussia'.[99] Martin Böhm stressed that Polish Prussia benefited from belonging to a free republic, instead of a monarchy where the king ruled by licence and arbitrary power.[100] The affirmation of self-government was not only directed against the new monarchy, but above all against interference from Warsaw: all writers agreed 'that our Prussia has special *Jura*, its own law and privileges separate from the Poles . . . and [we] do not merely obey the will of the Poles'.[101] As a free people, the Polish Prussians assembled their dietines, while the estates in neighbouring Brandenburg-Prussia had lost their powers of self-taxation and decision-making: the Polish Prussians 'cannot be forced into such obedience, but everything depends on their free will and politeness, not on the decisions of the Polish Sejm'.[102]

'Sovereignty' and 'freedom' had acquired a different meaning in the two parts of Prussia: in the new kingdom, both virtues were inherently bound to the existence of a strong monarch and to the grace of God, not to fundamental laws. All privileges therefore assumed the nature of concessions, granted by the grace of a divinely legitimised king, instead of immunities empowering nobles and burghers to be true citizens with an influence on their government. The foreign Brandenburger, it seemed, had become a Prussian king, with whom the estates identified as the 'father of their fatherland', who ruled them *legibus absolutus*, above their own ancient laws. In Polish Prussia, such an idea was utterly alien to the idea of free citizenship, where 'Lex regit Regem' – the law ruled the king.[103] Informal political activities below the level of the *Landtag* among East Prussian nobles and local representa-

---

[98] Philipp von Schröter, *Gründlicher Beweis daß das Westliche oder so genannte Polnische Preußen ein Groß-Herzogthum sey, aus zuverlässigen historischen Nachrichten und Urkunden* (Halle and Leipzig: Nisius, 1755), pp. 11, 19, 28.
[99] David Braun, *Ausführlicher Historischer Bericht vom Polnisch- und Preußischen Münz-Wesen* (Elbing: Bannehr, 1722), p. 61.
[100] Böhm, *Commentarius de Interregnis*, preface.
[101] Ibid., pp. 17, 36.
[102] Georg Peter Schultz, 'Variae Observationes', APT VIII. 46, p. 37.
[103] Böhm, 'Elenchus Manuscriptorum', Bibl. PAN Krak. 1936, folio 49v.

tions[104] could not compensate for the loss of true citizenship and local self-government, which the Polish Prussian estates successfully defended until the partitions in 1772–93.

The clash between the two Prussian constitutional identities was also obvious in day-to-day diplomacy. The Hohenzollern court-historian Besser wryly commented on the Danzigers, who received Frederick I with little enthusiasm after his coronation, when he visited on the way back to Berlin. He blamed the modesty of the reception on public opinion in the Commonwealth and the Polish monarch, who 'did not let them do more for the newly-crowned king'.[105] Not only did Besser underestimate the autonomy with which Danzig usually conducted its foreign relations, but he mistakenly attributed to the Polish Prussians a sentiment which was not there: 'that they had always considered Your Majesty as the protector of their freedoms'. Nothing could be further from the truth. Besser was, of course, a hired flatterer. Yet the fact that Hohenzollern panegyric literature so outspokenly recommended Polish Prussia as a future protectorate was alarming indeed for the Polish Prussian burghers, who sighed with relief in 1700 when the Brandenburgers left Elbing after two years of occupation: 'when Brandenburg troops at last evacuated the city in 1700, it was restored to its full freedom and the enjoyment of all its immunities'.[106] The sense of victory did not endure: Hohenzollern troops remained in control of Elbing's economically important hinterland.

After 1701, a contest emerged between two different political, historical and national Prussian identities. Throughout the eighteenth century, 'Prussian' and 'Prussia' came to assume different meanings. On a military and diplomatic level, the Prussian monarchy prevailed. The propagation of a new Prussian nation under the house of Hohenzollern succeeded in eclipsing the Prussian identity of Polish Prussia. The idea of a united Prussia was no longer fed by the memory of the rebellion against the Teutonic Knights of 1454, which had led nobles and cities to seek the protection of the Polish crown, but was usurped by the construction of a mythological kingdom, whose heir was the house of Brandenburg. Before the partitions of Poland-Lithuania, when Prussia was forcefully united under the Hohenzollern monarchy, Polish Prussia had yet to survive many years of warfare – battles against foreign intruders as well as civil wars. The conflict which has often been considered as decisive for breaking the power of Poland-Lithuania was the Great Northern War. It also fundamentally changed the attitudes of the burghers of Danzig, Elbing and Thorn towards the Commonwealth and its institutions.

[104] Neugebauer, *Politischer Wandel*, chapters 2–3, esp. pp. 87–125.
[105] Besser, *Preußische Krönungsgeschichte*, p. 63.
[106] 'Fata Civitatis Elbingensis Bellica conscripta a Samuel Gottlieb Fuchs', APGd, Rkps. Elbl. III, 255/452, p. 29, where it is shown that Brandenburg-Prussia was hardly regarded as the protector of the city's liberties.

# 8

# Centre versus province: the Royal Prussian cities during the Great Northern War

In 1701, while the courts of Berlin and Königsberg were busy preparing the coronation festivities, other rulers in Northern Europe had more serious matters to attend to. In 1697, the accession to the Swedish throne of fifteen-year-old Charles XII (1697–1718) aroused the interest of his neighbours in rethinking the balance of power in the Baltic. Denmark, under Frederick IV (1699–1730), aimed at the recovery of territories lost in wars with Sweden between 1643 and 1660; Russia, under Peter I (1682–1725), was equally keen to weaken Sweden's influence and gain access to the Baltic. In Poland-Lithuania, Frederick August, Elector of Saxony, had emerged victorious in the race for the Polish crown in 1697, after converting to Catholicism and outstripping the French candidate, François Louis de Bourbon, Prince of Conti. High hopes were attached to the new monarch, whose powerful presence gained him the name Augustus the Strong, and whose political ambitions, combined with the wealth and prosperity of Saxony, seemed to provide the Commonwealth with a welcome boost of strength after the lacklustre ending of John Sobieski's reign. In his coronation oath, Augustus promised to recover Livonia, and in particular the city of Riga, for the Commonwealth. In the autumn of 1698, after a meeting with Peter in Rawa, Augustus concluded an anti-Swedish alliance with Denmark. In January 1699, encouraged by the peace of Karlowitz between the emperor and the Ottoman Empire, which handed back Podolia and parts of the Ukraine to the Commonwealth, Augustus confirmed his official alliance with Denmark and Russia. In December, Saxon troops made their first assault on Swedish-occupied Riga. The optimism of the coalition partners, however, was rudely shattered when what seemed an easy enough expedition ended in a military fiasco. Charles XII forced the Danes to leave the alliance through the peace of Travendal in August 1700, and three months later Russia suffered a disastrous defeat at Narva, while the Saxons had to abandon their plans to reconquer Riga. The 1701 occupation of the Polish duchy of Courland by the Swedes officially opened the Great Northern War, which during the next two decades pushed the Commonwealth to the brink of disaster.

The Swedish occupation of Lithuania in 1702, the conquest of Warsaw and Cracow, the proclamation, in 1704, of Stanisław Leszczyński, the palatine of Poznań, as new king of Poland by the Swedish-led Confederation of Warsaw, and the Swedish occupation of Electoral Saxony resulted in Augustus's deposition in September 1706. It was only after the Russian victory over the Swedes at Poltava in July 1709 that Augustus could reclaim his throne. The price exacted for Russian support, however, was the tsar's influence on Polish affairs, the Russian occupation of Livonia, and Poland's continued military assistance against Sweden, confirmed in the Treaty of Thorn in December 1709. Russian control over the Commonwealth was once more asserted in 1716, when Augustus's designs to establish *absolutum dominium* and his encouragement of Prussian plans for the partition of the Commonwealth triggered a revolt against him by the confederation of Tarnogród. In 1717, under the 'protection' of Russian arms, the 'Silent Sejm' of Grodno decided to establish a standing army, limited at 16,000 troops for Poland and 8,000 for Lithuania. When the peace of Nystad officially ended the war, the Polish-Lithuanian Commonwealth was economically exhausted, and its international prestige had been ruined.

This war, and the reign of Augustus II, represent the greatest watershed in the relationship between the Prussian cities and the Polish monarchy before the partitions of 1772 and 1793 put an end to the long association of Royal Prussia with the Commonwealth. The period of the Great Northern War was also marked by a growing discrepancy between the Royal Prussian cities' attempt to uphold the fiction of an idealised Prussian past with its real or imagined liberties, and the political goals of a considerable part of the province's szlachta, which supported the transformation of the Commonwealth into a more coherent and unified body politic. Consequently, historians of Royal Prussia, such as Jerzy Dygdała, Hans-Jürgen Bömelburg and Stanisław Salmonowicz, have spoken of a general 'revival of Prussian particularism' in the eighteenth century.[1] The concept of 'particularism', however, is of doubtful value in characterising the objectives and ambitions of the Royal Prussian cities at any time in the history of the old Commonwealth. Dygdała has admitted that the popularity of local self-government was not just a Prussian phenomenon, but, at least under the Saxon kings, reflected a wider Polish-Lithuanian trend.

In reality, the ability of the urban politicians to conduct an independent policy diminished in inverse proportion to the fierceness of their rhetoric of 'particularism'.[2] In the last century of its union with the Polish-Lithuanian Commonwealth, a series of political and cultural changes swept through Royal Prussia and its cities.[3]

---

[1] Bömelburg, *Zwischen polnischer Ständegesellschaft*, pp. 145–86; Dygdała, *Życie polityczne*, pp. 18ff; Stanisław Salmonowicz, 'Prusy Królewskie w ustroju Rzeczypospolitej szlacheckiej, 1569–1772', *Acta Universitatis Wratislaviensis* 945, Historia LXVI (1988), 45–66.

[2] Dygdała, *Życie polityczne*, p. 241 and Stanisław Salmonowicz, 'Z dziejów walki o tzw. restauracji autonomicznych aspiracji Prus Królewskich w XVIII wieku', *Analecta Cracoviensia* 7 (1975), 436–8.

[3] For the history of Royal Prussian cities in the eighteenth century, see Edmund Cieślak, Zbigniew Nowak, Jerzy Stankiewicz and Jerzy Trzoska (eds.), *Historia Gdańska*, vol. III/1: '1655–1793' (Gdańsk: Instytut Historii PAN, 1993); Jerzy Dygdała, Stanisław Salmonowicz and Jerzy Wojtowicz (eds.), *Historia Torunia*, vol. II/3: 'Między barokiem i oświeceniem, 1660–1793' (Toruń: Instytut

As the flaws of the Commonwealth were exposed during the Great Northern War, and the debate began over its possible reform, so the Royal Prussians had to face up to both the decline of the political culture in which they had so long found a congenial home, and the Hohenzollern challenge to their identity as Prussians. Between the war, which had led to the devastation of their trade and prosperity by Polish, Saxon and Russian armies, and the crisis of the partitions, Royal Prussian attitudes changed substantially.

The friendly support Augustus had found in the Prussian cities cooled quickly when the urban politicians became aware of the king's ambitions in the Baltic war theatre. Remembering earlier royal projects – most notably under Sigismund III Vasa (1587–1632) – to build a Polish Baltic fleet and to contest Danzig's trade monopoly, the city did not welcome the king's expansionist intentions; nor did the majority of the local noble landowners. In the event of a renewed war with Sweden, their province would once more become the main battleground. The stationing of Saxon troops had already started in Royal Prussia, justified by the need to defend Elbing against the Brandenburg troops that had occupied the city in 1698. Several Polish envoys, however, doubted whether the king was serious in his intention to fend off the Brandenburgers, suspecting that 'the Saxons would not fight well against Brandenburg troops, as Germans would not like to hurt their countrymen: Germanos Germanis nil nocituros'.[4] Although proof of Augustus's secret deal with Brandenburg to occupy the city of Elbing was only discovered in the nineteenth century, burgomasters and council members possessed their own sources of information and were not easily fooled.[5] Anti-Saxon pamphlets and political verses, alleging that Augustus was not blameless in the 'Elbing-affair', appeared in several *silva rerum* of Thorn and Danzig burghers. After Brandt, the Brandenburg resident in Warsaw, had made it clear that Augustus II and the Elector Frederick had a 'harmonious understanding', and as Augustus did little to restore the city to the Commonwealth, many saw the augmentation of Saxon troops in Elbing as evidence for the Saxon king's pursuit of *absolutum dominium*.[6]

The old conflict between *majestas* and *libertas* – between the king's personal foreign policy goals, often pursued behind the Sejm's back, and the Commonwealth's opposition to any schemes that threatened higher taxation and strengthened the monarch's powers – entered a new phase and disempowered the party of senatorial constitutionalists who with little success had tried to reform the

---

Historii PAN and TNT, 1996). There is as yet no equivalent on Elbing: Andrzej Groth, et al. (eds.), *Historia Elbląga*, vol. II/1 (Gdańsk: Marpress, 1996), only covers the period until 1626.

[4] 'Diarium Electionis Wahl-Reichstag 1697', APT Kat.II, VI.20.

[5] Theodor Mörner, *Kurbrandenburgs Staatsverträge* (Berlin: G. Reiner, 1867); Gierszewski, *Elbląg*, p. 148; Ludwig Neubaur, 'Die Russen in Elbing, 1710–1713', *Altpreußische Monatsschrift* 53 (1916), 273. Neubaur reports that the Polish king suggested that the Elector of Brandenburg 'take the city either *par surprise* or in any other way'.

[6] Wanda Klęsińska, 'Okupacja Elbląga przez Brandenburgię w latach 1698–1700', *Rocznik Elbląski* 4 (1969), 117; and Bogusław Dybaś, *Sejm pacyfikacyjny w 1699 roku*, Roczniki TNT, no. 84 (Toruń: TNT, 1991), pp. 50–57.

Commonwealth during the seventeenth century. Bolstered by assurances of Russian support, the Polish king did not delay in reorienting his political activities towards Northern Europe. After Saxon troops under Jakob Flemming had advanced against Swedish-occupied Riga in December 1699, the rapidly degenerating relationship between Augustus and the Sejm resulted in the szlachta's refusal to grant any financial and military support to their king unless he pulled all Saxon troops out of the Commonwealth. Danzig had tried to prevent the quartering of Saxons by paying a lump sum towards the upkeep of the king's army, but when this failed in 1701 the city militia fought a skirmish to prevent Saxon soldiers from encroaching upon its lands.[7]

The Prussian cities continued to consider the war as Augustus's private conflict even after 1702. The Danzigers were particularly upset that the king had tried – unsuccessfully – to cajole them into expelling the Swedish resident ambassador Cuypercrona, and thus to curtail the city's customary right to pursue its own policy for the maintenance of its commerce and trade.[8] Danzig also insisted on taking measures against Saxon-Polish privateers, which earned the city the reputation of being well-disposed towards the Swedes and aroused Augustus's discontent with the Prussian cities. By 1703, however, the war caught up with them. At the same time as the Saxon troops stationed in Thorn had to surrender to the Swedes, Elbing was taken after Brandenburg-Prussian units had been forced to retreat and leave most of Warmia, including the episcopal palace in Heilsberg (Lidzbark), in Swedish control. Swedish troops first approached Danzig in the summer of the same year. As there was no hope that the king would send a relief force, the Danzigers desperately sought to mobilise foreign diplomatic support and to organise their own defence. After complex but unsuccessful negotiations with Berlin and the failure to win more than tentative diplomatic support from the Dutch and the English, Danzig entered into lengthy and financially burdensome negotiations with the Swedes. The threat of a full-scale occupation of the city by General Stenbock forced the city council in 1704 to join the Confederation of Warsaw, which supported Stanisław Leszczyński, Charles XII's candidate for the Polish throne.[9] This saved the city from occupation and destruction by war, although it could not protect the suburbs from Swedish garrisons. Ever new contributions, demands, exactions and taxes were presented and executed under constant military threat and drained the city of its financial resources.[10]

The relationship between the cities and Augustus remained tense. Danzig's position reflected rather closely the mood in the rest of the country, where

---

[7] 'Instruktion und Briefe an den Gesandten der Stadt Danzig in Warschau', APGd., Bibl. Archivi 300.R, Dd 18b, pp. 4–7.
[8] Hannes Saarinen, *Bürgerstadt und absoluter Kriegsherr. Danzig und Karl XII. im Nordischen Krieg* (Helsinki: Suomi Historiallinen Seura), p. 37.
[9] Alfons Wodziński, *Gdańsk za czasów Stanisława Leszczyńskiego 1704–1709* (Cracow: Gebethner and Wolff, 1929), p. 26.
[10] Löschin, *Geschichte Danzigs*, vol. I, pp. 111–27; Cieślak, *Historia Gdańska*, vol. III, p. 486.

enthusiasm for war with Sweden was clearly lacking. Only the szlachta in the Royal Prussian diet in 1701, facing an immediate threat to their landed estates, voted for a considerable increase in contribution for the crown army, while the major cities, above all Danzig, were resolved not to cede to royal pressure and refused to share the burden. Implicitly, therefore, the city joined the opposition to Augustus's policies which was growing in other provinces of the Commonwealth. The mood also changed in smaller Prussian towns, such as Marienburg, where in 1698 the city fathers had received Augustus with gifts of money and celebratory pomp organised around the traditional ceremony of hand-kissing in confirmation of loyalty; in 1705, however, when both Swedish and Commonwealth armies fought for possession of the town, several contemporary writers complained bitterly about the plundering of the city by Polish and Saxon troops.[11] Significantly, local chroniclers did not speak of rebellion against the Swedes, but against Augustus's soldiers, who deported several men from the Vistula delta and the Danzig and Marienburg river islands, starved the rural population, took by force any food and goods they could find, and collected contributions which 'had more resemblance to hostile plundering than protection'.[12] As a result of the continued financial burdens and demands for contributions, 'many poorer farmers had to abandon their property, commerce and trade in the city of Marienburg, which was impoverished to such an extent that many burghers fled the country to settle in the kingdom of Prussia, leaving behind deserted houses'.[13]

The emphasis on freedom from foreign domination was a common theme of political treatises and historical literature in Royal Prussia throughout the war. During the Polish Sejm of 1697, the szlachta had emphasised its dislike of the 'German troops' by demanding that the Royal Guard was to be formed from among Polish and Lithuanian troops, so that they would not be policed by foreigners and Protestants.[14] Not only the suspicious szlachta, but also urban magistrates were convinced that Augustus was plotting a coup against the Polish-Lithuanian constitution, to limit the powers of the hetmans and of the dietines (including the Prussian diet) and to increase the Saxon armed forces stationed on Polish soil. The king's main military adviser, field marshal Flemming, was suspected to be the author of a proposal to transform the Commonwealth into a hereditary monarchy.[15] There is evidence that the Prussian burghers rejected Augustus's policies in similar terms to the nobility: not because he employed German soldiers, but because he followed

[11] G. Berg, 'Marienburg im dritten schwedischen (nordischen) Kriege (1700–1721), *Mitteilungen des Westpreußischen Geschichtsvereins* 18 (1919), 2–10.

[12] Abraham Hartwich, *Herrn Abraham Hartwichs weyland Pastoris zu Bährenhof im Marienburgischen Werder Geographisch-historische Landesbeschreibung derer dreyen im Pohlnischen Preussen liegenden Werdern, als des Danziger-, Elbing- und Marienburgischen* (Königsberg: Eckert, 1723), pp. 439–40, 445.

[13] Berg, 'Marienburg', p. 10.

[14] 'Diarium Electionis', APT Kat. II, VI.20, folios 230v–231.

[15] Józef Gierowski, 'Pruski projekt zamachu stanu w Polsce w 1715 roku', *Przegląd Historyczny* 50 (1959), 753–4; the title of the anonymous pamphlet was: 'How to make the Polish throne hereditary and to introduce true freedom into this country'.

models of government which posed a threat to the basic philosophy and nature of the mixed form of government, the right of free election and the power of the diets and dietines. German or Saxon origin was synonymous with being foreign, thus neither Augustus nor his Saxon advisors were trusted to respect the constitution and freedoms of the citizens of the Commonwealth – including its urban citizens. When Thorn was defended by Saxon units during the Swedish siege, and the living conditions within the city grew worse, the citizens staged embittered demonstrations against the desperate defence of Thorn by the Saxon soldiers who 'do not behave towards the citizenry as if they were our friends, but our enemies'. In response to plundering by hungry Saxons, the burghers of Thorn organised squads to patrol burgher houses. When the Saxon commanders resisted pleas to surrender the city to the Swedes, the city fathers argued that they knew better what to do, 'since we belong more to this city than you'.[16] In his chronicle of Thorn, Heinrich Zernecke shows great indignation against the Polish-Saxon troops and the 'German dragoons', whose presence in the city he considered particularly ruinous.[17] After the Swedish defeat at the battle of Poltava in 1709, Danzig magistrates boycotted the commission of Augustus's foreign advisors summoned to judge the Prussian cities' behaviour during the war, because 'foreigners . . . do not know the constitution and customs of the Commonwealth and of the province of Royal Prussia'.[18]

Considering that in the early eighteenth century armies had grown in size and destructiveness, the Prussian province's immunity from military burdens and troops other than those raised in their own palatinates and cities was more important – but also less realistic – than ever before. In 1700, the Thorn professor Martin Böhm composed a pamphlet protesting the ancient right of Royal Prussia to employ its troops merely within the borders of the province, and only for self-defence. The idea that Polish or Saxon troops would be stationed in the province was considered a grave violation of the fundamental laws of the province.[19] Unable to foresee the consequences of the present war, Böhm ominously warned his fellow citizens to observe the province's ancient freedoms, such as the freedom from garrisons and from the duty of participation in the *levée-aux-armes* outside Royal Prussia's borders: 'the sinister fates which rolled over the Prussian lands many centuries ago teach us the importance of this privilege'. Servitude, he prophesied, always began with contributions to foreign armies which could easily be turned against the inhabitants to oppress their liberty. Böhm quickly added, however, that although Royal Prussia had separate laws, it was one 'with the body of the realm' and would rush to help the Commonwealth if the entire state was in danger of losing its freedoms to a foreign intruder.[20]

---

[16] Report of the Siege of Thorn, 24 May–14 October, 1703, APT Kat. II, IV.18, folio 20–1.

[17] Zernecke, *Historiae Thoruniensis*, p. 416.    [18] Wodziński, *Gdańsk za czasów*, p. 88.

[19] Martin Böhm, *Dissertatio ex Historia Prussica qua ostenditur, Borussos ad generalem Expeditionem extra fines suos non esse adstrictos defendit Johannes Hintz, Tempelburg[ii] Pom[eranus], sub praesidio M. Martini Böhm* (Thorn: Nicolai, 1700), folio Av.

[20] Ibid., folios A2, A4–A4v.

This treatise clearly repeats the urban elites' basic conviction that they formed an integral part of the republic, together with all other nations of the Commonwealth, and were ready for the defence of their common fatherland. By force of their own laws and privileges, however, they could not become part of an offensive and aggressive war. Adopting contemporary natural law arguments and following Hugo Grotius, Böhm stressed the refusal of Prussia's free citizens to serve as instruments of an absolute monarch. Deeply concerned for their commercial interests, the burghers felt threatened by a political development which pitched the cities' main trade partners, the Dutch, the English and the Swedes, against a Polish-Russian-Danish alliance. Beyond the commercial interest, however, a deeper political conviction, shared by the majority of the Commonwealth's szlachta, moved the burghers to oppose the war. Böhm protested that it was not the duty of the Prussians, incorporated under the safeguard of their liberties, to enter wars not approved by the whole republic; it was, however, the obligation of the king and the Commonwealth to defend Royal Prussia against any attack from outside. Privileges such as the freedom from garrisons and the general levy, therefore, were not mutual but one-sided, as the Prussians retained the freedom to decide whether they would remain under the Polish sceptre or choose another lord and master: '[The Prussians] did not transfer their allegiance in order to defend the kingdom [of Poland], but so that they would be defended by it.'[21] The warning that the allegiance of the Prussian cities to a king who endangered the safety and liberties of his subjects might cease altogether, and that Prussia could find a better protector of her rights, echoes in all writings of Prussian burghers during the Great Northern War.

Anti-Saxon attacks by the Polish szlachta on the courts of Warsaw and Dresden, often in the form of satires and mocking poems, were eagerly copied into the diaries and *silvae rerum* of burgomasters and council-members. Georg Austen and Petrus Düsterwald from Thorn, for example, translated into German a Polish pamphlet attacking Saxon troops, under the title 'Secrets of the present state [of Poland], obvious to everyone'. Not even the anti-Protestant bias of these verses prevented Düsterwald from approving their anti-monarchical thrust:

Polish lobster or everything goes backwards:

Everybody praises what ought to be criticised
everybody is overjoyed by what should make them weep
German troops are permitted to enter the kingdom for worse
while . . . the chamber [of envoys] is exposed to mockery . . .
Promising everything, delivering nothing
Distributing offices and taking them away again
Establishing commissions against troublemakers
Manning fortresses with heretics [i.e. Saxon Lutherans]
Avoiding calling the Sejm and holding mock senate councils

[21] Ibid., folio B3v.

Introducing the foreign army [the Saxons] under the pretext of war against the Elector of
  Brandenburg in order to weaken the szlachta
Plundering the riches of Poland and paying foreigners with them.[22]

The threat to liberty was considered to come mainly from the king, as Austen
continues: 'my king wants to give me balm which is mixed with the sweet poison of
sleepiness, which removes all spirit and senses'.[23] The king was also blamed for
'distributing Poland' to its enemies: to Brandenburg, to whom he 'gave the crown',
to Sweden, which 'strips [Poland] of its golden and silver dress', while the
Muscovites 'gain [Poland's] boots as reward'.[24]

   Despite the attempt by several Polish historians since the 1970s, particularly by
Józef Gierowski and Jacek Staszewski, to revise the hitherto exclusively negative
image of the Saxon period,[25] from a Polish Prussian perspective the rehabilitation of
Augustus II must have its limits. The unpredictability and secretive manoeuvring
of the king's foreign and domestic policies were legendary even among contemporaries, and although the picture of the king as a sinister plotter against the szlachta
and urban freedoms painted by the republican propaganda might not always be
borne out by the sources, there is no doubt that the Prussian burghers did not trust
their king. Why then did the burghers have such qualms about abandoning
Augustus? Why, although pressured into paying contributions to the Swedish
puppet-king, Stanisław Leszczyński, did the Swedes have to threaten severe
punishment before the citizens of Danzig abolished the customary prayer for
Augustus II in their Lutheran and Catholic churches?[26] The answer is that
although Danzig had no great love for Augustus, the city never surrendered the
legal source and guarantor of its precious liberties and one of the three necessary
elements of the well-balanced mixed form of government: a legally elected and
rightfully crowned king. After the defeat of the Saxon army at Fraustadt under
General Schulenburg, and the Swedish occupation of the Electorate in early 1706,
Augustus abdicated in September after his ministers signed the treaty of Altran-
städt. The news was barely believed in the city. Only now did the Danzigers agree
to abjure their previous oath; they still delayed recognising Leszczyński until he
was crowned, although he desperately tried to endear himself to the burghers. In
vain he appealed to the Danzigers' mercantile spirit, granting them a whole series of
economic privileges, enforcing their trade monopoly and protecting Danzig's
merchant fleet, in obvious contrast to Augustus.[27] Yet Rubach, the Brandenburg-

[22] Austen, 'Düsterwald, Encomia, Vituperia, Stylo lapidari scripta', APT Kat. II, XIV.71, pp. 110–11;
  see the Polish version in X. Froelich, 'Politische Poesien aus Polnisch-Preußen den Jahre 1697–1707
  angehörig', *Altpreußische Monatsschrift* 7 (1870), 540.
[23] Austen, 'Encomia', pp. 103f.   [24] Ibid., pp. 103–111.
[25] Józef Gierowski, 'Problematyka bałtycka w polityce Augusta II Sasa', in Trzoska, Jerzy (ed.), *Strefa
  bałtycka*, p. 51; Jacek Staszewski, 'Die polnisch-sächsische Union und die Hohenzollernmonarchie
  (1679–1763)', *Jahrbücher für die Geschichte Mittel- und Ostdeutschlands* 30 (1981), 28–34; and his *O
  miejsce w Europie* (Warszawa: PWN 1973).   [26] Wodziński, *Gdańsk za czasów*, pp. 12, 14.
[27] Gierowski, 'Problematyka bałtycka', p. 59.

Prussian delegate to Danzig, commented in one of his letters to Berlin that 'the happiness about the new king in the city is not genuine'.[28] Despite being personally rather well-liked by the burghers, he remained a king illegally forced upon them, not elected. As a result, Danzig never paid homage to king Stanisław, who also remained without any substantial support among the estates of Poland. Similarly, during the siege of Danzig in the war of succession in 1733–4 the city did acknowledge Leszczyński as king, since he was, in Danzig's opinion, legally elected, instead of Augustus III, who had been imposed upon them by Russian military force. Neither in 1704 nor in 1733 was the choice guided by national or personal preferences, but by constitutional arguments.

In face of such dogged support for the cause of the rightfully elected monarch, the city was bitterly disappointed in 1709, when Augustus, after Poltava opened the way for his return to the throne, decreed an amnesty for the nobility, including his arch-enemies, the Sapiehas and hetman Hieronym Lubomirski, but not for Danzig. It felt this injustice particularly strongly due to the attitudes of the Polish Prussian szlachta who in 1703 had first confederated at Stargardt in support of Augustus, but from 1707 had gone over to Leszczyński, to whom they allocated over 100,000 złp.[29] The contrast to the aftermath of the last Swedish wars, from 1655–60, could not have been greater. Instead of praise for its faithful allegiance and defence, Danzig, which had seen its treasury ransacked by unending demands for contribution and forced exactions, was accused of 'treacherous' negotiations with Berlin and Sweden. Such accusations were pressed by the very monarch who in 1698 had not raised any objections to the foreign occupation of Elbing and who in 1715 would plan the cession of Royal Prussia, Samogitia and Warmia to the kingdom of Prussia.[30] In 1709, a royal commission was ordered to Polish Prussia to investigate the burghers' attitudes during the reign of Leszczyński, for whose recognition Danzig alone was to be penalised. Despite voices at court which energetically disapproved of these sanctions, Augustus only backed down when the city agreed to reimburse him for the furniture which he had lost to the Swedes in 1704, and a payment of 600,000 fl.[31]

It is undeniable that this behaviour, encouraged by some of the Commonwealth's nobility, left deep scars. From this time the sources speak a very different language and radiate a much colder attitude towards the king than during the mid-seventeenth century. Prussian burghers' satires and lampoons grew much more cynical during the Great Northern War. Many Polish Prussian authors clearly thought that Augustus did not sufficiently respect their cherished privileges, and therefore redirected their appeal for recognition to the whole Commonwealth. Danzig, for

---

[28] Wodziński, *Gdańsk za czasów*, p. 60 (February 1707).
[29] Löschin, *Geschichte Danzigs* vol. I, p. 124; and Achremczyk, 'Konfederacja szlachty Prus Królewskich', 40.
[30] Gierowski, 'Pruski projekt zamachu', pp. 757ff.
[31] Cieślak, *Historia Gdańska*, vol. III, pp. 495–6.

example, responded to Swedish bullying by claiming that the city was 'a member indissolubly linked to the republic and the realm of Poland'. In particular the third estate and the artisans stressed that they would 'not separate themselves *a corpore Reipublicae*' – from the 'body of the republic'.[32] This was a most remarkable emphasis. During the seventeenth century, the city had stressed its loyalty to the Polish crown, to its kings; the republic had rarely been mentioned. After 1702, the Danzigers had no intention to sacrifice to the Swedes liberties which they shared with the republic – the mixed constitution, parliamentary life, the free election – and liberties which they considered singular and superior to Polish privileges – the participation of urban representatives in the Polish Prussian diet and all other special privileges of the province. If they wanted to safeguard their historical achievements, they knew that there was no realistic alternative to their existence within the constitutional framework of the Commonwealth.

The burgomaster of Danzig, Johann Ernst von der Linde, for example, stressed that his city was a 'free member of the Polish kingdom', and, according to the right and duty of Polish Prussia and her burghers, faithfully followed the will of the republic. In a letter addressed to a nobleman under a pseudonym, he wrote in 1712: 'Concerning public and private security, when the whole Republic deliberates about its fate, we equally demand that no Sejm can conclude anything without [the participation of] the estates of the Prussian Province, who are not the least member of the Republic.'[33] The right to self-government and equal participation in a confederative structure was the guiding principle for urban reform writers, who saw their traditions threatened by a Swedish absolute monarch, famous for his intransigence and ambition, on the one hand, and by their Saxon king's wayward plots on the other. The burghers of the major cities started to share in the common misfortune together with the whole republic, which had to acknowledge Polish Prussia's importance for the entire body politic. Looking for remedies in times of war and crisis, the defence of the whole republic became part of the burghers' political credo, and the habitual view that Danzig formed a union with the crown alone was replaced by the affirmation of Danzig's loyalty to the republic. This must be regarded as a significant modification of Danzig's political identity. During the Great Northern War, the city not only acquired a more distant relationship to the king, but expressed strong opposition to all centralising and levelling reforms directed against provincial privileges, be such reforms inspired by the king or the king's political party among the nobility. The desire for closer integration with the institutions of the Polish and Lithuanian nobility, which Polish historiography usually attributes to the Polish Prussian nobility, found its counterpart among the Prussian urban elites' aspirations to re-form the government of the Commonwealth into a well-functioning *forma mixta*, on the basis of the constitutionalist ideal of the sixteenth century.

[32] Saarinen, *Bürgerstadt*, p. 176.
[33] *Gratiani Severini Lipiński*, p. 24.

To Thorn and Elbing, the war offered even fewer political choices than to the richer Danzig. Thorn joined the Royal Prussian levy with '32 cavalrymen and two cannons', thus fulfilling the military obligations incumbent upon the city because of its land.[34] In 1703, the Swedes conquered Thorn and, after demanding the destruction of its fortification, sporadically returned until 1709, while troops under Russian, Swedish or Polish-Saxon command alternated in exhausting the town treasury and the neighbouring territories. These series of attacks on the city's resources were frequently described in political pamphlets, in allegories and self-critical satires. In the 'Foreigners' Carnival in Poland, 1701–1705', the Swedish king dines with the Russian Tsar, both being served the Polish eagle, 'spiced and baked'; the confederates of Warsaw provide the wine, and the Prussians prepare the bed for the night for the guests who 'soil their houses . . . but they prefer this to the Saxons'. The poor, however, watch in tears, asking 'there the Saxon, there the Swede – are they mad in the head?' The Lithuanians dance and jump around in Muscovite fashion (and the Cossacks fart), the Saxons, in accordance with their raw manners, dance in German, while the Prussians sing in mixed language and in bass voices, 'liber Hanns, nasz Kriegs-man, skoro szwarc bier pije' (dear John, our comrade, as long as he drinks dark beer).[35] The world was turned upside-down for the burghers of Thorn, and this satire authentically expresses an atmosphere of confusion and the disruption of the traditional loyalties between the province and its king. One unnamed author in Thorn ceated an allegory of the treacherous nature of war, where every carnival was followed by a masked ball. The Lithuanians and Poles pretended to be orphans, the palatine of Poznań (Stanisław Leszczyński) was dressed up as the king of Poland, the hetmans as Jews with a moneybag, the Sapieha family as impoverished szlachta, while the szlachta was disguised in peasant clothes. The same association was made in another anti-Augustus text: 'You did not want to be lords under a French king, therefore you are now peasants under the Saxon.'[36] Confusion and demoralisation was widespread among Thorn's citizenry, which deepened when the Polish Sejm formulated several charges against the council concerning the city's surrender to the Swedes of property stored in the city by noblemen – a repetition of the scenario of 1655.[37]

Elbing's citizenry, and particularly the council, reacted strongly to the approach of Brandenburg troops in 1698. This incident demonstrates the strong cohesion which occasionally still existed between the province's noble and urban elites. The refusal to open the city gates was justified by the 'oath that we swore to our king', supported by the Prussian szlachta's claim that Elbing was the 'antemurale of Poland against Brandenburg'.[38] When the city decided that further opposition was

---

[34] Wernicke, *Geschichte Thorns*, vol. II: *1698–1725*, p. 323.
[35] Austen 'Encomia', pp. 143–6. The satire catches very well the habit of Prussian peasants and burghers of mixing the Polish and German languages, which emphasises the authentically Prussian origin of this piece.    [36] Ibid., p. 147; Froehlich, 'Politische Poesien', p. 540.
[37] Wernicke, *Geschichte Thorns*, vol. II, pp. 330, 336.
[38] Gierszewski, *Elbląg*, p. 148.

useless, as neither Augustus nor the Prussian nobility would send any military aid, the council surrendered, but successfully refused to abjure their king and receive the Elector Frederick III of Brandenburg as their new lord.[39] In an apologetic letter, the city fathers accused the Republic of betrayal; despite their 'eternal connection with the Republic as long as it existed', the Polish king and the Rzeczpospolita had done nothing to help them. Prophetically, the Elbingers warned: 'The [Poles] could not have hurt themselves more than by separating themselves from an important member of their body and by opening the breast of the Prussian province, through which, come the time, the way will be opened towards the heart.'[40] After the Swedish occupation of 1703–10, and the Russian occupation of 1710–12, Saxon troops returned to the city. Within a decade, Böhm's affirmation that the Common-wealth and the king had a duty to defend all provinces and members of the body politic must have sounded like a voice from the distant past to the burghers of Elbing. The city had incurred debts of 70,000 thalers to Brandenburg alone, which, from 1703, occupied Elbing's landed estates. The city paid over 600,000 thalers to the Swedes and Russians during the war years, creating so many debts that 'even our grandchildren will not be able to repay them'.[41] Despite these troubles, precipitated by Augustus's readiness to hand the city over to Brandenburg, the presiding burgomaster Ramsey insisted in 1712, 'that we have great cause to thank God for liberating us from the Muscovite yoke . . . and for reinstating us under the benign wings of the Polish eagle'.[42] Such confirmations of allegiance notwithstand-ing, doubts did creep into many burghers' minds. The great sacrifices demanded of the cities in the name of the Commonwealth and by foreign powers, which had all claimed to protect their privileges and liberties before repeatedly breaking and violating them, left their marks.

After the Swedish defeat and Augustus's return to power in 1710, the Polish king repeatedly broke his oath to the *pacta conventa* by calling back his Saxon troops in even greater numbers than before. The republican response was the armed resis-tance by the Confederates of Tarnogród in 1715–16.[43] Royal Prussia could not help but become embroiled in this conflict. In 1716, Russian forces took up winter quarters in the territories and villages around the Prussian cities, demanding higher contributions than the Swedes and ordering Danzig to build privateering vessels, which the city rightly considered a threat to its international reputation as a reliable trading partner.[44] In the end, three ships were built, but never used for privateer-ing. Danzig summoned help in numerous letters to Warsaw, in which the city fathers emphasised their 'attachment to the most gracious king, senators and

[39] Ibid., p. 149; and Lengnich, *Geschichte der Lande Preußen*, vol. IX, p. 58.
[40] APGd, Rkps. Elbl. 369.1, no. 452, pp. 249–52.   [41] Gierszewski, *Elbląg*, p. 151.
[42] Neubaur, 'Die Russen in Elbing', p. 354.
[43] Józef Gierowski, *Między Saskim Absolutyzmem a Złotą Wolnością* (Wrocław: Ossolineum, 1953), pp. 302–15.
[44] Jerzy Trzoska, 'Der Streit zwischen dem Sachsen August II und Peter I um die Kaperschiffe von Gdańsk (1716–1721)', *Studia Maritima* 6 (1987), 81–105.

Republic, whose indivisible member the city is', and in a rare demonstration of solidarity the Polish–Lithuanian Diet backed the city against Russian pretensions.[45]

In the harsh political climate of the new century there was little respite for Polish Prussia. Although Russian mediation at the Silent Sejm of 1717 resolved the conflict between the Confederation of Tarnogród and Augustus, and ordered Saxon and Russian troops to leave Polish-Lithuanian territory, Royal Prussia and its three major cities had to submit, for the first time in their history, to regular, fixed military contributions to the Polish treasury. When in June 1719 Danzig insisted on monetary autonomy and refused to pay the quota demanded by the Sejm – and arbitrarily exaggerated by Jakub Rybiński, the general ordered to collect the taxes – it came to an exchange of hostilities between the urban militia and royal troops. The correspondence which preceded Rybiński's military action focuses extensively on historical arguments, as the city fathers rejected the Polish general's claim that in 1454 Royal Prussia had been conquered by the Poles – an opinion which was spreading among the Polish nobility during the eighteenth century. In response, Danzig pointed out that Prussia had always existed, even under the Teutonic Knights, as a 'distinct province' which had not joined the crown of Poland to be subjected to a new form of slavery: 'not to sail from Scylla into Charybdis, but to restore its former freedom, to maintain and augment it'.[46] The city found a supporter in Louis Mathy, the French resident, who in several letters to the king and the senate council deplored the illegal behaviour of criminals and haughty individuals with an anti-urban bias among the highest ranks of the Polish army, and warned:

As the king and the republic are incapable of protecting Danzig, . . . [the city,] tired of unending contributions, exactions and plundering, will at one point look for another protector, who might well be the Prussian king, if he just guarantees the same rights and privileges the city possesses under the Polish crown.[47]

Mathy, however, was wrong to doubt Danzig's political loyalty to Crown and Commonwealth. Most Polish Prussian burghers knew that an uncertain future under the Hohenzollerns would have to be purchased with their political freedoms, enough of which remained to be cherished. Augustus's endeavours to forge a lasting alliance with Brandenburg-Prussia did not find the Prussian cities' approval. On the contrary, a strong anti-Hohenzollern party in Danzig, under the combined leadership of burgomaster Johann Schmieden and the Lutheran minister Johann Schelgwig and supported by the crown treasurer Przebendowski, whipped up public opinion against Berlin.[48] Burghers who might have been attracted by more

[45] *Historia Gdańska*, vol. III/1: *1655–1793*, p. 499; also, Saarinen, *Bürgerstaat*, p. 324.
[46] *Responsio Civitatis Gedanensis ad scriptum quod circa irruptionem militum exercitus Regni Poloniae in Bona istius Civitatis patrimonialia sub Manifesti forma nomine ill. Domini D. Jacobi Sigismudi Rybinski Regni Venatoris & Generalis Locum-tenentis prodiit* (n.p., 1712), pp. 5–6.
[47] Cieślak, *Historia Gdańska*, vol. III, p. 506.
[48] Wodziński, *Gdańsk za czasów*, p. 41.

secure living conditions in the kingdom of Prussia were soon cured of such desires by the forced recruitment policies of Frederick William I's army, which also encroached upon Polish Prussian territories.[49] Nevertheless, the experience of the Great Northern War permanently undermined the former sense of security and self-esteem which had bound the Prussian cities to the Polish crown. The reaction was twofold: after the disaffection with the Saxon rulers and a brief revival of an all-Commonwealth identity, most urban citizens focused their concerns more exclusively on provincial and urban affairs, which was also reflected in intensified parliamentary activity in the Prussian Diet from the mid-eighteenth century. Not without reason did the urban governments come to the conclusion that the Polish king, now more than ever, considered the treasuries of the Royal Prussian cities as an easily accessible private resource from which he could improve the sorry state of his finances. From the Polish Prussian perspective, therefore, the conflict with the king and the central Sejm made the Commonwealth less of an exception in the European political context than outside observers and historians usually concede.

Among the many conflicts that riddled the relationship between the Polish Prussian cities and royal authority during the first half of the century, a final one deserves attention, because it had greater and longer-lasting repercussions for relations between the Prussian cities and the rest of the Commonwealth than any single incident: the so-called 'Tumult of Thorn' of 1724. It not only revealed the continued importance of religious issues among the common people, but also the unscrupulous exploitation of spiritual matters in the service of power politics in the era of the early Enlightenment. The late seventeenth century had seen the strengthening of Catholicism in the whole of Royal Prussia, with several important Protestant families, in particular Calvinists such as the Przebendowskis, converting to Catholicism. In 1718, the Sejm banned the last dissident, the Calvinist Piotrowski, from the chamber of envoys. Consequently, nobles and representatives from the larger cities, particularly in Great Poland and Royal Prussia, sought mutual support. In 1719, Polish dissident leaders assembled in Danzig and attracted attention by protesting against the suppression of non-Catholics in several letters to foreign European powers.

In this early phase, the most cautious among the Prussian cities was Thorn, which first refused to support the dissident movement with anything more than the signature of a common letter of protest addressed to the king, consciously shunning foreign contacts. In their *gravamina* the Polish dissidents repeated several points over and over again: Protestant pastors in Poland were frequently harassed, church buildings were closed and transferred to Catholic control, the construction of new ones was prohibited, Protestant schools were confiscated, the dying were visited by

[49] Robert Schück, 'Ein Conflict Friedrich Wilhelms I. mit der Stadt Danzig wegen der preußischen Werbungen aus dem Jahre 1728', *Zeitschrift für Preußische Geschichte und Landeskunde* 11 (1874), 471–82.

Catholic priests seeking to convert them. The most vexing discrimination for non-Catholic nobles was the exclusion from public appointments.[50] Most of these complaints might have reflected the situation of Protestants and their churches in other Polish or Lithuanian provinces, but not in the Royal Prussian cities, which actively discriminated against their own Catholic citizenry by barring them from elections to the higher urban offices.[51]

The historically-minded burghers had not forgotten the lesson they had learned in the previous century, when the combination of religiously-inspired strife among the Protestants and social protest against the urban magistrates in Danzig had led to the intervention of John Casimir in the 1650s and of John Sobieski in the 1670s, clearly demonstrating the kings' readiness to curtail the political competence of the city councils on a religious pretext.[52] The burghers were also aware of the fact that two wars and the repeated occupation of Thorn and Elbing by the Lutheran Swedes had tainted the reputation of their cities which were seen as 'Protestant traitors' by the increasingly paranoid Polish szlachta: from a Catholic perspective, three non-Catholic powers, Orthodox Russia, Lutheran Sweden and the Calvinist Hohenzollern dynasty, held the eighteenth-century Commonwealth more in thrall than ever.[53]

After 1719 tensions began to mount in Thorn, where the Jesuit College, situated in the middle of the old town, enjoyed great popularity among the middling and lower szlachta of Poland-Lithuania. The Protestant Gymnasium, whose greatest days in the early seventeenth century, when it attracted Protestant students from all over the Commonwealth, were long behind it, now suffered from a relatively low student intake. Several provocations by Jesuit pupils, who were infamous for their poor discipline, put serious strain on religious relations in the city. Moreover, speculations that the bishop of Kulm, Kretkowski, would soon visit the city to transfer the main Protestant Church of St Mary to the Catholics, were spreading. The encroachments on Protestant rights by various bishops of Kulm in the seventeenth century still lingered in people's memories. The news of the conversion of Augustus's son, Friedrich August, to Catholicism in preparation for his candidacy to the Polish throne after his father's death did nothing to relax the tension.[54] When in July 1724, during a procession by Benedictine nuns in honour of the Virgin Mary, a group of Jesuit pupils tried to force Protestant pupils to bow

---

[50] 'Pro Memoria der Gedrängten Evangelischen in Pohlen 1. Gravamina, 2. Desideria, 3. Fundamenta Desideriorum, 4. Media, Anno 1723', APGd, Bibl. Archivi 300.R, Nn 51, pp. 3–4.

[51] Stanisław Salmonowicz points out that Gotthold Rhode, whose work on the situation of Polish Protestants, *Brandenburg, Preußen und die Protestanten in Polen, 1640–1740* (Leipzig: von Hirzel, 1941), was not available to me, did not find one letter of complaint from the Lutherans of Thorn among the many *gravamina* that arrived in Berlin before 1724; *Historia Torunia*, vol. II, p. 405.

[52] Müller, *Zweite Reformation*, pp. 246–52.

[53] Jerzy Michalski, 'Sarmatyzm a europeizacja Polski w XVIII wieku', in *Swójkość i cudzoziemszczyzna w dziejach kultury polskiej* (Warsaw: PWN, 1973), p. 121.

[54] *Historia Torunia*, vol. II, p. 184. This chapter by Jerzy Dygdała provides one of the best accounts of the tumult.

down and cross themselves while the procession passed, a brawl ensued. After repeated attacks on Protestant boys by Jesuit pupils, the city militia intervened and arrested the main Catholic instigator. In an act of revenge, the Jesuits arbitrarily incarcerated a Lutheran pupil, which led to the attack by a Lutheran mob on the Jesuit College, whose interior was almost entirely destroyed. It was royal troops, stationed in the city, who protected the beleaguered Catholics, while the city council only set the city militia in motion when the damage could no longer be limited.

The intensity of Jesuit propaganda which followed, as well as the dismissiveness with which the magistrates treated the affair, aroused Polish Catholic opinion, especially in the Sejm, where the majority of the nobility called for severe punishment. Most reports and historical treatments of the incident are heavily tainted by nationalist and religious partiality, and their value lies more in the opinion they express than in their documentation of the actual events. Here is not the place to give a detailed analysis of either. But most historians agree that Augustus seized the opportunity which this affair offered him to win support and popularity among the Catholic nobility and to extend his hold over the royal cities in Polish Prussia.[55] Despite the intervention by field marshal Flemming and another friend of the city, crown treasurer Przebendowski, in favour of the magistrates, the king endorsed the verdict of the Sejm, which ordered the execution of burgomaster Gottfried Rösner and nine other members of the council and the citizenry. There has been a lot of speculation about why the city fathers expected to get away lightly, as in the past, when disputes between the king, the Sejm and the city were usually settled by paying more or less generous fines. Apart from its own experience, Thorn might also have looked at the example of Hamburg, where in 1719 a similar event led to the intervention of the Habsburg emperor in favour of the Catholic minority in the city. Provoked by rowdy Catholic school boys, a Lutheran crowd raided a newly built Catholic chapel, while the Senate and the leading Protestant clergy refused to intervene. Hamburg had to pay a hefty fine but escaped any other punishment, partly due to mediation by Protestant powers such as Brandenburg, Brunswick and Hanover.[56] Close contacts maintained between the Prussian cities and the scholarly and the Hanseatic merchant community in cities of the Holy Roman Empire make it most likely that the Thorn magistrates knew about this incident. The burgomasters also turned to foreign support after the strict verdict against Thorn became known, but this time without effect. Although in 1720 Hamburg had collected money in support of the 'persecuted Protestants in Poland', in 1724 and 1725, in

---

[55] Ibid., p. 197; Cieślak, in *Historia Pomorza*, vol. II/2: *1657–1815* (Poznań: Wydawnictwo Poznańskie 1984), pp. 163–6; for an unscholarly, anti-Polish and anti-Catholic view, see Heinz Neumeyer, in *Handbuch der Geschichte Ost- und Westpreußens*, vol. II/2 (Lüneburg: Institut Nordostdeutsches Kulturwerk, 1996), pp. 133–4.

[56] Joachim Whaley, *Religious Toleration and Social Change in Hamburg, 1529–1819* (Cambridge University Press, 1985), pp. 59–63.

order to calm religious tensions, Hamburg prohibited the distribution of Prussian pamphlets describing in detail the trial and public execution of the Lutherans in Thorn.[57] While Hamburg and states which had shown most indignation about the 'barbarous persecution' of Protestants in Poland did not hesitate to continue discriminatory policies against their own Catholic populations,[58] Thorn was forced to appoint several Catholics to the city council, the lay assessors' court and the constituted citizenry, and had to hand over the main parish church to Catholic control. The fact that Thorn did not send any representatives to the Prussian Diet or observers to the Sejm until 1734, however, was not caused by a Polish ban against the Thorners, but by their own reluctance fully to implement the 1724 decree. The most important political demand, that half the council had to be Catholic, was in fact never fulfilled. The largest number of Catholics ever elected into the city council was seven, as against eleven Protestants, and that was only for a short period in 1745. The council's anti-Catholic stance did not have exclusively religious motives; nor should it be interpreted in nationalist terms: one of the co-opted Catholics in the council, Casimir Leon Schwertmann, even supported the Protestant council's argument that fewer Catholics than Protestants in the city possessed the educational qualifications needed for recruitment into the top ranks of the magistracy.[59]

Traditional historiography has considered the Tumult of Thorn as yet more proof of the spreading of darkest xenophobia and intolerance in Poland, and a measure of the rapidly decaying relationship between the Royal Prussian burghers and the Catholic nobility.[60] In terms of public relations with Protestant Europe, the tumult was a disaster for Poland.[61] Brandenburg-Prussia's efficient propaganda machine made sure that it was not forgotten, sustaining the momentum that was gathering around an increasingly politicised 'dissident movement', which was diplomatically and financially supported by two of the later partitioning powers: Prussia and Russia. With the tumult, the lasting cliché of Poland-Lithuania as an unenlightened, 'medieval' Catholic environment began to be forged. It was, however, in the five decades after the end of the Great Northern War that the Polish Enlightenment and its political reform movement flourished; the economy re-

---

[57] Ibid., pp. 64–5.
[58] This was even pointed out in the famous pro-Lutheran publication 'Extraordynaryjna Rozmowa in Regno Mortuorum która była między Toruńskim Starszym Praesidentem Roesnerem . . . et Primum patrem Stemmatis ac Fundatorem Ordini Jesuitarum Ignatium de Loyola . . .', here used in manuscript form (Bibl. Kór. 1321), but printed in German, *Entrevue zwischen dem thornischen Oberpräsidenten Roessner . . . und Ignatio von Loyola* (1725); see Zofia Sinko, *Oświeceni wśród pól Elizejskich. Rozmowy zmarłych. Recepcja – twórczość oryginalna* (Wrocław, Warsaw, Cracow: Ossolineum, 1976), p. 170.
[59] *Historia Torunia*, vol. II, pp. 199–200.
[60] Franz Jacobi, *Das Thorner Blutgericht 1724* (Halle: Verein für Reformationsgeschichte 13, 1896); similarly Neumeyer, in *Handbuch der Geschichte Ost- und Westpreußens*, p. 134.
[61] In the Netherlands, for example, see L. R. Lewitter, ' "De Bloeddorst der Jesuiten": een Hollands pamflet uit 1725', *Spiegel Historiael. Maandblad voor Geschiedenis en Archeologie* 5 (1991), 231–8.

covered in the 1750s, and Warsaw rose to the status of a central European metropole at the crossroads of a Europe whose face was soon to change fundamentally under the concerted assault of Russia, Prussia and Austria during the Commonwealth's partitions of 1772–95.

# 9

# Myths old and new: the Royal Prussian Enlightenment

Enlightened Europe put little trust in Poland-Lithuania's ability to reform itself and abandon its main characteristics, the 'fanaticism and sedition', which according to Voltaire 'always animate [this] sad nation'.[1] Incompatible with the ideals of the Enlightenment,[2] Polish Catholicism was associated with intolerance and ignorance and blamed for the downfall of what had once been the largest central European power. Polish historians have often been the most severe judges of the Commonwealth's last decades. They contrasted the universalism of the Enlightenment and its culmination in the Declaration of the Rights of Man with the 'feudalism' of the Polish nobility's Sarmatian culture, which had to make way for more enlightened cultures, superior powers, and their more effective social, military and political organisations.[3] Such stereotypical views of the 'culture of difference' between East and West[4] were further reinforced by the Tumult in Thorn and the opportunity it gave to Russia and Prussia, who for their own purposes activated their propaganda machines and organised the resistance of the so-called dissidents against the Catholic majority. The most vociferous and polemic contemporary critic of Polish culture and society was Frederick II of Prussia, who began to prepare the ground for the dismemberment of Poland-Lithuania in order to gain the important territorial bridge between Brandenburg, Pomerania and his East Prussian provinces from 1752 at the latest, when he wrote in his testament: 'By right of political necessity, Royal [Polish] Prussia must be integrated into the Hohenzollern kingdom.' Poland was 'la dernière nation de l'Europe', and its weakness would allow its

---

[1] Larry Wolff, *Inventing Eastern Europe. The Map of Civilization on the Mind of the Enlightenment* (Stanford University Press, 1994), p. 265.

[2] On the Catholic Enlightenment in Poland, see chapters 7 and 10 of Richard Butterwick, *Poland's Last King and English Culture, 1732–1798* (Oxford: Clarendon Press, 1998).

[3] Müller, 'Epoka baroku i Sarmatyzmu', p. 230; Janusz Maciejewski, 'Uniwersalizm i swoistość polskiego oświecenia', in Kłoczowski, J. (ed.), *Uniwersalizm i swoistość kultury polskiej*, 2 vols., vol. II (Lublin: KUL, 1989), pp. 285–6; Mieczysław Klimowicz, *Literatura Oświecenia* (Warsaw: PWN, 1995), pp. 7–8; Michalski, 'Samatyzm', p. 131.

[4] Barbara Grochulska, 'The Place of the Enlightenment in Polish Social History', in Fedorowicz, A. (ed.), *A Republic of Nobles. Studies in Polish History* (Cambridge University Press, 1982), p. 244; Bömelburg, 'Polnische Wirtschaft', p. 243.

neighbours to eat it 'comme un artichot, feuille par feuille'.[5] In particular, Frederick's picture of a corrupt nobility and its ineffective monarchs, which was echoed with great authority by many apologists of the Polish Partitions, has proved extremely persistent.[6]

The one exception which historians have usually allowed to this picture was Polish Prussia: the presence of large numbers of German speakers and Lutherans in the towns led to the tendentious suggestion that Royal Prussia, as a 'German' or at least separate and independent province, was less hampered by Catholic, Polish resistance to the enlightened ways of the 'West', and to the conclusion that if the Enlightenment reached the Commonwealth at all, it found fertile ground only among the 'German burghers' of the Prussian province.[7] Some Polish historians, too, have followed this line of argument and have recognised Danzig, Thorn and Elbing as Poland's 'door to the Western Enlightenment'.[8] This narrow focus, however, ignores Polish Prussia's links to the home-grown Polish-Lithuanian reform movement, which produced a wealth of political, historical and religious-moral literature in the eighteenth century and saw the blossoming of Warsaw as a cultural centre of European status in its own right, as was recognised occasionally by contemporary men of letters, such as the Leipzig scholar Christian Gottsched who praised the generous sponsorship of arts and sciences in Poland in the 1750s. Joanna Jarzęcka has shown that many Polish history works were edited and printed in Leipzig and other cities, and that close contacts existed between scholarly societies and individual writers on both sides of the German-Polish borders.[9] As in the sixteenth and seventeenth centuries, Royal Prussia maintained its ability to integrate scholars from Silesia, Pomerania or Brandenburg, who settled in the province during the early eighteenth century and quickly became acquainted with Polish Prussian laws, history and the political situation in the Commonwealth.

Although the Polish Prussian cities seemed predestined for the transmission of German culture to their province, this influence was not always welcome there.

[5] R. Dietrich (ed.), *Die politischen Testamente der Hohenzollern*, Veröffentlichungen aus den Archiven Preußischer Kulturbesitz, vol. 20 (Vienna and Cologne: Böhlau, 1986), pp. 648 and 369–74. See the excellent analysis of Frederick's picture of Poland in Bömelburg, *Zwischen polnischer Ständegesellschaft*, pp. 205–12.

[6] Hans-Jürgen Bömelburg, 'Johann Georg Forster und das negative deutsche Polenbild', *Mainzer Geschichtsblätter* 8 (1993), 79–90.

[7] Typical for German historiography are Bernt Jähnig und Peter Letkemann (eds.), *Danzig in Acht Jahrhunderten. Beiträge zur Geschichte des hansischen und preußischen Mittelpunktes* (Münster: Copernicus-Verein, 1985) and Eduard Winter, *Frühaufklärung. Der Kampf gegen den Konfessionalismus in Mittel- und Osteuropa und die deutsch-slawische Bewegung* (Berlin: Akademie-Verlag, 1966). Obviously tainted by the political conditions of his period is Schieder, *Deutscher Geist*, pp. 94ff and 133.

[8] S. Salmonowicz, 'Gotfryd Lengnich. Szkic do portretu uczonego', in *Od Prus Książęcych do Królestwa Pruskiego* (Olsztyn: OBiWK, 1992), pp. 72–102; and his 'Prusy Królewskie i Książęcy jako terytoria 'styku' dwuch kultur (XVI–XVIIIw.)', in *Śląsk i Pomorze w stosunkach Polsko-Niemieckich od XVI do XVIII w.* (Poznań: Instytut Zachodni, 1987), pp. 69–92.

[9] Joanna Jarzęcka, *Obraz życia umysłowego Rzeczypospolitej doby saskiej (1710–1762)* (Gdańsk: PAN, 1983); and Władysław Konopczyński, *Polscy pisarze polityczni XVIII wieku* (Warsaw: PWN, 1966), pp. 140ff, 174.

## Myths old and new: the Royal Prussian Enlightenment

The universities of Saxony, Brandenburg and other German states, visited by Prussian burghers since the sixteenth century, continued to play an important role for the education of the young patriciate and the Lutheran clergy. But when the religious reform movement of Pietism spread from the newly founded university in Halle to Danzig and, to a lesser extent, to Thorn and Elbing, the Lutheran establishment clearly rejected it.[10] At the same time, the careers of many Prussian scholars show that the court in Warsaw or the familiar environment of their Prussian province usually proved a greater attraction for young, ambitious theologians, lawyers and politicians from Danzig and Thorn than Wittenberg, Jena or Halle.[11]

The Polish Prussian cities could nevertheless claim their fair share in the cultural phenomenon of the *Aufklärung*. This is particularly true in the disciplines of history and law. Konrad Jarausch has documented the increased interest of German scholars, societies and academies in local and provincial history, legal traditions and constitutions, which was linked to the institutionalisation of history as a university discipline, as well as to the 'historicisation of jurisprudence' at Halle and in Göttingen, where a new university was founded in 1734. From the 1730s, in places as far apart as Swedish Pomerania and Upper Austria, local scholars and officials began editing source collections of provincial and local privileges and constitutions.[12] But such an undertaking was no novelty to the Polish Prussian burghers. Ever since the fifteenth and early sixteenth centuries, the compilation of urban and provincial immunities had been one of the favourite tasks of the political writers of Danzig, Elbing and Thorn, and the publication of Royal Prussian constitutions and privileges continued unchecked to the end of the eighteenth century. References to sixteenth-century authors of such works as well as the standard seventeenth-century works by Hartknoch, Pastorius and others remained commonplace.

A new emphasis, however, appeared in Polish Prussian legal and historical works in the aftermath of the Great Northern War. The defence of the province's political, legal and constitutional particularities acquired a sharper edge, and even in historical works the focus shifted from a fascination with the origins of Prussia to the confrontation of the political challenges of the present. The man who contributed most to this change and influenced generations of historians with his prolific historical and legal writings on the privileges and special status of Polish Prussia

---

[10] S. Salmonowicz, 'Pietyzm na Pomorzu Polskim oraz w Wielkopolsce w pierwszej połowie XVIII wieku', *Rocznik Humanistyczny* 27 (1979), 95–8.

[11] Kocot, *Nauka prawa*, pp. 101–80; S. Salmonowicz, 'W kręgu Toruńskich erudytów osiemnastego wieku', in Zdrójkowski, Z., (ed.), *Księga Pamiątkowa 400-lecia Toruńskiego Gimnazjum Akademickiego*, vol. I: *XVI–XVIII w.* (Toruń: TNT, 1972), pp. 225–6.

[12] Konrad Jarausch, 'The Institutionalisation of History in Eighteenth-Century Germany', in Bödeker, H. E., Iggers, G. G., Knudsen, J. B. and Reill, P. H. (eds.), *Aufklärung und Geschichte. Studien zur deutschen Geschichtswissenschaft im 18. Jahrhundert* (Göttingen: Vandenhoeck und Ruprecht, 1986), pp. 34, 44.

and its cities was the Danzig lawyer, historian and politician Gottfried Lengnich (1689–1774). Early in his career he revealed the combative spirit with which he set out to fight for a strengthening of the political and economic status of his city and province:

> As the form of our government has changed, it is not enough to know what form our Republic once took, but it is of greater importance to know how it is now . . . What does it help us Prussians to know by heart the *servitutes urbanas et rusticas* [of Roman law], if we have not learned whether we are the Poles' equal brothers or their servants, and if we do not know how to . . . preserve our liberty?[13]

With these words, Lengnich invited his compatriots to reinvigorate their knowledge of the past in order to defend their present interests and rights more effectively. After studying law and history at the University of Halle under Christian Thomasius, Johann Peter Ludewig, Nicolaus Hieronymus Gundling and Christian Wolff – all leading natural law theorists – Lengnich returned to Danzig in 1713 to take up an appointment as professor at the local Gymnasium.[14] He was a major critic of the internal disarray in which he found the Commonwealth during the Great Northern War, and was utterly disillusioned with the malfunctioning of its parliamentary system, including the Prussian Diet. He attacked the Prussian estates for neglecting their republican tradition which they were unwilling or unable to preserve: 'It seems that the Prussians, against their own interest, show too much indifference. For over fifteen years they let pass the opportunity to deliberate and habitually decide about their future and their province's needs without even summoning their own Diet.'[15]

He compared the apathy of his contemporaries in the Saxon era with the concern of their busy forefathers, who 'never tired of convening several times during a year to deliberate extensively on how to advance the common good, to preserve the country's privileges and to prevent their corruption'. Lengnich's criticism was not entirely justified. During the first decades of Saxon rule, the delegation from Royal Prussia participating in the Polish Sejm reached record numbers, and it was not the nobility but the cities' representatives who made rare appearances, both at the provincial diet and as observers in Warsaw. Georg Peter Schultz, professor at the Gymnasium of Thorn, triumphantly reported in 1712 that 'the eagerness to protect their privileges [of the estates of Royal Prussia] has resulted in the celebration of their *conventus generalis* in 1700 without convocation by the king'.[16] Instead of

---

[13] Gottfried Lengnich, *Historia Prutena sub serenissmis Polonorum Regis Imperio facies ad fidem actorum publicorum descripta* (Danzig: Schreiber, 1728), praefatio; and *Polnische Bibliothec*, vol. II, part 9 (1719), pp. 244–5.

[14] Włodzimierz Zientara, *Gottfried Lengnich. Ein Danziger Historiker in der Zeit der Aufklärung*, vols. I and II (Toruń: UMK, 1995–6), with an extensive bibliography.

[15] Lengnich, *Geschichte der Lande Preußen*, vol. IX (1755), preface.

[16] 'Variae Observationes de Prussia Polonica', APT Kat. II, VIII. 46, p. 33. According to Salmonowicz, this was also the case in 1702 and 1716; 'Z dziejów walki', p. 441.

neglecting the political life and interests of the province, the estates aimed at a revival of the position of the provincial Prussian diet as it had existed in the fifteenth and early sixteenth centuries, before the union of Lublin.[17] Among the Prussian burghers, Lengnich became the most outspoken protagonist of this goal and a role model for other urban politicians who combined their widely publicised programmes with intense political activism during the last decades of the existence of the Polish-Lithuanian state. It was during the Enlightenment, which coincided with the decline of Poland-Lithuania's military and political influence in Europe, that the burgher elites of Polish Prussia underwent what Erik Ringmar has called a 'formative moment',[18] a crisis of their political and national identity which had a decisive impact on the image they forged of their own historical relationship with the Polish-Lithuanian Commonwealth and its monarch. Old identities and loyalties were becoming brittle and new ones had to be developed, as Poland's destruction became a probability. Lengnich was one of the central figures who prepared the way for a reorientation of the burghers' political, national and historical identity.

GOTTFRIED LENGNICH AND THE ENLIGHTENMENT IN POLISH PRUSSIA

The rediscovery of ancient laws and an awareness of their significance for a country's national identity and history were familiar features of the natural law school at Halle, where Lengnich had matured as a legal historian. In their attack on the domination of legal studies by Roman Law, his teachers, Thomasius and Gundling, had stressed the importance of a nation's particular legal tradition. The state of nature could only be overcome by the foundation of a civic society which produced the laws and constitutions best suited to its historical situation and character. Gundling wrote that 'law remains law and cannot be eliminated by force or by misguided legal judgements against the will of those who want to live according to a specific law'. Thus, no change of constitution could ignore the historical context – a principle which prefigures the writings of Edmund Burke on the French Revolution.[19] Lengnich would have thoroughly agreed with Burke that all changes to a constitution 'should follow the example of our ancestors. I would make repairs as nearly as possible in the style of the building. Political caution, a guarded circumspection . . . were among the ruling principles of our forefathers'.[20] The Halle school of natural law must have left a deep impression on the Danzig lawyer and historian: if laws gained their legitimacy from history, the Prussian

---

[17] Stanisław Achremczyk, 'Organizacja i funkcjonowanie sejmiku generalnego Prus Królewskich w XVIII wieku', *Acta Universitatis Nicolai Copernici*, Historia XVIII, *Nauki Humanistyczno-Społeczne* 128 (1982), pp. 129–30.     [18] Ringmar, *Identity*, pp. 89–91.
[19] Hammerstein, *Jus und Historie*, p. 264; and Georg G. Iggers, 'The European Context of Eighteenth-Century German Enlightenment Historiography', in Bödeker et al. (eds.), *Aufklärung und Geschichte*, p. 241.
[20] E. Burke, *Reflections on the Revolution in France*, edited by Conor Cruise O'Brien (Penguin Books, 1969), pp. 375–6.

incorporation privilege of 1454 was as valid and important in the eighteenth century as it ever had been. The nature of the contract with the Polish crown, which had guaranteed the free political voice and participation of the Prussian estates, including the cities, in the political life of the Commonwealth while safeguarding their right to run their own affairs, could not be changed without the consent of the Prussian Diet; hence the negative light in which Lengnich saw the changes that had occurred in 1569: 'The power of interpreting laws must be left to those who are entitled to legislate . . . The Prussians have never obeyed other laws than those which they, next to their rightful rulers, have given themselves.'[21]

The teaching of Thomasius and Gundling at Halle, which laid down the fundamental principles of an early modern *Rechtsstaat*, suited the Prussian burgher elites. The notion of liberty remained bound to a particular society, its corporate members and a legal framework, and to its citizens and their political rights. This status was at all times under threat from an arbitrary process of legislation, exercised either by a single ruler or by other central institutions. Corporate or individual freedom was only realised in a just, functioning society with a participatory constitution. In contrast to the Polish reform debate, which by the mid-eighteenth century revolved almost exclusively around the conflict between *majestas* and *libertas*, Lengnich's adaptation of natural law theory perceived provincial immunities and central power as the principal antipodes. Nevertheless, unlike Thomasius, who prohibited all acts of resistance against a constitutional monarch even if he abused natural law principles for his own selfish interests,[22] Lengnich explicitly pointed to the rebellion of 1454 as a justified act of resistance to the tyranny of central government: 'No doubt the Teutonic Knights would still be the rulers over the Prussian lands if they had not provoked their subjects to rebel against them through their unlimited government; but our ancestors did not suffer to be commanded by despots.'[23]

The influence of the cameralist notion of a 'well-ordered police state' was very different in Polish Prussia from in the Hohenzollern monarchy, where the new utilitarian ideal of the bureaucratic *Machtstaat* became the dominant inspiration. Even in eighteenth-century Polish Prussia, natural law ideas were tempered and mixed with older constitutional and confederative notions characteristic of Polish political culture. Lipsius had been as popular with Fredro and Opaliński as with Polish Prussian writers in the seventeenth century, and he remained a favourite author in the eighteenth century, because he defended a state based on moral and virtuous principles – not Hohenzollern rule according to the motto '*necessitas non habet legem*'. Lengnich had demonstrated that he derived little inspiration from the pragmatic principles of Prussian absolute monarchy when he rejected an academic career in Halle after Frederick William I's ascension to the throne in 1713.

[21] Lengnich, *Geschichte der Lande Preußen*, vol. II (1723), p. 6.
[22] Hammerstein, *Ius und Historie*, p. 76.
[23] Lengnich, 'Vom Abfall der Preußen von den Creutz-Herren', *Polnische Bibliothec*, vol. II, p. 249.

Lengnich was not impressed by his former teacher Christian Wolff, who in 1736 wrote a manual for monarchs recommending absolute rule and an all-powerful centralist state – the last thing a burgher from Danzig desired. The importance Lengnich attributed to the revival of Polish Prussia's self-government and the political strength of the cities separated him from Frederick William's police state, or the enlightened absolutism of Frederick the Great.

After his return from Halle, in 1718, Lengnich founded a new periodical with the title *Polnische Bibliothec welche von Büchern und anderen zur Polnischen und Preußischen Historie dienenden Sachen Nachricht giebt*, which was seen as a conscious effort to recreate in his city the cultural conditions which the young scholar had encountered in Halle, where he had contributed to Gundling's periodical *Neue Hallische Bibliothek*. Instead of Danzig, where it really appeared, the title page of *Polnische Bibliothec* claimed it was published in 'Tannenberg, where Władysław Jagiełło defeated the Teutonic Knights'. Considering the central role Prussian history played for Lengnich's multi-layered identity as a burgher of Danzig, a citizen of Royal Prussia and of the Polish crown, this emphasis on the defeat of the Order and the subsequent incorporation into the Polish kingdom seemed to continue traditional Royal Prussian patterns of self-definition. There are, however, crucial differences between Lengnich and his seventeenth-century predecessors, and the way they made use of Prussian and Polish history.

The idea that the Prussians had always ruled themselves had been at the heart of Hartknoch's research on the popular assemblies of the pagan Prussians: they cherished the freedom to decide their own matters without interference from a king or foreigners. Liberty was the core of the Polish Prussian constitutional programme for the present and future of the province. But in contrast to Hartknoch's myth of the Sarmatian origin of the Prussian nation, Lengnich had nothing but scorn for tales about the democratic Prussian assemblies, and he also ridiculed the myths of origin of the Polish nation and their legendary leader Lech. Almost half a century before August Ludwig Schlözer, professor of history at the Academy of St Petersburg, was awarded the prize of the *Naturforschende Gesellschaft* in Danzig in 1765, for a treatise that argued that the mythical founding father of the Polish nation never existed, Lengnich mocked Polish historians who still believed in such *fabulae*. Indeed, the political conflicts of the eighteenth century had become so formidable that the message of Hartknoch's mythical picture of Prussian-Sarmatian harmony was no longer relevant; instead, Lengnich called for the fighting spirit which in 1454 had guaranteed the survival of Prussian rights and liberties against the oppressive rule of the Teutonic Knights. Moreover, Lengnich consciously targeted the Polish-Sarmatian superiority complex: since the Poles, just like other tribes, had mixed with Goths and Vandals,[24] the Polish nobility had no

---

[24] *De Polonorum Majoribus Dissertationem praeside Godofredo Lengnich, D. eloquentiae et pres. PP in auditorio max. d. XXV. Sept. 1732, tuebitur Michael Hafft, Goldynga-Curonensis* (Danzig: Schreiber, 1732), paragr. I.

right to claim a monopoly of Sarmatian freedom over other nations, or to deprive others of equal, historically acquired liberties:

One might think that the Polish gentlemen who constantly speak about *libertas* would be much too conscientious to harm their fellow estates. However, events teach us that liberty must be even sweeter if one tries to prescribe laws to those over whom one has no power. It seems that our incorporation privilege now lies in an old chest with other useless treatises. Thus has our status changed.[25]

Analysing these changes in his *History of Royal-Polish Prussia*, the first major work exclusively focused on the political history of Royal and Polish Prussia, Lengnich devoted most attention to the two historical dates which essentially defined the relationship of Royal Prussia and Poland: 1454 and 1569. When the Prussian estates accepted the Polish king as their sovereign in 1454, according to Lengnich they did not surrender to the power of the republic as embodied in the Sejm, but formed a personal union with the Polish king alone. Quoting the original text of the incorporation privilege, which states that Prussia was 'integrated, reunited with, and incorporated into the Polish kingdom', Lengnich proceeds with his own peculiar interpretation: 'that the inhabitants owe obedience only to the king, and find themselves under the protection and government of the king alone. "Re-integration" means that Prussia did not subject itself to the kingdom, but only joined it . . . as if to fill a gap, to heal a mutilated body.'[26]

Far from clarifying medieval legal categories, Lengnich set out to exploit the equivocal character of the legal relationship between the province and the Commonwealth, which had been subject to heated debates from the late fifteenth century. In order to prove the historicity and longevity of the Prussian constitutions, Lengnich more than once overstepped the boundaries of historical truth, exaggerating the possibilities open to the Prussian estates in the fifteenth century for the conduct of an independent policy.[27] Reclaiming the application of laws and immunities which had never been used or had gone out of practice, such as the appointment of a separate governor of the Prussian province, the institution of an independent Prussian treasurer, or the function of the *Landesrat* as the highest legal instance for the whole province, Lengnich saw the incorporation of 1454 as a mutual contract between equals. But what good were separate laws and constitutions if there was no power to enforce them? Polish Prussia should remember it had once had the strength to stand alone; thus references to the separate Prussian republic are legion: 'I once showed that the province [of Prussia] under the rule of the Polish kings constituted a separate state. The most certain sign of it was its

---

[25] Lengnich, 'Immunitas Civitatum Prussiae a Jurisdictione Judicorum Tribunalitiorum Regni Poloniae & aliorum quorumvis praeterquam Regiorum . . .', *Polnische Bibliothec*, vol. I/5, p. 383.
[26] Lengnich, *Majorum Prussiae Civitatum pro Juribus suis vigilantis Interregno* (Danzig: Schreiber, 1764), p. 5.
[27] Jerzy Dygdała, 'Udział Gotfryda Lengnicha w Toruńskiej Konfederacji Dysydenckiej w 1767 roku', *Zapiski Historyczne* 42 (1977), 23–4; and Salmonowicz, 'Z dziejów walki', pp. 436–8 and 447–9.

special constitution . . . its own councillors, its own diets, its own laws and regulations concerning the government of the country.'[28]

Contrasting this approach with fifteenth-century notions of 'crown' and 'kingdom' in East Central Europe, Karol Górski has demonstrated the anachronism and artificiality of Lengnich's interpretation.[29] Taking into account that representatives of the Polish estates and cities had signed the incorporation document, and that in the fifteenth century the Polish monarchy had already been limited by various privileges for the nobility, guaranteeing protection of noble property and against arbitrary arrest, Lengnich's eighteenth-century vision of the events of 1454 is blurred. He constructed a utopia of Prussian self-government that went beyond a confederation of provinces and nations: before 1569, he stated, the Prussian Diet was not inferior to the Polish parliament, but fulfilled the same function for Prussia as the Sejm did for the Polish estates.[30] Lengnich went so far as to construct the existence of a Prussian diet during the period of the Teutonic Order's rule: 'even the Teutonic Knights did not touch our right to convoke a diet . . . a privilege which the Poles tried to destroy'.[31] In reality, although some consultative bodies had existed, the Teutonic Knights never tolerated an independently functioning Prussian diet. It was also clear from the incorporation treaty that Royal Prussia was to be part of the body of the Polish *regnum*, while Lithuania formed a separate legal and political entity. Lengnich, however, insisted that Prussia resembled Lithuania in status. From his perspective, it was not subjection, but parity which guaranteed the functioning of the body in its entirety: 'and [no member] could dictate to another . . . Ruthenia, Lithuania, Prussia, and Mazovia . . . they all relate to each other as equal members . . . although Ruthenia and Mazovia are much more closely knit together with Poland than Lithuania and Prussia'.[32]

Although he mainly blamed the nobility for the decline of Prussian liberties, he also rejected all attempts by Polish monarchs to undermine urban and provincial privileges through more uniform legislation. Thus, despite his contention that the Prussian cities had to obey the king alone, Lengnich formulated a more radical challenge to the king's authority than any previous Polish Prussian writer. As an active politician he also translated his political programme into reality. He tested the degree to which the Prussians were allowed to live according to their own rules and laws – the crux of the relationship between Prussia and the Polish crown. If legislation furthered urban and provincial interests, Lengnich was able to cooperate quite happily with the Polish nobility.

The conflict between the city of Danzig and king Augustus III in 1733–4

---

[28] Lengnich, 'Bescheidene Untersuchung', *Geschichte der Lande Preußen*, vol. II, p. 23.
[29] Karol Górski (ed.), *Związek Pruski i poddanie się Prus Polsce* (Poznań: Instytut Zachodni, 1949), pp. lxiii–lxiv.
[30] Lengnich, *Geschichte der Lande Preußen*, vol. II, p. 17.
[31] Lengnich, *Staats-Recht des Polnischen Preußens aus dem Lateinischen übersetzt von G. Künhold* (Danzig: Schreiber, 1760), pp. 368–9.
[32] Ibid., p. 11.

demonstrates Lengnich's political attitudes particularly well. In agreement with the majority of szlachta opinion in the Commonwealth, Danzig supported the election of Stanisław Leszczyński, for which it was rewarded with a costly siege by Russian forces, followed by substantial reparations. Augustus III, who was never fully reconciled with the city, exploited its political isolation, sending the Saxon councillor von Leubnitz, the Warmian bishop Grabowski and a royal commissar to Danzig, and between 1748 and 1752 they energetically intervened in the city's internal affairs. More successfully than John Sobieski seventy years earlier, Augustus supported the citizenry, mainly artisans and merchants, in their struggle for extended political participation against the patrician council and its lawyer elite, who were summoned before the royal assessorial court. It paid the king handsomely: individual council members and the citizenry spent several hundred thousand florins competing for royal favours.[33] The king and his chief Saxon minister, Heinrich von Brühl (1700–1763), made it clear that they had little respect for the magistrates' prerogatives. For the preservation of some of the city's key privileges, such as freedom from Saxon-Polish garrisons and full control over Danzig's trade and port, the city fathers repeatedly had to pay considerable sums of money.

Lengnich was a key player in these events – first as defender of the citizenry, and from 1750, when the full extent of the king's intentions to interfere in Danzig's internal affairs became obvious, as a spokesman of the city council, protecting the city's old constitution, which favoured the ruling elites. In his compilation of Danzig's laws and immunities, commissioned by the city but never published during his lifetime, Lengnich cautioned that the city 'can use its privileges even against its lord and king, in order to protect itself against unlimited rule'.[34] Augustus III forced the magistrates to accept a greater number of merchants and artisans in the city council and to agree to increased royal authority over administrative appointments and the conduct of the city's affairs. Patrician suspicions were fuelled by the fact that in 1749 Augustus III had successfully extended the power of his central ministerial government under Brühl in Electoral Saxony. While he could not accomplish similar reform plans in Poland-Lithuania as a whole, the king's policy of centralisation was temporarily successful in Danzig and, on the provincial level, in Great Poland, where the power of the general starosta was diminished.[35] This explains why Lengnich was not first and foremost a supporter of autonomy for Danzig, but defended the special status of the whole province. To attain autonomy for Danzig under the exclusive power of the king alone would even have obstructed Lengnich's main political goal: the revival of the provincial diet and Prussian noble and urban self-government, which was more likely if a consen-

[33] Edmund Cieślak, *Konflikty polityczne i społeczne w Gdańsku w połowie XVIII w. – sojusz pospólstwa z dworem królewskim* (Wrocław: Ossolineum, 1972), chapter VI, and his 'Gdańsk w polityce Augusta III', in Groth, A. (ed.), *W kręgu badań Profesora Stanisława Gierszewskiego* (Gdańsk: Marpress, 1995), pp. 95–108.
[34] Lengnich, *Ius publicum Civitatis Gedanensis*, p. 27.
[35] Jacek Staszewski, *August III Sas* (Warsaw: Ossolineum, 1989), pp. 220–1.

sus was built between Danzig and the provincial estates. From Lengnich's perspective, Danzig's privileges were no obstacle to the city's allegiance to the crown, but they helped to put the relationship on a viable, legal basis.

Not all Prussian burghers, however, were as opposed to centralisation as Lengnich. In his 1772 treatise on Polish and Royal Prussian laws, David Braun, the burgrave of Marienburg, criticised the weakness of the eighteenth-century kings of Poland and their dependence on noble factions in the senate. The majority of the Polish and Prussian nobles, he stressed, would support higher taxes if they went directly into the royal treasury, not the pockets of senators and other greedy nobles. Alluding to the great cities and their representatives – such as Lengnich – Braun attacked the 'great and the good' who blocked reform and the opportunity for Poland to recover.[36] In Danzig, too, the mass of the citizenry did not share Lengnich's resistance to royal authority. In gratitude to Augustus III, the guilds erected a monument in the Artushof which depicted the king as a senator in laurel wreath and a Roman toga. Merchants and artisans thanked their king for defending their democratic ideals against the oligarchic council. For others, this symbol might have been intended to humble the king of Poland and remind him that he was limited by the republic and its laws, including the privileges of the Prussian estates.

Lengnich's political actions, as well as his writings, made a lasting impression on many subsequent generations of historians. First, his contemporaries in Danzig and other cities eagerly picked up his historical construction of a separate, self-governing Prussian republic. Samuel Willenberg, professor at the Gymnasium, affirmed that 'the freedom of the Prussians was established when they were incorporated, but remained a free republic, without mixing with the Polish [republic]'.[37] In Elbing in 1741, Samuel Grüttner defended Prussia's freedom from any taxes imposed by the Polish Sejm and not unanimously passed by the Prussian Diet. He depicted the Prussian province as a free republic, 'where citizens rule', whose roots and privileges reached back beyond the Teutonic period. He agreed with Lengnich that negligence and ignorance on the part of the Prussian nobility had brought about the decline of liberties in their province. Grüttner's grudge against the nobility was motivated by the memory of the events of 1698, when king and republic failed to prevent the occupation of the city by Brandenburg troops – a violation of the fundamental principle that the Polish crown could not alienate any Royal Prussian territory to another state.[38]

In the past, German historiography has usually started out from the picture of Lengnich and his followers as 'separatist', German-oriented, anti-Polish and anti-

[36] David Braun, *De jurium regnandi fundamentalium in Regno Poloniae ratione* (Cologne: Braber, 1722), pp. 10–11, 26.

[37] Samuel Willenberg, 'Disputatio de Muneris Thesaurarii in Prussia Occidentali, antiquitate iuribus & praerogativis', *Das Continuirte Gelahrte Preußen* (1725), 227.

[38] Samuel F. Grüttner, *Tractatio iuris publici pruthenici de Prussia numquam et nulli tributaria* (Danzig: Schreiber, 1741), p. 34; Lengnich, *Polnische Bibliothec*, vol. II, part 5, pp. 487–8.

noble burghers and scholars, and some Polish historians have also accepted this judgement. In German works, Lengnich is still the most frequently quoted Polish Prussian writer of the pre-partition period. A selective reading of his treatises, often combined with an openly anti-Polish agenda, has ossified this approach, which still dominates most historical works on eighteenth-century Polish Prussia.[39] In retrospect, the Prussian patriciate's aspirations to join the Hohenzollern monarchy and rescue their 'German identity' seem natural to historians who wilfully, or because of their lack of familiarity with archival sources, ignore the long traditions that bound the province and its cities to the Commonwealth.[40] The Polish nobility has become notorious as a foreign and unenlightened enemy of the Prussian cities, engaged in a vicious nationality struggle between 'Poles' and 'Germans'. The reality, however, is different and much more complicated.

Lengnich was neither exhibiting a German identity, nor limiting his activities and interests to the affairs of his city and province. His links with the Polish reform movements were close and numerous, and it was his growing reputation in Poland which inspired Stanisław Poniatowski, palatine of Mazovia, to send his three sons to Danzig for tutoring; Lengnich thus played an important role in the education of the future king, Stanisław August Poniatowski, whose election in 1764 opened a period of enlightened reform. In 1740, Lengnich published a textbook of Polish history dedicated to his illustrious pupils under the title *Historia Polona a Lecho ad Augusti II mortem*, which was intended to 'educate the three youths so that they would understand the needs and problems of their fatherland, in order to lead the republic into a better future'.[41] Lengnich was not only aware of the need for Polish nobles to provide a solid civic political, historical and legal education for their sons, but was also influenced by Thomasius's plans to establish a university for the nobility (*Ritterakademie*) in Halle. In the 1750s Lengnich supported a similar project proposed by the scholar Christian Hanow, although in contrast to Stanisław Konarski's Collegium Nobilium, founded in Warsaw in 1740, it failed due to various political and financial constraints.

As the scholarly educator of Poniatowski's sons and a good citizen of the Polish-Lithuanian Commonwealth, Lengnich made sure that he taught them the constitution and ways of government of the republic, which, as he admitted, must have seemed odd and incomprehensible to foreigners. His criticism of Polish affairs attracted the interest of some of the leading figures of the Polish Enlightenment,

[39] For example, B. Jähnig, 'Bevölkerungsveränderungen und Landesbewußtsein im Preußenland', *Blätter für deutsche Landesgeschichte* 121 (1985), 115–55, and *Handbuch für Geschichte Ost- und Westpreußens*, vol. II/1, pp. 7–10; S. Sosin, 'Autonomia Prus Królewskich w ujęciu G. Lengnicha', *Gdańskie Zeszyty Humanistyczne. WSP w Gdańsku, Wydział Filol.-Hum.* 1 (1958), 9–25; Dygdała, *Życie polityczne*, p. 200; see Salmonowicz's criticism of this picture, in 'Gotfryd Lengnich. Szkic', pp. 95–6; likewise Zientara, *Gottfried Lengnich*, vol. II, p. 8.

[40] For a criticism of this school see Bömelburg's forthcoming 'Streitschrift', in *Nordost-Archiv* (1998), and my 'Politisches Landesbewußtsein und seine Trägerschichten im Königlichen Preußen', *Nordost-Archiv* NS 6, no. 2 (1997), 541–64.

[41] Lengnich, *Historia Polona a Lecho* (Leipzig: n.pub., 1740), preface.

such as the Polish Grand Chancellor and Bishop of Cracow, Andrzej Stanisław Załuski, and his brother Józef, founders of Poland's most famous eighteenth-century library. They invited Lengnich to Warsaw to discuss plans for a new Polish constitution which would raise the status and well-being of the burghers in the Commonwealth.[42] In 1734, after the interregnum and the armed conflict over the Polish throne between Stanisław Leszczyński and Augustus III, the Załuskis commissioned Lengnich to write an analysis of the Polish political institution of confederation. This gave the professor from Danzig the opportunity to criticise this legalised form of rebellion, which frequently led to internal strife and civil war, despite its usefulness as a means of crisis management during interregna, when the rule of majority vote in the confederation parliaments prevented a total paralysis of the political system. In fact, during the interregnum of 1763 and at the beginning of Poniatowski's reign, a reform party led by the Czartoryski family ran the country by confederation law for thirty months.[43] Lengnich's opposition to confederation thus demonstrates the problems inherent in refusing the authority of the Commonwealth and the confederated Sejm. He believed the Prussians had their own means to secure law and order between the death of a king and the coronation of his successor – their own diet and the *unio animorum* of the Prussian estates, which prescribed draconian laws against anyone who broke the public peace. Lengnich was particularly opposed to the principle of majority voting during confederations, as it worked to the detriment of minority interests such as those represented by the cities.[44] Without apparently perceiving the double standard of his approach, Lengnich promoted political reform in Poland while defending the *liberum veto* of the urban minorities in the Prussian Diet against the noble majority, a right which effectively blocked the legislative process throughout most of Augustus's III reign. Is it therefore true that the urban elites of Royal Prussia constituted a major obstacle to the reform of the Commonwealth and must at least in part be held responsible for its demise, as some Polish historians have asserted?[45]

It was with the help of the *liberum veto* that in the 1750s and early 1760s the so-called Prussian Patriots, with the support of the three major cities, hampered the success of a reform party in the province, which backed the introduction of central taxation and the appointment of the centralist reformer Paweł Mostowski as palatine of Pomerania. As a result of intense factional infighting, between 1713 and 1728, and again from 1735 to the end of the Saxon era in 1763, not one Prussian Diet was concluded successfully.[46] This political stalemate was not, however,

[42] Heinz Lemke, *Die Brüder Załuski und ihre Beziehungen zu Gelehrten in Deutschland und Danzig* (Berlin: Akademie-Verlag, 1958), p. 178; and Kurdybacha, *Stosunki kulturalne*, pp. 29–30.

[43] Butterwick, *Poland's Last King*, p. 158.

[44] *De Polonorum confoederationibus, praeside Godofredo Lengnich, . . . disputabit Carolus Ernestus Kettner, Gedanensis* (Danzig: Schreiber, 1735).

[45] Salmonowicz, 'Z dziejów walki', p. 456; J. Dygdała, *Polityka Torunia wobec władz Rzeczypospolitej w latach 1764–1772* (Toruń: Roczniki TNT, 1977), pp. 195–7.

[46] Dygdała, *Życie polityczne*, pp. 65–94.

entirely the fault of the Prussian urban and noble estates. Repeatedly the estates complained that the royal chancellery sent out the edict summoning the provincial diet too late, or without a given date. Thorn and Danzig occasionally failed to receive any summons at all, whereupon they refused to send any representatives.[47] The Prussian estates pointed to their privilege of the *ius indigenatus* and refused to accept 'foreign appointments' from among the court party. The king chose the way of least resistance by refusing to summon the Prussian Diet, or by interrupting it before it could oppose his designs. At the same time, Prussian burghers and nobles were locked into a permanent dispute over the attempt of several district assemblies, particularly in the relatively large palatinate of Pomerania, to send noble delegates directly from the district or palatinate *sejmiks* to the central Sejm, bypassing the provincial dietine.[48] This tendency both on the part of the nobility, who were trying to assert their independence from the provincial body, and of the king, who sought to devalue the Prussian provincial diet, deeply worried the cities: it was their only parliamentary forum, and they wanted no other.

Lengnich's concern for the political and economic status of the Prussian cities, however, found a ready reception when, in the later Saxon era, several Polish reformers rallied to improve the sorry state of the cities in the Commonwealth, which had been identified as one of the major causes of Poland's economic decline. In the late 1730s and 1740s, in an attempt to revive the economy, several local dietines called for an improvement of trades and crafts in the cities. Published in the 1750s, but written in the 1730s, Stefan Garczyński's *Anatomy of the Republic* argued for the lightening of burdens on peasants, support for urban trades and far-reaching religious toleration. The crusade for an elevation of the status of Polish cities in the journal *Monitor*, which was published from 1764 by the Saxon champion of the Polish Enlightenment Mitzler von Kolof and edited by Ignacy Krasicki and Adam Czartoryski, with contributions by Stanisław August himself, found wide appeal, especially among a Warsaw audience.[49] After 1764 the reform programme developed by the Czartoryskis under the influence of the Piarist Stanisław Konarski also found the king's support. His pro-urban attitudes were certainly not unconnected with the education he had received under Lengnich's tutelage. More than mere 'guardians of the door to the West', Lengnich and his intellectual entourage symbolised the symbiotic relationship between the natural law theory of the German Enlightenment and the Polish political reform movement; indeed, in their defence of the *liberum veto* they showed that the supposed standard-bearers of Western Enlightenment could uphold a constitutional principle usually seen as the epitome of unenlightened Polish obscurantism.

[47] Achremczyk, 'Organizacja i funkcjonowanie', p. 126.
[48] Dygdała, 'Sejmiki powiatowe województwa pomorskiego w czasach saskich i stanisławowskich', *Zapiski Historyczne* 52 (1987), 79–80; Achremczyk, 'Organizacja i funkcjonowanie', 121–47.
[49] Ewa Borkowska-Bagieńska, 'Nowożytna myśl polityczna w Polsce 1740–1780', in Staszewski, J. (ed.), *Studia z dziejów polskiej myśli politycznej*, vol. 4 (Toruń: UMK, 1992), pp. 31–45; Jarzęcka, *Obraz życia umysłowego*, p. 180; Butterwick, *Poland's Last King*, p. 166.

## Myths old and new: the Royal Prussian Enlightenment

### THE DEATH OF TRADITION: URBAN IDENTITY DURING THE COMMONWEALTH'S FINAL YEARS, 1764–1772

The mid-eighteenth century saw a revival of political initiative and parliamentary activity among the nobility as well as the burghers. However, contrary to Lengnich's predictions that the reanimation of the parliament would help to further provincial and urban interests, Prussian liberties received a substantial blow during the 1764 Convocation Sejm in Warsaw, which had little patience for the political programme of the Prussian Patriot Party. Despite a boycott of the Sejm by the anti-Czartoryski opposition, the Reform Party passed several laws which further assimilated the political structures of the Prussian province to the crown: the number of Polish Prussian envoys was reduced to thirty-eight, a third of their former strength; plans emerged for a new law court for Great Poland with authority over Prussia, including the cities; the restriction of the *liberum veto* was decided, especially in matters of taxation; so was the establishment of a treasury committee and the general and regular collection of taxes throughout the whole Commonwealth, including the Prussian cities. Finally, the Sejm further curbed the powers of the Prussian Diet by directly admitting envoys from the local dietines.

The reaction among the Prussian burgomasters and councillors was predictably strong. They denied that the 1764 Sejm, convened during the interregnum, had any power over Polish Prussia. Their own diet had been disrupted under the influence of Russian forces which aimed at preventing local dietines from taking any decisions against the Czartoryski faction.[50] Anti-Polish and anti-noble feelings ran high. Samuel Luther Geret (1730–97), an ambitious politician and Thorn's representative in Warsaw, was instructed to resist any attempt by the Polish Sejm to force the Prussian cities to join the pro-Czartoryski confederation, and to reject any restrictions on the *liberum veto*:

Maintaining equality during public assemblies, [cities] ought to have the same number of votes as the nobility, in order to prevent the nobles from oppressing them. Everything has to be settled *unanimi consensu* . . . If, however, the cities joined the confederation, they would hand over the means of their oppression, to further their own ruin. [51]

Judging by these political reactions, it is apparent that several decades of political propaganda by Lengnich, Schultz, Willenberg and others had prepared the burghers for the fight they now put up against the Sejm. The debate on the Prussian constitution was not the preserve of a few isolated academics: the enormous production of treatises bears witness to its wider relevance and political appeal.

---

[50] On the general diet in Graudenz, see 'Recessus 1764, 27.3. Graudenz, Conventus generalis ante-convocationalis', APGd 300.29/ 223, pp. 237ff; on Lengnich's reaction, Dygdała, 'Udział Gotfryda Lengnicha', p. 15.

[51] 'Briefbuch, 1762–1764. Brief der Stadt an Sekretär Geret (Warschau), 12.10.1764', APT Kat. II, I.47, pp. 879–80.

Historical images, real and invented traditions and legal fictions were now put to the test in the real world. In the summer of 1764, representatives of the Prussian Patriots met with Geret in Warsaw to discuss an appropriate response. Several of their projects and demands closely reflected suggestions found in the more radical Prussian literature. To fend off any attempt by the Polish Sejm to 'remodel the Prussian province into mere palatinates, on a par with Poznań, Kalisz and Cujavia', Geret proposed asking Russia for help and establishing a separate Duchy of Polish Prussia, with Catherine II's brother as grand duke.[52] A similar project had already been formulated in 1755 by Schröter in Elbing, who dedicated his treatise to Friedrich Franz of Anhalt-Dessau and Zerbst. Arguing that the Prussians, after their war of liberation from the Teutonic Knights, would not have wanted to be subject to another power, except for the protection of their self-government, he insisted that from 1454 Royal Prussia was an independent duchy whose ducal title was held by the Polish kings.[53] The fact that the Prussian Patriot Party appealed to Russia – not Prussia – to defend their constitutional immunities demonstrates that from a Polish Prussian perspective close relations with Catherine II seemed less threatening than the prospect of cooperation with Frederick II, whose annexation plans concerning Polish Prussia made him *persona non grata* in the province.

Political events and the agitation of the Prussian politicians, especially from Danzig and Thorn, sharpened the tone of some of the treatises the burghers used in defence of their liberties and what they regarded as their ancient rights, now under threat from the very reforms which were designed to revive the Commonwealth's political system and enable it to regain its position on the European stage. Several treatises contain quite detailed comparisons with the parliamentary systems of other European states, using the foreign context as a point of reference for the burghers' own political aspirations of good government and control of their own affairs. In Thorn, Geret compared the Royal Prussian diet with the status of the Irish parliament under the British crown.[54] He shared Lengnich's thesis that Royal Prussia was a separate body politic, subject to royal power alone, but in contrast to previous writers he used much more radical and polemical language: since Prussia was as separate a republic as Poland or Lithuania, the rule of the Polish king was limited by the government of the Prussian estates in the same way as the Polish Sejm circumscribed royal power in Poland. And just as the Poles would not tolerate Lithuanian interference in their own affairs, the Prussians could not accept any Polish dictate. In contrast to Poland and Lithuania, which was 'the king's prop-

---

[52] Samuel Luther Geret, 'Herrn Ludwig von Weyher aus der Ritterschaft von Preußen Erbherrn auf Langfuhr in Preußen, . . . in einem Sendschreiben an gedachten Herrn aus Lendeck vom [er]sten November 1771', *Die aus den Gräbern durchdringende Stimme derer vor zwey hundert fünfzig Jahren verstorbenen wahren und ächten Preußen* (Mitau: J. F. Hinz, 1774), p. 30; Dygdała, *Życie polityczne*, pp. 122, 127.

[53] Schröter, *Gründlicher Beweis*, pp. 11–12.

[54] Geret, 'Herrn Ludwig von Weyher', p. 21.

erty', the free republic of Prussia enjoyed liberties dating from pre-Teutonic times, which were superior to those of the Polish republic.[55]

Supporting Geret's approach, Schröter returned to the popular example of the Dutch nation which found independent statehood through an act of resistance to the Spanish tyrant: 'It would be absurd if the free Dutchmen or the Swiss, after the death of their generals, had subjected themselves to their enemies.'[56] Lengnich drew the same parallel, stressing the prosperity of Dutch cities and their burghers' political acumen: like the Dutch, the Prussians had justly resisted a tyrannical regime and, in 1454, found themselves independent and able to decide their own future. The Prussians could have established a separate republic of their own more easily than the Dutch, who were weak and had to fight against the formidable power of Spain: 'Why should they have failed to establish their own republic whereas the Dutch succeeded so happily a century later?' Instead, they sought protection under the Polish crown. Lengnich was rather economical with the historical truth when he wrote: 'all advantages which were gained over the Teutonic Knights were won by the Prussians alone . . . but they would have been much greater if they had only fought for their own liberty [and not in alliance with the Poles]'.[57]

Geret pointed out that only the vigilance and stubborn resistance of the burghers over centuries had preserved the Prussian liberties from complete destruction. In contrast to the Danzig burghers who resisted the Swedish Deluge in the 1650s and prided themselves on having served the Commonwealth as an *antemurale* against the foreign enemy, Geret now redefined this protective function. A year before the first partition, he was less concerned with protecting Poland-Lithuania from the Empress of Russia and the Hohenzollern king than with resisting the limitation and change of Prussian privileges. Assuming the identity of a Prussian nobleman, he wrote:

The fact that we have not become mere palatinates and pure Poles is due to our brothers from the [Prussian] cities, who, as estates of our fatherland, resist every attempt to interfere, change and undermine [our liberties]. For the protection of our constitution, liberties and immunities the cities are an *antemurale* in the same way as the Hungarians are for Christianity.[58]

The change of attitude since the seventeenth century is remarkable. Hartknoch's myth of the pagan republic was substituted with the historical and legal fiction of an independent Prussian state – not located in the legendary past, but as an aspiration for the future. Lengnich, Geret and their contemporaries instrumentalised the older myth of the constitutionalist superiority of the Prussian Sarmatians for a different, much more self-absorbed and introspective purpose. The Prussians no

---

[55] Geret, 'Beweis daß die Lande Preußen nicht unter der Republik Polen sondern unter dem König von Polen sind (1767)', *Die aus den Gräbern*, pp. 82–3.
[56] Schröter, *Gründlicher Beweis*, p. 12.
[57] Lengnich, 'Abfall der Preußen', *Polnische Bibliothec*, vol. II, pp. 294–6.
[58] Geret, 'Herrn Ludwig von Weyher', p. 11.

longer stood out for their ability to embrace Sarmatian political values and to provide the Commonwealth with cohesion. Instead, in the writings of these eighteenth-century patricians, the Prussian myth of liberty became an exclusive weapon for the defence of their legal, historical, political and national distinctiveness. While in 1700 Martin Böhm had still appealed to the spirit of solidarity between Poles and Royal Prussians to salvage the Commonwealth, Lengnich now suggested a strict separation of tasks: Prussia should not be forced to act on matters concerning Poland, nor should Poland intrude into Prussian affairs. It was no longer the common spirit of the Sarmatian form of government – the mixed constitution – but the particular character of each of the member-states of the confederation that was to be cultivated.

These arguments caught on among several nobles of the Patriot Party, which is a tribute to the influence of Lengnich and other urban writers on the political leadership of the Prussian estates. Under the leadership of Walerian Piwnicki and the brothers Goltz, the Patriots' fight against the implementation of the 1764 decrees gained a new importance as the means of building a new sense of identity. In a lengthy treatise of 1767 Geret appealed to Piwnicki, one of the most eloquent noble members of the Patriot Party, to have faith in Russian support and to continue the fight in the Sejm for the special status and constitution of Polish Prussia. Piwnicki felt obliged to honour the 'historic Prussian heroes' of the fifteenth and sixteenth centuries, remembering that 'the Prussians are a peculiar nation, with their own peculiar government, their own laws, with the power to administer their own justice and their own affairs'.[59] Protesting against the Polish contention that the Prussians were wreaking havoc in the Commonwealth and pushing the whole republic into anarchy by building a 'state within a state', Geret appealed to the principles of natural law and to European models of confederal systems, such as the Holy Roman Empire, the cantons of Switzerland, Lusatia's special status in Saxony, the seven provinces of Belgium, and the union between Ireland, Scotland and England. All these states, he asserted, accommodated territories and provinces, even separate nations, with their own peculiar laws and traditions, without descending into anarchy. It was only Polish arrogance, jealousy, and above all ingratitude, which caused such groundless accusations. At the time of incorporation in 1454, when they were themselves still 'arbitrarily' ruled by their king, the Poles were happy to follow the shining example of Prussian liberties, whereas the Prussians already possessed fully developed parliamentary institutions, which, in contrast to the Polish Sejm, even included the cities.[60] Now the Poles had forgotten what they owed the Prussians and were trying to deprive them of their superior political traditions.

---

[59] [Geret], *Vox Pruthenorum ad Illustr. atq. excell. dominum dominum Valerianum Piwnicki, ensiferum Terrarum Prussiae generalem inclytae commissionis Thesauri Regni Assessorem hoc tempore nuncium terrarum Prussiae in comitiis extraordinariis regni et delegatum ex his comitiis ad tractatum sub garantia sereniss. imperatricis Russiae conscribendum* (n.p., 1767), p. 7.    [60] Ibid., pp. 34–40.

## Myths old and new: the Royal Prussian Enlightenment

Piwnicki did not accept all of Geret's historically less than accurate observations, but he responded to his call to defend Prussian liberties. He belonged to a small group of noblemen who argued in favour of the Prussian cities' economic and political interests: payments he received from Danzig might have helped to convince him of the merits of this cause.[61] The picture of isolation from the provincial nobility which the cities often tried to conjure is more myth than reality. The cities had always found partisans among the noble estates. Piwnicki had the advantage of enjoying a good reputation not only among the Prussian nobility but also in Warsaw, where he maintained useful contacts with the king, the reform party and the Russian representatives. There were some successes. Rumours spread that the Prussian Diet might even recover the powers of an appeal court for the province alone.[62] Many Poles observed these developments with concern. In 1766, Kazimierz Rogaliński, the royal envoy to Royal Prussia, deplored the Patriots' political agitation in the Prussian Diet:

I doubt whether the Koran among the Turks, or the Talmud among the Jews receives such high esteem as the Prussian liberties, about which everyone says here that the whole of Europe envies them; but there are only a few people who really know and understand these laws, which often contradict each other . . . Klossman [the burgomaster of Thorn] is the local Solon, who knows them by heart and tells them what he wants them to know. They believe him and accept his head *pro codice legum* . . . A lot of spittle will be needed before such fanaticism can be rooted out.[63]

In the name of the Prussian Patriot Party, Michał Zboiński, starosta of Kowalewo (Schönsee), presented the Russian ambassador in Poland, Prince Repnin, with a plan for a Prussian confederation, modelled on the Prussian Union of 1454. With natural law arguments and references to the right of resistance, Zboiński attacked the king and the Reform Party as tyrants whom the Prussians must fight as once they had fought the Teutonic Knights. By confirming the decisions of the 1764 Convocation Sejm and by being the first king to refuse official recognition to the ancient liberties of the Prussian estates, the Patriots argued, Stanisław August had broken the contract concluded between the Prussian estates and the Polish crown in 1454.[64] References to the right of resistance and historical parallels with the Teutonic past abounded, as in the sermon celebrating the tricentenary of the rebellion against the Teutonic Knights held at the Elbing Gymnasium in 1754, which ominously alluded to the liberation of the Swiss and the Dutch from Habsburg oppression: no happy union between nations and states was possible

---

[61] Dygdała, 'Walerian Piwnicki', in *Polski Słownik Biograficzny* 26 (1981), 607–9.
[62] Geret summarised arguments in favour of such a court: 'Gedanken und Entwurf von einem wiederherzustellenden eigenen Tribunal für die Lande Preussen aufgesetzt, nachdem . . . kein Tribunal auch nicht vor einen Teil der Lande Preussen vorhanden war, im Jahr 1769', *Die aus den Gräbern*, pp. 112–24.
[63] Dygdała, *Życie polityczne*, p. 182.
[64] Ibid., p. 203.

without respect for each other's liberties and laws.[65] On the same occasion in Thorn, the Prussian liberties and resistance to tyranny also formed the central theme. The speaker, a member of the city council, appealed to his audience to remember the wisdom and fortitude of their ancestors, as well as the past clemency and goodness of their first Polish king, their only rightful lord and master.[66] In response to the strong opposition in Polish Prussia, Stanisław August chose a more conciliatory course in the province, which endeared him to the Thorn resident in Warsaw. In Geret's correspondence, the real foes soon became the Reform Party of the Czartoryski family and the centralisers, such as crown chancellor Andrzej Zamoyski, who effectively exposed the burghers' historical fiction of Prussia's personal union with the crown. He stressed that Polish kings in the fifteenth century were by no means independent of their estates, whereas the Prussian estates under Teutonic rule owed taxes and duties, and possessed no parliament of their own.[67]

The anti-reformist consensus among the Prussian estates and cities which the Convocation Sejm had established was soon broken over confessional issues. In the aftermath of the Tumult of Thorn, Protestants and Orthodox Christians felt more under siege than ever, as the crown tribunals were dominated by a growing number of Catholic clergy and an increasingly belligerent Catholic journalism, backed even by such eminent figures of the Polish Enlightenment as Józef Andrzej Załuski, who denounced non-Catholics as 'heretics'. After 1733, Protestant envoys were no longer tolerated in the lower chamber of the Sejm or admitted to public office in tribunals and commissions, and abandoning the Roman Catholic faith was prohibited by the death penalty, although this law was never applied in reality.[68] When the Sejm of 1736 confirmed these laws against non-Catholics, Poland-Lithuania seemed, at last, to have joined the rest of Enlightenment Europe, where confessional discrimination and harassment was widespread. It was the intense politicisation of religious issues during the years before the first partition and Russia's and Prussia's hostile rhetoric which marked the Commonwealth as a particularly intolerant, Catholic environment.

[65] *Ad solemnia saecularia Jubilaei Prussiae a plusquam Tyrannico Equitum Marianorum Imperio Liberatae Tertii eodem die quo ante hos trecentos annos Seren. ac potentissimo Poloniarum Regi Casimiro tum Elbingae praesenti iusiurandum solenni ritu datum fuit . . . interpres Joannes Langius Gymnasii Rector* (Elbing: Preuß, 1754), attached to APGd, Rkps. Elbl. 452, p. 78.

[66] Albin Kries, *Memoria saecularis diei quo ante hos trecentos annos Prussia excusso tyrannidis cruciferorum iugo in libertatem sese vindicatum i[u]vit ac deinde sub Seren. Poloniae Regum imperium ac tutelam concessit* (Thorn: Jungmann, 1754), folios M2 and O–Ov.

[67] Ludwig Prowe, 'Mitteilungen des Thorner Residenten am Warschauer Hofe Dr. S. L. von Geret (1765–1773)', *Die neuen Preußischen Provinizial-Blätter* 3rd series 10, no. 4 (1865), 509–30; Dygdała, *Życie polityczne*, p. 169.

[68] 'Pro Memoria der Gedrängten Evangelischen', APGd., Bibl. Archivi 300.R, Nn 51, folio 24v; Wojciech Kriegseisen, *Ewangelicy Polscy i Litewscy w epoce saskiej (1696–1763). Sytuacja prawna, organizacja i stosunki międzywyznaniowe* (Warsaw: Semper, 1996), p. 47.

Catholic Poland, however, was not ruled by superstitious, fanatic brutes, as the propaganda emanating from Berlin maintained, but its highly educated clerical establishment was recruited from among the eloquent representatives of the Catholic Enlightenment. Bishop Załuski, whose contacts with Enlightenment scholars are well known, stressed that strict laws against non-Catholics were necessary in the Commonwealth. Pointing to Russia and the Hohenzollern kingdom, the two foreign promoters of the Polish-Lithuanian dissident movement, Załuski stressed that religious tolerance was much more easily granted in a centrally controlled monarchy than in a free republic which relied on unanimity, and where dissent and disruption prevented the smooth functioning of the legislative process. The close link between religious dissent and political paralysis was the reason why the dissidents were regarded as traitors and enemies of the fatherland. Załuski was particularly keen on disproving that Poland-Lithuania had been happier or more powerful when it tolerated many religions in the sixteenth century – the main argument of dissident literature.[69] In 1764 Szymon Majchrowicz, a canon in Lwów, mounted an attack against Protestants on the basis of cameralist arguments: the happiness of all citizens, he insisted, could only be achieved in a Catholic state. Like Załuski, he cleverly mixed Enlightenment concepts, Pufendorf's natural law theory, and the Lipsian thesis that a multitude of religions weakened the cohesion and strength of a state.[70] As a result, the 1766 Sejm rejected the dissidents' demands for political and social equality.

On 20 March 1767, the dissident nobility of Poland concluded a confederation in the city of Thorn. The event was marked by the Russian court with the publication of a collection of grievances over the oppression of non-Catholics in the Commonwealth. To underline the importance of this event, Gottlieb Wernsdorff, Lengnich's contemporary and colleague at the Danzig Gymnasium, wrote a commentary on the religious guarantees granted to Royal Prussia and its cities in the mid-sixteenth century. Sharing other Prussian writers' erroneous premise that the Polish kings of the fifteenth and early sixteenth centuries ruled in an unrestricted manner, Wernsdorff reached a radically republican conclusion: in the Commonwealth constituted by the Union of Lublin in 1569, the laws and immunities which the Polish kings had passed before that date were invalid, unless the united republic confirmed them at a later stage. The Consensus of Sandomierz of 1570 and the Confederation of Warsaw in 1573, where the assembled nobility represented the republic, had confirmed the free exercise of religion for all Christian religions (with the exception of the Antitrinitarians), thus converting what was merely a royal guarantee into a fundamental law.[71] It was in breach of this law that the Catholics

---

[69] Ibid., pp. 42–3; Konopczyński, *Polscy Pisarze*, pp. 258, 263.
[70] Ibid., p. 248.
[71] Gottlieb Wernsdorff, *Eines evangelischen Mitgliedes der ehemaligen Conföderation zu Thorn ausführlicher Erweis der Gerechtsamen der Dissidenten in Polen und Widerlegung der neuesten Schriften welche Catholischer Seits wider die Rechte der Griechen und der Evangelischen herausgekommen sind* (Berlin, 1772), p. 10.

now persecuted and discriminated against Protestant citizens in the Commonwealth. The destruction of fundamental laws, however, could only spell disaster for
the whole Commonwealth. With reference to the discrimination against the Greek
Orthodox in the Commonwealth, Wernsdorff blamed the combination of Polish
political and Catholic religious oppression for the mid-seventeenth-century wars
and all subsequent conflicts which contributed to the decline of the fatherland: 'We
must not abominate the faithless Cossacks, but must look at the source of their
misery, which lies in our behaviour towards this free nation, our endeavour to force
them into a union [with Rome] and in our partiality towards the uniate Greeks. Do
they not tell us: *discite justitiam, moniti?*'[72]

In sharp contrast to earlier Prussian authors, Lengnich no longer singled out the
Cossacks for being particularly treacherous; they did not act so differently from
members of the Polish and Lithuanian nobility who in previous wars had collab-
orated with the enemy. Thus Lengnich showed considerable understanding for
their grievances and demands and put the blame for the Cossack rebellion squarely
on the attitudes of the Poles:

The Cossacks would never have decided to go to war against Poland if they had been treated
less harshly, or disciplined more thoroughly. Putting weapons into their hands, and then
disdainfully maltreating them and denying them justice, pushed them towards revenge.[73]

A supporter of *libertas legitima*, Lengnich resented the fact that the Cossacks had
fought and abandoned the Commonwealth; yet liberty abused, he warned, led to
the present state of disharmony and civil war between the estates of the realm: 'The
Poles have this peculiarity that distinguishes them from other nations, that they
wage war within their own country which others do abroad; this is called liberty and
is permitted in case somebody thinks his rights have been injured.'[74] The lesson to
be learned from the Cossack rising was not to lament about the pernicious nature of
the faithless Cossacks, but to consider the need for a comprehensive reform of the
Commonwealth to prevent it from further disintegration.

When in April 1767 the Prussian cities joined the confederation after some
hesitation, Lengnich did not seem to perceive the double standards of the burghers'
position. They closed ranks with the power that guaranteed the very status quo
which Lengnich had scorned in his writings. He soon realised, however, that
neither the Russians nor the dissident nobility showed serious support for urban
political and economic interests.[75] Although the Sejm of 1767, under Russian
pressure, ceded to the dissident demand for freedom of worship, it confirmed

---

[72] Ibid., p. 305.
[73] Lengnich, *Geschichte der Lande Preußen*, vol. VII, pp. i(verso)–ii.    [74] Ibid., p. iii.
[75] 'Instruction an Herrn Bgm. Christian Klossmann und Georg Adam Reyher Ratsmann von Thorn:
Graudenz, General Ante-Comitialis Landtag, 7. September 1767', APT Kat. II, VII.60, pp. 218ff;
'Recessus 1767 der in Thorn errichteten dissidentischen Confoederation', Bibl. PAN Gd. 1373, pp.
159–262; see also Dygdała, 'Udział Gotfryda Lengnicha', 26–30; Dygdała, *Polityka Torunia*, p. 101;
Bömelburg, *Zwischen polnischer Ständegesellschaft*, p. 170.

Catholicism as the state religion and rejected the most extreme Prussian demands which came from Thorn and its burgomaster Christian Klossmann, Geret's close associate and colleague. To what extent the urban confederates of Thorn had political rather than purely confessional grievances in mind is apparent from their publications. Part of Thorn's political programme went all the way back to the treaty of 1454, including the demand to restore the *Landesrat*, without a lower chamber but with a separate governor, treasurer and postal service, all of which was rejected as unrealistic. The greatest disappointment to Lengnich in particular, who had formulated more moderate demands for Danzig, which in contrast to Thorn had received a Russian guarantee of its liberties, was Stanisław August's lack of sympathy for the cities' aspirations. With what became a famous quote, during an audience of the Prussian cities' representatives he turned to them and urged them 'to stop harassing him about a separation of Prussia from Poland and acquire a Polish heart'.[76]

Russian and eventually also Brandenburg-Prussian help were bought for a high price. Not only did the Russians now consider parts of Polish Prussia as territory where they could station and feed their troops, demand financial compensation and interfere in the political process, but the confederation also contributed to the outbreak of the civil war which devastated Poland-Lithuania between 1768 and 1772, and culminated in the first partition. Neither of the warring parties – the confederation of Radom, supported by Russia, and the Catholic confederates of Bar – held any attraction for the Prussian burghers, and neither confederation assigned any meaningful role to the cities in their political programmes; nor was there an enthusiastic response to either confederation among the majority of the Prussian szlachta. Hans-Jürgen Bömelburg has convincingly shown that the readiness of the Prussian estates to collaborate with foreign powers was in fact less marked than among the confederates from other parts of Poland-Lithuania. In 1770, Frederick II's *cordon sanitaire*, which isolated Danzig from its hinterland and prepared the way for the Hohenzollern occupation of parts of Polish Prussia, ended the activities of the confederation armies in the province.[77]

What impact did the dispute about religious freedom have in the long run on the Prussian burghers' identity? This question cannot be answered without taking into account the changes which Polish national identity underwent during the eighteenth century. The burghers' quest for greater independence was fuelled by the enhanced exclusivity of a now thoroughly Catholicised and Polonised Sarmatian culture. A wider, socially more inclusive idea of citizenship spread in the Europe of the Enlightenment, which slowly dissolved the old political estate structures in Poland as elsewhere. Yet it substituted the old ideal of the multinational, Sarmatian Commonwealth with a new, much narrower and more exclusive idea of the Polish

---

[76] Dygdała, *Polityka Torunia*, p. 129.
[77] Bömelburg, *Zwischen polnischer Ständegesellschaft*, p. 180; Cieślak, in *Historia Pomorza* II/ 2, pp. 200–1.

nation. Towards the end of the eighteenth century, Polish peasants and burghers followed Tadeusz Kościuszko's patriotic appeals and rose against the Russian army, but the definition of Polishness increasingly excluded Lithuanians, Prussians, Ruthenians and other nations which in the past had participated in the Commonwealth's noble Sarmatian identity. State and nation became almost synonymous now, which led to the attempt to introduce uniform laws and central government for all parts, territories and provinces of the composite monarchy.[78] The Prussian burghers followed the same ideas, but with a different objective: the burghers who considered themselves the last defenders of the Prussian nation wanted to elevate their nation to the status of an independent *respublica*. Lengnich confirmed the need to subject all public life to the rule of law: but it had to be Prussian law, not Polish law, which guaranteed liberty from arbitrary government.

Sarmatism and the early modern political nation were not 'in a crisis'[79] but in a state of dissolution, especially in the non-Polish provinces. This opened several options to the Prussian burghers, who had to face the reality that they might soon be subjects of a new state which had nothing in common with their old laws and constitutions except the name of Prussia. Between a rock and a hard place, the Prussian burghers rallied to preserve their 'Prussian heart', as Geret so passionately recommended to the nobleman Ludwig von Wejher in 1771: 'But we must know the principles of our constitution and our state laws in order to know what our Prussian heart and our Prussian courage may accomplish.'[80] Instead of accepting Polish noble lifestyle and language, Polish law courts, Polish taxes and central reforms, Prussians ought to stand up for their national traditions. He spoke of Prussian nobles as '*Polacken*' – a clearly pejorative expression for Poles – and '*verpolackte Preußen*' who were seduced by the Poles, as if by 'the serpent in paradise'.[81] Depriving the Prussian burghers and estates of their ancient liberties meant the destruction of their identity. Geret was convinced that the Commonwealth had lost its former openness to other nations; hence the introspection and the retreat to the political virtues and history of their provincial and urban republics. Prussian burghers could identify with being a part of the old Sarmatian Commonwealth, but not of a Polish, Catholic state which was so obviously in decline, ridden with civil war and oppressed by foreign troops. It may have been this insight which made Lengnich refuse to defend the multinational republic which had housed his Prussian nation for over three hundred years. When he was asked by Stanisław August Poniatowski in 1772 to sharpen his wit and pencil and write a treatise refuting Hohenzollern claims to Royal Prussian territory, he declined.[82] The strong loyalty which had bound Polish Prussian burghers and citizens to the Commonwealth had become brittle.

---

[78] Jörg Hoensch, *Sozialverfassung und politische Reform in Polen im vorrevolutionären Zeitalter* (Cologne and Vienna: Böhlau, 1973), pp. 73–4.   [79] Maciejewski, 'Uniwersalizm i swoistość', pp. 285–6.
[80] Geret, 'Herrn Ludwig Weyher', p. 24.   [81] Ibid., pp. 6–7.
[82] Lemke, *Die Brüder Załuski*, p. 180; and Salmonowicz, 'Gotfryd Lengnich', p. 83.

## Myths old and new: the Royal Prussian Enlightenment

Little though the burghers might have been aware of the fact, their own cry for 'no new laws', their rejection of constitutional change and their staunch defence of their 'Prussian ways' were the exact mirror-image of the xenophobia and exclusivity of which they accused their Polish brothers:

Now everything assumed a Polish character, accompanied by corruption and disorder, as our children have no longer any opportunity to earn their bread in their province . . . the Prussians are no longer their own judges; a Volhynian, Ukrainian or Podolian is certainly very foreign for us Prussians; and have you ever seen a Pole who was not jealous of Prussians?[83]

In the light of such comments, Dygdała denied that the Prussian burghers had any intention of embracing the Enlightenment and its reforms: clinging to 'feudal', medieval privileges, or rather their fiction, the Lengnichs and Gerets of Polish Prussia sided with the reactionary, republican szlachta, rather than with a forward-looking reformist monarch. This argument overlooks, however, the vital changes in the use of political and philosophical concepts in Prussian burgher literature during the eighteenth century. The medieval principle that nothing was to be decided without the consent and representation of Prussian citizens was easily recast into the modern postulate of 'no taxation without representation'. Similarly, the debate among the confederates of Thorn about religious freedoms helped to transfer the medieval and early modern notion of corporate freedoms into a new mould of individual rights and personal liberty. When Wernsdorff, Lengnich's contemporary, defended Prussia's religious liberties, he suggested that the only remedy against the Catholic domination of the Polish state was the separation of state and church. Wernsdorff was the most outspoken defender of the need to exercise religion personally, freely, and unhampered by political dictate. Referring to Christian Thomasius's attack on superstition, he defined the free and equal citizenship of reasonable men as the most desirable of all forms of human existence: 'The freedom to choose any religion freely is an important element of the natural freedom of reasonable human beings in a free state. Religion concerns our souls, whereas political government is concerned with the state of our country.'[84] All grief and intolerance, he stressed, came from the erroneous assumption that the Polish state and Catholicism were inseparable.

In contrast to Lengnich, Wernsdorff saw the republic as the fountainhead of all law and considered legislation passed during an interregnum and during confederations, often against the king, as the most authoritative. This appeal to the Poles to rescue their traditional freedom and tolerance from the claws of the Catholic clergy, whose interest in control over the state was mainly motivated by economic interests, was not only explicitly anti-clerical, but was also rooted in the traditional loyalty to the Commonwealth of past generations of Prussian burghers. Wernsdorff

[83] Geret, 'Gedanken von einem wiederherzustellenden eigenen Tribunal', *Die aus den Gräbern*, p. 112.
[84] Wernsdorff, *Eines evangelischen Mitgliedes Erweis*, pp. 12–14.

appealed to his readers to think of Lithuanian, Ukrainian and Prussian non-Catholics who had repeatedly saved the Commonwealth and protected it against its foes: grand marshal Jan Firley, grand hetman Christoph Radziwill, the burghers of Danzig and many others. Wernsdorff's grievances were a declaration of love for the old Commonwealth built on a new, enlightened foundation.

Christian Windler, in his study of the development of civil society and public opinion in the eighteenth-century Alsatian city of Mühlhausen, has shown that the governing urban elite skilfully connected traditional corporate ideas of liberties and privileges with classical republican notions, natural law teaching and ideas of individual liberty, in order to 'legitimate the social and political status quo with old and new arguments'. The transition to the civil society of the French Revolution, however, could not succeed on the basis of the city's ancien régime of patrician clan rule.[85] Geret, Lengnich and their colleagues in the city councils of Thorn, Danzig and Elbing tried a similar trick, with the difference that Mühlhausen was taken over by revolutionary France, while their cities were conquered and annexed by the king of Prussia – Elbing in 1772, Danzig and Thorn in 1793. For if the relationship between Polish Prussia and Poland had come under serious strain in the eighteenth century, it was still preferred by the vast majority of the province's inhabitants to subjection under Frederick II. During his rule, the struggle between the two alternative Prussian identities even intensified. Despite its enlightened image, the Prussian monarchy did not herald the Enlightenment in Polish Prussia, but brought what Christian Klossmann, burgomaster of Thorn, called '*despotismo Beroliniense*'. He was not afraid to proclaim his choice: 'I would rather live under the Poles on 6 Huben of land than under the Prussians on 18: *insuportabilis servitus.*'[86] His colleague, Gabriel Weickhmann, protested no less vigorously when he demanded that the word 'violation' be added to the *Encyclopédie* citing the example of the Prussian annexation of Polish territory in 1772. For the inhabitants of Polish Prussia, as for the rest of Europe, 'Prussia' had acquired new connotations – none of which belonged to the Polish Prussian burghers' past: high taxes, burdensome garrisons, expropriation, a foreign bureaucracy, forced recruitment and a monarch who did not tolerate parliaments and confederations, and who had the means of preventing them. With Wernsdorff having prepared the way, the Polish Prussian idea of liberty soon lost its focus on corporate privileges, but echoed the writings of the late eighteenth-century Enlightenment, which had spread in Poland with the arrival first of the American and then of the French Revolution, emphasising the newly defined idea of sovereign state- and nationhood:

Every commonwealth, though its frontiers be most narrow, in respect of its rights in no way yields even to the most extensive kingdom . . . Every nation should be its own judge . . . A

---

[85] Christian Windler, 'Schwörtag und Öffentlichkeit im ausgehenden Ancien Régime. Das Beispiel einer elsässischen Stadtrepublik', *Schweizerische Zeitschrift für Geschichte* 46 (1996), 197–225.
[86] Bömelburg, *Zwischen polnischer Ständegesellschaft*, pp. 234–5.

foreign nation cannot prescribe rules for it, or set laws for it with a show of strength without violating its independence, which is the equal right of all countries in accordance with the laws of nature.[87]

Andrzej Popławski's defence of the principles of natural and international law was also reflected in a treatise refuting Hohenzollern attempts to justify the annexation, which Daniel Gralath wrote to a friend from Danzig:

> My Polish blood almost boiled over and invigorated me with new courage . . . as upright citizens of this commonwealth we cannot keep silent about the violations and the arbitrary application of power that are being paraded as justice . . . Why do these conquerors try to conceal their actions under a distorted interpretation of law, instead of clearly saying: we are a terrible power, such as Alexander and Ghengis Khan before us; what we want we take and we call it law![88]

With the straitjacket of the new Polish national idea on the one hand, and the threat of Hohenzollern despotism on the other, the burghers once more retreated to their own constitutionalist position. Even after the first partition, Geret still thought it possible to save the old union of a free and self-governing republic of Prussia with the Polish crown and the remains of the kingdom. Such a safe haven within the ruins of the Polish-Lithuanian republic could still be accomplished if the nobles and cities in Polish Prussia worked together once more: 'None of the unrest and devastations with which the Poles are faced would touch us and we could then be a secure harbour for the poor and plagued Poles, whose friends we shall remain forever, since we are inseparably united with the Polish crown.'[89]

But in the new context of the first partition, the survival of the Polish Prussian identity was no longer a realistic option. Most citizens of Danzig and Thorn had few illusions: Poland would most certainly be partitioned again, while the Prussian *cordon sanitaire* had not only destroyed Polish Prussia's recently recovered and flourishing economy, but had ruined the cities which were cut off from their economic hinterland and trade routes, burdened with high tolls and tariffs by an increasingly impatient bureaucracy in Berlin, and without effective support in Warsaw. In the end, the burghers' civic identity associated with their Prussian nationhood was not destroyed by the Polish kings and the 'jealous nobility', but by the despotism of the Prussian monarch, who thought the country was 'only

---

[87] The Polish physiocrat Andrzej Popławski, in Andrzej Walicki, *The Enlightenment and the Birth of Modern Nationhood. Polish Political Thought from Noble Republicanism to Tadeusz Kościuszko* (University of Notre Dame Press, 1989), p. 29.

[88] Daniel Gralath, *Gedanken von der Verjährung nach den Grundregeln der Naturgesetze. In einem Schreiben eines pommerellischen Juristen an seinen Freund K. auf Veranlassung der behaupteten Anspruchsrechte des Königes von Preußen an die Woywodschaft Pommerellen und mehrere zur Krone Polen gehörige Distrikte* (n.p., 1773), pp. 4–5, 40–41; see also Kocot, *Nauka prawa*, p. 210.

[89] Geret, 'Herrn Ludwig von Weyher', p. 30.

comparable to Canada'.[90] When in 1793 Hohenzollern troops entered Danzig and Thorn, the Prussian burghers of the Sarmatian republic had only one option – to forget that they had been free citizens of the Polish crown, in order to become obedient subjects of the Prussian king.

[90] Bömelburg, *Zwischen polnischer Ständegesellschaft*, p. 229.

# 10

# Conclusion

With the partitions of Poland-Lithuania, Sarmatian mythology lost its function as an umbrella identity for the various nations of the Commonwealth. Loyalty to a constitution, a common history and a common political culture receded into the background, to be replaced by a definition of Polish nationality in terms of language and ethnicity. After the partitions, the discrimination and chicanery against Polish-speakers and Catholics who, under the new regime of Berlin and Königsberg, had to suffer from harsher measures of expropriation and higher taxation than Protestants,[1] and their total exclusion from civil service careers, contributed to the increasing polarisation between 'Poles' and 'Germans'. The dissolution of the Polish-Lithuanian state made it even easier to mark the difference between a 'Western, civilised' part of Enlightenment Europe and a 'barbarian' East. Beyond that line was no longer just the Ottoman Empire, but the border was redrawn on the Memel and the Vistula rivers.

The national antagonism between Germans and Poles was not invented in 1772; in the past, Prussian historians had emphasised the German origins of the Teutonic Knights and of a majority of the population who had settled in the Prussian lands for centuries. From the sixteenth century language had been an issue, even in parliamentary debates, and many burghers had been eager to retain the use of German as one of their fundamental privileges. But the politically articulate elites, both in the cities and among the noble estates of the province, valued other, more important layers of identity, which defined their 'Prussian-ness' and which linked them historically, politically, and to some extent also culturally to the Commonwealth of Poland-Lithuania. Prussians were neither Germans nor Poles. The Prussian nation defined itself politically as a community of citizens who embraced the constitutional agenda of the multinational Commonwealth, even if burghers and nobles could not always agree upon the finer points.

It was only in the last decades of the Commonwealth's existence that loyalty to the Polish-Lithuanian state weakened, and the narrower definition of a Polish national character, triggered by the European Enlightenment, alienated a substantial part of the Polish Prussian nation, particularly among the urban elites. The Sarmatian idea had lost its former prestige and cohesive force. Although the

---

[1] Bömelburg, *Zwischen polnischer Ständegesellschaft*, p. 372.

Prussian burghers and nobles who cooperated with Russia during the Confederation of Thorn in 1767 did not betray the Commonwealth to a greater or lesser degree than the Polish and Lithuanian nobles, who had repeatedly concluded alliances with foreign powers, king and Sejm held it more strongly against the Prussians than against others. Prussian rhetoric and the strong defence of their 'old laws and liberties', as well as the survival of Protestantism in the province, had marked them out as troublemakers and separatists who could not be trusted.

From a Polish point of view, some developments in the Prussian province were indeed worrying. In response to intensified Polish and Catholic agitation in the 1760s, several urban writers rejected any association with the Poles. Philipp von Schröter, for example, refused to call his province 'Polish Prussia' – for him it was a separate duchy, after the model of the historical 'Grand Duchy of Lithuania'.[2] The Sejm considered repeated allusions to Prussian liberation from tyranny as direct attacks on the Commonwealth's overlordship and on the king himself. The burghers' negative focus on the union of Lublin, which in Lengnich's words 'oppressed the nobility, exhausted the cities, violated liberties, changed the constitution and was the basis for all subsequent novelties',[3] questioned the whole constitutional set-up of the Commonwealth. Many Poles feared that this could put similar ideas into Lithuanian heads. Further centralisation was the answer: Lithuania's special status was abolished in 1791.

By 1791, however, Polish Prussia had ceased to exist; only Danzig and Thorn had survived the Prussian onslaught of 1772 as islands in a hostile sea. Under these circumstances more than ever, urban politicians and lawyers insisted that the cities were independent republics, now deprived of their fatherland, the province, but willing neither to become integral parts of a reformed and centralised Polish rump-state, nor to accept a status equal to that of Polish cities.[4] Although Geret, the most vociferous defender of Thorn's liberties, knew of the 'bitterness of the Poles over the cities' presumptuous claim to independence', he wrote frankly about his dislike of 'Polish customs': 'It would be a scandal . . . and any Pole be damned if, with his Polish dress, he did enter our council chamber [in Thorn], since this would soon finish our good order, freedom, *Policey* and good reputation, and we would only follow Polish meanness and the demands of such a nobleman, starosta or palatine.'[5] Anyone appointed to the city council had to be 'at least [*sic!*] of the German nation'. Before 1793 such comments were the exception, but they indicate that external conditions were forcing the Polish Prussian elites to reorient themselves – in their political struggle as well as in their self-definition as a nation. A truly 'formative moment' had arrived.

Openly hostile to the measures of the Prussian monarchy, which 'sucked all life

[2] Schröter, *Gründlicher Beweis*, pp. 4–5.
[3] Lengnich, *Geschichte der Lande Preußen*, vol. II, p. 419.
[4] Bömelburg, *Zwischen polnischer Ständegesellschaft*, p. 378.
[5] Prowe, 'Mitteilungen des Thorner Residenten', p. 520.

# Conclusion

out of the once powerful Hanseatic cities' by cutting off their access to the Baltic through the Vistual delta,[6] Thorn and Danzig rallied in desperation to secure their economic and political survival. Despite their negotiators' awareness of Russia's unreliable policies and the deceitfulness of Repnin, Catherine II's negotiator in Poland, the cities turned for political support to Russia and England and refused to accept Hohenzollern rule: 'The free city government saw its most terrible enemy in Prussia . . . it is for this reason that the council of Thorn relies on Russia. There was no serious danger to the city from this empire.'[7] The citizenry joined in a widespread resistance movement, encouraging the city councils to withstand pressure from Berlin: the choice was between 'victory . . . or death, but enslavement is unworthy of us'.[8] The alternative to 'tyranny' was economic decline, which no guarantee by the Russian empress to preserve the cities' liberties could prevent. Elbing, occupied and incorporated into the Hohenzollern state in 1772, was unceremoniously informed that the Prussian monarch would 'treat the city in the same way as other cities of His Royal Majesty'.[9] Traditional liberties and constitutions, as well as the representation of the cities in a provincial diet, became null and void under the new rulers. State interference did not stop there: magistrates in cities under Brandenburg-Prussian rule were appointed by state officials; election, co-optation and urban self-government were abolished.[10]

Some burghers were quicker to redefine their place than others. Geret, the staunch defender of urban liberties, reacted to the news of the first partition in a letter to his colleague, burgomaster Klossman, with the words: 'God knows what tears these lines cost me. O fatherland, o father-city!'[11] In 1793, however, when Thorn was incorporated into the Prussian monarchy, he secured his place in the new state by dedicating to Frederick William II a treatise which traced the history of his city back to the Teutonic Order, which had 'planted the German nation into Prussia and built solid cities, by Germans for Germans', so that 'Prussia was an entirely German land' and Thorn a 'truly German, Prussian city'.[12] Geret's intention was to prevent the Prussian king from joining the newly formed province of West Prussia with the former Polish territories of Great Poland and Poznania, which the new Prussian rulers now called South Prussia and Netzedistrikt.

The old fighting spirit of the urban patriciate had not evaporated, but they adapted their political goals in tune with a changing political and national identity.

---

[6] Johanna Schopenhauer, *Jugendleben und Wanderbilder*, ed. W. Cosack, Gedanensia, Beiträge zur Geschichte Danzigs no. 3 (Danzig: T. Bertling, 1884), p. 42.

[7] Prowe, 'Mitteilungen des Thorner Residenten', p. 512.

[8] R. Damus, 'Die Stadt Danzig gegenüber der Politik Friedrichs des Großen und Friedrich Wilhelms II', *Zeitschrift des Westpreußischen Geschichtsvereins* 20 (1887), 58.

[9] Bömelburg, *Zwischen polnischer Ständegesellschaft*, p. 236.

[10] Harm Klueting, 'Stadt und Bürgertum', in Frühsorge, G., Klueting, H. and Kopitzsch, F. (eds.), *Stadt und Bürger im 18. Jahrhundert* (Marburg: Hitzeroth, 1993), p. 17.

[11] 'Briefe von Residenten und Deputierten der Stadt', APT Kat. I, 3373, p. 643.

[12] S. L. Geret, *Belehrende historische Nachricht von dem eigentlichen wahren Jahrhunderten hindurch bestehenden Vaterlande der Stadt Thorn* (n.p., 1795), pp. 21-3.

The old Commonwealth was lost, and the identification with Sarmatian Prussia was replaced with a German-Prussian identity; the success of this project is another story. The new rulers did not give the cities an easy ride. The core elements of the province's identity, the provincial diet and the structure of representative estates, were broken. Any attempts by the Hohenzollern kings to elicit loyalty by handing over limited consultation rights stopped short of involving the cities.[13] The urban reforms of 1809 did not change anything in this respect.

The confederation of nations of the old Commonwealth was replaced by the nineteenth-century nation-state of Prussia, in which the Polish-speakers and Catholics would remain second-class citizens at best, and an oppressed minority at worst. The modern principle of nationality has even less patience with diversity and dissent than Catholic nobles had in the Commonwealth's darkest hours. As Lord Acton put it, liberty and the tyranny of nationality are two incompatible concepts:

[Nationality] overrules the rights and wishes of the inhabitants, absorbing their divergent interests in a fictitious unity; . . . crushes all natural rights and all established liberties for the purpose of vindicating itself. . . . While the theory of unity makes the nation a source of despotism and revolution, the theory of liberty regards it as the bulwark of self-government, and the foremost limit to the excessive power of the State. . . . The co-existence of several nations under the same State is a test, as well as the best security of its freedom. It is also one of the chief instruments of civilisation; and . . . indicates a state of greater advancement than the national unity which is the ideal of modern liberalism.[14]

The eighteenth-century attempt by the burghers to carve out a new quasi-independent existence for a Polish Prussian nation-state remained a utopia, one of the many projects of failed state-building; an imaginary rather than an imagined community. Despite the noisy propaganda by Hohenzollern officials, who prided themselves on having turned the province from 'a moonscape, where civilised men live among the Poles as on a devastated island', into a flourishing province of the monarchy,[15] it is doubtful whether the Hohenzollern dynasty ever succeeded in eliciting as much genuine loyalty among the urban and noble estates as the Commonwealth had once done. What connected the Polish Prussian burghers to the Prussian monarchy was an uneasy compromise, similar to the arrangement which had reconciled the Ducal Prussian estates with Hohenzollern central power a century earlier; it was, in Milton's words: 'what more oft in Nations grown corrupt, And by their vices brought to servitude. Than to love Bondage more than Liberty, Bondage with an ease than strenuous Liberty.'[16] It is no coincidence that this was the exact opposite

---

[13] Neugebauer, *Politischer Wandel*, p. 118. Elections to the representative body of the citizenry remained under state control (p. 149).

[14] Lord Acton, 'Nationality', in *Essays in the History of Liberty. Selected Writings of Lord Acton*, 3 vols., ed. J. R. Fears, vol. I (Indianapolis: Liberty Fund, 1985), pp. 424–5.

[15] Theodor von Schön, in Robert Schmidt, *Städtewesen und Bürgertum in Neuostpreußen* (Könisgberg: Thomas und Oppermann, 1913), p. 14.

[16] Quoted by H. Koenigsberger, 'Schlußbetrachtung', p. 293.

to Sallust's motto – so popular with Polish and Royal Prussian writers in the seventeenth century – that it was 'better to live in perilous liberty than in quiet servitude': a principle which for over 300 years had provided political and constitutional cohesion for one of the largest and most diverse commonwealths of early modern Europe.

# Bibliography

I  MANUSCRIPT SOURCES

*Archiwum Państwowe w Toruniu (APT)*

*Katalog I*

3471, 3067 a–b      'Briefe an den Rath 1706–1707'

3067 a      'Gravamina der Thorner Handwerker' (1667)

3373      'Briefe von Residenten und Deputierten der Stadt'

*Katalog II*

I.47      'Briefbuch, 1762–1764, Brief der Stadt an Geret, 12.10.1764'

II.3      Acta Consularia

II.5      Acta Consularia, 'Ordinantz bey der Bürgerschafft betreffende'

II.4a      Acta Consularia

II.6      Acta Consularia

IV.13      Acta Consularia

IV.15      Acta Consularia

IV.18      'Beschreibung der Belagerung Thorns vom 24.5.–14.10.1703'

V.13      'Miscellanea Thoruniensia'

VI.20      'Diarium Electionis 1697'

VI.23      'Berichte vom Reichstag zu Warschau, Jan.–Oct. 1701'

VII.26      'Laudum Mariaeburgense' (8 July 1671), 'Urkunden und Lauda betr[effend] die Immunität der preußischen Städte, 1626–1742'

VII.32, 33, 34      'Akten der Ständetage Preußens' 1666–79; 16711–9

VII.60      'Instruction an Herrn Bgm. Christian Klossmann, 7. September 1767'

VIII.46      Georg Peter Schultz, 'Varia Observationes de Prussia Polonica' (1712)

XI.33, 35      'Thoruniensia' (1650–1700)

XII.3      Stroband, 'Tagebuch, 1600–1657' and 'Boxhornij Disputationes, 1645'

XII.5      Cretlovius, 'Tagebuch'

XII.12      Andreas Baumgarten, 'Stammbuch'

XIII.25      Simon Schultz, 'Tagebuch' (1619–76)

XIII.31–2, 37–46

# Bibliography

XIII.78     Johann Seger, ['Chronik']; 'Polnisch-Preußische Geschichte'

XIV.43–8     'Briefe an Bürgermeister Rösner'

XIV.49     'Briefe an Ephraim Praetorius' (1693–1720)

XIV.71     'Georg Austen Thorun[iensis] Boruss[us] continuata vero per P[etrus]. Düsterwald, Encomia, Vituperata . . . Collectanea quavis studio hic inserta'

*Archiwum Sczanieckich*

245     Silva Rerum

248     'Instrukcja sejmiku Kowalewskiego . . . 10.1.1654'

*Książnica Miejska w Toruniu (KM)*

10, R 8° 13

11, R 8° 14

37     Varia

40, R 4° 16     'Lectiones publicae habitae in celebri Gymnasio Thoruniensi conscripta a Joh[ann] God[fried] Rösnero, Ao. 1676–1678'

41, R 4° 17     Rösner, 'Collectanea'

113     Matrikel 1600–1817

129     Ephraim Pratorius, 'Presbyteriologia Thoruniensia'

130     'Arcana Magistratus Thoruniensis'

E 4° 465, adl. 3     'Reden des Georgius Niemierycz' (1659)

F 4° 57²     'Icon Animorum'

4788–837 (adl.3),

A fol. 57 adl. (1–49)     'Einladung zur Antritts-Vorlesung Hartknochs am 3.6.1677'

*Biblioteka Uniwersytetu Mikołaja Kopernika (UMK)*

501/ IV

537/ 2

*Archiwum Państwowe w Gdańsku (APGd)*

*Missiva*

300.27, no. 80     'Missiva der Stadt Danzig', 5.7.1669.

*Akta miasta Gdańska*

300.53, nos. 293 and 495

*Rękopisy Elbląskie*

369.1. nos. 131, 228, 234, 326, 452, 512, 3599

III, 255/452     'Fata Civitatis Elbingensis Bellica conscripta a Samuel Gottlieb Fuchs'

369.1, no. 856     'Apologia Elbingensium Civitatis (1626)'

369.1, no. 2910      'Discursus de Commerciis Regni Elbingam reducendis'
*Biblioteka Archivi*
300.R, nos. Bb 40, Gg 45, Hh 4, Ll 47, Ll 79, Ll 83, Ll.q 9, Ll.q 16b, N 38, Oo 28, R 2, T 14, Tq 25, Vv. q 21

300.R, Dd 18b      'Instruktion und Briefe an den Gesandten der Stadt Danzig in Warschau'

300.R, Nn 51      'Pro Memoria der Gedrängten Evangelischen in Pohlen 1. Gravamina, 2. Desideria, 3. Fundamenta Desideriorum, 4. Media, Anno 1723'

300.R, U 3      'Sententiae Criminales Nobilis Judicii Gedanensis Civitatis Primariae ab anno 1558 usque 1690'

300.R, Vv 171      'Responsum a Regentibus Prussiae', 10 December 1670


*Nucleus Lengnicha*
300.29, nos. 237–8


*Recesy Stanów Prus Królewskich*
300.29, nos. 136, 140–4, 157, 165, 202, 223, 277.


    *Biblioteka Polskiej Akademii Nauk w Gdańsku (Bibl. PAN Gd.)*

96      'Questiones Gedanenses' (1671)
399      'Descriptio Gentium'
403      'Vom Bürgerrecht'
540
538      Johann Kästner, 'Von der Abnahme des Handels in Dantzig'
616      'Adelsbriefe'
672      'Preußisches Haanengeschrey'
673      Georg Schröder, 'Tagebuch (1665–1703)'
755      Michael Behm, 'Diarium . . . durante bello svecico'
796      'Danziger Gelegenheitsgedichte'
755      ['Silva Rerum']
925      'Reisebeschreibung [Georg Schröders] von Dantzig nach Holland und Engelland'
1206
1336      'Acta Publica betreffend die kleineren Städte'
1373      'Recessus 1767 der in Thorn errichteten dissidentischen Confoederation'
1439      Friedrich Herzberg, Bäckermeisters in Elbing, 'Chronik' (1668–1704)
1527      'Geschichte Polens und Preußens' (1674–9)
1559–1559.I      Polemiken und Pasquillen (1697)
2460, adl. 3266      Hartknoch, 'Observationes in Res Prussorum'
2460–2461      Stadtgeschichte
Uph. fol. 92      'An Negotium immediatam Nobilitas Polona in Urbe Dantiscana sibi adferre possit?'

# Bibliography

Uph. fol. 104, 145     'Excerpta Conventualia Terrarum Prussiae, 1422–1655'
Nl 27.4, no. 9         von der Linde, 'Beschreibung der Pohlen Art und Policey'
NL 100. 8°, 193        Gazety Ulotne

### Biblioteka im. Czartoryskich (Bibl. Czart.)

*Teki Naruszewicza*
148 (microfilm 6680), 1–2 'Elogium Civitatis Elbingensis de Sueticis Armis detortis A.
                       1655'
IV.385                 'Akta za panowania Jana Kazimierza'
IV.478                 'Szembekiana (1723–34)'
IV.528                 'Akta sub Augusta II (1703–4)'
1662                   'Pisma różne od Zygmunta III do Jana III'
1883                   'Wiersze XVII wieku, Ein heimlich Pasquill darinnen die Dantz-
                       ker der beyden Städte Thorn und Elbing ihr Wappen durch-
                       ziehen und ihr eigeneß hochheben'
2027                   'Elias Riccius ex libris Biblioteki W. Wolski'
2314                   'Thorner Rechtsordnungen' (1634)
IV, 2475 and 1656      Silva Rerum (1655–67)


### Geheimes Staatsarchiv, Preußischer Kulturbesitz, Berlin Dahlem (GSta)

*XX. Hauptabteilung: Ehemaliges Staatsarchiv Königsberg, Etatsministerium (EM)*
13b; 25e, 7; 87a
111e; 114              'Briefe an den Kurfürsten' (1704)
178                    'Comitialia' (1670)
1358                   'Gravamina der drei Städte Königsberg' (1661)


*Ostpreußische Folianten (Ostpr. Fol.)*
720                    'Diarium Comitiorum Anno 1681' (Warsaw)


### Biblioteka PAN w Kórniku (Bibl. PAN Kór.)

152                    Johann (Jan) Clagius, 'Sarmatia sive de Originibus et An-
                       tiquitatibus primorum in Sarmatia Europaea populorum Dis-
                       sertatio Latinae de Prussia Historiae apparatus et libri I' (1662)
384, adl. 25           'Comparatio wolności Polskiey y Litewskiey z wolnością pos-
                       tronnych Xiążąt udzielnych et mianowicie rzeszy Niemieckiey
                       et Polonoborusse, A. 1680'


*Akta Działyńskich (1664–68)*
187, 384, 1169, 1195, 1286, 1318
1321                   'Extraordynaryjna Rozmowa in Regno Mortuorum'

# Bibliography

## Biblioteka PAN w Krakowie (Bibl. PAN Krak.)

| | |
|---|---|
| 368 | |
| 703 | 'Von dem Bürgerstand' |
| 1936 | Martin Böhm, 'Elenchus Manuscriptorum' |
| 2000 | 'Laudum Indigenatu' |

## Archiwum Diocezji Warmińskiej w Olsztynie (ADWO)

H.37      Adalbert Heide, 'Archiwum Vetus et Novum Ecclesiae Heilsber gensis ex variis Historiae Prussicae Scriptoribus' (1764)

*Braniewo Magistrat*
MSS 2 and 9

*Braniewo Księgi Miejskie i Gravamina*
Ee 112

## Archiwum Państwowe w Olsztynie (APO)

| | |
|---|---|
| XXV, 2/IV.27 | 'Briefwechsel mit Danzig' |
| XXV, 2/V.3 | 'Otto von Schlieben, politische Korrespondenz' (1632–99) |

## Archiwum Kościoły Jezuitów w Krakowie, Dom Pisarski

Pol. 56, Hist. (67)      'Relationen der Jesuitenkollegien Polens nach Rom' (1685–99)

## Wrocław Ossolineum (Ossol.)

| | |
|---|---|
| 1552/I | Rhetorik der Thorner Jesuiten (1684) |
| 1562 | Johann von Werden (Jan Verda), 'Indigenat Ziemi Pruskiej przez Jana Werda podkomorzego pomorskiego nowskiego starostę, odpis z druku' (1634/1647) |
| 3368 | |
| 9771 | Lengnich, 'Autograph' |

## British Library Manuscript Section

Egerton 2428      'Letters from Lord Plantamour, envoy to Berlin . . . to Blath wayt' (1701)

## II PRINTED SOURCES

*Abdruck etlicher Bedenken und Schriften so theils von wegen der Städte Königsberg übergeben,* Königsberg: n.pub., 1640.

Abel, Caspar, *Preußische und Brandenburgische Reichs- und Staats-Historie,* 2 vols., Leipzig: Heinrich Campen, 1735.

# Bibliography

Adlerhold, Germanus, *Das höchstgepriesene Preußen, oder umständliche Beschreibung und Verzeichnüs des herrlichen Landes Preußen, wie auch von dessen Beherrschung unter dem Marianisch-Teutschen Ritterorden, Ferner von der Erhöhung des preußischen Königthumbs zur Königlichen Würde, und Überschwemmung des königlich polnischen Preußens durch die Schwedische Kriegsflut; nebst einem Verzeichniß aller führnembsten Städte, Vestungen und Plätze*, Frankfurt and Leipzig: Buggel, 1704.

Althusius, Johann, *Politica Methodice digesta atque exemplis sacris & profanis illustrata*, Herborn: Corvinian, 1625.

*Amor Dei Morientis in Hominem sub Persona CODRI a scena repraesentatus a Iuventute Gymnasii Thoruniensis A. 1679, 31.3. directore Chr[istophori] Hartknoch, Gymnasii Professore*, Thorn: n.pub., 1679.

Bajerski, Adam, *Z Dotrzymanego Indygenatu Pruskiego dobro pospolite z niedotrzymanego uszczerbek y Ruina Prowincyi, przez Indigenę Pruskiego światu wywiedziona przydana Juris Correcti inter Fratrem & Sorores de Successione defensio*, n.p., 1696.

Barclay, John, *Icon Animorum Editio Indice, Capitum, Rerum & verbum, auctior*, Frankfurt: C. Hermsdorff, 1675.

Baumgarten, Andreas, *Theses Politicas de Majestate Principis limitata, praeside M[agistri] Johann Sartorio Gymn[asii] Thor[uniensi] P.P., proponit Antonius Baumgarten Thoruniensis, 1686 d[ato] 31. Januarii*, Thorn: Beck, 1686.

Behm von Behmfeldt, Michael, *De Indigenatu Sincera Collatio Jurium et Privilegiorum Poloniae et Prussiae Regiae ad sapentia Statuum Disidia mente bona, concordiae gratia scripta*, [Danzig], 1669.

Besser, Johann von, *Preußische Krönungsgeschichte oder Verlauf der Zeremonien mit welchen der Allerdurchl[auchte] Großm[ächtige] Fürst und Herr Hr. Friderich der Dritte Markgraf und Kurfürst zu Brandenburg die königliche Würde des von ihm gestifften Königreichs Preußen angenommen*, Cölln a. d. Spree: Ulrich Liebpert, 1712.

Blivernitz, Aaron, *Dissertatio juridico-politica de Cosacis an satius sit ad finiendum bellum Poloniae civile, rebelles Cosacos Morte prosequi, eosque funditus exstirpare, An vero Arte & perpetuis induciis cum eisdem pacisci ? ab Aarone Blivernitzio*, Lissa: n.pub., n.d. [1653].

Blomberg, Johann K. Baron, *An Account of Livonia, a Journey from Livonia to Holland in 1698, sent in letters to London*, London: Buck, 1701.

Böhm, M., *Q.D.B.V. Constantiam Choineciae ordinis Equitum Teutonicorum Mariano variis bellis robatam sub praesidio D[omini] M[agistri] Martini Böhm, publice exponit Simon A. Poltzin Chonecensis*, Thorn: Nicolai, 1699.

*Dissertatio ex Historia Prussica qua ostenditur, Borussos ad generalem Expeditionem extra fines suos non esse adstrictos defendit Johannes Hintz, Tempelburg[ii] Pom[eranus], sub praesidio M. Martini Böhm*, Thorn: Nicolai, 1700.

*Commentarius de Interregnis in Regno Poloniae a M[artino] Böhmio, professore Gymnasii Thoruniensis, concinnatus nunc e M[anuscrip]to editus ac quibusdam addimentis auctus*, Thorn: Beck, 1733.

Botsaccus, Joannes, *Botsaccus Redivivus, hoc est Moralia Gedanensia editio postrema*, Frankfurt and Leipzig: Johann H. Ellinger, 1678.

Braun, David, *Ausführlicher Historischer Bericht vom Polnisch- und Preußischen Münz-Wesen*, Elbing: Bannehr, 1722.

*De jurium regnandi fundamentalium in Regno Poloniae ratione videlicet de Comitus regni*

227

# Bibliography

*generalibus, Electionibus Regum, Juribus, Majestatis, commentatio brevis*, Cologne: Theodor Brabeus, 1722.

*De Scriptorum Poloniae et Prussiae Historicorum, Politicorum & J[uris] C[onsul]torum*, Elbing: Bannehr, 1723.

*Catalogus Lectionum et Operarum Publicarum in Athenaeo Gedanensi hoc cursu annuo expendiendarum proposito Januario ineunte*, Danzig: in Atheneo, 1688.

Centner, Gottfried, *Versuch, ob nicht aus der Geschichte älterer Zeiten der wahre Ursprung des nach und nach entstandenen Ansehens der polnischen Reichsstände und der Bürgermeister in den Städten in und außerhalb Deutschlands ausfündig gemacht werden*, Thorn: F. Kunzen, 1760.

Charitius, Andreas, *Commentario Historico-Literaria de viris eruditis Gedani ortis speciatim iis qui scriptis inclaruerunt*, Wittenberg: Impensis Ludovicianis, 1715.

Churchill, Awnsham (comp.), *A Collection of Voyages and Travels*, vol. 7: *A Description of Ukraine by Guillaume le Vasseur, sieur de Beauplan, containing several provinces of the kingdom of Poland, lying between the confines of Musvovy and the borders of Transylvania*, London: H. Lintot and J. Osborn, 1752.

Connor, Bernard, *The History of Poland in Several Letters to Persons of Quality*, London: D. Brown and A. Roper, 1698.

Conring, Hermann, *Exercitatio de Germanici Imperii Civibus quam ex discursibus praecipue praeside publice examinandam proponit C.C. Blume Wolfenbytanus*, Helmstedt: Müller, 1641.

*Exercitatio de Urbibus Germanicis D.O.M.A. praeside [H]ermanno Conringio praeceptore ac fautore plurimum honorando ex ejusdem privatis praecipue discursibus concinatam publice in Illustr[issima] Academia Julia 1641 defendit Gerardus Bode, Hamburgensis*, Helmstedt: Henning Müller, 1652.

*Cyriaci Thrasymachi De Iustitia Armorum Svevicorum in Polonos*, Hamburg: n.pub., 1655.

*Cyriacus Thrasymachus Andreae Nicanori amico suo S.P.D.*, Helmstedt: Henningus Mullerus, 1655.

*De scopo reipublicae Polonicae et domo Austriaca adversus F.M. Polonum*, Hamburg: n.pub., 1665.

*Continuirtes Gelehrtes Preußen*, Thorn: Nicolai, 1725.

Cureus, Joachim, *Newe Chronica des Herzogthumbs Ober und Nieder Schlesien Wahrhaffte und grüntliche Beschreibung*, Eißleben: Rätel, 1601.

Curicke, Reinhold, *Commentarius Iuridico-Historico-Politicus de Privilegiis*, Danzig: Förster, 1670.

*Der Stadt Dantzig Historische Beschreibung* [1645], Amsterdam and Danzig: Johann und Gillis Janssons von Waesberge, 1687.

Czölner, Basilius, *Disputatio Politica de Cive, ejus essentia et proprietatibus etc. quam C.B.D. Humanae Societatis praeside Basilio Czölner, Godofredus Zamelius respondens*, Thorn: Franciscus Schnellboltz, 1648.

*Das Bessere Zeiten hoffende Thorn i[n] e[inem] Senatu bey gehaltener Oration nach getroffener Raths-Kühr*, n.p., 1712.

*Denkschrift über das Verhältnis Preußens zu Polen [n.a. auch über die polnischen Ansprüche an Curland] verfaßt resp[ectiv] gezeichnet von Ilgen*, [Berlin]: n.pub., 1719.

Dietrich, R. (ed.), *Die politischen Testamente der Hohenzollern*, Veröffentlichungen aus den Archiven Preußischer Kulturbesitz, vol. xx, Vienna and Cologne: Böhlau, 1986.

# Bibliography

Drews, Johann, *Fasti Societatis Jesu res et personae memorabiles ejusdam societatis per singulos anni dies repraesentantes*, Braunsberg: Hisp. J. Padrivo, 1723.

Elsner, Johann Georg, *Einige Historische Anmerckungen von der Bürgermeisterlichen Würde in Thorn, als der Herr Anton Giering in ordentliche Rat-Küre 1738 zu derselben wie auch praesidierenden Ampte erhoben wurde*, Thorn: Nicolai, 1738.

Fredro, Andrzej Maksimilian, *Gestorum populi Poloni sub Henrico Valesio*, Danzig: G. Förster, 1660.

*Scriptorum Seu Togae et Belli Notationum Fragmenta*, Danzig: Förster, 1660.

*Militarium ad Harmoniam Togae Accomodatorum*, Amsterdam: Forster, 1668.

Gałęzowski, Casimir, *Iusta memoria spectatae dudum Nobilitatis Civitatum et Civium ducatus Prussiae*, Braunsberg: Weingärtner, 1650.

[Geret, Samuel Luther], *Vox Pruthenorum ad Illustr. atq. excell. dominum dominum Valerianum Piwnicki, ensiferum Terrarum Prussiae generalem inclytae commissionis Thesauri Regni Assessorem hoc tempore nuncium terrarum Prussiae in comitiis extraordinariis regni et delegatum ex his comitiis ad tractatum sub garantia sereniss. imperatricis Russiae conscribendum*, n.p., 1767.

*Die aus den Gräbern durchdringende Stimme derer vor zwey hundert fünfzig Jahren verstorbenen wahren und ächten Preußen*, Mitau: J.F. Hinz, 1774.

*Belehrende historische Nachricht von dem eigentlichen wahren Jahrhunderten hindurch bestehenden Vaterlande der Stadt Thorn*, n.p., 1795.

Gralath, Daniel, *Gedanken von der Verjährung nach den Grundregeln der Naturgesetze. In einem Schreiben eines pommerellischen Juristen an seinen Freund K. auf Veranlassung der behaupteten Anspruchsrechte des Königes von Preußen an die Woywodschaft Pommerellen und mehrere zur Krone Polen gehörige Distrikte*, n.p., 1773.

Groddeck, Gabriel, *De Scriptoribus Historiae Polonicae Schediasma literarium, quod divina favente gratia praeside Dn. M. Gabriele Groddeck P.P. ac Reipublicae Bibliothecarii fautore colendo, solenniori ritu submittit auctor Samuel Joachimus Hoppius*, Danzig: Stoll, 1711.

Grotius, Hugo, *De Antiquitate Reipublicae Batavicae*, Leiden: Elzevier, 1610.

Grüttner, Samuel F, *Tractatio juris publici Pruthenici De Prussia nunquam et nulli tributaria moderante viro nobilissimo atque excellentissimo D. Georg D. Seyler, 1740 publice submittit Author responsurus Samuel F. Grüttner Elbingensis*, Danzig: Schreiber, 1741.

Grunau, Simon, 'Preußische Chronik', in *Die preußischen Geschichtsschreiber des 16. und 17. Jahrhunderts*, 3 vols., vol. I: *Preußische Chronik*, Leipzig: Duncker und Humblot, 1876.

Gütthern, Christoph H, *Leben und Thaten Herrn Friederichs des Ersten Königes in Preußen, Markgrafen zu Brandenburg, des Heiligen Römischen Reichs Erzkämmerer und Churfürsten*, Breslau: Johann J. Korn, 1750.

Hacki, Franz J. (S.J.), *Regia Via ad Veritatem Christianae fidei manuducens*, Danzig: Aegidius Jansson, 1689.

[Hanow, Christoph (ed.)], *Preußische Sammlung allerley bisher ungedruckter Urkunden, Nachrichten und Abhandlungen, dadurch die Rechte und Geschichte der Kirchen, des Staats und der Gelehrten, besonders in dem Polnischen Preussen theils ergänzet, theils erläutert und verbessert werden zum gemeinen Besten herausgegeben von einem Liebhaber der Wahrheit*, 3 vols., Danzig: Schreiber, 1747–50.

Hartknoch, Christoph, *Disputatio Politica de Foederibus praeside Chr[istophori] Hartknoch, Antonius Fridericus à Medem Nobilis Prussus Autor*, Königsberg: Reusner, 1673.

# Bibliography

*Disputatio Politica De Incrementis et Decrementis Rerumpublicarum respondens Georg Friedrich a Kalnein*, Königsberg: Reusner, 1673.

*Disputatio Politica de Majestatis Regiae Impedimentis, sive apparentibus, sive veris. Quam adspirante Divino Numine et consentiente ampl[itudine] Facultate Philosophiae, in illi Albertina, praeses M. Chr. Hartknoch, et respond[ens] Jacobus Tydaeus Memela Prutenus*, Königsberg: Reusneri, 1674.

*Dissertatio de Forma Imperii Polonici*, Königsberg: Hallervorden, 1675.

*Dissertatio Historica de Idolatria et Aliis Superstitionibus ritibus Veterorum Prussorum sub praesidio M. Chr. Hartknochen, Passenheimensis Prussi, publico eruditorum examini submittit Friedericus Wernerus, Regiom[ontis] Prussus*, Königsberg: Reusner, 1675.

*De Republica Veterum Prussorum*, Königsberg: Reich, 1676.

*De Republica Polonica Libri Duo Polonicae Memorabiliora, posterior autem ius publicum Reipublicae Polonicae, Lithuanicae provinciarumque annexarum comprehendit. Opera & studio M. Christophori Hartknoch, Passenheimensis Prussi*, Frankfurt and Leipzig: Hallervorden, 1678; 2nd edn, Jena and Leipzig: Hallervorden, 1687; 3rd edn, Leipzig: Hallervorden, 1698.

*Respublica Polonica duobus libris illustrata*, Leipzig: Hallervorden, 1678.

*De Originibus Gentium Prussicarum Dissertatio III*. Königsberg: Reusner, 1679.

*Exercitationum Academicarum de Regno Poloniae prima, quam amplissimo philosophorum ordine consentiente in Ill[ustrissima] Pregelana praeside M[agistri] Christophoro Hartknoch*, Königsberg: Reusner, 1680.

*Alt- und Neues Preußen oder preußischer Historien zwei Theile mit sonderbarem Fleiß zusammengetragen durch M. Christophorum Hartknoch des Thornischen Gymnasii Professorem*, Danzig: Johann Schreiber, 1684; 2nd edn, Frankfurt (Oder) and Leipzig: Hallervorden, 1684.

*Preußische Kirchen-Historia, darinnen von der Einführung der Christlichen Religion in diese Lande, wie auch von der Conservation, Fortpflanzung, Reformation und dem heutigen Zustande derselben ausführlich gehandelt wird. Nebst vielen denckwürdigen Begebenheiten so sich biß an diese Zeiten in dem Kirchen-Wesen daselbst zugetragen, aus vielen gedruckten und geschriebenen Documenten, nicht allein den Inwohnern dieser Lande, sondern auch wegen der genauen Connexion deß Geschichts-Wesens, allen Teutschen zu gut, mit sonderbarem Fleiß zusammen getragen durch M. Christophorum Hartknoch des Thornischen Gymnasii Professoren*, Frankfurt and Leipzig: Simon Beckstein, 1686.

*Zwey Historische Disputationen die unter dem berühmten Preußischen Magister Christoph Hartknoch 1) durch W.Chr. von Nettelhorst Ao. 1674 von dem Ursprung der Preußen; 2) durch F. Werner Ao. 1675, von ihrem ehemaligen Götzendienst und abergläubigen Religions-, Hochzeits und Begräbnisgebräuchen abgehandelt worden, sind sowohl wegen ihres merkwürdigen und angenehmen Inhalts, als auch den damit verknüpften Nachrichten von der Herkunft der ältesten Familien in Preußen der Übersetzung aus dem Lateinischen ins Deutsche, und seiner nicht allein hierzu, sondern auch zu einem vollständigen Verzeichnis aller nachhero im Lande seßhaft gewordenen Edelleute angewandte Bemühung von Carl Johann von Caspari*, Königsberg: n.pub., 1755.

Hartknoch, Christoph (ed.), *Petri de Dusburg Ordinis Teutonici Sacerdotis Chronicon Prussiae, cum Anonymi cujusdam Continuatione, aliisque Antiquitatibus Prussicis C[hristoph] Hartknoch e MSS codicibus recensuit notisque illustravit*, Frankfurt and Leipzig: Hallervordi, 1679; 2nd edn, Jena: Nisius, 1679.

# Bibliography

Hartmann, Philip Jacob, *Respublica Prussiae*, Königsberg: Reusner, 1686; repr. in *Acta Borussica* II (1731), 1–54.

Hartwich, Abraham, *Herrn Abraham Hartwichs weyland Pastoris zu Bährenhof im Marienburgischen Werder Geographisch-historische Landesbeschreibung derer dreyen im Pohlnischen Preussen liegenden Werdern, als des Danziger-, Elbing- und Marienburgischen*, Königsberg: Eckert, 1723.

Hennenberger, Caspar, *Kurze und wahrhafftige Beschreibung des Landes zu Preußen*, Königsberg: Georg Osterbergern, 1584.

Herburt, Joannes, *Chronica sive historiae Poloniae compendiosa ac per certa librorum capita ad facilem memoriam recens facta descriptio*, Basileae: Oporiniana, 1571; 2nd edn, Regiomonti: Paul Nicolai, 1658.

Hermelin, Olaus, *Summi Polyhistoris Olaus Hermelini De Origine Livonorum disquisitio ad flagrantissima multorum desideria publicae publicae luci restituit M. Georgius Caspari Riga-Livonus*, Leipzig: Haeredes Johannis Grossii, 1717.

Hochstetter, Andreas Adam, *De Rebus Borussico-Polonicis praecipue vero Elbingensibus, occasione urbis mense Novembris 1698 occupata, praeside Dn. A.A. Hochstettero moralium Prof. P. Ordine respondit Fridericus Ludovicus Hochstetter, Neustadiensis*, Tübingen: J.C. Reist, 1699.

*Honor exequalis viro celeberrimo Dn. M. Christophoro Hartknoch, Gymnasii Thoruniensi Professori publico Clarissimo a rectore, professoribus ac visitationibus ejusdem Gymnasii*, Thorn: Beck, 1687.

Hoynovius, Michael, *Exercitatio Historica de Insignibus Prussiae, praeside Michael Hoynovius, Scholae Loebnic[ensae] Rector, respondens Heinrich Sivertz, Philos[ophiae] Stud[entus] Dantiscanus Prussus, in inclyte Academia Regiom[ontana]*, Königberg: Reusner, 1693.

Hutten, Ulrich von, 'Arminius', in *Die Schule des Tyrannen. Lateinische Schriften*, ed. Martin Treu, Leipzig: Reclam, 1991, pp. 191–206.

Iaenichius, Petrus (ed.), *Meletemata Thoruniensia seu Dissertationes varii Argumenti ad historiam maxime Polonicam et Prussicam spectantes*, 4 vols., Thorn: Johann Nicolai, 1726.

Jordanes [Jornandes], 'Chronica Iordani Episcopi Ravennatis civitatis, de origine ac vocabulis Gentis Gothorum edita ad Castalium, sumptaque ex auctoribus', in Jordanes, *Variarum libri XII & Chronicon ad Theodoricum Regem*, Lyon: J. Chouet, 1595.

Keckermann, Bartholomaeus, *Disputationes Practicae nempe ethicae, oeconomicae, politicae intra biennium ad Sectionum Philosophicarum cursum habitae in Gymnasio Dantiscano*, Hanover: Haeredes G. Antonii, 1612.

'De natura et proprietatibus historiae commentarius', in Keckermann, B., *Systema systematum*, Hanover: Haeredes Antonii, 1613.

Knipschildt, Philipp, *Tractatus Politico-Historico-Iuridicus de Civitatum Imperialium iuribus et privilegiis*, Ulm: Kühne, 1657.

König, Ernst, *Diatribe Politica de Majestate quam suprema majestate favente, in Gymnasio Thorn, praeside M. Ernesto König, subjicit Henricus Fibing, Svidnicio Silesius*, Thorn: Coepselius, 1671.

*Dissertatio Politica de Legibus Civitatis in genere, quam in Gymnasio Thoruniensi praeside M. Ernesto König subjicit Gabriel Nakielski Mariaeburgensis*, Thorn: Coepselius, 1675.

*Exercitatio Politica de Origine ac Rebus huic necessariis nominatim, territorio et publicis reditibus, praeside M[agistro] Ernesto König, Gymn[asii] Thoruniensis Rectore, Boguslaus ab Unruh, eques Polonus respondens*, Thorn: Coepselius, 1679.

231

# Bibliography

*Politica de Cive, et diversis hominum in civitate ordinibus, praeside Ernesto König, subjicit Christianus Wernigke, Elbingensis respondens*, Thorn: Johann Coepselius, 1680.

*Ad Bonarum Artium Patronos Virosque Doctos Provocatio a Decreto Abdicationis Thoruniensi M. Ernesti Königs*, Old Stettin: D. Starck, 1683.

Kojałowicz, Wojciech, *Historiae Lituanae Pars prior de rebus Lituanorum ante susceptam Christianam religionem conjunctemque Magni Lituaniae Ducatus cum Regno Poloniae libri novem*, 2 vols., Danzig: Förster, 1650.

Koryciński, Andreas z Pilczy, *Perspectiva Politica Regno Poloniae Elaborata per quam, quid & qualiter Regibus prospiciendum sit*, Danzig: Förster, 1652 (posth.).

Krantz, Albertus, *Vandalia*, Cologne: L. Soter alias Heil et Socii, 1519.

Kries, Albin, *Memoria saecularis diei quo ante hos trecentos annos Prussia excusso tyrannidis cruciferorum iugo in libertatem sese vindicatum i[u]vit ac deinde sub Seren. Poloniae Regum imperium ac tutelam concessit*, Thorn: Jungmann, 1754.

Kromer, Marcin, *Apologia contra obtrectatores quorundam*, n.p., 1556.

*Cromeri de origine et rebus gestis Polonorum libri XXX*, Cologne: Birckmann, 1589.

*Poloniae sive de situ, populis, moribus, magistratibus et respublica regni Poloniae libri duo* [1575], ed. Wiktor Czermak, Cracow: Gebethner i Wolff, 1901.

*Polska czyli o położeniu, ludności, obyczajach, urzędach i sprawach publiczynych Królewstwa Polskiego księgi dwie*, ed. Roman Marchwiński, Olsztyn: Pojezierze, 1977.

*Krótkie o Indygenacie Przeświętney Prowincyi Pruskiey obiaśnienie*, n.p. 1739.

Langius, Johann, *Ad solemnia saecularia Jubilaei Prussiae a plusquam Tyrannico Equitum Marianorum Imperio Liberatae Tertii eodem die quo ante hos trecentos annos Seren. ac potentissimo Poloniarum Regi Casimiro tum Elbingae praesenti iusiurandum solenni ritu datum fuit . . . interpres Joannes Langius Gymnasii Rector*, Elbing: Preuß, 1754.

Lengnich, Gottfried, *Polnische Bibliothec welche von Büchern und anderen zur polnischen Historie dienenden Sachen ausführlich Nachricht giebt. Erstes Stück*, Tannenberg 'wo Vladislaus Jagiello die Creutz-Herren schlug': n.pub., 1718.

*Geschichte der Lande Preußen Königlich-polnischen Antheils*, 9 vols., Danzig: Johann Daniel Schreiber, 1722–55.

'Bescheidene Untersuchung des königlichen Decrets so auf dem Reich-Tage zu Lublin A. 1569 wieder die preußischen Stände wegen Besuchung der Reichs-Tage und des Sitzens im Polnischen Senat und in der Land-Boten-Stube, abgesprochen worden', in Lengnich, G., *Geschichte der Lande Preußen*, vol. II (preface), Danzig: Johann Daniel Schreiber, 1723.

*Prutena sub serenissimis Polonarum Regis Imperio facies ad fidem actorum publicorum descripta*, Danzig: Schreiber, 1728.

*De Polonorum Majoribus Dissertationem praeside Godofredo Lengnich, D. eloquentiae et pres. PP in auditorio max. d. XXV. Sept. 1732, tuebitur Michael Hafft, Goldynga-Curonensis*, Gedani: Schreiber, 1732.

*De Polonorum confoederationibus, praeside Godofredo Lengnich, . . . disputabit Carolus Ernestus Kettner, Gedanensis*, Gedani: Schreiber, 1735.

*Historia Polona a Lecho*, Leipzig: n.pub., 1740.

*Majorum Prussiae Civitatum pro Juribus suis vigilantis Interregno*, Gedani: Schreiber, 1764.

*Jus publicum Civitatis Gedanensis*, ed. Otto Günther, Quellen und Darstellungen zur Geschichte Westpreußens 1, Danzig: Th. Bertling, 1900.

# Bibliography

Leo, Johannes, *Historia Prussiae*, Braunsberg: Collegium Societatis Jesu, 1725.

Lilienthal, Michael, *Schediasma praecipuis Prussicorum scriptoribus*, Königsberg: Reusner, 1758.

Lilienthal, Michael (ed.), *Erleutertes Preußen*, 4 vols., Königsberg: Hallervorden Erben, 1725–8.

de Linda, Lucas, *Descriptio Orbis et Omnium Rerumpublicarum*, Leiden: Petrus Leffen, 1655.

[Linde, Johann Ernst], *Gratiani Severini Lipiński ad V[incentum] C[onstantiunum] Starodobski Nob[ilem] Po[lonum] Epistola*, Danzig: n.pub., 1712.

Loccenius, Johannes, *Antiquitatum Sveco-Gothicarum cum huius aevi moribus, institutis ac ritibus indigenis pro renata comparatum libri tres*, Uppsala: H. Curio, 1670.

Ludewig, Johann Peter, *Verthaidigtes Preußen wider den vermeinten und widerrechtlichen Anspruch des Teutschen Ritter-Ordens und insbesondere dessen an. 1701 auf dem Reichstag zu Regensburg ausgestreutes unbefugtes Gravamen über die Königliche Würde von Preußen*, Mergentheim [Berlin]: n.pub., 1703.

Lydicius, Jacob, *Notitiae Ducatus Prussiae delineatio generalis & specialis, Jacobi Lydicii, Hohensteina-Prussi*, Wittenberg: H.D. Tobiae Mevii, 1677.

Malinowska-Kwiatkowska, Irina and Janusz Sondel (eds.), *Rewizja Nowomiejska Prawa Chełmińskiego 1580 (1814) zwana także Jus Culmense Emendatum lub Jus Culmense Polonicum*, Thorn: UMK, 1993.

Micraelius, Johannes, *Altes Pommernland, teutsch, wendisch, sächsisch, nebenst Historischer Erzehlung dero in Nähigsten Dreißig Jahren biß auff des letzten Hertzogen Bogislai XIV Todt, in Pommern vorgegangenen Geschichten*, Old Stettin: Georg Rheten, 1640.

Miechowita, Maciej, *De Duabus Sarmatiis Asiana et Europaeana*, Cracow: Vietor, 1517.

Murinius, Marcin, *Kronika Mistrzów Pruskich*, ed. Zenon Nowak, Olsztyn: Wydawnictwo Pojezierze, 1989.

Van der Mylen, Egidius, 'Antiqua Pomeranorum Respublica', in Rango, Martin (ed.), *Pomerania diplomatica sive de antiquitates Pomeranicae*, part III, Frankfurt (Oder): Renisch, 1707.

Mylius, Michael, *Exequiae Ill[ustrissimi] D[omini] D[omini] Magni Ernesti Comitis a Dönhof, Palatini Parnaviensis Torpat[ensis] Praefecti Elb[ingensis]*, Elbing: Bodenhausen, 1642.

Nemorecki, Johannes and Aramus, Daniel, *Orationes problema politicum de praecipuo Civitatum requisito seu Fine ex parte excutientes, ac in Encaenis Gymnasii Elbingensis publice inter alias habitae*, Elbing: Bodenhausen 1646.

Neugebauer, Salomon, *Historia Rerum Polonicarum libri quinque et ad Sigismundem III Poloniae Sueciaeque regem usque deducta libris decem*, Hanover: Danielis & Davidis Aubriorum nec non Clementis Schleichii, 1618.

Neunachbar, Johannes, *Gehorsames Lob-Opffer dem Chur- und Hochfürstlichen Stamme Dem Durchleuchtigsten Groß-Mächtigsten Fürsten und Herren H[erre]n Friedrich Wilhelm von Gottes Gnaden Marggraffen zu Brandenburg, Chur-Fürsten in Preußen, etc. etc.*, Thorn: Coepselius, n.d.

Niresius, Bernhard, *Dissertatio de Curonorum et Semgallorum republica tam vetere quam nova a. 1676 in Academia Regiomontis me praeside defendit B.J. Niresius Curonus*, Leipzig: Hallervorden, 1698.

Nixdorff, Jan, *Opuscula iuridico-practica Regnum Poloniae terrasque Prussiae regalis concernentia*, Danzig: Rhetius, 1685.

# Bibliography

Olizarovius, Aaron Alexander, *De Politica Hominum Societate libri tres*, Danzig: Förster, 1651.

Opaliński, Krzysztof, *Satyry*, ed. Lesław Eustachiewicz, Wrocław: Ossolineum, 1953.

Opaliński, Łukasz, *Obrona Polski (Polonia Defensa contra Joannem Barclaium)*, Danzig: Förster, 1648.

Orzechowski, Stanisław, *Quincunx*, Cracow: Łasarz Andrysowicz, 1564.

Pasek, Jan Chryzostom, *Memoirs of the Polish Baroque. The Writings of Jan Chryzostom Pasek*, ed., trans., with an introduction by Catherine S. Leach, Berkeley, Los Angeles, London: University of California Press, 1976.

Pastorius von Hirtenberg, Joachim, *Florus Poloniae seu Polonicae Historiae Epitome Nova*, Leiden: F. Heger, 1641.

*Ad nobilium Adolesc[entem] Sigismundum de Linda, Magnifici & Nobili Viri Adriani de Linda Burgrabii & Praeco[n]s[uli] Dant[iscani] Filium Epistola, de recte eloquentia Romanae studio*, Danzig: Georg Rhetii, 1649.

*Palaestra Nobilium*, Elbing: Corell, 1654.

*Orationes duae quarum prima inauguratis de praeciosis Historiae Autoribus altera de potissimis eiusdem argumentis agit*, Elbing: Corell, 1651–2; 2nd edn, Danzig: Georg Rhetius, 1656.

*In Obsessum a se & feliciter recuperatum Thorunium ingressu ipsis calendis Jan[uarii] A. 1659 celebrato. Intermixta alia complura ad praesentem Bellorum Polonicarum statum pertinentia*, Danzig: Rhetius, 1659.

Pommeresch, Johannes, *Discursus juridico-politicus de summo in civitatibus Imperio quem aeterni numinis gratia aspirante Johannis Pomereschi*, Greifswald: Jegeri, 1654.

Praetorius, Ephraim, *Athenae Gedanenses sive Commentarius historico-chronologicus succinctus, originem et constitutionem Gymnasii Dantiscani illustris continens*, Leipzig: J. O. Frider, Gleditsch et filium, 1713.

Praetorius, Matthaeus, *Orbis Gothicus, id est Historica Narratio omnium fere Gothici nominis populorum qua simul Gothicae Sarmaticae acceptam debere et originem*, Oliwa: Textor, 1688.

*Mars Gothicus id est Tractatus historicus: exhibens veterum Gothorum militam, potentiam, arma, machinas, exercitus, bellicas leges poenaesque militares etc*, Oliwa: Textor, 1691.

*Deliciae Prussiae Oder Preußische Schaubühne*, ed. William Pierson, Berlin: A. Duncker, 1871.

*Privilegium Civitatum Minorum Prussiae Occidentalis commentariolo Ill[ustratur], praemittitur de civitatibus minoribus introd[uctio] historica*, Danzig: Knoch, 1739.

Pufendorf, Samuel, *Einleitung zu der Historie der vornehmbsten Staaten so itziger Zeit in Europa sich befinden*, 2 vols., Frankfurt: Merian, 1682.

*De Rebus a Carolo Gustavi Sveciae rege gestis commentariorum libri septem*, Nuremberg: C. Riegel, 1696.

*Von den Thaten Carl Gustavs*, Frankfurt: Gleditsch, 1729.

*De Rebus Gestis Friderici Wilhelmi Magni, Electoris Brandenburgici Commentariorum libri novendecim*, 2nd edn, Leipzig and Berlin: Jeremias Schrey et haeredes H.J. Meyeri, 1733.

Radziwiłł, Stanisław Albrycht, *Pamiętnik o dziejach w Polsce (Memoriale Rerum Gestarum in Polonia, 1632–1656)*, 3 vols., ed. Andrzej Przyboś and Roman Zelewski, vol. III, Warsaw: PIW, 1980.

# Bibliography

Rango, Martin, *Origines Pomeranicas Clarissimorum Virorum nec non XXIV. Diplomata Vetusta Patriae antiquitates illustrantia*, Colberg: Bothius, 1684.

*Pomerania diplomatica sive de antiquitates Pomeranicae*, Frankfurt (Oder): Renisch, 1707.

[Rechenberger, Johannes], *Der unzeitige Haß gegen die Brauer und die unbedachtsame Liebe zur Contribution entdeckt von dem Wahrheitsliebenden*, [printed in Prussia]: n.pub., 1696.

*Reden des Georgius Niemierycz, Abgesandter der Zaporovvischen Kozaken vom Großfürstenthumb Reußlandt (13. April 1659) und Stefan Niemieryczen Obr[isten] über der Reuterey, Comm[andant] des Schlosses Krakau und Abgesandter, nach Außländischer Art dienendem Polnischen Kriegs-Heer*, n.p., 1659.

*Relatio de Nobile quodam Gedani decollato propter homicidium A. 1675 ex Epistola G[ener]osi D[omini] N.N. ex Prussia, ad G[ener]osi D[omini] N.N. in Poloniam prope Cracov[iae]*, n. p., 1676.

*Responsio Civitatis Gedanensis ad scriptum quod circa irruptionem militum exercitus Regni Poloniae in Bona istius Civitatis patrimonialia sub Manifesti forma nomine ill. Domini D. Jacobi Sigismudi Rybinski Regni Venatoris & Generalis Locum-tenentis prodiit*, n.p., 1712.

Röling, Johann, *Christliche Betrachtung des Todes worinn Boguslav Radziwill, des Hertzogthumbs Preußen Gouverneur, unverhofft doch selig verschieden*, Königsberg: Reusner, 1670.

Sachs, Jan [Franciscus Marinius Polonus], *De scopo Reipublicae Poloniae contra Conringium*, Breslau: Jacobi Treschneri Bibliopolae, 1665.

Sartorius, Johannes, *Theses politicas De Majestate Principis Limitata, praeside M. Joh[ann] Sartorius, Gymn[asii] Thor[uniensi] PP ad ventilandum proponis Antonius Baumgarten, Thoruniensis 1686, den 31. Jan[uar]*, Thorn: Beck, 1686.

Schlippenbach, Alexander Graf von, *Zur Geschichte der Hohenzollernschen Souveränität in Preußen. Diplomatischer Briefwechsel des Königs Karl Gustav von Schweden und dem Gesandten Grafen von Schlippenbach, 1654–57*, Berlin: E. Fleischel, 1906.

Schlözer, A. Ludwig, *Abhandlungen aus der polnischen Geschichte von der Ankunft des Lechs in Polen*, Leipzig: Jacobäer, 1770.

Schopenhauer, Johanna, *Jugendleben und Wanderbilder*, ed. W. Cosack, Gedanensia, Beiträge zur Geschichte Danzigs no. 3, Danzig: T. Bertling, 1884.

Schott, Andreas, *Tractatio Juris Publici de Indigenatu Polonorum ex jure publico Polonico deducta*, Danzig: G.M. Knoch, 1738.

Schröter, Philipp, *Gründlicher Beweis daß das Westliche oder so genannte Polnische Preußen ein Groß-Herzogthum sey, aus zuverlässigen historischen Nachrichten und Urkunden erwiesen von Philipp von Schröter, Elbingensi*, Halle and Leipzig: Nisius, 1755.

Schütz, Caspar, *Historia Rerum Prussicarum Wahrhaffte und eigentliche Beschreybung*, Danzig: Groß, 1599.

Schultz, Georg Peter, *Historia Interregni novissimi et comitiorum in Prussia Polonica A. 1738 celebratorum*, Danzig: Knoch, 1738.

Schultz, Georg Peter (ed.), *Das Gelahrte Preußen*, 4 vols., Thorn: Nicolai, 1722–1726.

Schultz [Szulecki], Johannes, *Disputationis Juris Publici de Polonia nunquam Tributaria quam praeside Joanni Schultzio die XVII Febr[uarii] 1681 placido Eruditorum examini submittit publice Johann Daniel Schlieff*, Danzig: Rhetius, 1681.

*Disputationis Juris Publici de Polonia nunquam Tributaria quam praeside Joanni Schultzio publice submittitur a Henrico Fredero*, Danzig: Haeredes Rhetii, 1694.

# Bibliography

*Tractatus historico-politicus de Polonia nunquam tributaria*, 10 parts, Danzig: Rhetii Haeredes, 1694.

*Serenissimo Domino Joanni III Poloniarum Regi*, Danzig: Rhetii Haeredes, 1694.

Schumann, Gabriel Friedrich, *Respublica Mixta An sit Irregularis in Inclyto Gedanensium Athenaeo [Johann Christoph] Rosteuscher disquiret publice G[abriel] F[riedrich] Schumann*, Danzig: Rhetius, 1689.

Schurtzfleisch, Konrad Samuel, *Dissertatio de origine Pomeranorum*, Wittenberg: Schrödter, 1673.

*Res Sueo-Gothicas recensebunt Conradus Samuel Schurtzfleisch & Johannes Bering*, Wittenberg: Schröderi, 1678.

Schurtzfleisch, Konrad Samuel and Daniel Tesmarus, *Origines Pomeranicas*, Wittenberg: Schrödter, 1673.

Seckendorff, Veit von, *Teutscher Fürsten-Staat*, Frankfurt and Leipzig: Johann Meyer, 1703.

Starowolski, Szymon, *Simonis Starovolsci Penu Historicum seu de dextra et fructuosa ratione Historias legendi Commentarius*, Venice: Zenarii Haeredes, 1620.

*Sarmatiae bellatores*, Cologne, n.publ., 1631.

*Mowa przeciw oczczercom Polski. Wybór z pism, Biblioteka Narodowa seria I*, no. 272, Wrocław: Zakład Ossolińskich, 1991.

Stella, Erasmus, *De Borussiae Antiquitatibus libri duo*, Basel: Joannes Frobenius, 1518.

Thamnitius, Conrad, *De Constantia Thoruniensium in obsidione probata oratio*, Thorn: Karnall, 1651.

Thegen, Georg, *Dicursus Politicus de Aristrocratia in Academia Regiomontana Patria consensu amplificanda Philos[ophiae] ord[inis] sub praesidio G[eorgii] Thegen respondens Adamus F. Hess, Brandenburgicus Prussus*, Königsberg: Reusner, 1686.

Thilo, Valentin, *Ad Panegyrin solemnem qua a Serenissimo ac potentissimo principe ac Domino Dn. Joanne Casimiro, Poloniae et Sveciae Rege ac Domino Dn. Friderico Wilhelmo Marchioni Brandenburgico munificentisssimo Borussiae Investituram, Rector et Senatus Academiae Regiomontanae*, Königsberg: Reusner, 1649.

Titius, Jo[hann] Petr[us], 'Oratione seculari de Prussia Seculum, sublata Cruciferorum Tyranniae, Libertatis sub Augustiss[imis] Polon[iae] Regibus tertium ordiente' (1654), *Acta Borussica* II (1731), 157–202.

*Jacobi Augusti Thuani Voluminum Historicorum Recensio*, Danzig: Rhetiana, 1685.

Trepka, Walerian Nekanda, *Liber generationis plebeanorum ('Liber Chamorum')*, Instytut Badań Literackich, Biblioteka pisarzów polskich seria B, no. 13, Warsaw: PAN, 1963.

*Urkunden und Aktenstücke zur Geschichte der inneren Politik des Kurfürsten Friedrich Wilhelm von Brandenburg*, Berlin: Duncker und Humblot, 1895–1915.

Venator, Johann Kaspar (Jäger), *Historischer Bericht vom marianisch-teutschen Reitterorden, wo und wie derselbe entsprungen*, Nürnberg: Knorz, 1680.

Voidius, Balthasar, *Erst-Jährliche Klag- und Ehren-Gedechtnis/ des Aller Durchleuchtigsten/ Hochgeborenen Fürsten/ Großmechtigsten Herren/ und glorwürdigsten Heldens von Mitternacht Gustavi Adolphi des anderen*, Elbing: Bodenhausen, 1633.

Waissel, Matthias, *Chronica alter Preußischer, Liffländischer und Curländischer Historien von dem Lande Preussen und seiner Gelegenheit*, Königsberg: Osterbergern, 1599.

Warszewicki, Krzysztof, *Christophori Warsevicii De optimo statu libertatis libri duo*, Cracow: Lazari, 1598.

# Bibliography

Werdenhagen, Johann Angelius von, *De rebuspublicis Hanseaticis Tractatus generalis et earum nob[ilis] cofoederatione tractatus specialis*, Leiden: Joannis Maire, 1631.

Wernsdorff, Gottlieb, *Eines evangelischen Mitgliedes der ehemaligen Conföderation zu Thorn ausführlicher Erweis der Gerechtsamen der Dissidenten in Polen und Widerlegung der neuesten Schriften welche Catholischer Seits wider die Rechte der Griechen und der Evangelischen herausgekommen sind*, Berlin: n.pub., 1772.

Willenberg, Samuel, 'Disputatio de Muneris Thesaurarii in Prussia Occidentali, antiquitate iuribus & praerogativis', *Das Continuirte Gelahrte Preußen* (1725), 227–30.

Zamehl, Gottfried, *Disputatio Politica de Cive, ejus essentia et proprietatibus, praeside Basilio Czölnero, Godofredu Zamelius respondens, Thorn: Karnall, 1648*.

*Studiosus Apodemicus, sive de peregrinationibus studiosorum Discursus Politicus*, Leiden: Jacobi Köhleri, 1651.

Zawadzki, Kazimierz, *Serenissimo ac Potentissimo Joanni III Poloniarum Regi Orthodoxo exilis tractatus super advertentiam defectuum in capitibus imperii Sarmatici*, Cracow: Franciscus Cezary, 1676.

*Serenissimo ac Potentissimo Ioanni III Poloniarum Regi orthodoxo Vere repraesentans Speculum Anomalium in Capitis Imperii Sarmatici a Casimiro Zawadzki Castellani Culmensi, Gubernatore Lipinensi*, Warsaw: Schreiber, 1690.

Zernecke, Jacob Heinrich, *Historiae Thoruniensis naufragae tabulae oder Kern der Thornischen Chronicke*, Thorn: Lauzer, 1711.

Das bey denen Schwedischen Kriegen Bekriegte Thorn oder Zuverlässige Erzehlung desjenigen was sich bey dieser Stadt im Jahre 1626, 1655, 1658 und 1703 in anfällen, Bloquier-, Bombardier- und Belagerungen denkwürdiges zugetragen; dabey ein nöthiger Anhang der Thornischen Chronicke, Thorn: n.pub., 1712; 2nd edn, Berlin: A. Haude, 1727.

## III  SECONDARY WORKS

Achremczyk, Stanisław, 'Związek małych miast Prus Królewskich, 1683–1772', *Zapiski Historyczne* 44 (1979), 25–45.

'Konfederacja szlachty Prus Królewskich w latach 1703–1709', *Zapiski Historyczne* 45, no. 3 (1980), 31–50.

*Reprezentacja stanowa Prus Królewskich w latach 1696–1772. Skład społeczny i działalność*, Rozprawy i Materiały Ośrodka Badań Naukowych im. Kętrzyńskiego w Olsztynie, Olsztyn: PAN, 1981.

'Organizacja i funkcjonowanie sejmiku generalnego Prus Królewskich w XVIII wieku', *Acta Universitatis Nicolae Copernici* 128, Historia XVIII (1982), 121–47.

*Życie polityczne Prus Królewskich i Warmii w latach 1660–1703*, Rozprawy i Materiały OBN im. Kętrzyńskiego w Olsztynie, Olsztyn: PAN, 1991.

Achremczyk, Stanisław, Marchwiński, R. and Przeracki, J. (eds.), *Poczet Biskupów Warmińskich*, Biblioteka Olsztyńska 23, Olsztyn: Instytut im. Wojciecha Kętrzyńskiego, 1994.

Acton, Lord, *Essays in the History of Liberty. Selected Writings of Lord Acton*, 3 vols., ed. J.R. Fears, vol. I, Indianapolis: Liberty Fund, 1985.

# Bibliography

Adam, Reinhard, 'Der Grosse Kurfürst und die Stände des Herzogtums Preussen nach dem Frieden von Oliwa', in *Acta Prussica. Abhandlungen zur Geschichte Ost- und Westpreußens, Festschrift zum 75. Geburtstag von Fritz Gause*, Beihefte zum Jahrbuch der Albertus-Universität 29, Würzburg: Holzner, 1968, 178–96.

Anderson, Benedict, *Imagined Communities. Reflections on the Origin and Spread of Nationalism*, London: Verso, 1983.

Arnold, Udo, *Studien zur preußischen Historiographie des 16. Jahrhunderts*, Bonn Bad-Godesberg: Wissenschaftliches Archiv, 1967.

'Geschichtsschreibung im Preußenland bis zum Ausgang des 16. Jahrhunderts', *Jahrbuch für die Geschichte Mittel- und Ostdeutschlands* 19 (1970), 74–126.

Arnold, Udo (ed.), *Die Stadt in Preußen. Beiträge zur Entwicklung vom frühen Mittelalter bis zur Gegenwart*, Lüneburg: Nordostdeutsches Kulturwerk, 1983.

Asch, Jürgen, *Rat und Bürgerschaft in Lübeck 1598–1669. Die verfassungsrechtlichen Auseinandersetzungen im 17. Jahrhundert und ihre sozialen Hintergründe*, Veröffentlichungen zur Geschichte der Hansestadt Lübeck vol. 17, Lübeck: Verlag Max Schmidt-Römhild, 1961.

Askenazy, Szymon, *Gdańsk a Polska*, Warsaw: Gebethner i Wolff, 1937.

Attman, Artur, *The Russian and Polish Markets in International Trade, 1500–1650*, Göteborg: Publications of the Institute of Economic History of Gothenburg University, 1973.

Back, Pär-Erik, *Herzog und Landschaft*, Lund: C.W.K. Gleerup, 1955.

Baczko, Ludwig, *Geschichte Preußens*, 6 vols., Königsberg: F. Nicolovius, 1792–1800.

Bär, Max, *Die Behördenverfassung in Westpreußen seit der Ordenszeit*, Danzig: A.W. Kafemann, 1912.

Bahlcke, Joachim, Bömelburg, H.-J. and Kersken, N. (eds.), *Ständefreiheit und Staatsgestaltung in Ostmitteleuropa. Übernationale Gemeinsamkeiten in der politischen Kultur vom 16.–18. Jahrhundert*, Leipzig: Universitätsverlag, 1996.

Baranowski, Henryk, *Bibliografia miasta Torunia*, Toruń: TNT, 1972.

Baron, Hans, *The Crisis of the Early Italian Renaissance. Civic Humanism and Republican Liberty in an Age of Classicism and Tyranny*, Princeton University Press, 1955.

Barycz, Henryk, *Andrzej Maksimilian Fredro wobec zagadnień wychowawczych*, Cracow: PAU, 1949.

'O właściwej roli i przemianach ideowych Uniwersytetu Królewieckiego', *Rocznik Olsztyński* 2 (1959), 245–63.

Barycz, Henryk (ed.), *Polska złotego wieku a Europa*, Warsaw: PWI, 1987.

Baryczowa, Maria, 'Augustyn Rotundus Mieleski – pierwszy historyk a apologeta Litwy', in Voisé, Waldemar (ed.), *Z dziejów Polskiej kultury umysłowej w XVI i XVII wieku*, Monografie z dziejów nauki i techniki no. 99, Cracow and Warsaw: PAN, 1976, 77–150.

Baumgart, Peter, 'Der Hof der Barockzeit als politische Institution', in Kauffmann, Gerhard, Spahr, Blake Lee and Wiedemann, Conrad (eds.), *Europäische Hofkultur im 16. und 17. Jahrhundert. Vorträge und Referate gehalten anläßlich des Kongresses des Wolfenbütteler Arbeitskreises für Renaissanceforschung vom 4.–8. 9. 1979*, general editor Martin Bircher, vol. VIII, Hamburg: Hauswedell, 1981, 25–43.

'Wie absolut war der preußische Absolutismus?', in Schlenke, Manfred (ed.), *Preußen. Politik, Kultur, Gesellschaft*, 2 vols., vol. I, Berlin: Rowohlt, 1981, 101–19.

# Bibliography

'Die preußische Königskrönung von 1701, das Reich und die europäische Politik', in Hauser, Otto (ed.), *Preußen, Europa und das Reich*, Cologne and Vienna: Böhlau, 1987, 65–102.

Baumgart, Peter (ed.), *Erscheinungsformen des Absolutismus. Verfassung und Verwaltung*, Germering: Stahlmann, 1966.

Baumgart, Peter and Schmädeke, Jürgen (eds.), *Ständetum und Staatsbildung in Brandenburg-Preußen. Ergebnisse einer internationalen Fachtagung*, Forschungen zur Brandenburgischen und Preußischen Geschichte, Berlin and New York: de Gruyter, 1983.

Behrens, C.B.A., *Society, Government and the Enlightenment. The Experiences of Eighteenth-Century France and Prussia*, New York: Harper and Row, 1985.

Below, Georg von, 'Zur Entstehung der deutschen Stadtverfassung', *Historische Zeitschrift* 58 (1887), 193–244; 59 (1888), 193–247.

Berg, G., 'Marienburg im dritten schwedischen (nordischen) Kriege (1700–1721)', *Mitteilungen des Westpreußischen Geschichtsvereins* 18 (1919), 2–10.

Bergmann, Robert, *Geschichte der ostpreußischen Stände und Steuern, 1688–1704*, Leipzig: Duncker und Humblot, 1901.

Berman, Harold, *Law and Revolution. The Formation of the Western Legal Tradition*, Cambridge, Mass.: Harvard University Press, 1983.

Bieniarzówna, Janina, *Mieszczaństwo Krakowskie XVII wieku*, Cracow: Wydawnictwo Literackie, 1969.

'Związki kuturalne Krakowa z Warmią XVI–XVIII w.', *Rocznik Olsztyński* 11 (1975), 31–62.

Bieniarzówna, Janina and Małecki, Jan (eds.), *Dzieje Krakowa*. Vol. II *Kraków w wiekach XVI–XVIII*, Cracow: Wydawnictwo Literackie, 1984.

Biskup, Marian, *Rozmieszanie własności ziemskiej województwa chełmińskiego i malborskiego w drugiej połowie XVI wieku (mapa i materiały)*, Roczniki TNT 60, no. 2 (1955), Toruń: TNT, 1957.

*Zjednoczenie Pomorza Wschodniego z Polską w połowie XV w.*, Warsaw: PWN, 1959.

*Prusy Królewskie w drugiej połowie XVI wieku*, Thorn and Warsaw: PAN, 1961.

'Über die Rolle und Bedeutung des Großgrundbesitzes der großen Städte von Königlich Preußen im 16. und 17. Jahrhundert', in *Problemy razvitiia feodalizma i kapitalizma w stranach Baltiki*, conference proceedings (14.–17. March 1972), Tartu: Tartu Ülikool, 1972, 263–5.

'Rola miast w reprezentacji stanowej Królestwa Polskiego i Prus Krzyżackich w XIV i XV wieku', *Czasopismo Prawno-Historyczne* 30 (1978), 87–121.

'Die Merkmale des entwickelten Nationalbewußtseins in Polen und seine Festigung im 14. und 15. Jahrhundert', *Jahrbücher für die Geschichte Osteuropas* 35 (1987), 372–83.

*Wojna Pruska czyli walka Polski z zakonem krzyżackim z lat 1519–1521*, Olsztyn: Wydawnictwo Pojezierze, 1991.

'Etniczno-demograficzne przemiany Prus Krzyżackich w rozwoju osadnictwa w średniowieczu', *Kwartalnik Historyczny* 2 (1991), 45–66.

Biskup, Marian (ed.), *Wybitni ludzie dawnego Torunia*, Warsaw, Poznań, Toruń: PWN, 1982.

*Toruń dawny i dzisiejszy. Zarys dziejów*, Warsaw: PWN, 1983.

# Bibliography

*Historia Torunia*, vol. I: *U schyłku średniowiecza i w początkach odrodzenia, 1445–1548*, Toruń: TNT, 1992.

Biskup, Marian, et al. (general eds.), *Historia Pomorza*, vol. II/1: '1464/66–1648/57', ed. and introduced by Gerard Labuda, Poznań: Wydawnictwo Poznańskie, 1976; vol. II/2: '1657–1815', ed. E. Cieślak, Poznań: Wydawnictwo Poznańskie, 1984.

Black, Anthony, *Guild and Civil Society in European Political Thought from the Twelfth Century to the Present*, Ithaca: Cornell University Press, 1984.

Blumhoff, E. 'Beiträge zur Geschichte und Entwicklung der westpreußischen Stände im 15. Jahrhundert', *Zeitschrift des Westpreußischen Geschichtsvereins* 34 (1894), 3–80.

Bodniak, Stanislaw, 'Młodzież polska w gimnazjum Gdańskim Akademickim', *Rocznik Gdański* 13 (1954), 38–52.

Böhme, Klaus-Richard, *Die Schwedische Besetzung des Weichseldeltas 1626–1636*, Jahrbuch der Albertus-Universität Königsberg, supplement 22, Würzburg: Holzner Verlag, 1963.

Bömelburg, Hans-Jürgen, 'Johann Georg Forster und das negative deutsche Polenbild', *Mainzer Geschichtsblätter* 8 (1993), 79–90.

*Zwischen polnischer Ständegesellschaft und preußischem Obrigkeitsstaat. Vom königlichen Preußen zu Westpreußen 1756–1806*, Schriften des Bundesinstituts für ostdeutsche Kultur und Geschichte vol. 5, Munich: Oldenbourg Verlag, 1995.

'"Polnische Wirtschaft". Zur internationalen Genese und zur Realitätshaltigkeit der Stereotypie der Aufklärung', in Bömelburg, H.-J. and Eschment, Beate (eds.), *'Der Fremde im Dorf'. Überlegungen zum Eigenen und zum Fremden in der Geschichte. Rex Rexheuser zum 65. Geburtstag*, Lüneburg: Institut Nordostdeutsches Kulturwerk, 1998, 231–48.

'Die königlich preußische bzw. westpreußische Landesgeschichte in der frühen Neuzeit – Probleme und Tendenzen. Eine Streitschrift', *Nordost-Archiv* (1998), forthcoming.

Bogucka, Maria, 'Walki społeczne w Gdańsku w XVI wieku', in Labuda, Gerard (ed.), *Szkice z Dziejów Pomorza*, Warsaw: Książka i Wiedza, 1958, 369–448.

'Towns of East Central Europe from the Fourteenth to the Seventeenth Century', in Mączak, Antoni, Samsonowicz, Henryk and Burke, Peter (eds.), *East Central Europe in Transition*, Paris and Cambridge: Cambridge University Press, 1985, 97–108.

'Gdańsk a Rzeczpospolita w XVI–XVII w.', *Acta Universitatis Wratislaviensis* 945, Historia LXVI (1988), 35–43.

'Miasta a życie polityczne w Polsce XVI–XVII wieku', in Kamler, Marcin et al. (eds.), *Władza i społeczeństwo w XVI i XVII wieku. Prace ofiarowane Antoniemu Mączakowi w sześćdziesiątą rocznicę urodzin*, Warsaw: PWN, 1989, 39–46.

Bogucka, Maria and Samsonowicz, Henryk, *Dzieje miast i mieszczaństwa w Polsce przedrozbiorowej*, Breslau, Warsaw, Cracow: Ossolineum, 1986.

Boockmann, Hartmut, 'Civis und verwandte Begriffe in ostdeutschen, insbesondere preußischen Stadtrechtsquellen', in Fleckenstein, Johanna and Stackmann, Karl (eds.), *Über Bürger, Stadt und städtische Literatur im Spätmittelalter*, Göttingen: Vandenhoeck and Ruprecht, 1980, 42–58.

*Die Marienburg im 19. Jahrhundert*, Frankfurt, Berlin, Vienna: Ullstein Propyläen, 1992.

Borawska, Teresa, 'Der Begriff des Indigenats im Streit um ein Zunftaufnahmegesuch in Allenstein 1523', *Zeitschrift für die Geschichte und Altertumskunde des Ermlands* 43 (1985), 7–19.

# Bibliography

Borkowska, Urszula, 'Uniwersalizm i regionalizm w Rocznikach Jana Długosza', in *Uniwersalizm i regionalizm w kronikarstwie Europy Środkowo-Wschodniej*, Lublin: Instytut Europy Środkowo-Wschodniej, 1996, 7–26.

Borkowska-Bagieńska, Ewa, 'Nowożytna myśl polityczna w Polsce 1740–1780', in Staszewski, J. (ed.), *Studia z dziejów polskiej myśli politycznej*, vol. IV, Toruń: UMK, 1992, 31–45.

Borowik, Jerzy, 'Pradzieje Pomorza a kontrowersje polsko-niemieckie', *Pamiętnik Instytutu Bałtyckiego* 3 (1930), 5–24.

Borowik, Jerzy (ed.), *Pamiętnik Instytutu Bałtyckiego*, vol. II, Seria 'Balticum', Thorn: Wydawnictwo Instytutu Bałtyckiego, 1929.

Borst, Arno, *Der Turmbau von Babel. Geschichte der Meinungen über Ursprung und Vielfalt der Sprachen und Völker*, 4 vols., Stuttgart: Hiersemann, 1957–63.

Borzestowski, Marian, 'Sprawa uchwalenia korektury pruskiej w obradach sejmiku generalnego Prus Królewskich 1580–1599', in Zdrójkowski, Zbigniew (ed.), *Księga Pamiątkowa 750-lecia Prawa Chełmińskiego*, 2 vols., vol. II, Toruń: UMK, 1988, 235–70.

Brauneder, Werner, 'Civitas et cives sancti Romani Imperii', in Lingelbach, Gerhard and Lück, Heiner (eds.), *Deutsches Recht zwischen Sachsenspiegel und Aufklärung. Rolf Lieberwirth zum 70. Geburtstag*, Rechtshistorische Reihe no. 80, Frankfurt, Bern, New York, Paris: Lang, 1991, 95–117.

Brough, Sonia, *The Goths and the Concept of Gothic in Germany from 1500 to 1750. Culture, Language and Architecture*, Mikrokosmos 17, Frankfurt, Bern, New York: Peter Lang, 1985.

Brunner, Otto, 'Stadt und Bürgertum in der europäischen Geschichte', in *Neue Wege der Sozialgeschichte. Vorträge und Aufsätze*, Göttingen: Vandenhoeck und Ruprecht, 1956, 80–96.

'Souveränitätsproblem und Sozialstruktur in den deutschen Reichsstädten der frühen Neuzeit', *Vierteljahrsschrift für Sozial- und Wirtschaftsgeschichte* 50 (1963), 329–60.

Brückner, Aleksander, *Dzieje Kultury Polskiej*, 4 vols., vol II: *Polska u szczytu potęgi*, Cracow: Nakładem Krakowskiej Spółki Wydawniczej, 1930; repr. Warsaw: Wiedza Powszechna, 1991.

Brückner, Alexander and Estreicher, Stanisław (eds.), *Encyklopedia Staropolska*, 2 vols., vol. I, repr. Warsaw: PWN, 1990; see 'Magdeburskie Prawo', 817–18.

Buława, Józef, 'Toruń w okresie potopu szwedzkiego w latach 1655–1660', MA dissertation, Nicolaus Copernicus University Toruń, 1957–8.

Burleigh, Michael, *Prussian Society and the German Order. An Aristocratic Corporation in Crisis, c. 1410–1466*, Cambridge University Press, 1984.

'The Knights, Nationalists and the Historians: Images of Medieval Prussia from the Enlightenment to 1945', *European History Quarterly* 17 (1987), 35–55.

*Germany Turns Eastward, A Study of Ostforschung in the Third Reich*, Cambridge University Press, 1988.

Butterwick, Richard, *Poland's Last King and English Culture, 1732–1798*, Oxford: Clarendon, 1998.

Bystroń, Jan Stanisław, *Megalomania Narodowa*, Warsaw, 1935; repr. Warsaw: Książka i Wiedza, 1995.

# Bibliography

Cackowski, Stefan, *Gospodarstwo wiejskie w dobrach biskupstwa i kapituły chełmińskiej w XVII–XVIII wieku*, 2 vols., Thorn: PAN, 1961.

Cackowski, Stefan, Dybaś, Bogusław, and Maliszewski, Kazimierz, (eds.), *Historia Torunia*, 2 vols., vol. II: *W czasach renensansu, reformacji i wczesnego baroku, 1548–1660*, Toruń: TNT, 1994.

Carsten, Francis L., *The Origins of Prussia*, Oxford: Clarendon, 1954.

*Geschichte der preußischen Junker*, Frankfurt: Suhrkamp, 1988.

Carstenn, Edward, *Elbings Verfassung zum Ausgang der polnischen Zeit*, Danzig: Kafemann, 1910.

*Die Geschichte der Hansestadt Elbing*, Elbing: Sauniers Buchhandlung (U. Brunk), 1937.

'Die preußischen Stände und das Königreich Polen 1454–1772', *Mitteilungen des Copernicus-Vereins* 45 (1937), 75–100.

Centner, Gottfried, *Gelehrte und Geehrte Thorner*, Thorn: Bergmann, 1763.

Chowaniec, Czesław, 'Poglądy polityczne rokoszan 1606-07 wobec doktryn Monarchomachów Francuskich', *Reformacja w Polsce* 11 (1924), 256–66.

Christiansen, Eric, *The Northern Crusades. The Baltic and the Catholic Frontier 1100–1525*, New Studies in Medieval History, London and Basingstoke: Macmillan, 1980.

Ciara, Stefan, *Senatorowie i dygnitarze koroni w drugiej połowie XVII wieku*, Breslau: Ossolineum, 1990.

Cieślak, Edmund, 'Przywileje Gdańska z okresu wojny 13-letniej na tle przywilejów niektórych miast hanzeatyckich', *Czasopismo Prawno-Historyczne* 6, no. 1 (1954), 61–122.

*Miasto wierne Rzeczypospolitej. Szkice gdańskie XVII–XVIII wieku*, Gdańsk: Wiedza Powszechna, 1959.

*Walki ustrojowe w Gdańsku i Toruniu oraz w niektórych miastach Hanzeatyckich w XV wieku*, Gdańsk: GTN, 1960.

*Walki społeczno-polityczne w Gdańsku w drugiej połowie XVII wieku. Interwencja Jana III Sobieskiego*, Gdańsk: GTN, 1962.

*Konflikty polityczne i społeczne w Gdańsku w połowie XVIII w. – sojusz pospólstwa z dworem królewskim*, Breslau: Ossolineum, 1972.

'Gotfryd Lengnich a walki polityczne w Gdańsku w połowie XVIII wieku', *Ars Historica* 71 (1976), 653–66.

'Miejsce Gdańska w Rzeczypospolitej szlacheckiej. Zarys problematyki', in Trzoska, J. (ed.), *Strefa Bałtycka w XVI–XVIII w. Polityka – Społeczeństwo – Gospodarka*, Gdańsk: Marpress, 1993, 37–50.

'Gdańsk w polityce Augusta III', in Groth, A. (ed.), *W kręgu badań Profesora Stanisława Gierszewskiego*, Gdańsk: Marpress, 1995, 95–108.

Cieślak, Edmund (ed.), *Studia gdańsko-pomorskie*, Gdańsk: GTN, 1964.

Cieślak, Edmund and Biernat, Czesław (eds.), *Dzieje Gdańska*, 2nd edn, Gdańsk: Wydawnictwo Morskie, 1975.

Cieślak, Edmund, Nowak, Zbigniew, Stankiewicz, Jerzy and Trzoska, Jerzy (eds.), *Historia Gdańska*, 3 vols., vol. III/1: '1655–1793', Gdańsk: Instytut Historii PAN, 1993.

Cieślak, Edmund and Rumiński, Józef (eds.), *Raporty rezydentów francuskich w Gdańsku w XVIII wieku, 1715–1719*, Gdańsk: GTN, 1964–76.

Cieślewicz, Michał, 'Pare uwag o indygenacie pruskim', *Zeszyty Naukowe Wydziału Humanistycznego Uniwersytetu Gdańskiego*, 3 (1974), 19–29.

# Bibliography

Cynarski, Stanisław, 'Sarmatyzm – ideologia i styl życia', in Tazbir, Janusz (ed.), *Polska XVII wieku. Państwo, społeczeństwo, kultura*, Warsaw: Wiedza Powszechna, 1974, 269–95.

'Uwagi nad problemem recepcji Historii Jana Długosza w Polsce XVI i XVII wieku', *Długossiana – Studia historyczne w pięcsetlecie śmierci Jana Długosza*, Cracow and Warsaw: PWN, 1980, 281–90.

Czacharowski, Antoni, 'Toruń średniowieczny (do roku 1454)', in Biskup, Marian (ed.), *Toruń dawny i dzisiejszy*, Warsaw, Poznań, Toruń: PWN, 1983, 31–131.

Czaja, Roman, 'Udział wielkich miast pruskich w handlu Hanzeatyckim do połowy XV wieku', *Zapiski Historyczne* 60, no. 2–3 (1995), 21–38.

Czapliński, Władysław, 'Gdańsk – Miasto Wierne', *Wiadomości Literackie* 31–32, no. 16 (1939), 9–10.

'Ideologia Satyr Krzysztofa Opalińskiego. Ekskurs w sprawie Autorstwa Broszury "Dyszkurs o pomożeniu miast w Polsce"', *Przegląd Historyczny* 47 (1956), 121–25.

*Rola magnaterii i szlachty w pierwszych latach wojny szwedzkiej*, Warsaw: PWN, 1957.

Czapliński, Władysław (ed.), *O naprawę Rzeczypospolitej XVII–XVIII w.*, Warsaw: PWN, 1965.

*O Polsce siedemnastowiecznej. Problemy i sprawy*, Warsaw: PIW, 1966.

Damus, Rudolf, 'Der erste nordische Krieg bis zur Schlacht bei Warschau. Aus Danziger Quellen', *Zeitschrift des Westpreußischen Geschichtsvereins* 12 (1884), 1–110.

'Die Stadt Danzig gegenüber der Politik Friedrichs des Großen und Friedrich Wilhelms II', *Zeitschrift des Westpreußischen Geschichtsvereins* 20 (1887), 1–213.

Davies, Norman, *God's Playground. A History of Poland*, 2 vols., vol. I: *The Origins to 1795*, New York: Columbia University Press, 1982.

Denzer, Horst, 'Pufendorfs Naturrechtslehre und der brandenburgische Staat', in Thieme, Hans (ed.), *Humanismus und Naturrecht in Berlin, Brandenburg und Preußen, Tagungsbericht Humanismus und Naturrecht in Berlin, am 18. und 19. Juni 1976*, Veröffentlichungen der Historischen Kommission zu Berlin, 48, Berlin: de Gruyter, 1979, 62–75.

*Deutsche Staatenbildung und deutsche Kultur im Preußenland*, ed. Landeshauptmann der Provinz Ostpreußen, Königsberg: Gräfe and Unzer, 1931.

Dhondt, Jan, *Estates or Powers. Essays in the Parliamentary History of the Southern Netherlands from the Sixteenth to the Eighteenth Century*, ed. Willem Blockmans, Heule: UGA, 1977.

Dietrich, Veit-Jakobus, *Johann Amos Comenius*, Hamburg: Rowohlt 1991.

Dittmann, Georg G., *Beyträge zur Geschichte der Stadt Thorn*, Thorn: n.pub., 1789; repr. Hamburg: Verein für Familienforschung in Ost- und Westpreußen, 1970.

Dobrzański, Jan and Kłoczowski, Jerzy (eds.), *Dzieje Lublina*, Lublin: Wydawnictwo Lubelskie, 1965.

Drabiński, Norbert, 'Z dziejów okupacji szwedzkiej Elbląga w latach 1626–1635', *Rocznik Elbląski* 2 (1963), 141–66.

Droysen, Johann Gustav, *Geschichte der preußischen Politik*, vol. III: *Der Staat des Großen Kurfürsten*, Leipzig: Veit, 1872.

Duchhardt, Heinz, 'Die preußische Königskrönung von 1701', *Herrscherweihe und Königskrönung im frühneuzeitlichen Europa. Festschrift für E. Kessel*, Wiesbaden: Steiner, 1983, 89–101.

# Bibliography

Dunajówna, Maria, 'Pierwsze Toruńskie Czasopismo Naukowe w XVIII w., *Das Gelehrte Preussen*', in Zdrójkowski, Zbigniew (ed.), *Księga Pamiątkowa 400-lecia Toruńskiego Gimnazjum Akademickiego XVI–XVIII wieku*, Toruń: TNT, 1972, 240–81.

Dwight van Horn, William, 'Suburban Development, Rural Exchange and the Manorial Economy in Royal Prussia, 1570–1700', Ph.D. diss., Columbia University, 1987.

Dworzaczek, Włodzimierz, 'Przenikanie szlachty do stanu mieszczańskiego w Wielkopolsce w XVI i XVII wieku', *Przegląd Historyczny* 47: 4 (1956), 656–84.

Dworzaczkowa, Janina, 'Kronika Pruska Szymona Grunaua jako źródło historyczne', *Studia Źródłoznawcze* 2 (1952), 119–46.

*Dziejopisarstwo gdańskie do połowy XVI wieku*, Gdańsk: GTN, 1962.

'Reformacja a problemy narodowościowe w przedrozbiorowej Wielkopolsce', *Odrodzenie i Reformacja w Polsce* 23 (1978), 79–101.

'"Panegyricus Carolo Gustavo" i jego tło polityczne', *Odrodzenie i Reformacja w Polsce* 27 (1982), 93–105.

Dybaś, Bogusław, *Sejm pacyfikacyjny w 1699 roku*, Roczniki TNT no. 84, Toruń: TNT, 1991.

Dygdała, Jerzy, 'Korespondencja rezydentów miasta Torunia', *Acta Universitatis Nicolai Copernici* Historia VIII (1973), 85–107.

'Udział Gotfryda Lengnicha w Toruńskiej Konfederacji Dysydenckiej w 1767 roku', *Zapiski Historyczne* 42 (1977), 9–30.

*Polityka Torunia wobec władz Rzeczypospolitej w latach 1764–1772*, Toruń: Roczniki TNT, 1977.

*Życie polityczne Prus Królewskich u schyłku ich związku z Rzecząpospolitą w XVIII wieku. Tendencje unifikacyjne a partykularyzm*, Roczniki TNT 81, no. 3, Warsaw, Poznań, Toruń: PWN, 1984.

'Sejmiki powiatowe województwa pomorskiego w czasach saskich i stanisławowskich', *Zapiski Historyczne* 52 (1987), 79–104.

*Adam Stanisław Grabowski (1698–1766). Biskup, Polityk, Mecenas*, Olsztyn: Rozprawy i Materiały OBN im. W. Kętrzyńskiego, 1994.

Dygdała, Jerzy and Mikulski, Krzysztof, 'Zmiany w elicie władzy Prus Królewskich w XV–XVIII wieku', in Dygdała, J. and Mikulski, K. (eds.), *Szlachta i ziemiaństwo na Pomorzu w dobie nowożytnej XVI–XX wieku, Materiały sympozjum w Toruniu 9 IV 1992*, Toruń: TNT, 1993, 7–29.

Dygdała, Jerzy, Salmonowicz, S., Wojtowicz, J. (eds.), *Historia Torunia*, 2 vols., vol. II/3: 'Między barokiem i oświeceniem, 1660–1793', Toruń: Instytut Historii PAN and TNT, 1996.

Eckerdt, Hans, 'Die kleinen Städte im Polnischen Preußen und die Städtetage des vorigen Jahrhunderts', *Altpreußische Monatsschrift* 9 (1872), 50–64.

Elliott, John, 'Revolution and Continuity in Early Modern Europe', in Parker, Geoffrey and Smith, Lesley M. (eds.), *The General Crisis of the Seventeenth Century*, London, Henley, Boston: Routledge and Kegan Paul, 1978, 110–33.

Ergang, R., *The Potsdam Führer. Frederick William I, Father of Prussian Militarism*, New York: Columbia University Press, 1941.

Essmanowska-Dworzaczkowa, Jolanta, 'Ruch szlachecki w Prusach Królewskich w I połowie XVI wieku', Ph.D. diss., Poznań University, 1951.

# Bibliography

Estreicher, Stanisław, 'Gotfryd Lengnich. Gdański prawnik i historyk', *Wiadomości Literackie* 31–32, no. 16 (1939), 21–2.

Etter, Else-Lilly, *Tacitus in der Geistesgeschichte des 16. und 17. Jahrhunderts*, Basel and Stuttgart: von Helbing and Lichtenhahn, 1966.

Evans, Robert J. W., 'Essay and Reflection: Frontiers and National Identities in Central Europe', *The International History Review* 14, no. 3 (1992), 441–660.

Evans, Robert J. W. and Thomas, Trevor (eds.), *Crown, Church and Estates. Central European Politics in the Sixteenth and Seventeenth Centuries*, London: Macmillan, 1991.

Faber, W, 'Die polnische Sprache im Danziger Schul- und Kirchenwesen', *Zeitschrift des Westpreußischen Geschichtsvereins* 70 (1930), 87–131.

Feckl, Karl-Ludwig, *Preußen im Spanischen Erbfolgekrieg*, Frankfurt, Bern, Chichester: Peter Lang, 1979.

Feldman, Józef, *Polska w dobie wielkiej wojny północnej, 1704–1709*, Cracow: Polska Akademia Umiejętności, Gebethner i Wolff, 1925.

Forstreuter, Kurt, 'Matthias Praetorius', in Krollmann, Christian (ed.), *Altpreußische Biographie*, vol. II, Marburg: Herder-Institut, 1967, 517.

Freylichówna, Janina, *Ideał Wychowawczy Szlachty Polskiej w XVI i początku XVII wieku*, Warsaw: Nakładem Naukowego Towarzystwa Pedagogicznego, 1938.

Fried, Pankraz, *Probleme und Methoden der Landesgeschichte*, Darmstadt: Wissenschaftliche Buchgesellschaft, 1978.

Friedrich, Karin, 'Better in Perilous Liberty Than In Quiet Servitude. The Idea of Freedom in the Writings of Two Protestant Burghers in Seventeenth Century Royal Prussia', in Poraziński, Jarosław (ed.), *Między Wielką Polityką a Szlacheckim Partykularzem. Studia z dziejów nowożytnej Polski i Europy ku czci Profesora Jacka Staszewskiego*, Toruń: UMK, 1993, 71–85.

'Facing Both Ways: New Works on Prussia and Polish-Prussian Relations', *German History* 15 (1997), 256–67.

'Politisches Landesbewußtsein und seine Trägerschichten im Königlichen Preußen', *Nordost-Archiv* NS 6, no. 2 (1997), 541–64.

Friedrichs, Christopher F., 'Citizens or Subjects? Urban Conflict in Early Modern Germany', in Chrisman, M. Usher and Gründler, Otto (eds.), *Social Groups and Religious Ideas in the Sixteenth Century*, Kalamazoo: Western Michigan University Press, 1978, 46–58.

*Urban Society in an Age of War: Nördlingen 1580–1720*, Princeton University Press, 1979.

'Urban Conflicts and the Imperial Constitution in Seventeenth-Century Germany', *Journal of Modern History* 58, supplement (1986), S98–S123.

*The Early Modern City, 1450–1750*, London and New York: Longman, 1995.

Fries, Friedrich, *Die Lehre vom Staat bei den protestantischen Gottesgelehrten Deutschlands und der Niederlande in der zweiten Hälfte des 17. Jahrhunderts*, Berlin: Ebering, 1912.

Froelich, X[aver], 'Politische Poesien aus Polnisch-Preußen den Jahren 1697–1707 angehörig', *Altpreußische Monatsschrift* 7 (1870), 535–44.

Frost, Robert I., *After the Deluge. Poland-Lithuania and the Second Northern War, 1655–1660*, Cambridge University Press, 1993.

'The Polish-Lithuanian Commonwealth and the "Military Revolution"', in Biskupski, Marian B. and Pula, James S. (eds.), *Poland and Europe: Historical Dimensions, I:*

# Bibliography

Selected Essays from the Fiftieth Anniversary International Congress of the Polish Institute of Arts and Sciences of America, East European Monographs, New York: Columbia University Press, 1993, 29–54.

'The Nobility of Poland-Lithuania, 1569–1795', in Scott, Hamish M. (ed.), The European Nobilities in the Seventeenth and Eighteenth Centuries, 2 vols., vol. II: Northern, Central and Eastern Europe, London and New York: Longman, 1995, 183–222.

'Potop a teoria rewolucji militarnej', in Muszyńska, Jadwiga and Wijaczka, Jacek (eds.), Rzeczpospolita w latach Potopu, Prace Instytutu Historii WSP w Kielcach no. 1, Kielce: WSP im. Kochanowskiego, 1996, 147–66.

Frühsorge, Gerhard, Klueting, Hans and Kopitzsch, Franz (eds.), Stadt und Bürger im 18. Jahrhundert, Marburg: Hitzeroth, 1993.

Fuchs, Karl Hans, Danzig im ersten nordischen Krieg, 1. Abschnitt, 1655/6, Danzig: A. Müller, 1935.

Fueter, Eduard, Geschichte der neueren Historiographie, Munich and Berlin: Oldenbourg, 1925.

Gallandi, Johann, Altpreußisches Adelslexikon, Königsberg: Gräfe and Unzer, n.d.

Garstein, Oskar, Rome and the Counter-Reformation in Scandinavia. Jesuit Education Strategy 1553–1622, Leiden: Brill, 1992.

Gause, Fritz, Die Geschichte der Stadt Königsberg in Preußen, 3 vols., Cologne, Vienna, Graz: Böhlau, 1965–72.

Gawlas, Sławomir, 'Stan badań nad polską świadomością narodową w średniowieczu', in Państwo, naród, stany i świadomości wieków średnich. Pamięci Benedykta Zientary, 1929–1983, Warsaw: PWN, 1990, 149–94.

Gawthrop, Richard L., Pietism and the Making of Eighteenth-Century Prussia, Cambridge University Press, 1993.

Gelderen, Martin van, 'Holland und das Preußentum: Justus Lipsius zwischen Niederländischem Aufstand und Brandenburg-Preußischem Absolutismus', Zeitschrift für historische Forschung 23 (1996), 29–56.

Gellner, Ernest, Nations and Nationalism, Oxford: Blackwell, 1983.

Gerlach, Jan, 'Inwentarz aktów sejmikowych Prus Królewskich', Kwartalnik Historyczny 41 (1954), 295–69.

'Język polski w obradach i korespondencji urzędowej w Prusach Królewskich w XVI–XVII w.', in Labuda, Gerard (ed.), Szkice z dziejów Pomorza, Warsaw: Książka i Wiedza, 1958, 163–86.

'Recesy toruńskie w Archiwum Ziem Pruskich', Zapiski Historyczne 24 (1958–9), 53–66.

'Elbląg – strażnikiem pieczęci Prus Królewskich 1503–1772', Rocznik Elbląski 2 (1963), 97–139.

'Grudziądz miejscem obrad sejmiku generalnego Prus Królewskich (1454–1772)', Rocznik Grudziądzki (1963), 7–33.

Gerstenberger, Heide, 'Was ist eine Stadt?', in Groth, Andrzej (ed.), Zwei Hansestädte Bremen und Danzig im Laufe der Jahrhunderte, Gdańsk: Marpress, 1994, 9–20.

Gierke, Otto, Johannes Althusius und die Entwicklung der naturrechtlichen Staatstheorien, Breslau: Marcus, 1902.

Gierowski, Józef, Między Saskim Absolutyzmem a Złotą Wolnością, Wrocław: Ossolineum, 1953.

# Bibliography

'Pruski projekt zamachu stanu w Polsce w 1715 roku', *Przegląd Historyczny* 50 (1959), 753–67.

'Szlachecki samorząd województw i ziem w XVI–XVIII w.', *Acta Universitatis Wratislaviensis* 945, Historia LXVI (1988), 151–9.

'Problematyka bałtycka Augusta II Sasa', in Trzoska, Jerzy (ed.), *Strefa Bałtycka w XVI–XVIII w. Polityka, Społeczeństwo, Gospodarka*, Gdańsk: GTN, 1993, 51–62.

Gierszewski, Stanisław, *Statystika Żeglugi Gdańska w latach 1670–1815*, Warsaw: PWN, 1963.

*Struktura gospodarcza i funkcje rynkowe mniejszych miast województwa pomorskiego w XVI i XVII w.*, Wydział nauk społecznych i humanistycznych, Seria monografii 22, Gdańsk: GTN, 1966.

*Chojnice*, Wrocław: Ossolineum, 1971.

*Obywatele miast Polski przedrozbiorowej*, Warsaw: PWN, 1973.

'Problematyka rozwoju mniejszych miast Prus Królewskich w XVII i XVIII wieku', *Zeszyty Naukowe Akademii Ekonomicznej w Krakowie* 70 (1974), 189–202.

*Elbląg – przeszłość i terazniejszość*, Gdańsk: Wydawnictwo Morskie, 1978.

Glemma, Tadeusz, *Stosunki kościelne w Toruniu w stuleciu XVI i XVII na tle dziejów kościelnych Prus Królewskich*, Toruń: TNT, 1934.

Glinski, Gerhard von, *Die Königsberger Kaufmannschaft des 17. und 18. Jahrhunderts*, Wissenschaftliche Beiträge zur Geschichte und Landeskunde Ost- und Mitteleuropas 70, Marburg: Herder-Institut, 1964.

Glomski, Jacqueline, 'Erasmus and Cracow, 1510–1530', *Yearbook of the Erasmus of Rotterdam Society* 17 (1997), 1–18.

Godlewski, Jerzy Romuald and Odyniec, Wacław, *Pomorze Gdańskie. Koncepcje obrony i militarnego wykonania od wieku XIII do roku 1939*, Warsaw: Wydawnictwo Ministerstwa Obrony Narodowej, 1982.

Goetz, Werner, 'Die Gegenwart der Vergangenheit im früh- und hochmittelalterlichen Geschichtsbewußtsein', *Historische Zeitschrift* 255 (1992), 61–97.

Goez, Hans-Werner, *Translatio Imperii*, Tübingen: Mohr, 1958.

Goldmann, Salka, *Danziger Verfassungskämpfe unter polnischer Herrschaft*, Leipzig: Teubner, 1901.

Górski, Karol, *Związek Pruski i poddanie się Prus Polsce. Zbiór tekstów źródłowych*, Poznań: Instytut Zachodni, 1949.

'Problematyka dziejowa Prus Królewskich, 1466–1772', *Zapiski Historyczne* 28, no. 2 (1963), 159–70.

'Die Anfänge einer Ständischen Vertretung der Ritterschaft im Ordensland Preußen im 15. Jahrhundert', in Arnold, Udo and Biskup, Marian (eds.), *Deutschordensstaat Preußen in der polnischen Geschichtsschreibung der Gegenwart*, Quellen und Studien zur Geschichte des Deutschen Ordens no. 30, Marburg: Elwert-Verlag, 1982, 218–36.

Górski, Karol (ed.), *Inwentarz aktów Sejmikowych Prus Królewskich 1600–1764*, Toruń: TNT, 1945.

Górski, Karol and Biskup, Marian (eds.), *Akta Stanów Prus Królewskich*, Toruń: Fontes TNT, 1955–1967; subsequent vols. ed. Marian Biskup and Irena Janosz-Biskupowa (1967–1996).

# Bibliography

Górski, Karol and Małłek, Janusz (eds.), *Prusy Królewskie i Prusy Książęce w XV i XVI wieku*, vol. I: *1466–1548, wybór tekstów*, Toruń: UMK, 1971.

Grajewski, H., *Jan Schultz-Szulecki i jego Tractatus historico-politicus de Polonia nunquam tributaria. Studium z dziejów polskiej literatury prawniczej*, Łódź: Zakładem Narodowym Ossolińskich, 1964.

Grochulska, Barbara, 'The Place of the Enlightenment in Polish Social History', in Fedorowicz, A. (ed.), *A Republic of Nobles. Studies in Polish History*, Cambridge University Press, 1982.

Grodziski, Stanisław, 'Obywatelstwo w szlacheckiej Rzeczypospolitej', *Zeszyty Naukowe Uniwersytetu Jagiellońskiego* 67, Prace Prawnicze, no. 12, Cracow: Uniwersytet Jagielloński, 1963.

Groth, Andrzej, et al. (eds.), *Historia Elbląga*, 2 vols., vol. II/1: '1466–1626', Gdańsk: Marpress, 1996.

Grunau Axel and Grunau Georg, *Die St. Georgen-Brüderschaft zu Elbing*, Wissenschaftliche Beiträge zur Geschichte und Landeskunde Ostmitteleuropas 21, Marburg: Herder-Institut, 1958.

Grzybowska, Teresa, *Artyści i Patrycjusze Gdańska*, Warsaw: DIG, 1996.

Grzybowski, Konstanty, *Teoria reprezentacji w Polsce epoki odrodzenia*, Warsaw: PWN 1959.

Grzybowski, Stanisław, *Jan Zamoyski*, Warsaw: PIW, 1994.

Günther, Otto, 'Zwei Miscellen zur Danziger Buchdrucker- und Literaturgeschichte im 17. Jahrhundert', *Zeitschrift des Westpreußischen Geschichtsvereins* 38 (1898), 149–52.

'Ein Nachtrag zu den Danziger Gustav-Adolf Liedern', *Zeitschrift des Westpreußischen Geschichtsvereins* 39 (1899), 165–7.

Gumowski, Marian, *Herbarz patrycjatu toruńskiego*, Roczniki TNT 74, no. 3, Toruń: TNT, 1970.

Haake, Paul, *August der Starke*, Berlin and Leipzig: Gebrüder Paetel, 1926.

'Der erste Hohenzollernkönig und August der Starke vor und nach 1700', *Forschungen zur Brandenburgischen und Preußischen Geschichte* 46 (1934), 381–90.

Haberkern, Eugen and Wallach, Joseph F. (eds.), *Hilfswörterbuch für Historiker*, 2 vols., UTB für Wissenschaften, Tübingen: Francke Verlag, 1987.

Hackmann, Jörg, 'Der Kampf um die Weichsel: Die deutsche Ostforschung in Danzig von 1918–1945', *Zapiski Historyczne* 58 (1993), 37–57.

*Ostpreußen und Westpreußen in deutscher und polnischer Sicht. Landeshistorie als beziehungsgeschichtliches Problem*, Wiesbaden: Harrassowitz, 1996.

Häussler, Reinhard, *Tacitus und das historische Bewußtsein*, Heidelberg: C. Winter, 1965.

Hagen, William, *Germans, Poles and Jews. The Nationality Conflict in the East, 1772–1914*, University of Chicago Press, 1980.

Haitsma Mulier, Eco, *The Myth of Venice and Dutch Republican Thought in the Seventeenth Century*, Assen: Gorcum, 1980.

Hammerstein, Notker, *Ius und Historie: ein Beitrag zur Geschichte des historischen Denkens an deutschen Universitäten im späten 17. und 18. Jahrhundert*, Göttingen: Vandenhoeck and Ruprecht, 1972.

Harasimowicz, Jan, 'Bürgerliche und höfische Kunstrepräsentation in Krakau und Danzig', in Engel, Evamaria, Lambrecht, Karen and Nogossek, Hanna (eds.), *Metropolen im Wandel. Zentralität in Ostmitteleuropa an der Wende vom Mittelalter zur Neuzeit*, Berlin:

# Bibliography

Akademie-Verlag, 1995.

Harasimowicz, Jan (ed.), *Sztuka miast i mieszczaństwa XV–XVIII wieku w Europie Środkowowschodniej*, Warsaw: PWN, 1990.

Hassinger, Erich, *Brandenburg-Preußen, Rußland und Schweden 1700–1713*, München: Isar-Verlag, 1953.

Hebbelmann, Georg, *Münster zur Zeit Christoph Bernhard von Galens (1650–1678)*, Westfalen im Bild, Historische Ereignisse in Westfalen 5, Münster: Landschaftsverband Westfalen-Lippe, 1992.

Heimann, Heinz-Dieter, 'Stadtideal und Stadtpatriotismus in der "Alten Stadt" am Beispiel der "Laudationes Coloniae" des Mittelalters und der frühen Neuzeit', *Historisches Jahrbuch* 111 (1991), 3–27.

Heinrich, Gerd (ed.), *Ein sonderbares Licht in Teutschland. Beiträge zur Geschichte des Großen Kurfürsten von Brandenburg 1640–1688*, Zeitschrift für Historische Forschung, supplement 8, Berlin: Duncker and Humblot, 1990.

Hellmuth, Eckhart, *Naturrechts-Philosophie und Bürokratischer Werthorizont. Studien zur preußischen Geistes- und Sozialgeschichte des 18. Jahrhunderts*, Göttingen: Vandenhoeck and Ruprecht, 1985.

Henshall, Nicholas, *The Myth of Absolutism. Change and Continuity in Early Modern European Monarchy*, London: Longman, 1992.

Herbst, Stanisław, *Toruńskie cechy rzemieślnicze*, Toruń: Nakładem Cechów Toruńskich, 1933.

'Polska kultura mieszczańska', in Walicki, Michał (ed.), *Studia Renesansowe* 1, Wrocław: Ossolineum, 1956, 9–29.

'Swiadomość narodowa na ziemiach Pruskich w XV–XVII wieku', *Komunikaty Mazursko-Warmińskie* 75, no. 1 (1962), 1–10.

Hernas, Czesław, *Barok*, Warsaw: PWN, 1980.

Heuer [Pfarrer], 'Der Thorner Pfarrer Simon Weiß, 1623–1688, ein Lebensbild aus stürmisch bewegter Zeit', *Mitteilungen des Nicolaus-Copernicus Vereins* 35 (1927), 1–23.

Hildebrandt, Reinhardt, 'Rat contra Bürgerschaft. Die Verfassungskonflikte in den Reichsstädten des 17. und 18. Jahrhunderts', *Zeitschrift für Stadtgeschichte, Stadtsoziologie und Denkmalpflege* 2 (1974), 221–41.

Hinrichs, Carl, *Preußentum und Pietismus. Der Pietismus in Brandenburg-Preußen als religiös-soziale Reformbewegung*, Göttingen: Vandenhoeck and Ruprecht, 1974.

Hintze, Otto, *Die Hohenzollern und ihr Werk. Fünfhundert Jahre vaterländische Geschichte*, 4th ed., Berlin: Paul Parey, 1915.

Hipler, Franz, 'Die Ermländische Bischofswahl vom Jahre 1549', *Zeitschrift für Geschichte und Altertumskunde des Ermlands* 11 (1897), 56–96.

Hirsch, Ferdinand, 'Zur Geschichte der polnischen Königswahl von 1669. Danziger Gesandtschaftsberichte aus den Jahren 1668 und 1699', *Zeitschrift des Westpreußischen Geschichtsvereins* 25 (1889), 20–63.

Hobsbawm, Eric and Ranger, Tim (eds.), *The Invention of Tradition*, Cambridge University Press, 1983.

Hoensch, Jörg K, *Sozialverfassung und Politische Reform. Polen im vorrevolutionären Zeitalter*, Cologne and Vienna: Böhlau, 1973.

Hubatsch, Walter, 'Kreuzritterstaat und Hohenzollernmonarchie. Zur Frage der Fortdauer

# Bibliography

des Deutschen Ordens in Preußen', in Conze, Werner (ed.), *Deutschland und Europa. Festschrift für Hans Rothfels*, Düsseldorf: Droste-Verlag, 1951, 179–99.

'Zur altpreußischen Chronistik des 16. Jahrhunderts', *Archivalische Zeitschrift*, (Bayerisches Hauptstaatsarchiv München), 50/51 (1955), 429–62.

'Deutschordenschroniken im Weichselland', *Ostdeutsche Monatshefte* 22 (1956), 713–18.

Huber, Wolfgang, *Kulturpatriotismus und Sprachbewußtsein. Studien zur deutschen Philologie des 17. Jahrhunderts*, Frankfurt, Bern, New York: Peter Lang, 1984.

Hundert, Gershon David, *The Jews in a Polish Private Town. The Case of Opatów in the Eighteenth Century*, Baltimore and London: Johns Hopkins University Press, 1992.

Jacobi, Franz, *Das Thorner Blutgericht 1724*, Halle: Verein für Reformationsgeschichte 13, 1896.

Jacobi, Richard, 'Thorn, Elbing, Danzig und die polnischen Königswahlen 1573–75', *Mitteilungen des Nicolaus-Copernicus Vereins* 15 (1907), 43–67.

Jacoby, Jörg, *Bogusław Radziwiłł. Der Statthalter des Großen Kurfürsten in Ostpreußen*, Wissenschaftliche Beiträge no. 40, Marburg: Herder-Institut, 1959.

Jähnig, Bernhart, 'Bevölkerungsveränderungen und Landesbewußtsein im Preußenland', *Blätter für deutsche Landesgeschichte* 121 (1985), 115–55.

'Die landesgeschichtliche Forschung des Preußenlandes (Ost- und Westpreußen) seit 1960 im Überblick', *Jahrbuch für die Geschichte Mittel- und Ostdeutschlands* 38 (1989), 81–141.

Jähnig, Bernhart and Letkemann, Peter (eds.), *Danzig in Acht Jahrhunderten. Beiträge zur Geschichte des hansischen und preußischen Mittelpunktes*, Münster: Copernicus-Verlag, 1985.

Janiszewska-Mincer, Barbara, 'Otto von Gröben – przywódza opozycji stanów w Prusach Książęcych', *Komunikaty Mazursko-Warmińskie* 1, no. 75 (1962), 143–62.

'Zwycięstwo opozycji Pruskiej na konwokacjach landratów w latach 1615–16', *Komunikaty Mazursko-Warmińskie* 2, no. 80 (1963), 233–52.

*Stosunki Polsko-Niemieckie w latach 1515–1772*, Bydgoszcz: Wydawnictwo Udzielniale WSP, 1997.

Janiszewska-Mincer, Barbara and Mincer, Franciszek, *Rzeczpospolita Polska a Prusy Książęce w latach 1598–1621*, Warsaw: PWN, 1988.

Janosz-Biskupowa, Irena, *Archiwum Ziem Pruskich. Studium Historyczne*, Roczniki TNT 77, no. 3, Toruń: TNT 1974.

Jarausch, Konrad, 'The Institutionalisation of History in Eighteenth-Century Germany', in Bödeker, H.E., Iggers, G.G., Knudsen, J.B. and Reill, P.H. (eds.), *Aufklärung und Geschichte. Studien zur deutschen Geschichtswissenschaft im 18. Jahrhundert*, Göttingen: Vandenhoeck and Ruprecht, 1986, 31–48.

Jarochowski, Kazimierz, *Dzieje panowania Augusta II od śmierci Jana III do chwili wstąpienia Karola XII na ziemie polskie*, Poznań: Wydawnictwo Poznańskie, 1856.

'Polityka brandenburska w pierwszych latach wojny Karola XII i misja Przebendowskiego w r. 1704', in *Nowe opowiadania i studia historyczne*, Warsaw: Gebethner i Wolff, 1882.

*Sprawa Kalcksteina 1670–72*, Poznań: Żupański, 1883.

Jarzęcka, Joanna, *Obraz życia umysłowego Rzeczypospolitej doby saskiej (1710–1762)*, Gdańsk: PAN, 1983.

Joachimsen, Paul, *Geschichtsauffassung und Geschichtsschreibung in Deutschland unter dem Einfluß des Humanismus*, 2 vols., Beiträge zur Kulturgeschichte des Mittelalters und der

# Bibliography

*Renaissance*, ed. Walter Goetz, Leipzig and Berlin: Teubner, 1910.

Jöcher, Christian Gottlieb, *Allgemeines Gelehrtenlexikon*, Leipzig: n.pub., 1750–1; repr. Hildesheim: Olms, 1960.

Johannesson, Kurt, *The Renaissance of the Goths in Sixteenth-Century Sweden*, Berkeley: University of California Press, 1991.

Jonasson, Gustav, 'Karl XII und Polen, 1700–1706', in Cieślak, E. and Olszewski, H. (eds.), *Changes in Two Baltic Countries. Poland and Sweden in the Eighteenth Century*, Poznań: UAM, 1990, 137–46.

Jones, Guernsey, *The Diplomatic Relations between Cromwell and Charles X Gustavus of Sweden*, inaugural diss., Lincoln and Nebraska: State Journal Co., 1897.

Kalisch, Johannes and Gierowski, J. (eds.), *Um die Polnische Krone*, Berlin (East): Akademie-Verlag, 1962.

Kamieński, Andrzej, *Stany Prus Książęcych wobec rządów Brandenburskich w drugiej połowie XVII wieku*, Olsztyn: OBN im. Wojciecha Kętrzyńskiego, 1995.

Kamińska, Anna, *Brandenburg-Prussia and Poland 1669–1672*, Marburger Ostforschungen 41, Marburg: Herder-Institut, 1983.

Kamińska, Krystyna, *Sądownictwo Miasta Torunia do połowy XVII wieku na tle ustroju sądów niektórych miast Niemiec i Polski*, Warsaw, Poznań, Toruń: PWN, 1980.

Kamińska-Linderska, Anna, 'Lenno Lębork i Bytów na tle stosunków polsko-brandenburskich (1657–1670)', *Studia i Materiały do Dziejów Wielkopolski* 6 (1960), 65–122.

Kamiński, Andrzej S., *Konfederacja sandomierska wobec Rosji w okresie poaltransztadskim, 1706–1709*, Prace Komisji Nauk Historycznych no. 23, Wrocław: PAN, 1969.

'The Polish-Lithuanian Commonwealth and its Citizens', in Potichnyj, Peter J. (ed.), *Poland and Ukraine. Past and Present*, Edmonton and Toronto: The Canadian Institute of Ukrainian Studies, 1980, 32–57.

'The *Szlachta* of the Polish-Lithuanian Commonwealth and their Government', in Banac, Ivo and Bushkovitch, Peter (eds.), *The Nobility in Russia and Eastern Europe*, New Haven: Yale Consortium on International and Area Studies, 1983, 17–45.

*Republic versus Autocracy. Poland-Lithuania and Russia 1686–1697*, Cambridge, Mass.: Harvard University Press, 1993.

'Imponderabilia społeczeństwa obywatelskiego Rzeczypospolitej Wielu Narodów', proceedings of the conference 'Rzeczpospolita wielu narodów i jej tradycje', Instytut Historii Uniwersytetu Jagiellońskiego, Cracow 15–17 September 1997 (forthcoming).

Kausche, Dietrich, 'Zur Geschichte der brandenburgisch-preußischen Statthalter', *Forschungen zur Brandenburgischen und Preußischen Geschichte* 52 (1940), 1–25.

Kawczyński, *Polnisch Preußen zur Zeit des zweiten schwedisch-polnischen Krieges von 1655–1660*, Braunsberg: n.pub., 1868.

Kestner, Ernst, 'Aus Thorns Schwedenzeit', *Beiträge zur Geschichte der Stadt Thorn* 9 (1882), 198–220.

Kętrzyński, Wojciech, 'Martin Cromers Rede über das preußische Indigenat', *Altpreußische Monatsschrift* NS 17 (1880), 343–52.

Keyser, Erich, *Geschichte der Stadt Danzig*, Schriften des Göttinger Arbeitskreises, no. 11, Kitzingen (Main): Holzner, 1951.

Klemp, Aleksander, *Protestanci w dobrach prywatnych w Prusach Królewskich od drugiej połowej XVII do drugiej połowie XVIII wieku*, Gdańsk: GTN, Ossolineum, 1994.

# Bibliography

Klempt, Adalbert, *Die Säkularisierung der universal-historischen Auffassung. Zum Wandel des Geschichtsdenkens im 16. und 17. Jahrhundert*, Göttingen: Musterschmidt, 1960.

Klesińska, Wanda, 'Archiwum Miasta Elbląga', *Rocznik Elebląski* 1 (1961), 73–96.

'Okupacja Elbląga przez Brandenburgię w latach 1698–1700', *Rocznik Elbląski* 4 (1969), 85–121.

Kletke, Karl, *Quellenkunde der Geschichte des Preußischen Staates: Die Quellenschriftsteller zur Geschichte des Preußischen Staates*, Danzig and Berlin: Schröder, 1858.

Klimowicz, Mieczysław, *Literatura Oświecenia*, Warsaw: PWN, 1995

Klonder, Andrzej, 'Szlachta a Królewszczyzny Prus Królewskich za Stefana Batorego (1576–1586)', *Zapiski Historyczne* 52, no. 3 (1987), 75–95.

'Prusacy na sejmie 1579–1580. Ostatnia próba przekreślenia Unii Lubelskiej', in Kamler, A., et al. (eds.), *Władza i społeczeństwo w XVI i XVII wieku. Prace ofiarowane Antoniemu Mączakowi w sześćdziesiątą rocznicę urodzin*, Warsaw: PWN, 1989, 248–60.

Koch, Hannsjoachim W., *A History of Prussia*, London: Longman, 1978.

Koch, Walther, *Die Hof- und Regierungsverfassung Friederichs I, 1697–1710*, Untersuchungen zur deutschen Staats- und Rechtsgeschichte no. 136, Breslau: M. and H. Marcus, 1926.

Kocot, Kazimierz, *Nauka prawa narodów w Ateneum Gdańskim*, Wrocław: Wrocławskie Towarzystwo Nauk, 1965.

Koczy, Ludwig, *Dzieje wewnętrzne Torunia*, Toruń: Nakładem Magistratu Miasta, 1933.

Koenigsberger, Helmut G., *Politicians and Virtuosi*, London: Hambledon, 1986.

'Republicanism, Monarchism and Liberty', in Oresko, Robert, Gibbs, Graham C., Scott, Hamish M. (eds.), *Royal and Republican Sovereignty in Early Modern Europe. Essays in Memory of Ragnhild Hatton*, Cambridge University Press, 1997, 43–74.

Koenigsberger, Helmut G. (ed.), *Republiken und Republikanismus im Europa der Frühen Neuzeit*, Schriften des Historischen Kollegs, Kolloquien 2, Munich: Oldenbourg, 1988.

Kohn, Hans, *The Idea of Nationalism*, New York: Collier, 1967.

Konopczyński, Władysław, 'Prusy Królewskie w unji z Polską, 1569–1772', *Roczniki Historyczne* 3 (1927), 111–41.

*Polscy pisarze polityczni XVIII wieku*, Warsaw: PWN, 1966.

Koser, Reinhold, 'Das Jubiläum der preußischen Königskrone', *Hohenzollern-Jahrbuch. Forschungen und Abbildungen der Hohenzollern in Brandenburg-Preußen* 4 (1900), 2–22.

Kossmann, Oskar, *Die Deutschen in Polen seit der Reformation*, Marburg: Herder-Institut, 1978.

Kot, Stanisław, 'Hugo Grotius a Polska w 300-lecia dzieła o prawie wojny i pokoju' in *Polska złotego wieku a Europa*, ed. Henryk Barycz, Warsaw: PIW, 1987, 577–614.

'Descriptio Gentium Poetów Polskich XVII wieku', in *Polska złotego wieku a Europa*, ed. Henryk Barycz, PIW, 1987, 834–73.

'Wenecja w oczach Polaków na przestrzeni dziejów', in *Polska złotego wieku a Europa*, ed. Henryk Barycz, Warsaw: PIW, 1987, 307–22.

Kramm, Heinrich, 'Streiflichter auf die Oberschichten der mitteldeutschen Städte im Übergang vom Mittelalter zur Neuzeit, Zur Frage des Patriziats', in Rössler, Hellmuth (ed.), *Deutsches Patriziat 1430–1740*, Büdinger Vorträge 1965, Limburg (Lahn): L.A. Starke, 1968, 125–56.

# Bibliography

Kraus, Andreas, 'Grundzüge barocker Geschichtsschreibung', *Historisches Jahrbuch* 88 (1968), 54–77.

Krause, [Prediger], 'Nachrichten über Matthäus Praetorius', *Beiträge zur Kunde Preußens* 7 (1825), 336–65.

Krawczyk, Antoni, 'Źródła informacji do *Respublica Polonica* Krzysztofa Hartknocha', *Annales Universitatis Mariae Curie-Skłodowska* 40, section F (1985), 117–41.

Kriegseisen, Wojciech, *Sejm Rzeczypospolitej Szlacheckiej (do 1763 roku)*, Warsaw: Wydawnictwo Sejmowe, 1996.

*Ewangelicy Polscy i Litewscy w epoce saskiej (1696–1763). Sytuacja prawna, organizacja i stosunki międzywyznaniowe*, Warsaw: Semper, 1996.

Krollmann, Christian, *Die Selbstbiographie des Fabian von Dohna nebst Aktenstücken zur Geschichte der Sukzession der Kurfürsten von Brandenburg*, Verein für die Geschichte der Provinz Preußen, Leipzig: Duncker and Humblot, 1905.

Krollmann, Christian (ed.), *Altpreußische Biographie*, 12 vols., vols. I–II: Königsberg: Gräfe und Unzer, 1936; following vols., Marburg: Herder-Institut, 1967.

Kumke, Carsten, *Führer und Geführte bei den Zaporoger Kosaken*, Forschungen zur osteuropäischen Geschichte, Osteuropa-Institut an der FUB, Historische Veröffentlichungen no. 49, Berlin: Duncker and Humblot, 1993.

Kunisch, Johannes, *Absolutismus*, Göttingen: UTB, 1986.

Kurdybacha, Łukasz, *Stosunki kulturalne polsko-gdańskie w XVIII wieku*, Gdańsk: Towarzystwo Przyjaciół Nauk, 1937.

Kurdybacha, Łukasz (ed.), *Historia wychowania*, 2 vols., Warsaw: PWN, 1967.

Kutrzeba, Stanisław, *Historia ustroju Polski w zarysie*, Lwów: Nakładem Księgarnii Polskiej Połonieckiego, 1905.

*Gdańsk – przeszłość i teraźniejszość*. *Prace zbiorowe*, Lwów: Ossolineum, 1928.

Kwiatkowska, Irena, 'Das sächsische Recht in der polnischen juristischen Literatur des 17. Jahrhunderts', in Lingelbach, G. and Lück, H. (eds.), *Deutsches Recht zwischen Sachsenspiegel und Aufklärung. Rolf Lieberwirth zum 70. Geburtstag*, Rechtshistorische Reihe no. 80, Frankfurt, Bern, New York, Paris: Peter Lang, 1991, 95–117.

Laassonen, Pentti, 'Die Anfänge des Chiliasmus im Norden', *Pietismus und Neuzeit* 19 (1993), 19–45.

Labuda, Gerard (ed.), *Historia Pomorza*, 2 vols., vol. II/1: '1464/66–1645/57', Poznań: Wydawnictwo Poznańskie, 1976.

Łaska, Janina, 'Stosunek Gdańska do Elektora Brandenburskiego w początkowym okresie "potopu" Szwedzkiego', *Rocznik Gdański* 27 (1968), 5–29.

Leinz, Josef, 'Ursachen des Abfalls Danzigs vom Deutschen Orden unter besonderer Berücksichtigung der nationalen Frage', *Westpreußen-Jahrbuch* 13–14 (1963–4), 1–59.

Lemke, Heinz, *Die Brüder Załuski und ihre Beziehungen zu Gelehrten in Deutschland und Danzig*, Studien zur Frühaufklärung, Quellen und Studien zur Geschichte Osteuropas 2, Berlin (East): Akademie-Verlag, 1958.

Lepszy, Kazimierz, *Prusy Książęce a Polska w latach 1576–1678*, Cieszyn: Drukarnia Dziedzictwa, 1932.

Letkemann, Peter, 'Die Geschichte der westpreußischen Staatsarchive', *Beiträge zur Geschichte Westpreußens* 5 (1976), 5–96.

# Bibliography

Leube, Hans, *Kalvinismus und Luthertum im Zeitalter der Orthodoxie*, 2 vols., Leipzig: n.pub., 1928; repr. Aalen: Scientia Verlag, 1966.

Lewitter, Lucjan R., 'Russia, Poland and the Baltic, 1697–1721', *Historical Journal* 11 (1968), 3–34.

'"De Bloeddorst der Jesuiten": een Hollands pamflet uit 1725', *Spiegel Historiael. Maandblad voor Geschiedenis en Archeologie* 5 (1991), 231–8.

Lipiński, Edward, 'Rozprawa "O pomnożeniu miast w Polsce" z roku 1648', *Zeszyty Naukowe Szkoły Planowania i Statystyki* 1 (1953), 115–42.

Litwin, Henryk, 'W poszukiwaniu rodowodu demokracji szlacheckiej. Polska myśl polityczna w piśmienictwie XV i XVI w.', in Sucheni-Grabowska, A. and Żaryn, M. (eds.), *Między monarchą a demokracją. Studia z dziejów Polski XV–XVIII wieku*, Warsaw: Wydawnictwo Sejmowe, 1994, 13–53.

Löschin, Gotthilf, *Geschichte Danzigs*, 2 vols., Danzig: Albertinische Buch- und Kunsthandlung, 1822–3.

Lüdtke, Franz, *Polen und die Erwerbung der preußischen Königswürde durch die Hohenzollern*, Bromberg: Richard Krahl, 1912.

Lutman, Roman, 'Położenie prawne Gdańska w dawnej Rzeczypospolitej Polskiej', *Rocznik Gdański* 1 (1927), 59–82.

MacDonogh, Giles, *Prussia, The Perversion of an Idea*, London: Mandarin, 1994.

Maciejewski, Janusz, 'Uniwersalizm i swoistość polskiego oświecenia', in Kłoczowski, J. (ed.), *Uniwersalizm i swoistość kultury polskiej*, 2 vols., vol. II, Lublin: KUL, 1989, 271–97.

Maercker, Hans, *Geschichte der ländlichen Ortschaften und der drei kleinen Städte Thorns*, Quellen und Darstellungen zur Geschichte Westpreußens 2, Danzig: T. Bertling, 1899–1900.

Mager, Wolfgang, 'Respublica und Bürger: Überlegungen zur Begründung frühneuzeitlicher Verfassungsordnungen', *Der Staat*, supplement 8 (1987): *Res Publica. Bürgerschaft in Stadt und Staat*, 67–84.

Maisel, Witold and Zdrójkowski, Zbigniew (eds.), *Prawo Starochełmińskie 1584 (1394)*, Teksty Prawa Chełmińskiego w przekładach polskich, no. 2, Toruń: UMK, 1985.

Maliszewski, Kazimierz, *Jakub Kazimierz Rubinkowski. Szlachcic, mieszczanin, toruński erudyta barokowy*, Roczniki TNT 81, no. 1, Warsaw, Poznań, Toruń: PWN, 1982.

'Kształtowanie się stereotypu Niemca i obrazu krajów niemieckich w potocznej świadomości sarmackiej od XVI do połowy XVIII wieku', in Wajda, Kazimierz (ed.), *Polacy i Niemcy. Z badań nad kształtowaniem heterostereotypów etnicznych*, Toruń: Adam Marszałek, 1991, 7–44.

'Obraz krajów obszaru niemieckojęzycznego w Polskiej prasie pisanej doby późnego baroku', *Acta Universitatis Wratislaviensis* 1136, Historia 79 (1991), 55–68.

'Mieszczańskie formy i metody komunikacji społecznej w wielkich miastach Prus Królewskich w XVII–XVIII wieku', *Zapiski Historyczne* 57, no. 4 (1992), 39–62.

'Stosunki religijne w Toruniu', in Cackowski, S. Dybaś, B. and Maliszewski, K. (eds.), *Historia Torunia, vol. II: W czasach renensansu, reformacji i wczesnego baroku, 1548–1660*, Toruń: TNT, 1994, 270–6.

Małłek, Janusz, *Ustawa o rządzie (Regimentsnottel) Prus Książęcych z roku 1542*, Toruń: UMK, 1967.

*Prusy Książęce a Prusy Królewskie w latach 1525–1548*, Warsaw: PWN, 1976.

# Bibliography

'Powstanie poczucia odrębności w Prusach i jej rozwój w XV i XVI wieku', in *Dwie Części Prus*, Olsztyn: Wydawnictwo Pojezierze, 1987, 9–17.

'Eine andersartige Lösung. Absolutistischer Staatsstreich in Preußen im Jahre 1663', *Parliaments, Estates and Representation* 10, no. 2 (1990), 177–87.

'Bikameralismus in Ordenspreußen, Königlich-Preußen und Herzogtum Preußen vom 15. bis zum 18. Jahrhundert', in Blom, H. W., Blockmans, W.P. and de Schlepper, H. (eds.), *Bicameralisme tweekamerstelsel vroeger en nu handelingen van de internationale conferentie ter gelegenheid van hel 175-jarie bestaan van de eerste Kamer der Staaten-Generaal in de Nederlanden*, The Hague: SDU, 1992, 175–87.

'Das Königliche Preußen und der Brandenburg-preußische Staat in den Jahren 1525–1772', in *Preußen und Polen. Politik, Stände, Kirche und Kultur vom 16. bis zum 18. Jahrhundert*, Mainzer Philosophische Fakultätsgesellschaft, Stuttgart: Steiner Verlag, 1992, 45–57.

'Die Entstehung und Entwicklung eines Sonderbewußtseins in Preußen während des 15. und 16. Jahrhunderts', in *Preußen und Polen*, 71–81.

'Einwirkungen der polnischen Kultur auf das Herzogtum Preußen im 16. Jahrhundert', in *Preußen und Polen*, 137–49.

'Die Ständerepräsentation im Deutschordensstaat (1466–1525) und im Herzogtum Preußen (1525–1566/68)', in Boockmann, Hartmut (ed.), *Die Anfänge der ständischen Vertretungen in Preußen und seinen Nachbarländern*, Historisches Kolleg, Kolloquien 16, Munich: Oldenbourg, 1992, 101–20.

'Polityka miasta Królewca wobec Polski w latach 1525–1801', *Komunikaty Mazursko-Warmińskie* (1992), 247–55.

Mańkowski, Tadeusz, *Genealogia Sarmatyzmu Polskiego*, Warsaw: Towarzystwo Wydawnicze 'Łuk', 1946.

Maschke, Erich, *Das Erwachen des Nationalbewußtseins im deutsch-slawischen Grenzraum*, Leipzig: J.C. Hinrichs, 1933.

'Preußen, das Werden eines Stammesnamens', in *Domus Hospitalis Theutonicorum*, Quellen und Studien zur Geschichte des Deutschen Ordens vol. 10, Bonn-Bad Godesberg: Verlag Wissenschaftliches Archiv, 1970, 158–87.

Mason, Roger A, 'Chivalry and Citizenship. Aspects of National Identity in Renaissance Scotland', in Mason, Roger A. and MacDougall, Norman (eds.), *People and Power in Scotland. Essays in Honour of T. C. Smout*, Edinburgh: John Donald, 1992, 150–73.

Matysik, Stanisław, 'Elias Konstantyn Schröder. Gdański prawnik i sekretarz królewski z XVII wieku. Życie i dzieło', *Czasopismo Prawno-Historyczne* 6 (1954), 153–75.

Melton, Edgar, 'The Prussian Junkers, 1600–1786', in Scott, Hamish M. (ed.), *The European Nobilities in the Seventeenth and Eighteenth Centuries*, 2 vols., vol. II: *Northern, Central and Eastern Europe*, London and New York: Longman, 1995, 71–109.

Melton, James Van Horn, *Absolutism and the Eighteenth-Century Origins of Compulsory Schooling in Prussia and Austria*, Cambridge University Press, 1988.

Menke-Glückert, Emil, *Die Geschichtsschreibung der Reformation und Gegenreformation. Bodin und die Begründung der Geschichtsmethodologie durch Barthel Keckermann*, Leipzig: J.C. Hinrichs, 1912.

Michalski, Jerzy, 'Sarmatyzm a europeizacja Polski w XVIII wieku', in *Swójkość i cudzoziemszczyzna w dziejach kultury polskiej*, Warsaw: PWN, 1973, 113–68.

# Bibliography

Mika, Marian J, 'Udział Poznania w sejmach Rzeczypospolitej od końca XV w. do 1791 r.', *Studia i Materiały do dziejów Wielkopolski i Pomorza* 6 (1960–1), 257–302.

Mikulski, Krzysztof (ed.), *Urzędnicy Prus Królewskich XV–XVIII wieku*, Wrocław: Ossolineum, 1990.

Mirow, Jürgen, *Das alte Preußen im deutschen Geschichtsbild seit der Reichsgründung*, Berlin: Duncker und Humblot, 1981.

Mocarski, Zygmunt, *Kultura Umysłowa na Pomorzu*, Toruń: Nakładem Instytutu Bałtyckiego, 1931.

*Książka w Toruniu do roku 1793*, Toruń: Magistrat Miasta Torunia, 1934.

Mörner, Theodor, *Kurbrandenburgs Staatsverträge von 1601–1700*, Berlin: G. Reiner, 1867.

Mokrzecki, Lech, 'Dyrektor Gimnazjum Elbląskiego Joachim Pastorius (1652–1654) i jego poglądy na historię', *Rocznik Elbląski* 4 (1969), 59–83.

*Studium z dziejów nauczania historii*, Wydział nauk społecznych i humanistycznych 46, Gdańsk: GTN, 1973.

'Zainteresowanie historyczne Jerzego Wendego, rektora Gimnazjum Akademickiego w Toruniu 1695–1705', in Zdrójkowski, Zbigniew (ed.), *Księga Pamiątkowa 400-lecia Toruńskiego Gimnazjum*, vol. I: *XVI–XVIII w.*, Toruń: TNT, 1992, 315–47.

Mokrzecki, Lech and Kubik, Kazimierz, *Trzy wieki nauki gdańskiej. Szkice z dziejów XVI–XVIII w.*, Gdańsk: GTN, 1969.

Motekat, Helmut, *Ostpreußische Literaturgeschichte mit Danzig und Westpreußen*, Munich: Schild-Verlag, 1977.

Müller, Michael G., 'Zur Frage der Zweiten Reformation in Danzig, Elbing und Thorn', in Schilling, Heinz (ed.), *Die reformierte Konfessionalisierung in Deutschland. Das Problem der Zweiten Reformation*, Gütersloh: Mohn, 1986, 251–65.

'Discursus in der Religions-Sache der Preußischen Städte. Ein Dokument zur Geschichte von Konfession und Politik im Königlichen Preußen im 16. Jahrhundert', in Poraziński, Jarosław (ed.), *Między wielką polityką a szlacheckim partykularzem. Studia z dziejów nowożytnej Polski i Europy ku czci Profesora Jacka Staszewskiego*, Toruń: UMK, 1993, 177–88.

'Wielkie miasta Prus Królewskich wobec parlamentaryzmu polskiego po Unii Lubelskiej', *Czasopismo Prawno-Historyczne* 45 (1993), 257–68.

*Zweite Reformation und Städtische Autonomie im Königlichen Preußen. Danzig, Elbing und Thorn in der Epoche der Konfessionalisierung (1557–1660)*, Berlin: Colloquium, 1998.

Müller, Wiesław, 'Epoka baroku i sarmatyzmu', in Kłoczowski, Jerzy (ed.), *Uniwersalizm i swoistość kultury polskiej*, 2 vols., vol. I, Lublin: Katolicki Uniwersytet Lubelski, 1989, 217–40.

Muhl, John, 'Danziger Bürgergeschlechter im ländlichen Besitz', *Zeitschrift des Westpreußischen Geschichtsvereins* 71 (1934), 89–113.

Nachama, Andreas, *Ersatzbürger und Staatsbildung. Zur Zerstörung des Bürgertums in Brandenburg-Preußen*, Frankfurt, Bern, New York: Lang, 1983.

Nadolski, Bronisław, *Życie i działalność B. Keckermanna*, Toruń: TNT, 1961.

*Ze studiów nad życiem literackim i kulturą umysłową na Pomorzu w XVI i XVII wieku*, Warsaw, Wrocław, Cracow: PWN, 1969.

Naworski, Zbigniew, 'Indygenat w Prusach Królewskich 1454–1772', *Czasopismo Prawno-Historyczne* 35 (1983), 31–57.

# Bibliography

'Uwagi o roli prowincji Pruskiej w strukturze federacyjnej Rzeczypospolitej w XVII wieku', *Zapiski Historyczne* 53 (1988), 131–42.

*Sejmik Generalny Prus Królewskich 1569–1772. Organizacja i funkcjonowanie na tle systemu zgromadzeń stanowych prowincji*, Toruń: UMK, 1992.

Neubaur, Ludwig, 'Die Russen in Elbing, 1710–1713', *Altpreußische Monatsschrift* 53 (1916), 273–366.

Neugebauer, Wolfgang, *Politischer Wandel im Osten. Ost- und Westpreußen von den alten Ständen zum Konstitutionalismus*, Stuttgart: Steiner, 1992.

Neumaier, Klaus, *Jus Publicum. Studium zur barocken Rechtsgelehrsamkeit an der Universität Ingolstadt*, Ludovico Maximilianea Forschungen 6, Berlin: Duncker und Humblot, 1974.

Neveux, Jean-Baptiste, *Vie spirituelle et vie sociale entre Rhîn et Baltique au XVII siecle, de J. Arndt à P.J. Spener*, Paris: Klincksieck, 1967.

Nippel, Wilfried, 'Bürgerideal und Oligarchie. "Klassischer Republikanismus" aus althistorischer Sicht', in Koenigsberger, H. (ed.), *Republiken und Republikanismus im Europa der Frühen Neuzeit*, Schriften des Historischen Kollegs, Kolloquien 11, München: Oldenbourg, 1988, 1–18.

North, Michael, 'Englische Reiseberichte des 17. Jahrhunderts als Quelle zur Geschichte der königlich-preußischen Städte Danzig, Elbing und Thorn', in Letkemann, P. and Jähnig, B. (eds.), *Thorn. Königin der Weichsel*, Göttingen: Vandenhoeck und Ruprecht, 1981, 197–208.

'The Export Trade of Royal Prussia and Ducal Prussia, 1550–1650', in Heeres, W. G. et al. (eds.), *From Dunkirk to Danzig. Shipping Trade in the North Sea and the Baltic, 1350–1850*, Hilversum: Verloren Publishers, 1988, 383–90.

Nugel, Otto, 'Der Schöppenmeister Hieronymus Roth', *Forschungen zur Brandenburgischen und Preußischen Geschichte* 14 (1901), 393–479.

Ochmann, Stefania, *Sejmy lat 1661–2. Przegrana batalia o reformę ustroju Rzeczypospolitej*, Wrocław: Wydawnictwa Uniwersytetu Wrocławskiego, 1977.

Ochmański, Jerzy, 'The National Idea in Lithuania from the Sixteenth to the First Half of the Nineteenth Century: The Problem of Cultural-Linguistic Differentiation', *Harvard Ukraininan Studies* 10 (1986), 301–15.

Odyniec, Wacław, *Starostwo Puckie 1546–1678*, Gdańsk: GTN, 1961.

*Dzieje Prus Królewskich 1454–1772*, Warsaw: PWN, 1972.

Oestreich, Gerhard, *Strukturprobleme der frühen Neuzeit. Ausgewählte Aufsätze*, Berlin: de Gruyter, 1969.

*Neostoicism and the Early Modern State*, Cambridge University Press, 1982.

Ogonowski, Zbigniew (ed.), *700 Lat Myśli Polskiej. Filozofia i Myśl społeczna XVII wieku*, 2 vols., Warsaw: PWN, 1979.

Olejnik, Karol, *Stefan Batory*, Warsaw: PWN, 1988.

Olszewski, Henryk, *Doktryny prawno-ustrojowe czasów Saskich, 1697–1740*, Warsaw: PWN, 1961.

'Ustrój polityczny Rzeczypospolitej', in Tazbir, Janusz (ed.), *Polska XVII wiek*, Warsaw: PWN, 1974, 60–93.

Opaliński, Edward, 'Die Funktionen regionaler Amter im Machtsystem der polnischen Adelsrepublik in der zweiten Hälfte des 16. und in der ersten Hälfte des 17. Jahrhun-

# Bibliography

derts. Das Beispiel der Woiwodschaften Łęczyca und Sieradz', in Bahlcke, J., Bömelburg, H.-J. and Kersken, N. (eds.), *Ständefreiheit und Staatsgestaltung in Ostmitteleuropa. Übernationale Gemeinsamkeiten in der politischen Kultur vom 16.–18. Jahrhundert*, Leipzig: Universitätsverlag, 1996, 65–80.

Opas, Tomasz, 'Z problemu awansu społecznego mieszczan w XVII–XVIII w.', *Przegląd Historyczny* 65, no. 3 (1974), 465–75.

Opgenoorth, Ernst, *Friedrich Wilhelm. Der Große Kurfürst von Brandenburg*, 2 vols., Göttingen: Musterschmidt, 1971/78.

'Nervus Rerum: Die Auseinandersetzungen mit den Ständen um die Staatsfinanzierung', in Heinrich, Gerd (ed.), *Ein sonderbares Licht in Teutschland. Beiträge zur Geschichte des Großen Kurfürsten von Brandenburg 1640–1688*, Zeitschrift für Historische Forschung, supplement 8, Berlin: Duncker and Humblot, 1990, 99–112.

Opgenoorth, Ernst (ed.), *Handbuch der Geschichte Ost- und Westpreußens*, 3 vols., Lüneburg: Verlag Nordostdeutsches Kulturwerk, 1994–7.

Oracki, Tadeusz, *Słownik biograficzny Warmii, Mazur i Powiśla od połowy XV do 1945 roku*, Warsaw: Instytut Wydawniczy PAX, 1963.

Orlich, Leopold von, *Geschichte des preußischen Staates im 17. Jahrhundert mit besonderer Beziehung auf das Leben Friedrich Wilhelms des Großen Kurfürsten*, Berlin: F. Dümmler, 1838–9.

Othmer, Sieglinde C., *Berlin und die Verbreitung des Naturrechts in Europa. Kultur- und sozialgeschichtliche Studien zu Jean Barbeyrac's Pufendorf-Übersetzung und eine Analyse seiner Leserschaft*, preface by G. Oestreich, Einzelveröffentlichungen der Historischen Kommission zu Berlin 30, Berlin: de Gruyter, 1970.

Paczkowski, Josef, 'Der Große Kurfürst und Christian Ludwig von Kalckstein', *Forschungen zur Brandenburgischen und Preußischen Geschichte* 2 (1889), 103–209.

Pawlak, Marian, *Dzieje Gimnazjum Elbląskiego w latach 1535–1772*, Olsztyn: Wydawnictwo Pojezierze, 1972.

'Młodzież elbląska w Toruńskim Gimnazjum Akademickim w XVII–XVIII w.', in Zdrójkowski, Z. (ed.), *Księga Pamiątkowa 400-lecia Toruńskiego Gimnazjum Akademickiego*, Toruń: TNT, 1972, 207–24.

*Studia uniwersyteckie młodzieży z Prus Królewskich w XVI–XVIII wieku*, Toruń: UMK, 1988.

Pazyra, Stanisław, *Miasta polskie*, 2 vols., Warsaw: PWN, 1965–7.

Penners-Ellwart, Hedwig, *Die Danziger Bürgerschaft nach Herkunft und Beruf 1536–1709*, Wissenschaftliche Beiträge zur Geschichte und Landeskunde Ostmitteleuropas no. 13, Marburg: Herder-Institut, 1954.

Petersen, Peter, *Geschichte der Aristotelischen Philosophie*, Leipzig: Meiner, 1911; repr. Stuttgart: Frommann (Holzboog), 1964.

Pfeiffer, Ernst, *Die Revuereisen Friedrichs des Grossen besonders die Schlesischen nach 1763*, Berlin: n.pub., 1904; repr. Vaduz: Kraus, 1965.

Piskorska, Helena, *Organizacja władz i kancelarii miasta Torunia do 1793 roku*, Toruń: TNT, 1956.

Piwarski, Kazimierz, 'Sprawa pruska za Jana III Sobieskiego 1688–89', *Kwartalnik Historyczny* 43 (1929), 153–86.

'Polityka bałtycka Jana III w latach 1675–1690', in Halecki, Oskar (ed.), *Księga pamiąt-*

# Bibliography

*kowa ku czci Profesora Wacława Sobieskiego*, Cracow: PAU, 1932, 197–265.

*Dzieje polityczne Prus Wschodnich 1621–1772*, Gdynia: Instytut Bałtycki, 1938.

*Dzieje Prus Wschodnich w czasach nowożytnych*, Gdańsk, Bygdgoszcz: Instytut Bałtycki, 1946.

'Plan rozbioru Rzeczypospolitej w dobie "potopu" (Polityka dworu Hohenzollernów wobec Szwecji i Rzeczypospolitej w latach 1655–57)', *Sprawozdania PTPN* 19 (1955), 253–6.

'Das Interregnum 1696–1697 in Polen und die politische Lage in Europa', in Kalisch, J. and Gierowski, J. (eds.), *Um die polnische Krone*, Berlin (East): Akademie-Verlag, 1962, 9–44.

Pniewski, Władysław, *Język polski w dawnych szkołach gdańskich*, Gdańsk: Towarzystwo Przyjaciół Nauki i Sztuki, 1938.

Pocock, J.G.A, *The Machiavellian Moment. Florentine Political Thought and the Atlantic Republican Tradition*, Princeton University Press, 1975.

Poraziński, Jarosław, *Sejm Lubelski w 1703 r.*, Roczniki TNT no. 83, Toruń and Warsaw: PWN, 1988.

Prowe, Ludwig, 'Mitteilungen des Thorner Residenten am Warschauer Hofe Dr. S.L. von Geret (1765–1773)', *Die neuen Preußischen Provinzial-Blätter* 3rd series, vol. 10, no. 4 (1865), 509–30.

Pryshlak, Maria O., 'Forma Mixta as a Political Ideal of a Polish Magnate: Łukasz Opaliński's Rozmowa Plebana z Ziemianinem', *Polish Review* 26 (1981), 26–42.

'The Well-Ordered State in the Political Philosophy of the Polish Aristorcracy', Ph.D. diss., Columbia University, 1984.

Ptaśnik, Jan, *Miasta i mieszczaństwo w dawnej Polsce*, Warsaw: PIW, 1949.

Rachel, Hugo, *Der Große Kurfürst und die ostpreußischen Stände, 1640–88*, Staats- und Sozialwissenschaftliche Forschungen no. 24, part 1, ed. Gustav Schmoller and M. Sering, Leipzig: Duncker and Humblot, 1905, 1–344.

Raeff, Marc, *The Well-Ordered Police State. Social and Institutional Change through Law in the Germanies and Russia, 1600–1800*, New Haven and London: Yale University Press, 1983.

'Some Observations on the Work of Hermann Aubin (1885–1969)', in Lehmann, H. and van Horn Melton, J. (eds.), *Paths of Continuity. Central European Historiography from the 1930s to the 1950s*, Cambridge University Press, 1994, 239–49.

Rausch, Walter (ed.), *Die Städte Mitteleuropas im 17. und 18. Jahrhundert*, Beiträge zur Geschichte der Städte Mitteleuropas 5, Linz: Ludwig-Boltzmann Institut für Stadtgeschichtsforschung, 1981.

Recke, Walter, 'Der Danziger Hof in Warschau und seine Bewohner', *Mitteilungen des Westpreußischen Geschichtsvereins* 24, no. 2 (1925), 17–40.

Renan, Ernest, 'Qu'est-ce qu'une nation?', in Woolf, Stuart (ed.), *Nationalism in Europe, 1815 to the Present: A Reader*, London and New York: Routledge, 1996.

Riabinin, Jan, *Rada Miasta Lublina*, Lublin: TPNL, 1935.

Riedesel, Erich, *Pietismus und Orthodoxie in Ostpreußen*, Schriften der Albertus-Universität 7, Königsberg and Berlin: Ost-Europa Verlag, 1937.

Ringmar, Erik, *Identity, Interest and Action. A Cultural Explanation of Sweden's Intervention in the Thirty Years War*, Cambridge University Press, 1996.

# Bibliography

Roding, Juliette, 'Dutch Architects in Danzig and the Southern Baltic in the 16th and 17th Centuries', *Tijdschrift voor Skandinavistiek* 16, no. 2 (1995), 223–34.

Rombowski, Aleksander, 'Szkolnictwo Polskie w Toruniu w XVI–XVIII w.', *Studia i Materiały do Dziejów Wielkopolski i Pomorza* 6 (1960), 54–108.

Roos, Hans, 'Das Ständewesen in Polen (1505–1772)', in Gerhard, Dietrich (ed.), *Ständische Vertretungen in Europa im 17. und 18. Jahrhundert*, Göttingen: Vandenhoeck und Ruprecht, 1969, 310–67.

Rosenberg, Hans, *Bureaucracy, Aristocracy and Autocracy. The Prussian Experience, 1660–1815*, Cambridge, Mass.: Harvard University Press, 1966.

Rousseau, Jean-Jacques, *The Government of Poland*, trans. and with an introduction by W. Kendall, Indianapolis and New York: Bobbs-Merrill, 1972.

Rowell, Steven C., *Lithuania Ascending. A Pagan Empire Within East-Central Europe, 1295–1345*, Cambridge University Press, 1994.

Rymaszewski, Zbigniew, *Sprawy Gdańskie przed sądami zadwornymi oraz ingerencja królów w gdański wymiar sprawiedliwości XVI–XVIII w.*, Wrocław: Ossolineum, 1985.

Saarinen, Hannes, *Bürgerstadt und absoluter Kriegsherr. Danzig und Karl XII. im Nordischen Krieg*, Helsinki: Suomen Historiallinen Seura, 1996.

Salmonowicz, Stanisław, 'W kręgu Toruńskich erudytów osiemnastego wieku', in Zdrójkowski, Z. (ed.), *Księga Pamiątkowa 400-lecia Toruńskiego Gimnazjum Akademickiego*, vol. I: *XVI–XVIII w.*, Toruń: TNT, 1972, 225–41.

*Toruńskie Gimnazjum Akademickie w latach 1681–1871. Studium z dziejów nauki i oświaty*, Poznań: PTPN, 1973.

'Z dziejów walki o tzw. restauracji auttonomicznych aspiracji Prus Królewskich w XVIII wieku', *Analecta Cracoviensia* 7 (1975), 433–57.

'Nauczanie filozofii w Toruńskim Gimnazjum Akademickim 1568–1793', in Szczucki, Lech (ed.), *Nauczanie filozofii w Polsce w XV–XVIII wieku*, Wrocław, Warsaw, Cracow: Ossolineum, 1978, 137–97.

'Pietyzm na Pomorzu Polskim oraz w Wielkopolsce w pierwszej połowie XVIII wieku', *Rocznik Humanistyczny* 27 (1979), 95–105.

'Jerzy Piotr Schultz, 1680–1748', in Biskup, Marian (ed.), *Wybitni ludzie dawnego Torunia*, Warsaw, Poznań, Toruń: PWN, 1982, 105–9.

'Stany Prus Królewskich wobec Korony w XVII–XVIII wieku', *Acta Universitatis Nicolai Copernici* Historia XVIII, Nauki Humanistyczno-społeczne 128 (1982), 105–19.

'Jesuitenschulen und Akademien im Königlichen Preußen vom 16. bis zum 18. Jahrhundert', *Zeszyty Naukowe Wydziału Humanistycznego Uniwersytetu Gdańskiego, Pedagogia i Historia Wychowawcza* 15 (1985), 15–27.

'O roli i formach reprezentacji stanów w państwie brandenbursko-pruskim doby absolutyzmu', *Czasopismo Prawno-Historyczne* 37 (1985), 163–70.

'Prusy Królewskie i Książęce jako terytoria styku dwuch kultur (XVI–XVIIIw.)', in Czubiński, Antoni and Kulak, Zbigniew (eds.), *Śląsk i Pomorze w stosunkach polsko-niemieckich od XVI do XVIII w. XIV Konferencja Wspólnej Komisji Podręcznikowej PRL-RFN Historyków. 9.–14. VI. 1981 r.*, Poznań: Instytut Zachodni PTPN, 1987, 69–92.

'Das königliche Preußen im öffentlichen Recht der polnisch-litauischen Republik, 1569–1772', *Studia Maritima* 6 (1987), 41–60.

# Bibliography

'Idea federacyjna i samorządowa w dawnej Rzeczypospolitej', in *Pamiętnik XIII Powszechnego Zjazdu Historyków Polskich, Poznań 6–9 września 1984 roku*, part II: 'Sprawozdania i sympozjów', Wrocław, Warsaw, Cracow: Ossolineum, 1988, 61–6.

'Prusy Królewskie w ustroju Rzeczypospolitej szlacheckiej, 1569–1772', *Acta Universitatis Wratislaviensis* 945, Historia LXVI (1988), 45–56.

'Życie religijne luteranów toruńskich w XVII–XVIII w.', *Odrodzenie i Reformacja w Polsce* 34 (1989), 115–130.

'Nauczanie prawa i polityki w Toruńskim Gimnazjum Akademickim od XVI do XVIII wieku', *Czasopismo Prawno-Historyczne* 23 (1991), 53–85.

'Gotfryd Lengnich. Szkic do protretu uczonego', in *Od Prus Książęcych do Królestwa Pruskiego*, Olsztyn: OBN im. Kętrzyńskiego, 1992, 72–102.

'Jerzy Forster a narodziny stereotypu Polaka w Niemciech', in *Od Prus Książęcych do Królestwa Pruskiego*, Olsztyn: OBN im. Kętrzyńskiego, 1992, 112–20.

*Polacy i Niemcy wobec siebie. Powstawy, opinie, stereotypy*, Olsztyn: OBN im. Kętrzyńskiego, 1993.

Samsonowicz, Henryk, 'Der Deutsche Orden und die Hanse', in Fleckenstein, Johann and Hellmann, Manfred (eds.), *Die geistlichen Ritterorden Europas*, Sigmaringen: Thorbecke, 1980, 317–28.

Saring, Hans, 'Ein unbekannter Bericht über die Danziger Politik des Großen Kurfürsten, 1662', *Mitteilungen des Westpreußischen Geschichtsvereins* 33 (1934), 53–8.

Sarnowska-Temeriusz, Elżbieta, *Świat mitów i świat znaczen. Maciej K. Sarbiewski i problemy wiedzy o starożytności*, Warsaw: PAN, 1969.

Schellhase, Kenneth, *Tacitus in Renaissance Political Thought*, Chicago and London: University of Chicago Press, 1976.

Schevill, Ferdinand, *The Great Elector*, University of Chicago Press, 1947.

Schieder, Theodor, *Deutscher Geist und ständische Freiheit im Weichselland. Politische Ideen und politisches Schrifttum in Westpreußen von der Lubliner Union bis zu den polnischen Teilungen, 1569–1772/93*, Danzig: Gräfe und Unzer, 1940.

'Die preußische Königskrönung von 1700 und die politische Ideengeschichte', in *Begegnungen mit der Geschichte*, Göttingen: Vandenhoeck und Ruprecht, 1962, 183–209.

*Nationalismus und Nationalstaat. Studien zum nationalen Problem im modernen Europa*, ed. Otto Dann and Hans-Ulrich Wehler, Göttingen: Vandenhoeck, 1991.

Schilling, Heinz, 'Reformation und Bürgerfreiheit. Emdens Weg zur calvinistischen Stadtrepublik', in Moeller, B. (ed.), *Stadt und Kirche im 16. Jahrhundert*, Gütersloher Verlagshaus, 1978, 128–61.

'Der libertär-radikale Republikanismus der holländischen Regenten', Schröder, Hans-Christian (ed.), *Politischer Radikalismus im 17. Jahrhundert*, Göttingen: Vandenhoeck and Ruprecht, 1984, 498–553.

'Gab es im späten Mittelalter und zur Beginn der Neuzeit in Deutschland einen städtischen Republikanismus? Zur politischen Kultur des alteuropäischen Stadtbürgertums', in Koenigsberger, H. (ed.), *Republiken und Republikanismus im Europa der Frühen Neuzeit*, Schriften des Historischen Kollegs, Kolloquien 11, Munich: Oldenbourg, 1988, 101–43.

# Bibliography

*Civic Calvinism in North-West Germany and the Netherlands*, special issue of *Sixteenth-Century Journal*, vol. 17: *Essays and Studies*, Missouri: Sixteeenth-Century Journal Publishers, 1991.

'Confessionalisation in the Empire: Religious and Societal Change in Germany between 1555 and 1620', in Schilling, H. (ed.), *Religion, Political Culture and the Emergence of Early Modern Society. Essays in German and Dutch History*, Leiden: Brill, 1992, 205–45.

*Die Stadt in der Frühen Neuzeit*, Enzyklopedie Deutscher Geschichte 24, Munich: Oldenbourg, 1993.

Schilling, Heinz (ed.), *Die reformierte Konfessionalisierung in Deutschland. Das Problem der Zweiten Reformation*, Gütersloh: Mohn, 1986.

Schmidt, Heinrich, 'Zur Vorstellungswelt deutscher Städte im 17. Jahrhundert', in Wegener, Werner (ed.), *Festschrift für K.G. Hugelmann zum 80. Geburtstag*, 2 vols., vol. II, Aalen: Scientia, 1959, 501–21.

Schmidt, Robert, *Städtewesen und Bürgertum in Neuostpreußen*, Königsberg: Thomas und Oppermann, 1913.

Schmoller, Gustav, *Deutsches Städtewesen in älterer Zeit*, Bonner staatswissenschaftliche Untersuchungen 3, Bonn and Leipzig: K. Schröder, 1922.

Schneppen, Hans, *Niederländische Universitäten und deutsches Geistesleben, von der Gründung der Universität Leiden bis ins 18. Jahrhundert*, Münster: Aschendorff, 1960.

Schönwälder, Karen, *Historiker und Politik. Geschichtswissenschaft im Nationalsozialismus*, Historische Studien 9, Frankfurt and New York: Peter Lang, 1992.

Schorn-Schütte, Luise, 'Territorialgeschichte – Provinzialgeschichte – Landesgeschichte – Regionalgeschichte. Ein Beitrag zur Wissenschaftsgeschichte der Landesgeschichtsschreibung', in Jäger, Helmut et al. (eds.), *Civitatum Communitas. Studien zum europäischen Städtewesen. Festschrift für Heinz Stoob*, Cologne and Berlin: Böhlau, 1984, 390–416.

Schramm, Gottfried, *Der Polnische Adel und die Reformation*, Wiesbaden: Franz Steiner, 1965.

'Staatseinheit und Regionalismus in Polen-Litauen (15.–17. Jahrhundert)', *Forschungen für Osteuropäische Geschichte* 11 (1966), 7–23.

'Danzig, Elbing, Thorn als Beispiele städtischer Reformation, 1517–1558', in Fenske, H., Reinhard, W. and Schulin, E. (eds.), *Historia Integra. Festschrift für Erich Hassinger zum 70. Geburtstag*, Berlin: Duncker und Humblot, 1977, 125–54.

'Szlachta a Państwo na przekładzie Brandenburgii i Rzeczypospolitej obojga narodów w XVII wieku', *Zapiski Historyczne* 49 (1984), 29–50.

'Polen, Böhmen, Ungarn: Übernationale Gemeinsamkeiten in der politischen Kultur des späten Mittelalters und der frühen Neuzeit', in Bahlcke, J., Bömelburg, H.-J. and Kersken, N.(eds.), *Ständefreiheit und Staatsgestaltung in Ostmitteleuropa. Übernationale Gemeinsamkeiten in der politischen Kultur vom 16.–18. Jahrhundert*, Leipzig: Universitätsverlag, 1996, 13–38.

Schück, Robert, 'Ein Conflict Friedrich Wilhelms I. mit der Stadt Danzig wegen der preußischen Werbungen aus dem Jahre 1728', *Zeitschrift für Preußische Geschichte und Landeskunde* 11 (1874), 471–82.

Schumacher, Bruno, *Geschichte Ost- und Westpreußens* (1937), ed. Walther Hubatsch, 6th edn, Würzburg: Holzner-Verlag, 1977.

# Bibliography

Schwinges, Rainer Christoph, 'Primäre und "sekundäre" Nation, Nationalbewußtsein und sozialer Wandel im mittelalterlichen Böhmen', in Grothusen, Klaus-Detlev and Zernack, Klaus (eds.), *Europa Slavica – Europa Orientalis, Festschrift für Herbert Ludat*, Berlin: Duncker und Humblot, 1980, 490–532.

Selle, Götz von, *Geschichte der Albertus-Universität zu Königsberg in Preußen*, Göttinger Arbeitskreis, Würzburg: Holzner, 1956.

Seraphim, August, 'Eine politische Denkschrift des Burggrafen Fabian von Dohna 1606', *Forschungen zur Brandenburgischen und Preußischen Geschichte* 24 (1911), 109–46.

Serczyk, Jerzy, 'Krzysztof Hartknoch (1644–1687) toruński historyk Pomorza', *Rocznik Toruński* 3 (1969), 55–88.

'Warsztat historyczny K. Hartknocha, 1644–1687', in Zdrójkowski, Z. (ed.), *Księga Pamiątkowa 400-lecia Toruńskiego Gimnazjum Akademickiego*, Toruń: TNT, 1972, 283–311.

'Obraz zakonu krzyżackiego w historiografii Toruńskiej okresu wczesnego Oświecenia', *Acta Universitatis Nicolai Copernici*, Historia IX, Nauki humanistyczne, no. 58 (1973), 159–74.

'Krzysztof Hartknoch, profesor Gimnazjum Akademickiego w Toruniu', in Biskup, Marian (ed.), *Wybitni Ludzie Dawnego Torunia*, Warsaw, Poznań, Toruń: PWN 1982, 81–8.

Serczyk, Jerzy and Tomczak, A. (eds.), *Dzieje Historiografii Prus Wschodnich i Zachodnich do 1920 roku. Kierunki, ośrodki, najwybitniejsi przedstawiciele*, Toruń: TNT, 1989.

Sheehan, Margaret, *The Rise of Brandenburg-Prussia*, Lancaster Pamphlets, London: Routledge, 1995.

Simson, Paul, 'Westpreußen und Danzigs Kampf gegen die polnischen Unionsbestrebungen in den letzten Jahren des Königs Sigismund August, 1568–1572', *Zeitschrift des Westpreußischen Geschichtsvereins* 37 (1897), 1–176.

Sinko, Zofia, *Oświeceni wśród pól Elizejskich. Rozmowy zmarłych. Recepcja – twórczość oryginalna*, Wrocław, Warsaw, Cracow: Ossolineum, 1976.

Skalweit, Stephan, 'Das Herscherbild des 17. Jahrhunderts', *Historische Zeitschrift* 184 (1957), 66–80.

Skinner, Quentin, *The Foundations of Modern Political Thought*, 2 vols., vol. II: *The Age of Reformation*, Cambridge University Press, 1978; 6th edn, 1996.

Slósarczyk, Kazimierz, 'Sprawa zespolenia Prus Królewskich z Koroną za Jagiellonów, 1454–1572', *Roczniki Historyczne* 3 (1927), 92–110.

Smith, Anthony, *National Identity*, London and New York: Penguin, 1991.

Sobieski, Wacław, 'Za kim opowiadziały się Prusy Królewskie w roku 1655', *Pamiętnik V Zjazdu Historyków Polskich w Warszawie, 28.11.–4.12.1930*, Lwów: Polskie Towarzystwo Historyczne, 1930, 296–301.

*Der Kampf um die Ostsee*, Schriften des Baltischen Instituts 5, Serie Balticum, ed. Józef Borowik, Leipzig: Markert and Petters, 1933.

Sommerfeldt, Gustav, 'Zur Geschichte des Pommerellischen Woiewoden Graf Gerhard von Dönhoff', *Zeitschrift des Westpreußischen Geschichtsvereins* 43 (1901), 219–68.

Sosin, Stanisław, 'Autonomia Prus Królewskich w ujęciu G. Lengnicha', *Gdańskie Zeszyty Humanistyczne. WSP w Gdańsku, Wydział Filol.-Hum.* 1 (1958), 9–25.

Staszewski, Jacek, 'Groźba saskiego abzolutyzmu 1697–1706', *Sprawozdania TNT* 22 (1968), 43–4.

# Bibliography

*O miejsce w Europie*, Warsaw: PWN 1973.

'Die polnisch-sächsische Union und die Hohenzollernmonarchie (1679–1763), *Jahrbücher für die Geschichte Mittel- und Ostdeutschlands* 30 (1981), 28–34.

*August III Sas*, Warsaw: Ossolineum, 1989.

'Stanisław Leszczyński – inny niż znany', in Trzoska, Jerzy (ed.), *Strefa Bałtycka w XVI–XVIII w. Polityka, Społeczeństwo, Gospodarka*, Gdańsk: GTN, 1993, 63–70.

Stolleis, Michael (ed.), *Hermann Conring 1606–1681*, Historische Forschungen 23, Berlin: Duncker and Humblot, 1983.

Stone, Daniel, 'The End of Medieval Particularism: Polish Cities and the Diet, 1764–89', *Canadian-Slavonic Papers* 20 (1978), 194–207.

Strauss, Gerald, *Law, Resistance and the State. The Opposition to Roman Law in Reformation Germany*, Princeton University Press, 1986.

Sucheni-Grabowska, Anna, 'Społeczność szlachecka a państwo', in *Polska w epoce Odrodzenia*, Warsaw: Wiedza Powszechna, 1986, 13–107.

Święciochowski, Bolesław, 'Stosunek Augusta II do Gdańska w latach 1697–1698', *Rocznik Gdański* 24 (1967), 91–123.

Sysyn, Frank, 'Ukrainian-Polish Relations in the Seventeenth Century: The Role of National Consciousness and National Conflict in the Khmelnytsky Movement', in Potichnyj, Peter J. (ed.), *Poland and Ukraine. Past and Present*, Edmonton and Toronto: The Canadian Institute of Ukrainian Studies, 1980, 58–82.

*Between Poland and the Ukraine. The Dilemma of Adam Kysil, 1600–1653*, Cambridge, Mass.: Harvard University Press, 1985.

Szafran, Przemysław, 'Warsztat Historyka Reinholda Curicke, dziejopisarza Gdańska XVII wieku w świetle jego księgozbioru', *Libri Gedanenses* 2 (1970), 87–126.

Szczuczko, Witold, 'Izba niższa generalnego Prus Królewskich 1548–1562', in Nowak, Zenon (ed.), *W kręgu stanowych i kulturalnych przeobrażeń Europy Północnej w XIV–XVIII wieku*, Toruń: UMK, 1988, 137–48.

*Sejmy koronne 1562–1564 a ruch egzekucyjny w Prusach Królewskich*, Toruń: UMK, 1994.

Szczygiel, Ryszard, 'Udział magnaterii w urbanizacji ziem Polskich w XVI wieku', *Acta Universitatis Wratislaviensis* 945, Historia 66 (1988), 249–56.

Szelągowski, Adam, *Sprawa północna w wiekach XVI i XVII*, Lwów: Nakładem B. Polonieckiego, 1904.

Szorc, Aloizy, *Dominium Warmińskie 1243–1772. Przywileje, prawo chełmińskie na tle ustroju Warmii*, Olsztyn: Wydawnictwo Pojezierze, 1990.

Szwagrzyk, Józef, 'Ludność Prus Książęcych wobec traktatu Welawsko-Bydgoskiego, 1657–1660', in Gierowski, J. (ed.), *O naprawę Rzeczypospolitej XVII–XVIII w. Prace ofiarowane Władysławowi Czaplińskiemu w 60 rocznice urodzin*, Warsaw: PWN, 1965, 177–88.

Szymczak, Barbara, 'Sejmiki Prus Królewskich wobec Księstwa Pruskiego i polityki elektora Fryderyka Wilhelma w latach 1648–1668', *Przegląd Historyczny* 86, no. 2 (1995), 167–77.

Targosz, Katarzyna, *Hieronym Pinocci. Studium z dziejów kultury naukowej w Polsce w XVII wieku*, Monografie z dziejów nauki i techniki 41, Wrocław: Zakład Historii Nauki PAN, 1967.

Tazbir, Janusz, 'Zainteresowania nowym światem w miastach Prus Królewskich w XVI–XVIII w.', *Zapiski Historyczne* 35 (1970), 31–45.

# Bibliography

'Sarmatyzacja katolicyzmu', *Studia Staropolskie* 29 (1970).

*Arianie i katolicy*, Warsaw: PWN, 1971.

'Polish National Consciousness in the Sixteenth to the Eighteenth Century', *Harvard Ukrainian Studies* 10 (1986), 316–35.

*Reformacja w Polsce*, Warsaw: Książka i Wiedza, 1993.

Thadden, Rudolf von, *Die brandenburgisch-preußischen Hofprediger. Ein Beitrag zur Geschichte der absolutistischen Staatsgesellschaft in Brandenburg-Preußen*, Berlin: de Gruyter, 1959.

Tippelskirch, Egloff von, *Die Statthalter des Großen Kurfürsten*, Institut für Politik und Internationales Recht der Universität Kiel 1 / 31, Quackenbrück: Trute, 1937.

Töppen, Max, *Geschichte der preußischen Historiographie von Dusburg bis auf Schütz*, Berlin: Verlag Wilhelm Hertz, 1853.

'Die Elbinger Geschichtsschreiber', *Zeitschrift des Westpreußischen Geschichtsvereins* 32 (1893).

'Historische Lieder, mitgeteilt von Max Toeppen', *Zeitschrift des Westpreußischen Geschichtsvereins* 39 (1899), 168–70.

Töppen, Max (ed.), *Akten der Ständetage Preußens unter der Herrschaft des Deutschen Ordens*, Leipzig: Duncker und Humblot, 1878–86.

Tomczak, Andrzej (ed.), *Dzieje historiografii Pomorza Gdańskiego i Prus Wschodnich 1920– 1939 (1944), Materiały sesji w Toruniu 15–16 IX 1991 r.*, Toruń: TNT, 1992.

Treitschke, Heinrich, 'Das deutsche Ordensland Preußen', *Preußische Jahrbücher* 10 (1862), 95–151.

*Origins of Prussianism* (1862), London: Allen and Unwin, 1942.

Trestik, Dusan, 'Moderne Nation, hochmittelalterliche politische Nation, frühmittelalterliche Gens und unsere genetische Software. Der Fall Mitteleuropa', in Bues, Almut and Rexheuser, Rex (eds.), *Mittelalterliche Nationes – Neuzeitliche Nationen*, Wiesbaden: Harrassowitz, 1995, 161–81.

Trzoska, Jerzy, 'Der Streit zwischen dem Sachsen August II und Peter I um die Kaperschiffe von Gdańsk (1716–1721)', *Studia Maritima* 6 (1987), 81–105.

Tümpel, Ludwig, *Die Entstehung des brandenburgisch-preußischen Einheitsstaates im Zeitalter des Absolutismus 1609–1806*, Breslau: Marcus, 1915; repr. Aalen: Scientia, 1965.

Tymieniecki, Kazimierz, *Dzieje Torunia. Praca zbiorowa z okazji 700-lecia miasta*, Toruń: TNT, 1933.

Tync, Stanisław, 'Sekretarz Toruński Jan Sachs, patriota polski', *Tygodnik Toruński* 42–9 (1924), see pp. 1–2 in vols. 42, 44–7 and 49.

*Dzieje Gimnazjum Toruńskiego*, 2 vols, vol. II: *1600–1660*, Roczniki TNT no. 53, Toruń: TNT, 1949.

Ulewicz, Tadeusz, *Sarmacja. Studium z Problematyki słowiańskiej w XV i XVI wieku*, Biblioteka Studium Słowiańskiego, Cracow: Uniwersytet Jagielloński, 1950.

Vetulani, Adam, *Lenno Pruskie. Od traktatu Krakowskiego do śmierci księcia Albrechta, 1525–1568*, Cracow: PAU, 1930.

Vota, J. [pseud. for Klopp, Onno], *Der Untergang des Ordensstaates und die Entstehung der preußischen Königswürde*, Mainz: Kirchheim, 1911.

Waas, Adolf, *Die alte deutsche Freiheit. Ihr Wesen und ihre Geschichte*, Munich and Berlin: R. Oldenbourg, 1939.

# Bibliography

Waddington, Albert, *L'acquisition de la Couronne Royale de Prusse par les Hohenzollern*, Paris: Ernest Leroux, 1888.

Walczak, Ryszard, 'Konfederacja Gdańska, Elbląga i Torunia 1615–1623', *Rocznik Gdański* 15–16 (1956–57), 247–88.

Walicki, Andrzej, *The Enlightenment and the Birth of Modern Nationhood. Polish Political Thought from Noble Republicanism to Tadeusz Kościuszko*, University of Notre Dame Press, 1989.

Walker, Mack, *The German Home Towns, 1648–1871*, Ithaca: Cornell University Press, 1972.

Walther, Rolf, 'Die Danziger Bürgerschaft im 18. Jahrhundert nach Herkunft und Beruf', *Zeitschrift des Westpreußischen Geschichtsvereins* 73 (1937), 67–170.

Waschinski, Emil, 'Das Thorner Land- und Stadtschulwesen', *Zeitschrift des Westpreußischen Geschichtsvereins* 56 (1912), 1–139.

*Das kirchliche Bildungswesen in Ermland, Westpreußen und Posen vom Beginn der Reformation bis 1773*, 2 vols., vol. II: *Klosterschulen*, Schriften der Baltischen Kommission zu Kiel, Breslau: Hirt, 1928.

Wdowiszewski, Zygmunt, 'Regesty Przywilejów Indygenatu w Polsce, 1519–1793', *Materiały do Biografii, Genealogii i Heraldiki Polski* 5 (1971), 8–78.

Wermke, Ernst, *Bibliographie der Geschichte von Ost- und Westpreußen bis 1929*, 3 vols., Aalen: Scientia-Verlag, 1958–62.

Wermter, Manfred, 'Die politische Vorstellungswelt der Stände im königlichen Preußen, insbesondere in Danzig um 1500', *Acta Borussica* 3 (1983–84), 102–46.

'Die Bildung des Danziger Stadtterritoriums in den politischen Zielvorstellungen des Rates der Stadt Danzig im späten Mittelalter und der frühen Neuzeit', in Arnold, Udo (ed.), *Ordensherrschaft, Stände und Stadtpolitik*, Lüneburg: Nordostdeutsches Kulturwerk, 1985, 81–124.

Wernicke, Julius, *Geschichte Thorns aus Urkunden*, 2 vols., Thorn: Ernst Lembeck, 1842.

Whaley, Joachim, *Religious Toleration and Social Change in Hamburg, 1529–1819*, Cambridge University Press, 1985.

Wichert, Ernst, 'Die politischen Stände Preußens, ihre Bildung und Entwicklung bis zum Ausgang des 16. Jahrhunderts', *Altpreußische Monatsschrift* 5 (1868), 213–42, 419–64.

Windler, Christian, 'Schwörtag und Öffentlichkeit im ausgehenden Ancien Régime. Das Beispiel einer elsässischen Stadtrepublik', *Schweizerische Zeitschrift für Geschichte* 46 (1996), 197–225.

Winter, Eduard, *Frühaufklärung. Der Kampf gegen den Konfessionalismus in Mittel- und Osteuropa und die deutsch-slawische Bewegung*, Berlin: Akademie-Verlag, 1966.

Wippermann, Wolfgang, *Der Ordensstaat als Ideologie. Das Bild des Deutschen Ordens in der deutschen Geschichtsschreibung und Publizistik*, Historische Kommission zu Berlin 24, Berlin: Colloquium Verlag, 1979.

Wisner, Henryk, *Najjasniejsza Rzeczpospolita. Szkice z dziejów Polski szlacheckiej XVI–XVII wieku*, Warsaw: PWN 1978.

Wodziński, Alfons M., *Gdańsk za czasów Stanisława Leszczyńskiego 1704–1709, 1733–1734*, Cracow: Gebethner i Wolff, 1929.

*Polnisch Preußen und Danzig in den ersten Jahren der Regierungszeit Augusts II*, Warsaw: Gebethner i Wolff, 1933.

# Bibliography

Wolff, Larry, *Inventing 'Eastern Europe'. The Map of Civilization on the Mind of the Enlightenment*, Stanford University Press, 1994.

Wundt, Max, *Die deutsche Schulmetaphysik des 17. Jahrhunderts*, Heidelberger Abhandlungen zur Philosophie und ihrer Geschichte 29, Tübingen: Mohr, 1939.

Wyduckel, Dieter, *Princeps Legibus Solutus. Eine Untersuchung zur frühmodernen Rechts- und Staatslehre*, Berlin: Duncker und Humblot, 1979.

Wyrobisz, Andrzej, 'Zatargi mieszczan ze starostami soleckimi w XVI, XVII i XVIII wieku', *Małopolskie Studia Historyczne* 12 (1969), 365–76.

Wyrozumski, Jerzy, 'Geneza senatu w Polsce', in Matwijowski, K. and Pietrzak, J. (eds.), *Senat w Polsce. Dzieje i teraźniejszość. Sesia naukowa, Kraków 25–26 maja 1993*, Warsaw: Kancelaria Senatu RP Biuro Informacyjne, 1993, 21–34.

Załęski, Stanisław, *Jezuici w Polsce*, 6 vols., Lwów: N. D. Ludowej, 1900.

Zdrójkowski, Zbigniew, 'Korektura pruska – jej powstanie, dzieje oraz jej rola w historii polskiej jurysdykcji i myśli prawniczej, 1598–1830', *Czasopismo Prawno-Historyczne* 13 (1961), 109–57.

*Zarys dziejów prawa chełmińskiego 1233–1862*, Thorn: UMK, 1983.

Zdrójkowski, Zbigniew (ed.), *Studia Culmensia Historico-Juridica, Księga Pamiątkowa Prawa Chełmińskiego*, 2 vols., Torun: UMK, 1988–90.

Zernack, Klaus, 'Der historische Begriff "Ostdeutschland" und die deutsche Landesgeschichte', *Nordost-Archiv NS* 1, no. 1 (1992), 157–74.

Zernack, Klaus (ed.), *Polen und die polnische Frage in der Geschichte der Hohenzollernmonarchie 1701–1871, Referate einer deutsch-polnischen Historiker-Tagung vom 7.–10. November 1979 in Berlin*, Einzelveröffentlichungen der Historischen Kommission 33, Berlin: Colloquium Verlag, 1982.

Zernack, Klaus and Biskup, Marian (eds.), *Schichtung und Entwicklung der Gesellschaft in Polen und Deutschland im 16. und 17. Jahrhundert. Parallelen, Verknüpfungen und Vergleiche*, Vierteljahresschrift für Sozial- und Wirtschaftsgeschichte, supplement no. 74, Wiesbaden: Steiner Verlag, 1983.

Zielińska, Teresa, *Magnateria polska epoki saskiej*, Wrocław, Warsaw, Cracow: Ossolineum, 1977.

Zielińska-Melkowska, Krystyna, *Przywilej Chełmiński 1233 i 1251*, Torun: UMK, 1986.

Zientara, Benedykt, 'Struktury narodowe średniowiecza. Próba analizy terminologii przedkapitalistycznych form świadomości narodowej', *Kwartalnik Historyczny* 84 (1977), 287–311.

'Świadomość narodowa w Europie Zachodniej w średniowieczu. Powstanie i mechanizmy zjawiska', in Gieysztor, A. and Gawlas, S. (eds.), *Państwo, Naród, Stany w Świadomości Wieków Średnich. Pamięciu B. Zientary 1929–1983*, Warsaw: PWN, 1990, 11–26.

Zientara, Włodzimierz, *Gottfried Lengnich, ein Danziger Historiker in der Zeit der Aufklärung*, 2 vols., Toruń: UMK, 1995–6.

Zillessen, Horst (ed.), *Volk, Nation und Vaterland. Der deutsche Protestantismus und der Nationalismus*, Gütersloher Verlagshaus, 1970.

# Index

# Index

# Index

# Index

Great Poland (Wielkopolska), 25, 56, 98, 163, 184
Greece, 77
Grodno, 172
Grotius, Hugo (1583–1645), 60, 69, 113, 117, 155, 157Grunau, Simon (1470–1530/37I), Prussian chronicler, 81–3
Grüttner, Samuel, political writer from Elbing, 199
Gryphius, Andreas (1616–64), 86
Grzymułtowski, Krzysztof (1620–87), palatine of Poznań, 39
guilds, 67, 112–3, 199
  political representation of, 65, 67, 69
Gundling, Nicolaus Hieronymus (1671–1729), 192, 194, 195
Gustav II Adolf (1594–1632), king of Sweden (from 1611), 85, 87, 121, 142

Habsburg, house of, 3, 6, 28, 60, 88
  candidature in Poland, 111
  policies of, 186, 207
  Spanish succession and, 162
Hadiach (Hadziacz), Treaty of (16 September 1658), 125, 126, 130
Halicz, 166
Halle, 75, 167, 194–5
  law studies at, 191, 193
  Neue Hallische Bibliothek, 195
  University of, 167, 191, 192, 200
Hamburg, 47, 147, 186, 187
Hanoverian dynasty, 149
Hanow, Christoph (1695–1773), professor in Danzig, 43, 200
Hanseatic League, The
  cities of, 63, 107, 186, 219
  decline of, 21
  Prussian towns in, 20–1, 58, 66, 78
  Wendish Circle of, 21
Hartknoch, Christoph (1644–1687), 17, 51, 70, 79, 80, 101–6, 138
  constitutional theory of, 97–101, 116–17
  Königsberg, in, 96, 159
  myth of Prussia of, 102–6, 107, 109, 160, 165
  social thought of, 99, 101–2, 105
Heide, Adalbert (1706–65), priest in Heilsberg, 82
Heidelberg, 75
Heilsberg (Lidzbark Warmiński), 82, 174
Helmoldus (d. after 1177), author of Chronica Slavorum, 82, 105, 168
Helmstedt, 48, 61, 68, 75
Hennenberger, Kaspar (1529–1600), pastor and historian, 82, 164
Henri of Valois, king of Poland (1573–4), king of

France (Henri III, 1574–89), 16, 153
Henrician Articles, 98, 154; see also Pacta conventa
Henry, prince (1726–1802), brother of Frederick II, 12
Herder, Johann Gottfried (1744–1803), 7
Herodotus, 84, 89
Hetmanshchyna, 125
Hobbes, John, 59, 113
Hohenzollern, 49, 59, 83, 173, 183–36, 358
  despotism, 215, 220
  historical mythology, 164–7, 168, 170
  historiography, 2, 6, 14, 149, 159–60, 161, 168–9
  mythology, historical, 164–7, 168, 170
  political theory, 150, 154–5, 156
  rule over Ducal Prussia, 4, 97, 148–54, 168
  see also Brandenburg; Duchy of Prussia
Holy Roman Empire, The 104, 122, 125, 153, 156, 186, 206
  armies of, 138
  and Brandenburg-Prussia, 148, 154, 160, 162
  cities in, 52, 64–6, 70, 110, 113
  constitution of, 4, 9, 118
  and Danzig, 17
  German character of, 70, 86, 92, 94
  German provinces of, 4, 13, 14
  political structure of, 57, 64, 67
  and Pomerania, 94–5
  religious conflict in, 14–15
homagium eventuale, 150, 167
Honigfelde, battle of (1629), 121
Hosius, Stanisław (1504–79), bishop of Warmia and cardinal, 34, 56
Hoverbeck, Johann von (1606–82), Brandenburg-Prussian diplomat, 164
Huguenots, 156
Humanism, 71–2, 80
Hungary, 47, 72, 205

interregnum, 115, 154
  of 1572, 15
  of 1733, 201
  of 1763–4, 201, 203
Ireland, 204, 206
Isabella of Castile and Aragon (1451–1504), 71
Israel, 166
Italy, 57, 71, 108
iius indigenatus, 66, 130, 151, 202
  debate about, 36–40, 41–5
  defence of, 40, 45
  definition of, 26, 34–5, 37
  Ducal Prussian, 39–40
ius terrestre, 109
Ivan IV, the Terrible (1530–84), grand duke of

# Index

# Index

# Index

# Index

# Index

# CAMBRIDGE STUDIES IN EARLY MODERN HISTORY

*Henry IV and the Towns: The Pursuit of Legitimacy in French Urban Society, 1589–1610*
S. ANNETTE FINLEY-CROSWHITE
*The Limits of Royal Authority: Resistance and Obedience in Seventeenth-Century Castile*
RUTH MACKAY
*Defiled Trades and Social Outcasts: Honor and Ritual Pollution in Early Modern Germany*
KATHY STUART
*The Other Prussia: Royal Prussia, Poland and Liberty, 1569–1772*
KARIN FRIEDRICH


Titles available in paperback marked with an asterisk*

The following titles are now out of print:
*French Finances, 1770–1795: From Business to Bureaucracy*
J. F. BOSHER
*Chronicle into History: An Essay in the Interpretation of History in Florentine Fourteenth-Century Chronicles*
LOUIS GREEN
*France and the Estates General of 1614*
J. MICHAEL HAYDEN
*Reform and Revolution in Mainz, 1743–1803*
T. C. W. BLANNING
*Altopascio: A Study in Tuscan Society 1587–1784*
FRANK MCARDLE
*Gunpowder and Galleys: Changing Technology and Mediterranean Warfare at Sea in the Sixteenth Century*
JOHN FRANCIS GUILMARTIN JR
*The State, War and Peace: Spanish Political Thought in the Renaissance 1516–1559*
J. A. FERNÁNDEZ-SANTAMARIA
*Calvinist Preaching and Iconoclasm in the Netherlands, 1544–1569*
PHYLLIS MACK CREW
*The Kingdom of Valencia in the Seventeenth Century*
JAMES CASEY
*Filippo Strozzi and the Medici: Favor and Finance in Sixteenth-Century Florence and Rome*
MELISSA MERIAM BULLARD
*Rouen During the Wars of Religion*
PHILIP BENEDICT
*The Emperor and His Chancellor: A Study of the Imperial Chancellery Under Gattinara*
JOHN M. HEADLEY
*The Military Organisation of a Renaissance State: Venice c. 1400–1617*
M. E. MALLETT AND J. R. HALE
*Neostoicism and the Early Modern State*
GERHARD OESTREICH
*Prussian Society and the German Order: An Aristocratic Corporation in Crisis c. 1410–1466*
MICHAEL BURLEIGH

Lightning Source UK Ltd.
Milton Keynes UK
UKOW04f0627110118
315932UK00001B/27/P